ARISTOPHANES
AN AUTHOR FOR THE STAGE

Original title: *Aristofane autore di teatro,*
English translation by KEVIN WREN.

ARISTOPHANES
AN AUTHOR FOR THE STAGE

Carlo Ferdinando Russo

London and New York

Italian edition, *Aristofane autore di teatro*,
first published 1962
by G. C. Sansoni, Firenze

Revised Italian editions published 1984, 1992

Revised and expanded English edition
first published 1994
by Routledge
11 New Fetter Lane, London EC4P 4EE

Simultaneously published in the USA and Canada
by Routledge
29 West 35th Street, New York, NY 10001

First published in corrected paperback 1997

Italian edition © 1962, 1984, 1992 Carlo Ferdinando Russo
English edition © 1994 Carlo Ferdinando Russo

Typeset in Garamond by
Ponting–Green Publishing Services, Chesham, Bucks
Printed and bound in Great Britain by
T.J. International Ltd, Padstow, Cornwall

British Library Cataloguing in Publication Data
A catalogue record for this book is available from
the British Library

Library of Congress Cataloguing in Publication Data
A catalogue record for this book is available from the
Library of Congress

ISBN 0–415–01082–9 (hbk)
ISBN 0–415–15404–9 (pbk)

To my Hekamede, curly-locked, transoceanic
(*Iliad* XI and XIV)

CONTENTS

PREFACE

Aristophanes continues to gather suitors, and in recent years I too have kept biting, or rather nibbling, at the strings of his comedies. Some time ago, moreover, at the theatre at Syracuse, I strove to acquaint myself with the historical dawn of comedy, when in the times of Miltiades and Aristides comedy was legitimized and first admitted to the official contests.

When I started work on *Aristophanes, an Author for the Stage*, I was living in Forio d'Ischia-Pithekoussai, where along with Giorgio Buchner and David Ridgway I savoured the Celebration Cup of Nestor and Aphrodites for Olympiad XIV of 724, and with Ingeborg Bachmann and Wystan Auden discussed *Acharnians* and the poetics of Aristophanes. From Pithekoussai I moved to another Mediterranean environment, accepting an appointment in Bari after my years with Giorgio Pasquali at the Scuola Normale di Pisa and in Florence, and then as an afternoon lecturer in Cologne.

The aim of my work on Aristophanes was to point out the theatrical properties inherent in the Word. During the preparatory phases, the University library – so much appreciated by Eduard Fraenkel, professor at Bari throughout the 1960s – offered me Granville-Barker's *Prefaces to Shakespeare*, with its innovative introduction addressed to the 'new scholarship'. In 1929, John Dover Wilson had acclaimed this theatrical philologist as follows:

> It is one of the most important literary discoveries of our age that Shakespeare wrote, not to be read, but to be acted; that his plays are not books, but, as it were, libretti for stage performance. It is amazing that so obvious a fact should so late have come to recognition.

Every comedy is indeed a 'libretto', or rather a work of thought designed for theatrical execution. Take *Clouds* and *Frogs*, for instance, both bruised and revised by the author in response to pressing demands. Whereas these comedies simply confound the desk-bound reader, they reward anyone who takes their theatrical properties into account, ranging from the three professional and the amateur actors to the very 'strings of the comedy' themselves, which the author was obliged brusquely to pull: on the one hand when *Clouds* was defeated and subsequently revised, and again when Sophocles

xi

descended into Hades at a point when the text of *Frogs* was already prepared for the stage.

The functional manuscript of the stage-author is even more apparent in the case of *Wasps*. The comedy has been transmitted in a state of disorder, so to speak, the result of an accident occurring *chez* Aristophanes! Certain elements of the manuscript are evidently out of place, and within its overall habitat there even emerges a fossil, a structural form consisting of 18 × 2 tetrameters with a phosphorescent alarm-signal at its centre. In recent years, because of the efforts of Dutch scholars, certain new materials have illuminated the deep scansion and the acting style of the prologue of *Peace*, a comedy which prior to the parabasis puts on display a compositive outline of unmitigated purity made up of 36 × 2 trimeters divided midway by an extra metre ὦ ὤ. The classicist, none the less, remains enchanted by the Byzantine archetype and prepares editions devoid of metrical and dramaturgical directions yet full of sigla, lists and variants of arguable utility: 'What an ass that master of Byzantine school is', exclaimed the professor of dramaturgy August Wilhelm von Schlegel; 'but I have found a better master, a source as new as it is old: the text of the poet.' Today, Thomas Gelzer, Jean Irigoin, Giuseppe Mastromarco and Hans-Joachim Newiger are close to the autograph of the Athenian dramatist himself.

In the dramaturgical bibliography you will find a work by an evergreen archaeologist, Curt Fensterbusch, the founder of the modern Aristophanic stage. In one of my many letters to Fensterbusch, I once enquired: 'Why did you not refer more explicitly in your 1912 dissertation to the two theatres of Aristophanes – the theatre of Dionysos and the Lenaian precinct – as you did in 1932 under the heading *Theatron* in Pauly–Wissowa?' He replied immediately: 'My professor, Ulrich von Wilamowitz-Moellendorff, refused to tolerate the slightest mention of the two theatres. Hence, I was forced to tone down that particular aspect, indeed to hide it almost completely.' That aspect has not been abandoned here, and I have also recorded its essential traits. Besides, in modern times the Lenaion generally receives greater attention, thanks to *Acharnians* 504: οὑπὶ Ληναίῳ τ'ἀγών, 'the contest is in the Lenaion'. Anyone who is unwilling to listen to *Acharnians* should at least listen to Albin Lesky, who in 1968 drew attention to the pregnant and localizing value of this expression, an expression which is almost as concrete as the religious stone found in Athens on which are inscribed the names of Aristophanes' companions, including his faithful poet-didaskalos Philonides.

Aristophanes, an Author for the Stage has found a congenial translator in the linguist Kevin Wren, whom I had the good fortune to encounter at the Faculty of Science along with his collaborator, Elena Palazzo of Magna Graecia. With my transoceanic spouse Adele Plotkin, art teacher and graduate of Yale University School of Design, I discussed the composition and decomposition of *Frogs* and the staging of the comedies. I have also received unfailing support from Raffaele Ruggiero with Flavio Rizzo, and sensitive suggestions from Eric W. Handley and Sebastiano Timpanaro.

I am grateful to Kenneth J. Dover, Aristophanist *par excellence*, who immediately, and with great enthusiasm, expressed the idea that the book should be translated, and my thanks also go to the Aeschylean Oliver Taplin, who recently seconded the idea.

In this English edition you will find some afterthoughts, and certain proposals: the theatrical seasons, comedy legitimized in the time of Miltiades and Aristides, the historiographical *Knights* and finally Aristophanes' naval career and his role as coryphaeus in *Acharnians*.

According to Thucydides, Pericles once said to the Athenians: 'By celebrating games and festivals throughout the year, we have procured the greatest distraction for our minds, providing relief from fatigue' (II.38.1). *Clouds* releases an analogous message for the entire year, a message which privileges the joys of spring, in the theatre of Dionysos. Yet the greatest entertainment and most pungent jokes are left to 'Aristophanes in the heavens, to the Universal Author, the Colossus of wit': words annotated at the end of *Geständnisse*, after Plato, by the self-mocking Heinrich Heine. Heine was christened 'the earthly Aristophanes' by his compatriots.

What I wish to say is that when faced with Aristophanes all critics tend to feel like Dikaiopolis at *Acharnians* 367, before the kitchen chopping-block: ὁ δ'ἀνὴρ ὁ λέξων οὑτοσὶ τυννουτοσί, 'he who is about to speak is as tiny as this'.

C.F. Russo
Florence, 'La Belfagoriana'

1

THE THEATRICAL SEASONS
AND
THE DAWN OF COMEDY

The two annual theatre seasons surface more than once from within the texture of Aristophanic comedy. Regarding the seasons and the two separate audiences, the playbills which the author releases from this or that comedy are of great significance.

The extant comedies number 11, out of an overall total of 40. Here they are, with the theatrical seasons when known: *Acharnians*, Lenaia 425, *Knights*, Lenaia 424, *Clouds*, Dionysia 423, *Wasps*, Lenaia 422, *Peace*, Dionysia 421, *Birds*, Dionysia 414, *Lysistrata*, 411, *Thesmophoriazusae*, 411, *Frogs*, Lenaia 405, *Assemblywomen*, 392, *Plutus*, 388. The Lenaian contests took place between the end of January and the beginning of February, the Dionysian between the end of March and the beginning of April. From the end of the sixth century, tragedy had already installed itself at the Dionysian contests, whereas the comic contests did not begin until 486. At the Lenaia, however, the comic dramatists had the upper hand, with official contests beginning around 440 (the tragic contests around 432). The Dionysia, in which the dithyrambic contests also took place, were organized by the eponymous archon, the Lenaia by the archon basileus.

In *Acharnians* and *Clouds*, the playbills are launched at particularly sparkling moments of the action. In *Clouds*, the Clouds are exhorted to appear, and the excellence is proclaimed of the variegated spring season:

> Rainclad virgins, let us stir to gaze upon the glowing land of Pallas, a region of heroes loved by Cecrops, home of the cult, and of its ineffable rites, in whose sacred ceremonies the temple doors swing wide to admit the initiated, bearing gifts to the celestial gods. In every season, there are processions, sacrifices and banquets in Athens; and when springtime arrives, it is time for the feast of Bromios, the excitement of resounding choruses, the deep-quivering Muse of the flauts.
>
> (298–313)

By contrast, the playbill of *Acharnians*, which was performed in winter, is prosaic and punctilious: it proclaims and confirms the Athenian, hence non-Hellenic, identity of the audience, without failing to mention the site of the

1

contest open to such a restricted public, 'the purest wheaten flour'; the theatre of Dionysos, on the other hand, could house around fifteen thousand people. Here, the first actor is speaking, and the moment is a political one:

> Don't wish me ill, O gentleman spectators, that I, poor beggar, should come to speak before the Athenians about the city, in a tragi ... comedy, for even tragicomedy can distinguish righteousness, and the words I speak will be hard, yet righteous. This time Kleon won't be able to slander me, accusing me of speaking ill of the city in the presence of foreigners, because we are here alone. The contest is in the Lenaion and the foreigners are absent: the tributes haven't come, and not even the city's allies. Now, we are alone, the purest wheaten flour.
>
> (495–511)

There are three different expressions referring to the absentees: 'the foreigners', 'the tributes' and 'the allies' ('the tributes' were put on display in the orchestra prior to the performance, when the theatre of Dionysos was full). Just as many expressions are used to describe the occasion itself: 'we are here alone', 'the contest is in the Lenaion', 'Now, we are alone, the purest wheaten flour.' The mention of the precinct in which the contest took place would have increased the author's freedom of speech and rendered the comedy all the more political in the eyes of the Athenians. In *Knights*, Aristophanes demands the ληναΐτης roar, 'the roar proper to the Lenaion'. In *Acharnians*, the protagonist, promoter just previously of κατ'ἀγροὺς Διονύσια (202), is as topographical as a Baedeker.

And 'Les Belles Lettres' render homage to our Baedeker: 'c'est le concours du Lénaion'. The others, however, envision a formular decline: 'the Lenaian contest, the contest of the Lenaia'. As remarked in the preface, Albin Lesky, reviewing the second edition of Pickard-Cambridge, has issued a warning regarding the topographical eloquence of οὑπὶ Ληναίῳ τ'ἀγών. In the same passage, line 510 reads οὑπὶ Ταινάρῳ θεός, 'Poseidon, the god worshipped in the sanctuary of Tenaros', and it is known that in this sanctuary the Spartans did actually worship the god. At the end of the century, in the comic poet Sannyrion, Μέλητον, τὸν ἀπὸ Ληναίου νεκρόν is topographical and theatrical to the maximum degree: see chapter 4 on *Knights*.

The strings linking the protagonist to the contest precinct also link the orphan-character in *Birds* to the theatre of Dionysos, since civil ceremonies were held in the theatre prior to the contests, and held there alone. Solemn and vital as it was, the theatre of Dionysos is never actually named: 'a great swarm of goddesses move forward singing' (297). This eccentric stage-direction is given by the master of ceremonies, Socrates, a moment prior to the song of the twenty-four 'Virgin Clouds', advancing from the sky towards the powerful city of Pallas, or rather towards the corridor of the theatre of Dionysos. The solemn Dionysian contests in fact opened with virgins and noble young women moving in procession towards the Dionysian orchestra.

Our Baedeker is always on the alert, and in the Dionysian *Peace* is highly punctilious regarding the Lenaian *Wasps* from the previous year: a number of lines from the parabasis of *Peace* are identical, or extremely similar, to lines from the parabasis of *Wasps*: cf. *Peace* 752 and 754–60 with *Wasps* 1029–37. One variant is significant: 'but all along I stood up to the monster, fighting for you *and for the islands*'. 'And for the islands', adds the poet in the Dionysian *Peace*, since the audience this time includes the allies from the islands, not the Athenians alone.

There exists another refined contact between dramas, this time between Euripides and Aristophanes, between *Andromeda*, with Perseus in flight, and *Thesmophoriazusae*: 'I am Echo . . . she who took part in the contest last year, I too, in this very same place, for Euripides', thus *Thesmophoriazusae* 1059–61, on the lips of Echo, previously one of the characters of Euripides' *Andromeda*. The theatre in which *Andromeda* was performed must have been the theatre of Dionysos, since it alone was equipped with a flying-machine (the Lenaion, a makeshift theatre, would not have availed itself of this particular device). Besides, Euripides never took part in the contests of the Lenaia, where his enemies, the comic dramatists, were masters of the house.

Comic dramatists are masters by nature: the Greek comic dramatists, for instance, would have been free to consign their works just a couple of months prior to performance. However, they remain the slaves of events: Aristophanes found himself under urgent obligation to revise *Frogs* because of Sophocles' death, and *Peace* on account of the deaths of the two warlords; *Wasps* had to be revised on account of the trial of the pacifist strategos Laches, whereas at the last moment nine lines were added to *Assemblywomen*, after a draw unfavourable to the author.

'The greatest distraction for our minds, providing relief from fatigue', the words of Pericles (Thucydides II.38.1): and the machine of the theatrical season went into motion six to nine months prior to the winter Lenaia and the springtime Dionysia, when between June and July, at the beginning of the Attic year, the choregoi were appointed – a financial weight, fair enough, but a sure source of popularity. Nikias, for example, 'sought popular trust as a choregos and obtained many first places, never once meeting defeat' (Plutarch, *Nikias* 3.1.3). A fully fledged season at the Dionysia – tragedy comedy dithyrambs – required a mass of 1165 choral voices; the dithyrambic choruses alone employed 500 men and 500 boys.

It was the duty of both archons to choose between the aspirant poets. Plato writes:

Mad would be the city that allowed you to do the things which have just been mentioned, before the archons have judged whether it is opportune or not to allow you to perform your compositions. Hence, children of the sweet Muses, show your choral songs to the archons along with

3

ours, and if the things you have said seem equal to or better than those we have said, then shall we award you the chorus.

(Laws 817d)

A dialogue on admission to the theatre is to be heard in *Frogs* 89–97, during a debate between Herakles and the god of the theatre: 'Are there not other striplings here who compose tragedies as well, over ten thousand of them, more verbose than Euripides by a mile?' 'Aborted little clusters they are, chatterboxes, "academy of swallows", craft-spoilers; they disappear far quicker than you'd think if they manage to obtain a chorus, the one time they've peed on Tragedy. A spermatic poet you wouldn't find any longer even if you went looking for him, just one who can make an original locution sound out.'

In *Peace*, out of joy for peace, the sarcasm aimed at mediocre tragedians is particularly strong: 'Karkinos, unexpectedly, gained admission'; 'In spring the swallow chirps happily and Aeschylus' two little grandchildren, Morsimos and Melanthios, fail to gain admission. O Muse, launch a nice gob of spit at them.' And again: 'Muse, you who have driven war away, dance with me, for I am your friend; and if Karkinos asks you to dance with his sons, pay him no heed, don't enter into their company, instead treat them like domestic quail, dwarfed dancers with porcupine necks, pellets of goat dung, inventors of artificial dance figures' (*Peace* 781–817).

The Baedeker is even more punctilious than Professor Eduard Fraenkel: consider, for example, the political brio of Lenaian comedies such as *Acharnians*, *Knights* and *Wasps* (Lamachus, Kleon, the lawcourts), first brought to light by the graduating Friedrich Leo in 1863, in comparison to the Dionysian Panhellenic comedies such as *Peace*; *Lysistrata*, whose contest remains unknown, must also have been Panhellenic. Political brio apart, it is also the dramaturgy of comedies for the makeshift Lenaian theatre which apparently distinguishes them from those performed in the theatre of Dionysos. The Dionysian protagonist remains within the environment of the theatre from the beginning of the comedy to its end. When he is not on-stage, he stays within the structures of the stage and never makes use of the public side corridors, in so far as they lead out of the theatre. The other Dionysian characters, after exiting by the corridor, disappear for good. The characters of Dionysian comedies, with the exception of the divine Tumult in *Peace*, are all governed by the theatrical unity proper to the environment in which the comedies were performed.

By contrast, the Lenaian protagonist is active both in and outside the theatre: he exits by the corridor, re-enters by the corridor, and provides an account of what has happened in the mean time in some extra-theatrical location. The other characters behave in the same way. The exits normally take place during the parabasis. The characters in the Lenaian comedies expand the dramatic action beyond the theatre itself. Only in *Frogs*, which is set for the most part in the nether world, is there no such action.

Extra-theatrical actions are also to be found in *Assemblywomen* and *Plutus*: in *Assemblywomen*, even the chorus has its moment of escape. In these, the two final comedies, the setting is made up of the normal little bourgeois houses, as in comedies of certified Lenaian origin, although, with the one exception of *Clouds*, the setting of the Dionysian comedies is more characteristically of an eccentric variety: the sky, a cave, a copse, the city of the birds. In *Lysistrata* the setting is the Acropolis, in *Thesmophoriazusae* the Thesmophorian temple: the contests of these two comedies may indeed remain unknown, but they conform none the less to the theatrical unity of the milieu in which they were performed.

In 1917, the German archaeologist August Frickenhaus, discussing the stage-properties of the Greek dramas, stated as a preamble to his rapid analyses of Aristophanes that the attempt to find some scenic distinction between Lenaian and Dionysian comedies is a pointless enterprise, and cited in his favour the scenic unity of plays which Shakespeare composed for radically differing theatres. The reference to Shakespeare is an interesting one, considering that one of the most secure findings of modern Shakespearian scholarship is precisely the scenic, and linked stylistic and ideological, distinction existing between dramas conceived first for one theatre, then for another, then for yet another again, first for one public, then for another.

Comedies designed for the two different contests naturally have a common foundation: articulation into, and composition in, blocks. From *prologue* to *exodos*, these blocks are represented by the *parodos, agon, parabasis, episodes, agon II* and *parabasis II*.

They are blocks which a 25-year-old philologist, the geometric Dr Thadeusz Zieliński, illustrated in colour in his brilliant work dedicated to Otto Ribbeck, *Die Gliederung der altattischen Komödie* (Leipzig, 1885): taking the tragic poets as his starting-point, he made designs of seven Aristophanic comedies, from *Acharnians* to *Frogs*. They are blocks probably written progressively by the author on the basis of functional acting units (indeed, revising *Frogs*, the author changed the position of one of these blocks): dialogue on the one hand and parts for the chorus alone on the other (see chapter 15, 'The disorderly *Wasps*'). They are blocks some of which were rather antique for Aristophanes' time: the parabasis, glorious and magnificent, was on its way out of the orchestra and into the museum, as the prologue flowered next to the scenic façade, into which the actor would retire to allow the chorus to deliver the parabasis. The chorus is normally indifferent to the scenic façade, whereas the actor penetrates as far as the spectators seated in the front row.

While the actor would have been employed for an action framed by a σκηνή, the choreutai were nomads, countryfolk. At most one might have met them in the open air, in procession. During the parabasis, moreover, the actors are in a state of lethargy, whereas during the prologue the choreutai are straining for the green light.

At a certain point in the official evolution of comedy, a moment of systematization must have arrived: the information office of the prologue would have developed along with the increase in the number of actors and of the σκηνή, while at the Lenaia in 442 a competition between the comic actors was begun, fifteen years before Aristophanes' début.

The parabasis may frequently be polemical, but neither does the prologue lack its shafts: *Acharnians*, at the very outset, tips acid over some of the dramatists from the previous year, and instead compliments the stripling Aristophanes from the previous year; at the beginning of *Frogs*, the front-ranking comic dramatists feel the sting, then the petals of the tragic daisy are plucked, and plucked too are those tart clusters which merely tickle tragedy, rather than fertilizing it, as did Euripides.

Such shafts apart, Aristophanes also adorns his prologue with songs, or with singable pieces, at least. In *Peace, Birds, Thesmophoriazusae, Frogs*, the iambic undergrowth opens out into a lyrical glade, or almost: the rhythmic flight of Trygaeus in *Peace*; voice of voices, the most spectacular in Greek theatre, in *Birds*; the small chorus for Agathon in *Thesmophoriazusae*; and finally the hymns and dialogues of the frog-swans. The frogs are invisible, creatures of voice and sound – of voice and sound clearly audible in the theatre.

And this is precisely the point: in the prologues, the most important lyrical displays are in each case assigned to invisible singers, or rather, the space proper to the actors is never usurped by outsiders, even by those of appropriate rank. This reserved space is protected even in *Assemblywomen*: dominated by a dictatoress, the women of the chorus appear gradually in the course of the prologue. Yes, the chorus appears during the prologue. However, this is merely a joke, for although the female chorus does appear, it remains silent, confused with the women actors.

At the end of the prologue, the aforementioned chorus of men disguised as women – later disguised as men, through an irony of the plot – rather than gearing itself up for a march, goes into reverse, leaving the theatre and making its way to the city with the female followers of the dictatoress. It is at this point, and this alone, that the chorus begins to sing, although it could already have done so during the prologue. Aristophanes in fact never allows the prologue to be touched by bodies historically extraneous to the scenic façade.

The truth is that the chorus of the polis is disintegrating, that the polis itself is disintegrating. Athenian man is becoming less than a man. The chorus of *Plutus* does not enter the theatre out of any impulse of its own; the choreutai are treated like muscles, driven by a colossus. Who is this colossus? Not the coryphaeus, but the first actor. And who is the first actor? A slave promoted to the rank of autonomous character, an individual whom one has not encountered until now, if not in embryo in *Frogs*. In *Plutus*, the Byzantines' favourite (*Lysistrata* was the most neglected), the chorus sings under its breath rather than with full voice, and it is also teasingly affirmed that it will sing out once it leaves the theatre.

As early as *Knights*, the actor is allowed to taste another of the chorus' finest dishes, closing the prologue, not in trimeters, but rather in long, sonorous tetrameters. A minor theft at the expense of the glorious corps of the choreutai.

The lucid and ardent Dr Thadeusz Zieliński outlined the issue in half a page: 'Maybe one of the most recent parts of Ionic comedy is the prologue. Not so much because we could do without it in many cases – *Wasps*, for example – or by analogy to tragedy, where the prologue became indispensable at a relatively late stage: it is enough to think of Kratinos, who began his Βοῦκολοι with a dithyramb, i.e. with a choral part. The prologue, moreover, was not adapted to the regulations of epirrhematic composition, in so far as it lacked a chorus.' Ribbeck's student concludes: 'the prologue remains free, free as the wind, its form as loose as its content: it is impossible to provide a structure design for the prologue, so let us not refer to this matter again'.

Yet the prologue, too, is subject to the slide-rule of Adrian Leverkühn, *Doktor Faustus*, the composer who says: 'I am bound by a willed constriction to order, therefore I am free' – as much liberty as there is in a cage dominated explicitly by numbers such as the parabasis, in which the tetrameters are not always 16 and not always 20, but sometimes 16 and sometimes 20.

Gottfried Hermann, in *Elementa doctrinae metricae* (1816), was the first modern scholar dealing with the parabasis to have glimpsed another slide-rule when in *Birds* he recognized the 63 agonistic tetrameters corresponding to 63 tetrameters, and so forth. In such a way, he first touched on the epirrhematic agon (with respect to *Lysistrata*, too).

In 1964, Daniel Holwerda illuminated the outline of the prologue by recuperating from the ancient metrician Heliodorus an extra metre, ἰὴ ἰή, between trimeters 235–6 of the celestial prologue of *Peace*. We finally understand, therefore, that the celestial moment, thanks to the roar let loose by the god of war, is scanned into two identical sections composed of sixty-three trimeters.

This is not all: Holwerda has also recuperated the interrogative τί φής; extra metre after line 25 of the first tableau, whereby this line now winks at line 25 in the accompanying tableau! Here we have chosen to leave aside the recovery of the colours proper to dialogue and monologue.

Prior to the Dutch, however, the most innovative were the Germans: it was Ritschl's student, Otto Hense, who in 1870 indicated and discussed the ὣ ὥ extra metre in the 72-trimeter passage preceding the parabasis of *Peace*. This fine iambic structure is divided by this exclamation, a fact already noticed by Heliodorus. Hense went ahead, noting that the first 36 trimeters of the dialogue concern politics, Kleon-Hyperbolus, the second 36 art, Sophocles-Kratinos, and that the two trimeters in fourteenth position always represent a turning-point, with ἴθι νυν. Hense said that through his responsive analyses Heliodorus had worked back to the editorial signs of the Alexandrians, but that it was also a short step from the Alexandrians to the autographical signs of the Athenian dramatists themselves.

The dramatic prologue is situated at the gates of western culture, at the beginning of the first book of the *Iliad*, in those hexameters that Plato in the Academy called τῆς Ἰλιάδος τὰ πρῶτα: a retrospective, Apollonian *prologue*, characterized by an abrupt shift in respect to the proem and by an interrogative typical of the dramatic prologuist: 'which of the gods had Agamemnon and Achilles contend?'. The soliloquizing narrator provides the answer himself; the hurricane Agamemnon is introduced; Apollo lets loose a wave of unimaginable evil. Does this perhaps remind you of the desperate scourges which afflict Athenian drama from the prologue onwards?

The first book of the *Iliad* is a prolusion. One is presented with the many high-ranking personalities concerned, in earthly, marine and celestial environments. The scourge is followed by an entrance march – the army of the dispute, called up by Achilles, effectively a minor *parodos*. Then, the oracle of Calchas reigns over a *proagon* of driving tension, during which Agamemnon becomes even more bearish and hurricanelike (53–120).

Out of this *proagon* an *agon* is born, divided into four alternating sections each opening curtly, with insults worthy of a drama conceived for the Lenaia: 'Drunkard, dog-eyes, heart of a deer, plunderer!'. From line 121 onwards, Achilles and Agamemnon consume respectively 32 and 31 hexameters. At the end, Agamemnon curses the equality of the contest, an equality which the Attics termed *isegoria*, pride of their comedy, and pride also of the German philologists who first brought it to light. In an 'aside', the *dea ex machina*, Athena, pulls Achilles' hair in the dark. The umpire Nestor intervenes, and like an old coryphaeus turns first to one champion, then to the other.

Now comes the *second prologue*, delivered by Achilles: 27 hexameters of historical soliloquy regarding the actions completed, with an interrogative opening, 'what is it that I am recounting?'; and 21 dialogical hexameters addressed to his mother, informing her of the acts she must perform in Olympus. This is followed by a minor *second contest* between Zeus and Hera, umpired by Hephaistos (539–94).

The *exodos* is a professional one: Hephaistos, Apollo on the lyre, and the Muses singing. The parade is preceded by that 'inextinguishable laughter' of the gods which disturbed Plato so. The gods are united in κῶμος for an entire day (the duration of a comedy), and laugh also at seeing the disabled architect in the role of breathless cupbearer. The gods, as a group, laugh nowhere else in the *Iliad*, nor does one encounter the group of Hephaistos, Apollo and the Muses: 'and all day long, until the sun went down, they enjoyed the feast, together delighted in the banquet, in the superb lyre of Apollo, in the Muses singing with sweetest voice, alternating one for the other'.

After the first agon, and the extension involving Nestor, the assembly had dissolved and Achilles moved away. Now, half-way through the song, there is a radical change of course – the rapid dispatching, in ten hexameters, of a boat bearing a captain and twenty oarsmen to Crisa to placate Apollo (in comedy, the coryphaeus expresses his best wishes for the protagonist's extra-theatrical journey at the beginning of the parabasis).

After an interval on land, the boat arrives at the port of Crisa at hexameter 432. The only seafaring scene in the *Iliad* is sacred throughout. As soon as the boat arrives, there is a procession towards the altar of Apollo, hymns all day long, a paean (the only one dedicated to Apollo in Homer), the god himself participating joyfully from on high, youths filling the craters to the brim.

The boat takes to sea again the day after. The first dawn is described, although eleven days have already passed, and then Apollo sends the wind: an accelerated return, a joyful 'stretto' between the wind of the poetic god and the propitious sound of waves circling the prow, and with the 'stretto' of hexameters 479–87 the captain is once again in port.

The captain of the mission goes by the name of Odysseus, and was chosen from amongst three kings. His mission, central as it is, sixty-six hexameters long, bears all the features typical of the ancient parabasis, and it was inarguably at the beginning of the fifth century that the parabasis was to implant itself at the centre of official comedy (previously, it would have been a preamble). The 20-year-old Aristophanes, captain on his own behalf now that he has requested a chorus for the first time with *Knights* (424), intones a historical, parabatic march for official comedy entering into its third age (the leader Magnes, Crates and Kratinos), and alludes to the solitary captain, Odysseus, who did not leap aboard ship on the day of the false embarkation (B 169–71). Neither has Aristophanes leapt haphazardly on to the ship, and so at this climax of anapaestic 'stretto' desires a great roar, the applause of eleven oars. Today, the poet's ship has driven off the epic, oracular scourge of Typhon-Kleon; yesterday Odysseus drove off the scourge unleashed by 'Dog-eyes'. Today, the guardian knights have baptized and distinguished the new poet, who hates as they hate; yesterday a godfather gave to a new-born child the name of hate, Odysseus, or 'he who hates' (τ 406–12).

The Aristophanic character of the Paphlagonian has an ancestor in the pre-author of Chios; in Homer, the Paphlagonian king has a son, Ἁρπαλίων, the 'thief', whereas Kleon is Ἁρπαγᾶς. The father of the Homeric 'thief' is a figure worthy of Ariosto: he dies, is resurrected and bears a name suited both to a trade conducted at the πύλαι (*Knights* 1247 and 1398) and to the exploits of Pylos; that name is Πυλαιμένης. In Homer, Harpalion meets an extravagant end (N 650–9).

The simile used in the parabasis to describe Kratinos, who crushes his adversaries, is also to be found in the Meleager episode, when the wild Caledonian boar launched by Artemis lands and tears up by the roots trees laden with fruit (the rare προθέλυμνος in both texts). Meleager appears in the ninth book, with its exceptional hero who plays the lyre and sings the exploits of a contemporary war: the hero is Achilles.

In the *Iliad*, there is the Apollonian, seafaring Odysseus, and the Odysseus who does not leap aboard ship. In the *Odyssey*, the Phaeacians demand insistently of the stranger, 'why do you not take part in our contest, you who seem to know so much about it?'. And the guest replies in exactly the same terms as, later, Aristophanes is to reply, 'because the gods do not concede their favours to everyone!' (χαρίεντα διδοῦσιν, in Aristophanes χαρίσασθαι). Yet Odysseus performs an experiment and wins, imitating the others without unveiling his own identity. Shortly afterwards, however, Alcinous spurs on the reluctant guest to renounce his *anonymity*. Odysseus agrees, and thenceforth is a poet in his own right, with his own adventures, no longer merely a listener to the adventures sung by Demodocos (θ 133–233 and 536–86). Today, Aristophanes' behaviour is identical to that of Odysseus.

Once the short anapaestic march has come to an end, there appears the first ode dedicated to the equestrian Poseidon, whose prototype is the Homeric Poseidon astride the horses on the sea: the lauds addressed to the horses are not without some references to the praise for the horses dictated by the Muse in the Catalogue of Ships.

The Iliad, *at the very outset, passes from a prologue to a proagon and agon, arriving eventually at a joyful exodos. Midway, there is a seafaring scene, sacred and filled with hymns, under the guidance of Odysseus. With this interlude as his model, the new author for the stage wished to present his own apprenticeship in the parabasis as if it had been a seafaring one, whereas for some time the physiognomy of that particular book from the* Iliad *had been impressed on to the face of comedy, legitimizing it.*

Let us return to another young man, Zieliński, to the point at which, citing *Wasps*, he writes that in many cases the prologue might just as well be ripped up. I myself would take part in this ripping game, *Acharnians* in hand, were not the term more correctly 'dismembering', amidst the disgruntled cries of Dante's Pier della Vigna. The prologue has its roots set deep in the tree; on one occasion, it is even recalled in the second part of a drama (*Peace*). Any character sooner or later to appear on-stage in the course of the comedy is provided with off-stage vital force during the prologue: Demos in *Knights*, for instance, or the creditors in *Clouds*. If you rip up the prologue, you are left with nothing more than the spontaneous outdoor spectacle of more ancient times. The prologue of *Clouds* even foresees the presence of Chaerephon amongst its characters (he is struck out in the revised and unfinished text containing instead the two Arguments); and the two prologues of *Frogs*, although they were updated with great haste, do nevertheless resolve the relationship between the recently deceased Sophocles and the two other Greats.

To conclude our discussion of the prologue-parabasis: in *Knights*, the prologue depends on a parabatic expedient. The hymn in the parabasis opens invariably with a phrase such as 'Poseidon, come here!', 'Acharnian Muse, come here', 'Zeus, amongst the chorus I am calling you', etc. Fraenkel

(*Parabasenlieder* in the 1962 volume) and others think that pre-literary comedy always began with this kind of sacred invocation, resembling the above-mentioned invocation near the altar of Apollo in the *Iliad*. In *Knights*, two actor-prologuists call 'here', as if he were a god, a man who is simply walking outside the Lenaian precinct. As one can see, *Knights* appears to imitate the parabatic invocation, in a terrestrial manner: instead of invoking a god, it invokes a man. It is as if the prologue were saying, we actor-prologuists, although of recent appearance, are in no way inferior: we avail ourselves of the same powers of attraction as do our twenty-four colleagues in the chorus.

The unknown passer-by who is drawn marvellously into the theatre precinct is the first actor, assigned the role of leading man. Towards the end of the comedy, his name is disclosed, an excellent and artificial name, Agoracritos, which in reality was that of an extremely fashionable sculptor, Phidias' favourite student. For the moment, the presumed Agoracritos functions as *artifex ex machina*, and during the second parabasis melts down and remodels Demos (δῆμος/δημός, 'fat'; the verb expressing the act of fusion is a technical one). The *artifex* then restores Demos to the Acropolis, ancient, envied and extolled, its doors wide open to all the Hellenes, as in the period of the Dionysia. Aristides, Miltiades and the trophy of Marathon are evoked in the anapaests. The audience sings a paean, crying out its joy.

The transfiguration is intended principally as a celebration of theatre. Indeed it was precisely in the period of Aristides and Miltiades that comedy in its defined and regular form first developed, when Chionides and other comic dramatists had finally been admitted in 487–486 to the Dionysian contests in the theatre of the Acropolis. The comic dramatists, now worthy to enter the theatre of the tragedians, would have ennobled their work by subjecting it to a formal resetting, philo-Homeric in style, all of which goes to explain the zeal of the captain Aristophanes/Odysseus.

Athens, too, is remodelled in a furnace *ex machina*. Homer, in his 'parabasis', had staged a great Apollonian fire for *fat*-embellished meat, a powerful paean lasting the entire day. In Aristophanes, the paean is addressed to the renewed good fortune of Athens. 'The theatre intones a paean for our recent good fortune.... Come, raise a cry of joy, as the Athens of old appears, marvellous, renowned Athens, home of the illustrious Demos.'

The renewed good fortune of Athens is essentially a reworking of Homer. Once a social scourge is allayed, in Homer there breaks the *first* 'rosy-fingered dawn': 'rosy-fingered', or rather stained with purple like one who has finally sat down to write with his tablet, stylus and purple ink. On his part, the new captain Aristophanes celebrates the Homeric dawn of comedy, whose history he has just recounted from the times of Aristides and Miltiades, leaving aside the previous, adverse stage when comedy was not held in great esteem, as we have been told by Aristotle.

Here are the relevant passages from Aristotle's *Poetics*:

As in the serious genre Homer was the poet *par excellence* . . . so too was he the first to reveal and mark down the fundamental outlines of comedy (σχήματα ὑπέδειξεν), expressing in dramatic poetry, not personal invective, but the laughable . . . the successive changes which took place in tragedy, and those who produced them, are not unknown to us. However, the same cannot be said of comedy, since from the outset it was not taken seriously. It was only at a later stage that the archon allowed the poets a company of comic actors and choreutai; until then, the comic dramatists were volunteers. Information regarding the comic poets, in the strictest sense, is available only from the period in which comedy had to some degree achieved its definitive form (σχήματα). As to who introduced the comic mask and the prologue, however, and who increased the number of actors, as to all this and other factors too, no information has survived.

(*Poetics* 48b34–49a1 and 49a37–49b9)

In the context of the inextinguishable laughter of the gods, Plato also found fault with the contest between Achilles and Agamemnon, with the seductress Hera in the *Iliad*, book XIV, and with the interlude involving Ares and Aphrodite (*Republic* 389–90bc). In *Lysistrata*, Myrrhine behaves like an Aphrodisiac Hera, seducing her husband Kinesias for purposes of war, whereas for Aeschylus and Euripides, locked in artistic combat in *Frogs*, the renowned ἔρις is commemorated, and Achilles recalled, furious at the outrage (*Frogs* 877 and 992). The inextinguishable laughter of the gods returns for Hephaistos alone in the adultery scene criticized by Plato, in which the smith invites the gods to enjoy the spectacle of the imprisoned Ares and Aphrodite (although the goddesses decline this audacious invitation).

A gifted and witty poet, juggling with διαστήτην in the proem of the *Iliad*, imagined a dispute διὰ στήτην, for a girl. Parodying himself, through the dispute between knights over a mare at the end of the race in the Games, Homer alluded to the agon in the first book. And in their time the ancient scholiasts noticed the 'comedy of Thersites'.

In conclusion, pre-author and all authors in one: 'whosoever by virtue of his art is a tragic poet must also be a comic poet' (*Symposium* 223d); 'amongst all these fine tragic poets the first didaskalos and the pioneer was Homer' (*Republic* 595c); 'if you knew out of art and science how to speak of Homer, you would know at the same time how to speak of all poets, for the poietic is a single whole' (*Ion* 532c). Lastly, Plato, scalpel in hand, delivering a lecture: 'If you were to cancel the parts pertaining to the poet, lying between those of the characters, you would be left with the opposite form, the form of tragedy' (*Republic* 394b).

2

CHRONOLOGY OF AN APPRENTICESHIP

1 Pillars and chronological clues

In *Knights* 542–3, Aristophanes chooses to define as a period of apprenticeship the activity which pre-dates the Lenaian contest of 424, in which he made his official début with *Knights*. The import of this apprenticeship, during which the author did not present his comedies personally, is discussed briefly in section 6 of this chapter.

The extant 425 Lenaian comedy aside (*Acharnians*, staged victoriously by the didaskalos Kallistratos), the chronology of Aristophanes' apprenticeship rests on two separate pillars:

(a) 'ever since the Virtuous and the Inverted received great praise here . . . and I had to expose them – I was still unmarried and not allowed to give birth – and another girl took them and adopted them instead': thus Aristophanes in *Clouds* 528–31, on his own unofficial début. The scholiasts on *Clouds* 529 provide the title of the comedy 'of the Virtuous and the Inverted', Δαιταλῆς, or *Banqueters*, and transmit that Aristophanes came second in the list. Anon., *De comoedia* III communicates that Aristophanes made his début with the didaskalos Kallistratos, during the archontate of Diotimos, in 427. The contest remains unknown.

(b) 'I myself know well how much I suffered at Kleon's hands on account of last year's comedy', lines 377 and 378 of the Lenaian *Acharnians* from the year 425. It emerges directly from *Acharnians* 503–5 that 'last year's comedy' was not performed at the Lenaia. The scholiast on *Acharnians* 378 provides the title, Βαβυλώνιοι, whereas the *Suda* reports that *Babylonians* was staged by Kallistratos and confirms the date as 426. The place-list remains unknown: the current opinion, that *Babylonians* came first, is examined in section 5 of this chapter.

In short: 427, unofficial début with *Banqueters*, didaskalos Kallistratos, second place, contest unknown; Dionysia 426, *Babylonians*, didaskalos Kallistratos, place-list unknown; Lenaia 425, *Acharnians*, didaskalos Kallistratos, first place; Lenaia 424, official début with *Knights*, first place.

Some clues have led modern chronologers of Attic comedy to accept that Aristophanes was present at other contests in the years 426–425. In theory, along with the Lenaian contest in 426 and the Dionysian in 425, there is also the Dionysia in 427, should *Banqueters* prove to be Lenaian, that is: we know that the Lenaian contest took place in the seventh Attic month, hence preceding the Dionysian, which took place in the ninth. The clues are as follows:

(a) 'Antimachos, choregos at the Lenaia, sent me off without refreshments': *Acharnians* 1155;

(b) before his official début 'the poet . . . secretly helped other poets (ἑτέροισι ποηταῖς) . . . penetrated into other people's stomachs (εἰς ἀλλοτρίας γαστέρας)': lines 1018 and 1020 of *Wasps*, a 422 comedy staged by Philonides. The scholiast on *Wasps* 1018 reads: 'he presented some dramas through Philonides and Kallistratos; the first drama he presented personally was *Knights*'. *Vitae Aristophanis* 2 reads: 'Aristophanes presented the first dramas through Kallistratos and Philonides . . . although he later competed personally.' Further erudite witness, apparently regarding the apprenticeship, is discussed at the beginning of section 6 of this chapter.

The passage quoted from *Wasps* implies the existence of at least a fourth comedy during the years. of apprenticeship, whose didaskalos was not Kallistratos. The *Vitae* and scholiast apart, it is evident that the plurals in 1018 and 1020 are not generic, but must effectively be plurals. In any case, the contest without refreshments recalled in *Acharnians* 1155 in itself implies that Aristophanes was present at the Lenaia of 426, in which Eupolis had the first of his three Lenaian victories (see section 4). It can be ruled out that the passage from *Acharnians*, from the year 425, alludes to a choregos from the distant 427, in particular to the choregos of the successful *Banqueters*.

2 The contest without refreshments

It would not be so significant were an objection such as the following to be made against the contest 'without refreshments': why did the Dionysian *Babylonians*, staged two months later by Kallistratos, fail to lodge a complaint against the Lenaian choregos of 426? No, indeed, it would not be so significant, for the Acharnian chorus dedicates the entire satirical stasimon 1150–73 to this selfsame Antimachos, hence implying that *Babylonians* would have made only passing reference to him, if it was in time to do so at all. Nor would it be significant to object that the Lenaian *Acharnians* of 425 refers to the Dionysian *Babylonians* as to 'last year's comedy', implying that in 426 Aristophanes took part in the Dionysian contests alone. The poet, who most certainly did not write with his chronologers specifically in mind, is referring to the comedy last performed, the comedy which scandalized Kleon so. Hence, it is more than likely that Aristophanes was present at the Lenaia of 426.

All that can be said about the 426 Lenaian comedy is that its choregos was Antimachos. It cannot even be said with any degree of certainty that Philonides was the didaskalos, since he might have adopted that role, if not at the Dionysia of 427, at least at that of 425. Besides, it is not very prudent to bring up the name of Philonides when discussing the years of apprenticeship: the *Vitae Aristophanis* and the scholiast on *Wasps* 1018 do indeed mention him, but it is possible that in each case one is dealing with an inference from the frequent use Aristophanes made of Philonides from 422 onwards. The two different scholiasts on *Clouds* 531, for example, assert that *Banqueters* of 427 was entrusted to 'Philonides *and* Kallistratos' (even if one replaces the καί with an ἤ, it remains clear that this is simply conjecture). Regarding the years of apprenticeship, it is possible, on the basis of *Wasps* 1018 and 1020, to speak in terms of a 'poet'-didaskalos other than Kallistratos alone. Should this other didaskalos – as mentioned previously – not have handled the 426 Lenaian comedy, he might have been assigned a 425 Dionysian comedy instead. Further reference is made to this passage from *Wasps* in section 6.

Acharnians 299–302, while it does not testify to the presence of Aristophanes at the Dionysia of 425, does not exclude it either. In these lines, the poet indeed announces the upcoming anti-Kleonine *Knights*. However, his abnormally sudden announcement is made on-stage in January–February 425, when the composition of a comedy for the imminent March–April contest would already have been an accomplished fact, and the poet's attention already have turned to the succeeding contests. It is also true that Aristophanes would have been in some anxiety to announce the hard lesson he had reserved for Kleon, since neither *Acharnians* nor some other imminent comedy (as one may deduce from *Wasps* 1029–31) responds adequately to whoever was responsible for denouncing and persecuting the poet after the performance of *Babylonians* at the preceding Dionysia of 426. In section 6, certain considerations are offered as to why Aristophanes should have chosen *Knights* in particular as the comedy of his official début: at the end of section 5, other considerations are offered on the Dionysia of 425.

3 'Ever since the Virtuous and the Inverted'

As already mentioned, the contest of *Banqueters* remains unknown. In the parabasis of the *Second Clouds* Aristophanes re-evokes the comedy of his secret début, in the following context:

> Spectators, I shall freely tell you the truth, in the name of Dionysos, by whom I was bred. May I win and may I be judged a good poet, since considering you to be intelligent spectators, and this the most acute of my comedies, I felt it was right that you should be the first to relish it (πρώτους ἠξίωσ' ἀναγεῦσ' ὑμᾶς, line 523), this comedy which had cost me so much hard work. And yet I was forced to withdraw, defeated by buffoons – treatment I did not deserve. It is precisely for this that I reprove judicious people such as yourselves, for whom I had done so much. Despite everything, however, I would never betray those who are

15

intelligent amongst you. For ever since (ἐνθάδε) the Virtuous and the Inverted received great praise from people whom it is in itself a pleasure to entertain (οἷς ἡδὺ καὶ λέγειν, line 528), and I had to expose them – I was still unmarried and not allowed to give birth – and another girl took them and adopted them instead, and you brought them up generously and educated them well, since then I have had a sure guarantee of your understanding. So now, like Electra of old, comes this comedy, seeking spectators no less judicious: she will know well how to recognize the lock of her brother's hair the very moment she casts her eyes upon it.

It is known that *Clouds* was defeated at the Dionysian contest of 423 and that this parabasis from the *Second Clouds* was intended to vindicate the comedy during its performance in subsequent years. When the poet requested a chorus for *Clouds* from the archon in the summer of 424, he opted for the Dionysian contests, which were staged two months after the Lenaian. For the *Second Clouds* also, he chose the Dionysia, in order to address himself to the spectators *first* to have been offered *Clouds*: 'first', since in the summer of 424 Aristophanes had no intention of presenting the comedy to the audience of the upcoming Lenaian contests.

Aristophanes allows the fact that both comedies were presented at the Dionysia to pass teasingly as a compliment, as though he preferred the audience of the Dionysia to its rigorous and solemn contest. The compliment he offers to 'people whom it is in itself a pleasure to entertain' conveys the pleasure and sense of privilege felt at being admitted to the contest at least, and all the more so in the case of admission to a Dionysian contest. The greater consideration which the dramatists reserved for the Dionysian contests, under State control half a century earlier than those of the Lenaia, is reflected also in some Greek inscriptions discovered in one of the great libraries of Rome. In these inscriptions (*IG* XIV.1097 and 1098), which deal with fifth- and fourth-century poets, the Lenaian first places are preceded by the Dionysian, the Lenaian second places by the Dionysian, and so forth. Even when a Lenaian place-list pre-dates the corresponding Dionysian list considerably, the latter is given precedence.

The compliment 'people whom it is in itself a pleasure to entertain' is made as part of a reference to *Banqueters*. Aristophanes' choice of the same contest for both versions of *Clouds* is here made to pass also as a trusting preference for the spectators who had heaped praise on 'the Virtuous and the Inverted'.

The parabasis of the *Second Clouds*, composed in 419–417, invokes *Banqueters* from the year 427 and not *Acharnians*, *Knights* or other victorious comedies, because *Banqueters*, as the most important of the fragments demonstrate, must have dealt with an issue similar to that of the two *Clouds*: 'So now, like Electra of old, comes this comedy [the *Second Clouds*], seeking spectators no less judicious: she will know well how to recognize the lock of her brother's hair the very moment she casts her eyes upon it [the audience favourable to *Banqueters*]'. In short, *Banqueters* is not mentioned in pathetic terms as a début comedy, but because Aristophanes wishes mischievously to make his choice of the same contest pass as a gesture of esteem for the audience at that contest.

In the case of my début also, he might have said, I did not present myself at the Lenaia in January–February, but waited for the Dionysia in March–April instead. I waited for spring, for 'in every season, there are processions, sacrifices and banquets in Athens; and when springtime arrives, it is time for the feast of Bromios, the excitement of resounding choruses, the deep-quivering Muse of the flauts', thus *Clouds* 310–13, discussing the spring-time Dionysia.

'Ever since the Virtuous and the Inverted received great praise from people whom it is in itself a pleasure to entertain': scholars who, unlike us, cannot be suspected of partisanship regarding the two distinct Aristophanic theatres interpret ἐνθάδε as 'im Dionysostheater', 'on this spot', 'in the theatre', rejecting the tautologous, if not improper, interpretation of ἐνθάδε as 'in Athens'. The theatre of Dionysos, or rather the theatre housing the Dionysian contests alone: 'right here', the place in which *Clouds* competed in the contest of the Dionysia. The Lenaian *Acharnians* 140, through ἐνθαδὶ ἠγωνίζετο regarding a bad tragic poet, alludes instead to the Lenaion, where tragedy was admitted in 432. In *Clouds* 955, and at many other points, ἐνθάδε refers to the site of the dramatic action, in *Frogs* 783 to the zone reserved for the spectators, in *Clouds* 869 to the scenic façade, and so forth. In the parabasis generally, ἐνθάδε cannot but express 'here, here in the theatre'. During the parabasis, and especially during parabases of a personal kind (of which the parabasis of *Clouds* is the most outstanding example), one is necessarily in the theatre. When ἐνθάδε clearly means 'in Athens', the scenic milieu of the comedy is never Athenian (*Peace* 611 and 671, *Birds* 755, 757, 1455 and 1458).

It might be worth while to point out that the scholars, to a man, either mishandle or alter the πρώτους in *Clouds* 523, forgetting that the Dionysian contests took place after those of the Lenaia. Mishandled or altered, too, is οἷς ἡδὺ κτλ. in line 528, since no attention is paid to the fact that from the point of view of an artist writing for the theatre alone admission to a contest was satisfaction enough in itself.[1]

4 Supremacy overthrown, or the new poets of 428–426

The firm current opinion that *Babylonians* came first at the Dionysia of 426 is based on the so-called 'list of victors' of the Dionysian comic contests. Both the Dionysian and the Lenaian lists need to be re-examined, particularly since a fragment, published in 1943, of the so-called 'Fasti' has made it possible to establish that Hermippus – the name directly preceding the mutilated API in the Dionysian list – consigned a victory at the Dionysia, certainly his first, in 435, and has also indirectly confirmed that Pherekrates, who precedes

Hermippus in the list, won for the first time in 437. A serious disappointment for those chronologers who, attributing a victory in 426 to Ἀρι[στοφάνης took it upon themselves to lower Pherekrates and Hermippus' first victories to 431 and 430–427.

These marble lists (*IG* II².2325) are the architrave inscriptions of a monument to the contests erected most probably in 278, in whose interior were displayed the so-called 'Didaskalai' (*IG* II².2319–23). These fragmentary pieces, which were found mainly on the southern slopes of the Athenian Acropolis, list on different columns the poets (tragic and comic) and winning actors in accordance with the year of their first victory (although no chronological indications are provided), and beside the name of the poet or actor, the sum-total of his victories. Sometimes neither the names nor the figures have survived, sometimes only the name, sometimes only the figures (in the ensuing calculations it is presumed that the contests took place regularly each year and that on every occasion the first prize was actually awarded).

For the twenty-eight-year period 486–459 (Euphronios had his first victory in 458, as transmitted by the 'Fasti' (*IG* II².2318, col. II)), the Dionysian list contains the names of nine poets: this implies that in the course of their career these nine poets came first at least twenty-eight times. The list attributes eleven victories to Magnes and four to another four poets. Hence, the remaining four, whose names and victories have not been preserved (although the first was definitely Chionides, victorious in 486), must have come first four + *at least* nine times. However, should the first places of these four poets exceed thirteen, then the victories of some of the nine poets from 486–459 would have to be transferred to the year 457 and those following: Magnes, for example, victorious for the first time in 480, and again in 472, might also be assigned one of the nine victories remaining after 458. The list goes on in this way (for practical reasons I shall add the year of the first victory, where it is definitely known; the three missing names are referred to as Poet A, Poet B and Poet C):

<458> Euphronios one victory, Ekphantides four, Kratinos six, Diopeithes two, Krates three, <446> Kallias two, Teleikleides three, Poet A one, Poet B, Poet C, <437> Pherekrates, <435> Hermippus. Hermippus is followed by: a mutilated API, Eupolis, Kantharos (victorious in 422: cf. *IG* II².2318, col. V), Phrynichos, Ameipsias (the noted 414 victory was perhaps his first), Plato, a mutilated ΦΙΛ, Lykis and Leukon. After Leukon, the last poet on the second column, there are two empty lines. The third column lists Nikophon, Theopompos, Kephisodorus and a poet . . .I[, and therefore contains gaps. The fourth column is full of gaps. According to Lysias XXI.4, Kephisodorus had a victory in 402, which scholars think was his first.

In the thirty-six-year period 458–423 – 423 is the date of the noted victory of Kratinos, definitely his last – the list mentions eight poets sharing a total of twenty-two victories and includes another six with *at least* six successes. If the victories of poets from the period 486–459 were not consigned after 458, then the six poets, prior to Kantharos, to whom I have ascribed *one* victory, must by 424 have won a minimum of another eight times. The reference is to a minimum, since a couple of victories consigned by the poets preceding the aforementioned six might have come later than 422, or rather 421, in so far as first place in 421 is known to have gone to Eupolis.

Therefore, if one accepts the by now current integration 'Αρι[στοφάνης, victorious in 426, and the equally current attribution of first place in 424 to Eupolis, then the eight first places are to be assigned to Poets B and C, victorious around 443–440, and to Pherekrates and Hermippus, victorious in 437–435 (Poet C is almost certainly Lysippos, who won in about 440: cf. *IG* XIV.1097). Hence, within a period of eighteen to sixteen years, four dramatists must have consigned four + at least eight victories, and only in 426 would an uninterrupted series of successes pertaining to half a dozen older poets have been interrupted by a new poet (who made his début in 427), and in 424 by another, who had made his début in 429 at 17 years of age (the year of his début is transmitted by Anon., *De comoedia* 10, which is normally precise regarding débuts: Pherekrates' début, for instance, has been indirectly confirmed by the new fragment of the 'Fasti').

Is this vision of things convincing? The fact that Pherekrates and Hermippus, poets held in great esteem, accumulated a considerable number of victories should hardly come as a surprise: Hermippus wrote no fewer than forty comedies, and won four times at the Lenaia, Pherekrates twice – in their entire Lenaian career. Perhaps what might appear surprising is the uninterrupted series of victories consigned in 443–427 by a restricted circle of poets.

In any case, let us examine the record of first places at the contemporary Lenaian contests. The contest was inaugurated in 445–442 with a victory by Xenophilos, who had no further success. He was followed by Telekleides with five victories, Aristomenes with two, Kratinos with three, Pherekrates with two, Hermippus with four, Phrynichos with two (first victory in 428; début in 429, according to Anon., *De comoedia* 10), Myrtilos (Hermippus' brother) with one and Eupolis with three (first victory in 426). The last six lines of the list's first column are full of blanks (Eupolis was definitely followed by Aristophanes, victorious in 425; from the year of Aristophanes' victory and from that of Phrynichos' début, one may deduce the dates of Phrynichos', Myrtilos' and Eupolis' first places and the approximate date of the single victory consigned by the founding father Xenophilos). The second column mentions Poliochos with one victory (around 411), Metagenes and Theopompus with two, Polyzelos with four, Nikophon and Apollophanes with one, Ameipsias, Nikokare, Xenophon, etc.

During the seventeen–fourteen-year period 445/442–429 only six poets, with a career of seventeen victories, dominated the Lenaian contests. In 428 a new poet surfaced who had made his début in 429, followed by Myrtilos in 427, Eupolis in 426 and Aristophanes (undoubtedly rather young) in 425, 424 and 422 (in 422 with *Proagon*, under the name of Philonides). No information survives regarding the Lenaian contest of 423.

The clarity of the Lenaian records adds probability to the conjectural record of first places put forward regarding the Dionysia. The supremacy of the older and more mature poets, at the Dionysia as at the Lenaia, was only interrupted during the years 428–426, by poets who had just made their début, such as Phrynichos, Aristophanes and Eupolis. Until then, although the Lenaian contests had allowed for a larger number of poets since 445–442 (five poets at the Dionysia and five at the Lenaia), and hence for a calmer atmosphere in competition, none of the new poets had managed to gain first place: between 442–440 approximately and 428–426 the Lenaian and Dionysian first places went alternatively to half a dozen old or mature masters (with an average of six to four victories each), including Kratinos, Telekleides, Pherekrates and Hermippus. After 424, however, Lenaian victories consigned by the older poets are extremely rare and admissible only if one dates the single victory of the founding father Xenophilos to 442 rather than 445: in such a case, *three* victories, and three alone, can be ascribed to the old poets, in 423 (no documentation), 421 and the years following (no documentation). Pherekrates, active until around 414, was present at the Lenaia of 420, and definitely did not gain first place (cf. Plato, *Protagoras* 327d; Hermippus, one of the main poets of the preceding years, along with Pherekrates, is treated demeaningly by Aristophanes in the parabasis of *Clouds* from 419–418). The same must have been the case at the Dionysia, and not only because of the reduction in the number of poets from five to three, in force at both the Lenaia and the Dionysia from 425 at least (cf. Argument I to *Acharnians*, and also section 7 of this chapter).

This phenomenon might indicate that the judges and public recognized almost immediately the value of new poets such as Phrynichos, Aristophanes and Eupolis. One should note that in those years the hitherto stable nature of the Athenian public had undergone considerable alteration, due to the mass of country people which the Peloponnesian war, which broke out in 430, had displaced from country to city. Poets making their first appearance, many of whom must have been extremely young, had immediate success in this period, before this public, in an epoch in which six poets took part in the contests and no longer ten: the old or mature masters went into a gradual but steady decline.

The poet API[in the Dionysian list, therefore, might easily be Aristophanes and not, for example, Aristomenes, for the additional reason that should this thesis prove untrue, Aristophanes' name could not appear until after that succeeding Kephisodorus, i.e. towards 400–395, if not even later. All told, a highly improbable idea.

5 *Babylonians*, or concerning the superstition of the moderns

In the 426–422 period, the only definite Dionysian victories are those of Kratinos and Kantharos, in 423 and 422. This implies that Eupolis' victory must date to 425 or 424, Aristophanes' to 426 or 425. There is no evidence of either poet participating at the Dionysia of 425. As seen in section 2 above, there is nothing to exclude Aristophanes' having entered a comedy at the Dionysia of 425 (it should be remembered that of the 40 known Aristophanic comedies evidence exists for the performance of around 15 alone), and likewise Eupolis. That Eupolis was present at the Dionysian contests of 424, and was also victorious, has been deduced by some modern scholars from the inferences of the scholiasts on *Wasps* 1025 and *Peace* 763. These inferences are far from convincing. However, Eupolis must have won, once at least, in the years 425 or 424. Indeed, he could have won either in 425 or in 424, and Aristophanes either in 426 or in 425. In brief, if Aristophanes did not win in 426, Eupolis could only have won in 424.

Regarding the outcome of the contest of 426, we have sufficient evidence: the Lenaian *Acharnians* from 425, staged ten months after *Babylonians*. Prior to employing *Acharnians* as a means to unveiling the fortune of *Babylonians*, a preliminary statement is required: were *Babylonians* to have been victorious, this would imply that a series of Dionysian victories on the part of the older poets would have been clamorously interrupted, since the comedy's success would have been the first consigned by a new poet at the Dionysia since 436, to a poet who was also rather young, having made his début no earlier than 427.

The opening anapaests of the parabasis of *Acharnians* read: 'ever since our didaskalos has come to stand at the head of comic choruses he has never once said a word to the spectators about how skilled he is'. In the parabasis of *Acharnians* all the anapaests are dedicated to personal affairs, likewise the iambic trimeters 377–82 and 502–3 and the satirical stasimon deriding the Lenaian choregos Antimachos. *Acharnians*, indeed, is the comedy richest in personal references made outside the parabasis directly by the protagonist himself. Apart from the stasimon against Antimachos, the personal references all relate directly to *Babylonians*. Let us take a look, within the overall surrounding contest (the italics indicate the beginning and end of the personal passages, besides those of the parabasis):

> I'll say whatever I wish in favour of the Spartans. Although I'm really terribly afraid, for I know the taste of our country-folk, I know that they're always delighted whenever some impostor lauds them and the city, rightly or wrongly as the case may be, although they have no idea that they're being bought and sold. And as for the old folk, I know what's in their soul, they've no other wish than to bite with their vote. *I know well* what I suffered at Kleon's hands on account of last year's comedy. Having dragged me into the Boulē he slandered me, vomiting

a stream of lies, a real Cycloboros, a flood: I almost perished caught up in his slimy *tangles*. Allow me before speaking, therefore, to dress myself in the most pitiable fashion possible.

Thus trimeters 369–84. Trimeters 497–507 read:

Don't wish me ill, O gentlemen spectators, that I, a poor beggar, should come to speak before the Athenians about the city, in a tragi. . .comedy, for even tragicomedy can distinguish righteousness, and the words I speak will be hard, yet righteous. *This time* Kleon won't be able to slander me, accusing me of speaking ill of the city in the presence of *foreigners*, because we are here alone. The contest is in the Lenaion and the foreigners are absent: the tributes, as you know, haven't come, and not even the city's allies. Today, we are alone.

Anapaests 628–64 of the parabasis read:

ever since our didaskalos has come to stand at the head of comic choruses, he has never once said a word to the audience about how good he is. Yet since he has been slandered by his enemies before the Athenian public ready to decide, accused of deriding our city and of insulting the people, he has no alternative other than to defend himself before the Athenian public ready to change its mind. The poet asserts that he has done you much good service: thanks to him you are no longer so easily taken in by exotic speeches, you have ceased to develop a taste for adulation and have given up behaving like imbeciles. Once, in order to adulate you, the ambassadors of the cities christened you 'crowned with violets', and with that single 'crowned' put you all on the point of your behinds; and if in order to solicit you, someone referred to Athens as 'gleaming', thanks to that single 'gleaming' he got everything he desired, gratifying you with the lustre . . . of sardines. Through these actions he has done you much good service, also in showing you what kind of democracy reigns in the allied cities. And this is why now the people of the cities who must bear you the tributes will come desiring to see the fine poet who has dared to speak the language of righteousness to the Athenians. The news of his glorious courage has spread so far that even the King, sounding out the Lacedaemonian ambassadors, asked them first which of the two peoples was strongest at sea, and then for which the poet had reserved his disapproving words; since, he observed, the men of his country have much improved and that people, with such an adviser, were sure to win the war. This is why the Lacedaemonians have invited you to make peace, and demand Aegina! They couldn't care less about the island, but hope in this way to make off with your poet. Be on your guard, then, and never part from him, for he will defend the cause of righteousness in his comedies! He promises to teach you many fine things, in order to make you happy, without adulating you, without bribes, without tricks or clever schemes, without flattery, just by teaching you of the finest things.

Let Kleon devise his intrigues, plot against me as he will: goodness and justice will be my allies! I will never be caught acting as he does towards the city, as a coward and arch-queer!

Perhaps line 5 of *Acharnians* refers to the performance of *Babylonians*: 'what was that joy rising to the point of ecstasy? Ah, I recall. Within my breast my heart beat for joy when I saw Kleon spit out the five talents. How I rejoiced, and how I wish the Knights well for this exploit, worthy of Greece it is!' Line 15 refers to 'this year's' shows, which would seem to imply that the preceding ones were staged the year before. The interesting thing, in any case, is that in the parabasis and in the other personal passages regarding the comedy from the year before, the poet never takes the chance to counter Kleon's slander by referring to a triumphal verdict delivered by the judges of *Babylonians*, or even to the comedy's being definitively favoured by the public. He seems rather to feel obliged to explain the constructive intention of the comedy, as if it had not been well enough understood. While he does not moan about the audience, as he does in *Wasps* after the failure of *Clouds*, he does not exalt it either; nor does he let fall an expression such as that employed in *Clouds* regarding *Banqueters*, second in the place-list: 'ever since the Virtuous and the Inverted received great praise here'. One should bear in mind that *Babylonians* would have been Aristophanes' first victorious comedy, in an environment which had not seen a victory on the part of a new poet since 435.

Strange, strange indeed the reserve of Aristophanes: not a word said of his fresh and clamorous success with the Athenians, instead fanciful boasting regarding his fame with the King of Persia and with the Spartans. Strange, strange indeed the behaviour of the audience and judges: shortly before, the audience would have expressed its enthusiasm for *Babylonians*, and the judges awarded it victory; soon afterwards, along comes Aristophanes with his success 'slandered by his enemies before the Athenians ready to decide', to such an extent that Kleon had subsequently 'dragged [him] into the Boulē'.

In the fourth century at least, it appears that a popular assembly was held in theatre a day after the Dionysian contests, in order to discuss the archon's running of the event, and to consider any offence which might have arisen in the course of the festivities grave enough to lead to a denunciation, before the assembly, for public outrage (cf. Demosthenes, *Midias* 8–10). If the assembly seconded the denunciation, judicial proceedings were undertaken in the relevant seat. In the case of *Babylonians*, should one accept that such a practice already actually existed in the fifth century, the assembly in the theatre of Dionysos seconded Kleon's denunciation and Kleon brought the defendant before the Boulē. The Boulē, however, allowed the defendant to go free.

'This time' – says the protagonist of the Lenaian *Acharnians* – 'Kleon won't be able to slander me, saying that I have spoken ill of the city in the presence of foreigners. Because we are alone, the contest is in the Lenaion, and no foreigners are present: as you know, the tributes have not arrived, and not even the allies from the cities.' And the coryphaeus in the parabasis: 'Athenians, the poet has shown you what kind of democracy reigns in the allied cities. Hence, now the people of the cities who must bear you the tributes will come desiring to see [in theatre] the fine poet who has dared to speak the language of righteousness to the Athenians [in *Babylonians*, particularly].'

Whether an appointment with the allies in the theatre for the Dionysia of 425 is here implicit or not, it is in any case certain that the language of *Acharnians* does not lend itself to the idea of *Babylonians* having been a triumph. On the contrary, it excludes the idea of a triumph.

Aristophanes' first Dionysian victory must have taken place in 425, two months after his Lenaian victory over Kratinos and Eupolis with *Acharnians*. In the summer of 425, after these triumphs, the poet decided to request a chorus personally from the archon for the year 424 at least, or rather for *Knights*. The second triumph at the Dionysia must have been particularly rewarding, since it was the first to be consigned in that particular environment by a new poet since 435. At the Lenaia, the supremacy of the older poets had been shattered in 428 by Phrynichos, in 427 by Myrtilos and in 426 by Eupolis. Phrynichos won for the first time at the Dionysia after 421, Aristophanes in 425 and Eupolis, therefore, in 424; all three won first at the Lenaia and then at the Dionysia. First place at the Dionysia of 426 must therefore have gone to one of the old poets. The fact that Aristophanes presented two comedies in 425 is by no means unusual: the same is true of 426 and 422, and certainly of 424 and 423 also. This is discussed further on.

The Dionysia of 425 has never been considered in regard to Aristophanes, not so much because there is no evidence of his presence there, but because when at the end of an age-old dispute it became evident that not only in the fourth century but also in the fifth the names of the poets, not those of the didaskaloi, were inscribed in the so-called list of victors, it was automatically assumed that the list testified to the victory of *Babylonians*, staged by Kallistratos, after which nothing more was thought or said. This attribution would undoubtedly have been influenced by the persistent tendency to reduce the gap between the couple Pherekrates–Hermippus and Aristophanes, and also – why not indeed? – to reward as soon as possible the new recruit Aristophanes, hence establishing in one fell swoop that the Athenians were also willing to honour liberally the champion of their allies.[2]

To the ancient scholars, it emerged that *Banqueters* had come second in the place-list; they also knew the title of this 426 Dionysian comedy, whereas the *Suda* provided the name of the didaskalos. Regarding the place-list . . . silence: a silence which naturally does not imply a non-victory for *Babylonians*, but one which is peculiar, none the less. In the imperial anthology of Aristophanes' works, one of the reasons why the latest comedy, *Plutus*, was chosen must have been that it was the last with which the author had competed personally (cf. Argument III.4 to *Plutus*). Would *Acharnians*, the most ancient comedy in the collection, not have been 'chosen' because it was the first victory in the most absolute sense, and *Knights* because it was the first under Aristophanes' name? These are naturally hypotheses, which it is assuredly no pleasure to make, particularly when *Acharnians* might also have been chosen on account of the triad Aristophanes, Kratinos and Eupolis. The victory of *Babylonians*, however, is something less than a hypothesis. It is a superstition, which no consideration of ours is destined to affect, since the temptation to interpret a perfectly neutral text in a manner favourable to the few proven facts is so strong as to erase completely from scholars' minds the many other facts which have not been proven.

A victory a year earlier or a year later is obviously a trifle. However, it is better to pursue such trifles than to trust in those who have heard the thunder of liberal applause in the theatre of *Babylonians*, those who maintain that the Dionysian list provides an exact calendar record of the victory of *Babylonians* – the list which chronologers and 'historians' of literature prefer not to analyse, disdaining such 'ancillary' labour, although it contains *all* the instruments necessary for an accurate historical treatment of the rise of the new poets and the decline of the old.

Be that as it may, a better-founded chronology of Aristophanes' apprenticeship in the years 427–425 might perhaps be the following (angle brackets denote the new results and deductions; square brackets denote the current doctrine):

1 <Dionysia> 427: unofficial début with *Banqueters* produced by Kallistratos; second in place-list, first place to a pre-Aristophanic poet;
2 Lenaia 426: one comedy [*Centaur*] produced by a didaskalos [Philonides]; Eupolis' first victory after his début in 429 and also the third Lenaian victory of a new poet after Phrynichos' success in 428 (début 429) and that of Myrtilos in 427;
3 Dionysia 426: *Babylonians*, produced by Kallistratos, [victorious]; <victory of a pre-Aristophanic poet>;
4 Lenaia 425: *Acharnians* produced by Kallistratos, victorious over Kratinos and Eupolis; <first victory in Aristophanes' career>;
5 <Dionysia 425: a victorious comedy, produced by a didaskalos; second victory in Aristophanes' career and first affirmation at the Dionysia for a new poet since 435, followed by Eupolis' first Dionysian victory in 424>.

At least one of the two comedies presented at the Lenaia 426 and Dionysia 425 was entrusted to a didaskalos other than Kallistratos. In the summer of 425, Aristophanes asked the archon personally for a single chorus at least, that of *Knights*.

During the period of his apprenticeship, Aristophanes was definitely active on-stage in the course of his own comedies, one moment as a choreutes, another as the leader of a semi-chorus, and yet again as the coryphaeus of *Acharnians*: this is discussed in the following section.

6 The navarchs of 427–425 and the navarch of 424

Banqueters, *Babylonians* and *Acharnians* were entrusted to the didaskalos Kallistratos, therefore, and at least one of the two conjectural comedies from 426–425 to a different didaskalos. This implies that *Knights* was followed by another thirty-four comedies. Theatrical information exists regarding eleven comedies alone: Dionysia 423, *Clouds*, didaskalos Aristophanes (discussed further on), Lenaia 422, *Wasps*, didaskalos Philonides, Lenaia 422, *Proagon*, with Philonides as official author and didaskalos, Dionysia 421, *Peace*, didaskalos Aristophanes, Lenaia 414, *Amphiaraus*, didaskalos Philonides, Dionysia 414, *Birds* and Dionysia 411, *Lysistrata*, didaskalos Kallistratos, Lenaia 405, *Frogs*, didaskalos Philonides, 388, *Plutus*, didaskalos Aristophanes. After *Plutus* Aristophanes entrusted *Kokalos* and the *Second Aiolosikon* to his son Araros.

Anon., *De comoedia* II, having informed us that Aristophanes made his début under the archon Diotimos, with Kallistratos (the title is not provided), goes on:

τὰς μὲν γὰρ πολιτικὰς τούτῳ φασὶν αὐτὸν διδόναι, τὰ δὲ κατ᾽ Εὐριπίδου καὶ Σωκράτους Φιλωνίδῃ. διὰ δὲ τούτων νομισθεὶς ἀγαθὸς ποιητής, τοῦ λοιποῦ <αὐτὸς> ἐπιγραφόμενος ἐνίκα. ἔπειτα τῷ υἱῷ ἐδίδου τὰ δράματα, ὄντα τὸν ἀριθμὸν μδ΄, ὧν νόθα δ΄.

According to the data and material at our disposal, this hearsay transmitted by the Anonymous, if it alludes to the period of the apprenticeship alone, is invalidated by *Acharnians*, a comedy 'against Euripides' entrusted to Kallistratos, whereas if it alludes to Aristophanes' whole career, *Wasps* entrusted to Philonides is contrary neither to Euripides nor to Socrates. Perhaps the source is referring only to comedies which Aristophanes was able to cede to didaskaloi, such as *Proagon*, for instance, whose characters, according to the scholiast on *Wasps* 61, included Euripides? Argument I to *Thesmophoriazusae* reads: 'this drama is also one of those composed against Euripides'. Does this imply that *Thesmophoriazusae* – for which no theatrical information survives – was also ceded to Philonides? These are all hypotheses, and dangerous ones into the bargain. Moreover, apart from the fact that the Anonymous is apparently referring to the period of the apprenticeship alone, it would also appear that Aristophanes did not cede his last comedies to his son, but rather entrusted them to him as didaskalos (Argument III.5–7 on *Plutus*, and see also the end of the present section). In short, the means at our disposal are insufficient to allow for a correct interpretation of the hearsay which has been referred to us by the Anonymous. And pure hearsay it is, for it seems that neither the Anonymous nor his sources are in a position to verify their information: if one examines the short treatise thoroughly, it becomes clear that the various φασίν of the Anonymous indicate that some of the information is hypothetical. In general, this article on Aristophanes is rather summary and brief: note, for example, ὄντα κτλ. summing up the entire career of the dramatist, or the fact that Kallistratos, with an elliptical γάρ, is immediately defined as a 'political' didaskalos, without a single reference to the title of the début comedy; note also the hasty inaccuracy of τοῦ λοιποῦ ἔπειτα κτλ. There is likewise the fact that the tradition of the text, preserved in the Estensis and Aldine, is of no particular value.

Another source, the Venetus 427 and the Aldine, reads: ὑποκριταὶ Ἀριστοφάνους Καλλίστρατος καὶ Φιλωνίδης, δι' ὧν ἐδίδασκε τὰ δράματα ἑαυτοῦ· διὰ μὲν Φιλωνίδου τὰ δημοτικά, διὰ δὲ Καλλιστράτου τὰ ἰδιωτικά. The exact contrary of the Anonymous, albeit lacking the specification that the word 'private' is intended to indicate the dramas against Euripides and Socrates. Even if one transposes the names of Philonides and Kallistratos, the aforementioned incongruity does not disappear altogether. The most striking aspect of this source, which definitely refers to Aristophanes' entire career, is its description of the didaskaloi as 'actors'. The second scholiast on *Clouds* 531 asserts that Aristophanes' unofficial début was seen to by 'Kallistratos and Philonides, who later became actors of Aristophanes'. Worse than voyaging in the dark.

Nevertheless, the distinction between dramas which are 'public and political' and others which are 'private' must have its roots somewhere, roots of a scholastic kind. Perhaps the forty Aristophanic comedies were indeed divided, empirically, in this way for the schools of the period; and perhaps the 'private' comedies were those with the greatest tendency towards the literary and cultural. According to the most ancient scholars, the *greater part* of the latter comedies were staged by Philonides, and the greater part of the 'public and political' by Kallistratos. However, for Anon., *De comoedia*, and perhaps for his sources too, the transmitted distinction could no longer be satisfactorily verified, because of the sparse theatrical information then surviving. It is in any case strange that the distinction should be mentioned, apparently at least, with reference to the period of apprenticeship alone. However, let us repeat, the Anonymous' article on Aristophanes bears all the signs of having been the fruit of a compendium.

Should we modern scholars, with the means at our disposal, set out to make a distinction between the two didaskaloi, we could say little other than that Philonides appears to have been assigned the Lenaian dramas alone and Kallistratos, with the exception of *Acharnians*, the Dionysian: in 414, for example, *Amphiaraus* was staged by Philonides at the Lenaia, while Kallistratos was preparing the staging of the Dionysian *Birds*. It must be admitted, however, that this distinction has feet of clay.

In conclusion: after *Knights*, Philonides was didaskalos thrice, 'author' once, Kallistratos didaskalos twice, Araros didaskalos twice and Aristophanes himself didaskalos thrice. No information survives regarding the other twenty-three comedies, one at least of which was never performed, i.e. the *Second Clouds*. It is not improbable, however, that Aristophanes may have used Kallistratos and Philonides (and perhaps others too) more often than appears to be the case: 'afterwards he *also* competed in person' (*Vitae Aristophanis*).

More than one contemporary dramatist said that 'Aristophanes was born at the fourth day of the month', and the scholiast on Plato, *Apology* 19c, comments, 'he passed his entire life labouring for others . . . . Herakles, too, was born on the fourth day of the month'. The dramatists mentioned were apparently referring to the period of apprenticeship, since the *Vitae* alludes to them after having said: 'Aristophanes' first dramas were staged through Kallistratos and Philonides.' In any case, following the rout of *Clouds* in 423, Aristophanes mischievously depicted that particular period of his career, in *Wasps* 1017–18, as one during which he was extremely benevolent towards the spectators, not appearing himself, perhaps, but 'helping other poets in secret'. Certainly, the greater part of the spectators (leaving aside the 'many who went in total amazement to the poet, asking him why for some time he had not requested a chorus in his own name': *Knights* 512f.) did not know that the poet active in 427–425 was Aristophanes. The reason for this is that it was the didaskalos and not the poet – if the didaskalos was not the poet himself – whom the herald invited personally to 'introduce the chorus' into the theatre. The herald also proclaimed the name of the victorious poet-didaskalos at the end of the contest, the poet-didaskalos whom the archon promptly crowned in the theatre. 'Desiring to present his son Araros to the spectators, through him Aristophanes entered the two comedies after *Plutus*.'[3]

After *Knights*, Aristophanes' recourse to didaskaloi would have done nothing to damage his reputation. By then Kallistratos and Philonides would have been almost synonymous with Aristophanes, given that neither had ever worked with any consistency for other poets. To us it does not appear that Kallistratos, whom Aristophanes used at the very beginning of his 'secret' career, was himself a comic poet: more precisely, either he was not a comic poet or, if at some point he had been, he had later specialized as a didaskalos. That Aristophanes should refer to him as a 'poet' in that particular passage from *Wasps* is perfectly natural. Neither does Philonides appear to have been particularly prolific: the *Suda*, which informs us that 'he was first a painter', attributes three comedies to him. In the thirteenth line of the second column of the list of victorious comic poets at the Dionysia, there stands a mutilated ΦΙΛ. Some infer Phil[onides, others Phil[ilios: if the name is Philonides, one should not forget that Aristophanes might have ceded him one of his comedies, as he had in the case of *Proagon*, for instance. It appears that this particular Dionysian first place cannot be dated any earlier than 413.

It is not in the least surprising that Aristophanes should so often have resorted to didaskaloi, considering the intensity and extent of his work. Besides, we know nothing of his rivals' behaviour in this respect: the only definite information is that Eupolis entrusted the *Autolycus* of 420 to a didaskalos. The instruction of the choreutai and actors alone required considerable time and energy. Or was it that Aristophanes lacked the skills necessary to meet all the demands of production? This much has been deduced by some scholars from *Knights* 515–16: νομίζων κωμῳδοδιδασκαλίαν εἶναι χαλεπώτατον ἔργον ἁπάντων. Here, however, Aristophanes is saying that the *art of comedy*, the creation of comedy, the work of the dramatist, is most difficult of all: also, in the technical sense διδάσκαλος means the author of theatrical works. For Aristophanes' use of this term, see *Acharnians* 628, *Knights* 507, *Peace* 734, 737, 738, 829, *Birds* 912, 1403, *Thesmophoriazusae* 30, 88, *Second Thesmophoriazusae*, fr. 334, *Plutus* 797, and cf. Harpokration I, p. 96, 4–9. In *Assemblywomen* 809 χοροδιδάσκαλος means the instructor of the chorus (regarding ἔργον cf. at least *Clouds* 524). What we call the 'didaskalos', Plato's *Ion* 536a called ὑποδιδάσκαλος, and Photius under this particular entry reads: ὁ τῷ χορῷ καταλέγων. διδάσκαλος γὰρ αὐτὸς ὁ ποιητής, ὡς Ἀριστοφάνης. However, the ποιητής Aristophanes 'for the first time began to διδάσκειν' in *Knights* (*Wasps* 1029).

Of greater interest is the third argument by which Aristophanes, in the parabasis of *Knights* 542–4, justifies his prudent three-year apprenticeship (first argument: the art of comedy is difficult; second argument: the public is voluble and difficult): 'first of all one must be an oarsman, then take the helm, after that stand at the prow and observe the winds and lastly govern the ship oneself'. This passage is particularly interesting, since *Clouds* 530, 'I was still unmarried (παρθένος) and not allowed (οὐκ ἐξῆν) to give birth' – uttered regarding the first 427 comedy which 'another girl (παῖς ἑτέρα) took and adopted' – in practice expresses the third argument of *Knights*: I was still an oarsman and not allowed to steer, to be a navarch. The image from *Clouds* leaves no room for speculation, either regarding Aristophanes' age or regarding a hypothetical minimum age for admission to the dramatic contests. Similarly, with respect to *Knights* 512–13, 'as to the total amazement of the many of you who came to the poet, asking him why for some time (πάλαι) he had not requested a chorus in his own name', it is by no means true that πάλαι implies 'since the poet has reached the legal age'; more probably it implies 'since his comedies have begun to go well'.

The continued delay after *Babylonians* and after the ensuing incident with Kleon (and after *Acharnians* also, if one allows for a comedy at the Dionysia of 425; nevertheless the request for a chorus would have had to be forwarded in the summer of 426, for this comedy as well as for the eventually victorious *Acharnians*) was perhaps the result of a calculated decision to appear officially with the authoritative chorus of the knights against the most powerful man in Athens. The coryphaeus of *Knights* 507–11 utters the following:

> if one of the old comic poets [this does not refer to the didaskaloi employed during the years of apprenticeship] had tried to constrain us

knights to address the public in the parabasis, he wouldn't have got away with it so lightly. But this time the poet is worthy because he hates the same people as we do and because he dares to speak the truth, and marches generously against Typhon and Hurricane [i.e. Kleon].

On-stage in *Acharnians* 299–302, in January–February 425, the coryphaeus had suddenly exclaimed: 'I hate you even more than Kleon, whose hide I'll have to make shoes for the knights!' In *Wasps* 1029 and 1031 and *Peace* 754, Aristophanes contentedly dwells on the fact that his official career began with the attack on Kleon.[4]

And now, arriving at the seafaring *Knights* 542–3, who steer a course towards an apprenticeship pursued on the stage also: (1) as oarsman, (2) as helmsman, (3) observing the winds from the prow: i.e. the author is playing court to comedy on-stage as a choreutes, next standing at the head of a semi-chorus and finally at the head of the chorus as a whole (the latter was certainly the case in *Acharnians*).

The 'helmsman' leads directly to the corps of twenty-four choreutai, which appears soon afterwards (546), during the invocation to the 'eleven oars' (the choreutai are grouped as follows: 11 + 11 + 1 + 1). The parabasis of *Peace* offers an image of Aristophanes coming out 'in previous years' at the end of successful performances and 'gathering the mask/the costume' (τὴν σκευήν; at *Knights* 1324 and *Frogs* 108, 'mask/costume' of the actor; the mask-makers appear in *Knights* 232). The parabasis of *Wasps* 1018–22 provides another self-portrait: Aristophanes has secretly poured a series of comic inventions into other people's bellies, in the manner of the soothsayer Eurycles, who spoke through other people's bellies. Likewise the poet, in the period of his apprenticeship, bridled the Muses of others, not his own.[5]

In any case, the passage from *Knights* quoted above – 'as to the total amazement of the many of you who came to the poet' – indicates that the 'secret' career was not a secret at all: at least after *Babylonians* and the ensuing incident with Kleon, Aristophanes' name must have slipped out somehow. One should note that the parabasis of *Acharnians*, made public in the theatre by Kallistratos, when it defends and praises the διδάσκαλος and the ἄριστος ποιητής as 'Aeginetan', does not defend the selfsame Kallistratos who had brought *Babylonians* before the public ten months before, just to be slandered by Kleon and generally misunderstood. Little does it matter should the most ignorant of the spectators of *Acharnians* – imitated by modern scholars – have attributed the Kleon affair entirely to the didaskalos who had brought the chorus into the theatre; little does it matter either should they have expected Kallistratos to be the author of *Knights*, heralded in *Acharnians*. The 'secret' poet of *Acharnians*, writing the first personal parabasis of his career (cf. *Acharnians* 628f.), would certainly not have concealed himself to such an extent that he would have referred to Kallistratos alone, hence Aeginetan etc., expressing himself, so to speak, in the spirit of the General Register Office. In defending and praising the διδάσκαλος and the ἄριστος ποιητής the author defended and praised the διδάσκαλος (i.e. the ποιητής) of *Babylonians* and the previous comedies ('ever since our διδάσκαλος has come to stand at the head of comic choruses', *Acharnians* 628), the 'Aeginetan': the Aeginetan seriously for officials of the Register Office alone.

Athenians – says the Acharnian coryphaeus – do not accept the Spartans' offer of peace; the Spartans want peace only in order to take possession of the island of Aegina, or rather, along with the island, to make off with the poet, since they have heard from the King of Persia that whoever has this particular poet on his side is sure to win the war.... Let us think for a moment: Aristophanes was definitely Athenian, from the city deme; perhaps his father Philippus' holding lay on Aegina; the Spartans were not requesting the cession of Aegina but simply autonomy for the island, occupied by the Athenians and assigned to its cleruchy. In the semi-serious admonition not to make peace and consign Aegina to the Spartans might there not be a touch of light-hearted preoccupation regarding the holding on the island?

After *Babylonians*, perhaps Kleon had dragged Kallistratos alone before the Boulē, and not Aristophanes, since he was indignant that the city and the people had been offended in the theatre in the presence of the foreigners (cf. *Acharnians* 503). Yet *Acharnians* naturally replies in the name of the author of *Babylonians*: the personal parabasis and the mention of Aegina put *the poet* in the limelight, at least for those who are aware that the poet and coryphaeus were one and the same.

If this problem is regarded as still worth pursuing, it will be worth while referring to *Wasps*, despite the fact that it is a comedy from the official period of Aristophanes' career. After the failure of *Clouds* at the Dionysia of 423 (with Aristophanes himself as didaskalos), the poet competed at the Lenaia the following year with two comedies, *Proagon* and *Wasps*. Apparently to evade a norm prescribing one comedy per author (this is discussed further on), Aristophanes ceded *Proagon* to Philonides, didaskalos of its fellow-competitor *Wasps*, and Philonides passed to all effects as the author of *Proagon*. In itself, this expedient demonstrates that the copyright and public responsibility for a work entrusted to a didaskalos – in this case *Wasps* – belonged none the less to the author. Additional internal proof of the latter is provided by *Wasps* 1016–42, 1043–59 and 1284–91: the coryphaeus speaks of the artistic career of the ποιητής before and after *Knights* and of the failure of *Clouds*, whereas the chorus, in the first person and in Aristophanes' name, speaks of the Kleon affair provoked by *Babylonians*. All highly personal and extremely hurtful facts which *Proagon*, ceded to Philonides at the same contest, apparently did not mention at all.

Note that the chorus of *Acharnians* 299–302 speaks in the first person, as does the chorus of *Wasps* 1284–91; in the parabasis of *Acharnians*, the coryphaeus speaks in the third person, as in the parabases of *Knights*, *Wasps* and *Peace*, moving to the first person in *Acharnians* 659–64 and *Peace* 754–74.

31

The coryphaeus of the highly personal parabasis of *Clouds* speaks in the first person throughout. This implies that there is no distinct expressive practice for comedies assigned to didaskaloi, not even in the case of *Acharnians*, whose author was the new recruit Aristophanes: the chorus and the coryphaeus always speak in the first or third person, in the *poet's* name.[6]

Regarding Araros' acting as his father's didaskalos, yet another controversy has emerged. Argument III of the extant *Plutus* reads: '*Plutus* is the last comedy that Aristophanes put into competition under his own name [cf. scholion *Plutus* 173]. Desiring to present his son Araros to the spectators [cf. *Vitae Aristophanis* 10], through him Aristophanes presented the remaining two, *Kokalos* and *Aiolosikon*.' The Dionysian 'Fasti' relative to 387 record a victory of] PΩC. Scholars are unanimous in identifying the latter as Ara]ros, particularly as only three letters are missing. Regarding Araros, the *Suda* says: διδάξας τὸ πρῶτον ὀλυμπιάδι ρα', i.e. he made his début in 375–372. If the text of the *Suda* is not corrupt, and the date therefore correct, victory at the Dionysia of 387 is to be assigned to Aristophanes, with Araros as didaskalos. The comedy would have been *Kokalos* (if the 388 *Plutus* was Lenaian, then strictly speaking *Kokalos* might already have been staged at the Dionysia of 388). Some scholars are bemused by the fact that having put only one more comedy into competition for his father, *Aiolosikon*, Araros should have waited for ten years before competing with a comedy of his own. This is why they reject the findings of the *Suda* and assign first place at the Dionysia of 387 to a comedy by Araros. Should this be true, then Araros would have made his début and won, not in the 101st Olympiad, but rather in the 98th, in the years 387–384. The fragments of the 'Fasti', engraved from 346 onwards, and the parallel material do not make it possible for one to establish whether the name of the didaskalos was engraved or that of the poet.

The question remains open, therefore. Strictly speaking, one should also take into account the hypothesis that *Kokalos* and *Aiolosikon* were fellow-competitors, and that Araros would have figured as author of the winning comedy and as didaskalos of the other.

3

ACHARNIANS

1 Aristophanes, the coryphaeus

In chapter 1, the Lenaion was indicated as the site on which comedies were performed for the contests of the Lenaia alone. A passage was also quoted which polemically emphasizes the fact that the audience of *Acharnians* was composed exclusively of Athenians, and that 'the contest takes place in the Lenaion': further evidence is provided in section 1 of chapter 4 on *Knights*.

Argument I.37–40 reads: (τὸ δρᾶμα) ἐδιδάχθη ἐπὶ Εὐθύνου ἄρχοντος ἐν Ληναίοις διὰ Καλλιστράτου· καὶ πρῶτος ἦν· δεύτερος Κρατῖνος Χειμαζομένοις, οἳ οὐ σῴζονται· τρίτος Εὔπολις Νουμηνίαις. The victory of *Acharnians* was apparently Aristophanes' first success, at the beginning of the third year of his career: if the considerations made in section 5 of the preceding chapter are indeed correct, then the Dionysian first place mentioned in the victors' list would not have been consigned in 426, but rather in 425, two months after the first place with *Acharnians*.

Acharnians is the only extant comedy from the period of Aristophanes' apprenticeship, during which – as remarked previously – he did not present his comedies personally, but preferred to appear in the chorus. In this, the fourth comedy of the apprenticeship, 'our διδάσκαλος who is at the head of the chorus' lets the audience know for the first time how skilled he is: Ἐξ οὗ γε χοροῖσιν ἐφέστηκεν τρυγικοῖς ὁ διδάσκαλος ἡμῶν / οὔπω παρέβη πρὸς τὸ θέατρον λέξων ὡς δεξιός ἐστιν (628–9). This professional and extremely ambiguous expression, although it is intended to refer to the secret author, characterizes him none the less as the leader of the chorus, or rather as the *coryphaeus*, soon to become the mouthpiece of the ποιητής (633, 644, ποιητὴν τὸν ἄριστον, 654).

The Acharnian coryphaeus speaks like Aristophanes once more when he begins a dialogue with the first actor-Dikaiopolis: 'I hate you even more than I hate Kleon, whose hide I'll have to make shoes for the Knights' (299–302). Hence, it is the coryphaeus who sets the key for the well-known theme of personal ambiguity discussed in the preceding chapter.[1]

2 The identity of characters in Aristophanes

Regarding the protagonist of *Acharnians*, it would now be more useful to ask why his name should appear at such a late stage, and why in that particular position: the name Dikaiopolis is to a considerable extent a 'speaking name'. To add grist to his own mill, Cyril Bailey would have us believe that Aristophanes himself was the first actor of *Acharnians* and observes that adjectives in -πολις are not applied to people, but rather to districts or states. In Pindar, *Ol*. 2.8, however, ὀρθόπολις is attributed to Theron, 'who governs the State well', and the character in *Plutus* 901, who bears the siglum Δίκαιος in the manuscripts, is implicitly considered φιλόπολις, and so forth. The name Δικαιόπολις, moreover, rather than the 'Righteous Citizen', is intended more expressively as Δίκαιος περὶ τὴν πόλιν, he who is righteous towards the city, he who renders the city righteous, or as a model for the entire city (cf. 971). Just as Aristophanes, in *Babylonians*, 'dared to speak the language of righteousness to the Athenians', and promised always to 'defend the cause of righteousness in [his] comedies', and to have 'righteousness as [his] ally, and never be found acting like Kleon towards the city, as a coward and arch-queer' (the Acharnian coryphaeus in 645, 655, 661–4), on-stage today it is Dikaiopolis who knows and speaks 'righteousness' (317, 500f., 562; cf. *Knights* 510, which might *also* allude to Dikaiopolis), and the comedy's plan, as normal, is that of saying 'useful things', χρηστά. Is it really casual therefore that his speaking name should appear so late, in line 406?

Or might it not be that this character, on-stage since the beginning of the comedy, has just identified himself with the author of *Babylonians* (in lines 377–82, to be precise), with the poet accused of 'deriding the city in his comedies and of insulting the people' (*Acharnians* 631), accused by Kleon of ἀδικία εἰς τοὺς πολίτας (according to the scholion on 378), of being anything other than righteous towards the city? And might it not also be because Dikaiopolis, soon afterwards, having asked Euripides for the rags of Telephus, should figure as the protagonist of a tragicomedy of righteousness aimed, not 'against the city', as in *Babylonians*, but rather against unspecified individuals in Athens (cf. 496–518)? His programmatic name, therefore, already known to the audience, might be intended to offset the range of the polemic. Is it mere coincidence, moreover, that Dikaiopolis should make no reply when Euripides' Servant asks him 'who are you?' (395), but instead waits for a few minutes before invoking Euripides at the top of his voice, Δικαιόπολις καλῶ σ' ὁ Χολλῄδης ἐγώ? Euripides, the poet of the 'righteous' Telephus, and the poet and father of heroes χωλοί.

Aristophanes' normal practice in presenting speaking names – or names rendered thus – seems to exclude any idea of casualness. Either these names appear after some delay and then go on to 'speak' coherently in the direction established, at times enriching themselves with new allusions, or else, when they appear with little delay or immediately, at first seem to 'speak' in one manner, but then in another which is more profoundly significant. The speaking name which is more or less delayed – beginning with that of the protagonist of *Acharnians* – is not *as a rule* a historical one, whereas the apparent division of a nominal personality is usually executed by recourse to well-known historical names. In the case of Agoracritos in *Knights*, one encounters both of these games: on the one hand, that of *Clouds* (Pheidippides), *Wasps*, *Birds*, *Peace* and *Assemblywomen*, on the other that of *Knights* (the Paphlagonian), *Clouds* (Strepsiades) and *Lysistrata*.

The protagonists of *Birds* only receive their two names at 644–5. In *Wasps* 133–4, the names of the still-inactive protagonists appear at the end of what is substantially indirect stage representation of their exploits, and also with some effect, after lengthy preparation: the clausula of 133, Φιλοκλέων, would undoubtedly have been pronounced clearly and distinctly (cf. 77), since with a glance towards the amused audience the Servant adds: 'just like that, by Zeus' (134a). The Servant prologuist of *Peace* does not mention the name of his master Trygaeus. Rather it is Trygaeus himself, on-stage since 82, who decides to disclose his name in line 190, at the request of the celestial doorman: 'I am "Grape-harvester", a vine-dresser of quality, neither a spy nor an evil-doer.' At the end of the comedy, however, the 'grapes' he is to 'harvest' are those of a beautiful maiden going by the name of Harvesthome (*Peace* 1339–40). The name Φειδ-ιππίδης appears in *Clouds* 67: indeed it is invented after the youth has already been characterized as a horseman. When the name is heard for the last couple of times, in lines 1143 and 1229, it is the first part of the compound that 'speaks': the father deludes himself into believing that his erstwhile horseman, now sophist son has become his 'piggybank'. And Pheidippides, formerly anointed and wearing a long mane like a true horseman, emerges from the reflectory wearing instead the long and filthy mane of the sophists ὑπὸ τῆς φειδωλίας (cf. *Clouds* 835). The name of the protagonist of *Assemblywomen* also appears with some delay, in line 124, and one might almost say that by virtue of her 'nominal' fate Praxagoras disappears prematurely from the stage, to govern permanently the off-stage zone of the Agora (cf. 711–16). Aristophanes' normal practice with delayed speaking names can be observed in miniature in the case of the minor roles: the Peasant in *Acharnians*, for example, is mentioned in 1028 after around ten lines, lamenting tragically: 'I've lost my eyes weeping over the oxen; if you care for Δερκέτης Φυλάσιος [even the demotic seems to have speaking qualities], quickly, anoint my eyes with peace.' Perhaps this character, whose eyes are so little 'open', might also have worn an appropriate mask.

The name of the Paphlagonian is heard at once – in line 2 (the character appears in 235) – and at first is apparently just the name of a slave of foreign birth; the name, however, does *not* 'paphlagonize', and begins to seethe only at line 19. Naturally the seething voice of the actor would have explained well in advance the choice of this apparently historical name; and should anyone have failed to understand, not only does the poet provide an explanation, but he also seems to enjoy himself in doing so. The protagonist of *Clouds* remains anonymous until 134, despite the confidences he has shared with the spectators. The eventual mention of his name would undoubtedly have provoked a wave of laughter, for it emerges that the bearer of this Pindaric, high-sounding, noble, historical name, which generates a resolution in the severe line in which it appears, is no more than a countryman whose sole preoccupations hitherto have been his debts and his unhappy marriage to a noblewoman. However, the name is explained in 1455 as meaning 'Enemy of justice', and this has been substantially clear since line 434. Amongst the extant comedies, only in *Lysistrata* are the spectators already aware – through the title – of the name of the presumed protagonist of the comedy (the case of the personified Plutus in *Plutus* is different): this is why it appears in line 6 without delay. However, the spectators would not immediately have interpreted the name as meaning 'Army dissolver', for the added motive that the extremely common historical name Lysistratus was that of an Athenian personality frequently mentioned by Aristophanes, notorious at the time for his vices, physical frailty and cowardice. At the beginning, therefore, the protagonist, furnished with a typically male name, could be a woman possessed of exceptional male energy and athletic prowess (her name appears in combination with a χαῖρ', ὦ Κλεονίκη, alluding probably to the noted philo-athletic ὦ καλλίνικε χαῖρε: cf. *Knights* 1254): obviously there was no need for this woman to wear a mask more or less resembling the afore-mentioned Lysistratus. The second and more profound meaning of the name is alluded to – with a reference to Lysistratus himself – at the climax of the action in 1105 (see also 554): the reference to Lysistratus is a mischievous one, since it is made by a Laconian, and the Laconians were a race of notorious pederasts. The Sausage-seller in *Knights* is called Agoracritos only in line 1257, as a 'man of the Agora'. Yet Agoracritos is also the name of a historical personality of the time, whose value is naturally positive. When the name of the present Agoracritos is repeated after the second parabasis, he has become a man of honour, one who works miracles, the best agoretes in Athens (cf. 1335, 1373).

In the case of the non-speaking names of protagonists and important characters in Aristophanes, the mode of presentation is different. Historical names appear immediately, with the one exception of Kleisthenes, which appears about fifty lines into the text (but cf. *Thesmophoriazusae* 574): Euripides, Socrates, Hierokles, Meton, the poet Kinesias, Agathon, Aeschylus and Lamachus. The name Lamachus also suggests 'the warlike' and hence is of considerable resonance in *Acharnians*, and also in *Peace*, in which Lamachus may not appear as a character but in which, amongst other things, a warlike youth at the end of the comedy defines himself as the son of Lamachus (1290, cf. 1293 and the playful reference in 473). The immediate naming of historical personalities is not always casual. At times – as in *Thesmophoriazusae* 4, for instance – it is designed to help the spectators identify at once the approximate portrait mask being worn by the actors: it is unlikely that the audience would have found itself in the position, let us say, of Euripides' Relative, who had never seen the poet Agathon and hence was unable to recognize his mask (cf. *Thesmophoriazusae* 30–4, 97; the reverse at *Knights* 230–4). As remarked in chapter 2, Aristophanes availed himself of real historical personalities, from his own deme, the Kydathenaion: not only was he frequently paired with the didaskalos Philonides, but often either cites or adopts Amphitheos and Simon, both from the thiasus of Herakles (*Acharnians* 45 and *Knights* 242).

Common names also appear immediately: the 'slave' and 'master' in the second line of *Plutus*, however, remain anonymous until 624 and 336 respectively (although Chremylos could be a speaking name); in *Thesmophoriazusae*, the future protagonist, along with the immediately identified Euripides, is described as Euripides' Relative in 74 – his anonymity is intentional (cf. 584 and 861). The delayed identification of the character is undoubtedly calculated, and so too the expressive focus on his 'old man's' mask in line 63 (after 59–62). Hence, among the roughly thirty characters identified, like him, either with some or with great delay, there stand out: Dikaiopolis, Agoracritos, Strepsiades, Trygaeus, Peisetairos and Euelpides, Praxagora, Karion and Chremylos. The remaining non-anonymous Aristophanic characters, around forty, are all named approximately ten lines before or after their entrance.

There are around eighty anonymous characters, including the identifiable Herakles, Aiakos and Pluton in *Frogs* and the servants Nikias and Demosthenes in *Knights*. The latter two rather exceptional servants are a case apart: obviously, they could not have been called by their historical names, given the overall conception of the comedy, nor were they provided with nicknames. Instead, they wear what are to all intents and purposes portrait masks, rounded out for the spectators by dialogue teeming with personal allusions: their colleague, the Paphlagonian, does not wear a portrait mask. Any other characters who remain anonymous do so for stylistic motives, almost always because it is a waste of time to name a short-lived, insignificant or categorial character (including a series of 'women' or 'old women' in the 'feminist' comedies), or because there are specific reasons for which it is better not to do so: perhaps the first Ambassador of *Acharnians* remains anonymous because the entire Persian delegation exists on an unreal level. In *Assemblywomen* and *Plutus* some of the characters are left anonymous for clearly allegorical-gnomic reasons.

3 Some notes on sigla and on the theatrical texts

Phenomena associated with the representation of the comedies include: the anonymity of certain characters, the late identification of many, the lack of nominal apostrophes for some parts of the dialogue, and the insufficient or openly lacking stage-directions. Costumes, masks, gesture and décor, however, would immediately have put the spectators at their ease. After a palaeographical and philological examination of all the dialogical texts of antiquity, Jean Andrieu has provided sound technical evidence to support the thesis that classical drama was intrinsically designed for the spectator, adding that the dramatist must never have had the contemporary reader in mind, for he did not insert into the body of the dialogue elements indispensable to him or, indifferent to his drama's destiny after the contest, externally add this material to the copy for eventual circulation: in the text one would have found the diacritical distinction of the lines alone and never any sigla or stage-notes.[2]

Aristophanes, to give just one example, undoubtedly did not write with the reader in mind. Yet in allowing to circulate what was presumably a text of the kind mentioned above it cannot be said that he manifested indifference towards the interests of contemporary professionals, who were furnished sooner or later with the text of the unperformed *Second Clouds*. The exact differentiation of lines, the stylistic and scenic expressiveness of the dialogue, the verisimilar naturalness of the characters' appearances, and above all experience of contemporary stage-technique would have made it possible for the by no means large circle of contemporary specialists (in practice, artists and men of letters) to decipher the naked text, understood as the economic transcription of stage-diction. These readers were not afflicted with problems concerning the identities of characters or their physical appearance, not even in the case of comedies such as *Assemblywomen* or *Plutus* in which the inexpressiveness of the dialogue and the unusual practice governing the characters' entrances might at times appear bewildering: only to readers from subsequent epochs, however, without taking into account that such bewilderment might also be due to the corruption or loss of diacritical signs, or to other more serious mishaps. Jean Andrieu himself knows well – since he continually draws one's attention to it – that the ancient reader was an active one, a decipherer, and that the later introduction of sigla marked a change in the psychological dispositions governing intellectual life.

Furthermore, the Aristophanic text, since it was conceived to be (and as long as it remained) a vitally speaking and musically and figuratively evocative text, was (and remained) a text in which no sigla were assigned. In any case, it was not always feasible to assign sigla, given the large number of anonymous characters and those left intentionally anonymous for long periods. Plato, who wrote exclusively for the reader, definitely did not provide sigla for his characters, even those of the dramatic dialogues: in *Laws*, indeed, the dialogue is constructed in such a way that the reader comes gradually to unveil the setting and to discover the exact identity of the interlocutors. Our editions, which fret themselves to provide nominal sigla immediately, and to foretell the setting, are friends neither of Plato nor of the truth. Just as the spectator 'should not hear immediately everything that he's shortly going to see with his own eyes' (*Thesmophoriazusae* 5f.), so the ancient reader was left uninformed. One should also consider that the Platonic text would not always have lent itself to sigla, in so far as the 'type' of the characters is not always clearly defined and the style itself sees to distinguishing the homonymous characters. In fact, in the case of the Greek dialogue texts it is the very style of the literary genre itself, progressively more and more refined, which renders sigla superfluous, or rather would not have encouraged the author to invent a system of nominal sigla.

Even were a dramatist to have felt compelled to invent a system of sigla in the course of his work, he would have thought most probably of a system of algebraic sigla designed for the actors. He knew that he had only a few actors, differently endowed and from different categories. For the author and his didaskalos, the artistic evaluation and calculation of the parts was of prime importance, and it was also useful for the actors to have at hand a manuscript indicating rapidly their progressive appearances as 'masks': the parts left without sigla, or in which different kinds of sigla were employed, were intended for the chorus. It did not seem necessary to include these highly probable algebraic sigla, whose nature was categorial and value functional, in the modest edition designed to be read, since they were strictly linked to the interests of the performance itself. Papyrus 1176 of the Italian Society, prior to AD 60, attests to the existence of such sigla in new comedy (apparently, they are already to be seen in the Hibeh papyrus 180 from the years 270–240), and it is by no means improbable that this latter represents the propagation of a technique developed in more ancient stage-exemplars (themselves destined to disappear), a technique which in the field of Latin is known to have been typical of fourth-century bookshop editions.[3]

These algebraic sigla were extremely well suited to the masked actors used by the dramatists, and hence to Aristophanes himself. Not only is his corps of characters normally larger than that of tragedy, but he also has a sizeable crowd of 'type' characters and few historical or mythical ones. What was required for the theatre exemplar were algebraic signs for the first, second and third actors and indications regarding the masks.

It is also true that in the case of the principal non-historical or mythical characters of any given comedy the spectators would have been more lastingly impressed by the mask worn, and by the 'type' and voice, than by the character's proper name, which was almost always late in being heard: on the other hand, they would already have known the names of the actors. Aristophanes himself liked to re-evoke his own or other dramatists' characters for the audience through typological or figurative descriptions such as 'Typhon and Hurricane', 'the jag-toothed Hound', 'Chills and Fevers', 'the Virtuous and the Inverted', 'a drunken bawd that Phrynichos invented first' and 'the Paphlagonian tanner' (*Knights* 511, *Wasps* 1031 and 1038, *Clouds* 529, 555 and 581). If a proagon was held for comedy a few days prior to staging, as it undoubtedly was for tragedy, on that occasion the non-historical or mythical names of the characters would not have been disclosed to the audience, who would have been far more interested in hearing immediate descriptions such as the examples provided above. At the proagon, the actors appeared without their masks, and it was they who provoked the public's curiosity, the first, second and third actors, whom the dramatist must have entered algebraically into his own manuscript and into the manuscript intended for the theatre.[4]

The almost systematic nominal sigla to be found in the Byzantine manuscripts (apart from the occasional sigla on the papyri from the third century onwards) are on the contrary the expression of an editorial civilization with a conscious mission for book-production and a radically different form of theatrical life. In general, the first Alexandrians seem not to have deemed it necessary to interpret the diacritical signs. They might perhaps have attempted to integrate or correct those that had been lost or corrupted in the mean time, or at most have provided a list of the characters. However, since the theatrical texts were still fairly much alive for them, they were far more concerned with researching information in Aristotle on the contest, the eponymous archon, the didaskalos, if there was one, and the place-list, with establishing the colometry and so forth.[5]

The exemplars to have reached Byzantium must at times have been ill equipped or unequipped with diacritical signs; and to this, or rather to this also, is to be ascribed absent or false dialogue divisions in the Byzantine manuscripts. Very many diacritical signs – principally due to inept scenic interpretation – were translated with false sigla; many were honourably left mute. Some of the sigla are exaggeratedly erudite – Kephisophon in *Acharnians*, Nikias and Demosthenes in *Knights* and Mnesilochos in *Thesmophoriazusae*, for instance. Others, however, are remarkably acute: the sigla for *Knights* 234 and *Birds* 267, for example (except in the Ravenna manuscript). The scholia which the Byzantines transcribed into the margins of their own editions are frequently in contrast with the sigla which they themselves ascribed, and often it is the scholiasts who are correct. However, scenotechnical or scenic interpretations of these scholia rarely reflect either the theatrical civilization or the stagecraft of Athens in the fifth and fourth century, but rather those of the theatre and public shows of the epochs in which the individual scholiasts lived and worked: for example, the involved and intricate *ekkyklema*, the caged fighting cocks for the two Arguments, and nomenclature such as πάροδος for εἴσοδος, παραχορήγημα, and so forth. Neither do the seven interlinear stage-notes in some Byzantine manuscripts have what could be described as an ancient appearance: these are discussed below, and so too the principal sceno-technical and scenic scholia.

In modern critical editions the list and sigla are obviously tolerable and in general not really that bad, as long as they are not expressed in Latin or placed between angle brackets. The essential thing is that the reader should not be led into believing that the 'correct' sigla are even a conjectural restoration of the sigla that Aristophanes himself omitted to append to the reader's copy, but included, in that same copy, in an opening list of the characters (this is Victor Coulon's opinion, I, p. xxxi). Next to our list, there should instead *always* be a sign indicating which of the actors available should be entrusted with the listed character; and this might be repeated alongside the sigla whenever the dialogue becomes more complex and delicate. More effectively than nominal sigla, these signs, to the perceptible advantage of textual and dramaturgical criticism, would remind the reader of the quality of actors employed in Aristophanes, of the economy governing their lines and of the author's customary practice in assigning them roles: in *Knights* 234 and 1254, *Clouds* 886–92 and 1102–12 and so forth, the inclusion of such signs would have rendered the scholars more prudent and responsible. It was most certainly the interpretation of Greek tragedy as a 'literary' form, not a theatrical one governed, as seen later, by an artistic and economic syntax regarding the actors, which dictated the later aesthetic theory of dramatic structures involving three actors and no more.

It must be said, however, that some sigla are illegitimate beyond the shadow of a doubt: I refer in particular to the sigla of intentionally delayed speaking names. No one dares to anticipate the siglum of Agoracritos to line 150 for the protagonist of *Knights* (but, faithful to the mechanical Byzantine copyist almost everyone goes on to assign him the siglum of the Sausage-seller after 1257), or to give a Youth in *Peace* the siglum of the son of Lamachus. And whereas it would indeed be convenient to be able to anticipate the sigla of Dikaiopolis, Strepsiades, Pheidippides, Trygaeus, etc., in such cases the apparatus would be obliged to indicate the line from which these precocious, anti-artistic sigla were drawn, and this would also be necessary in the case of characters such as Prometheus in *Birds* and Poverty and Plutus in *Plutus*, who at first conceal their identity from the other characters (and from the spectators) – further confirmation of the fact that the Aristophanic text is not technically designed to be provided with sigla. To give an example of a different kind, premature assignation of sigla has also led to false divisions being made in the dialogue: regarding *Wasps*, for instance, certain modern editors (and some of the pre-Byzantine manuscripts), because they have given the Servant the siglum of Sosias from the very first line, go on to divide lines 74–85 amoebically, given that in line 78 Sosias is apostrophized directly in the course of a remark. But, as the lively context makes perfectly clear, the Sosias apostrophized is no more than an imaginary spectator: the fact that the slave is actually called Sosias does not emerge until line 136. In the manuscripts there is not even the shadow of a diacritical sign. In that era, moreover, Sosias was not yet typically a servant's name. Another example: some modern editors – the Oxonians, for instance – follow the Ravenna in affixing the sigla XOP. to the songs in *Thesmophoriazusae* 104, hence adding a 'chorus of Agathon' to the list of characters; in the known treatise on the dramatic contests, again Oxonian, Agathon's chorus tends to be interpreted as a supplementary one also. However, as the scholiasts had already pointed out, one is dealing neither with a chorus nor with a small chorus, but rather with Agathon himself, rehearsing without the slightest accompaniment his still

41

imperfect melodic composition. To insert, as Coulon does, a ὡς Χορός into the text between discreet round brackets is entirely improper. One should keep to the text, the metre: 'Must I then identify you through your song?', says Euripides' Relative in *Thesmophoriazusae* 144–5 to Agathon, who is reluctant to identify himself.

To declare the precociousness of some of the sigla in our modern editions would be the expression of a merely formal rigour. A more substantial rigour would be expressed were one to provide numbered signs for the character-actors and also to develop a more streamlined apparatus – of greater variety and significance, however, than Teubner's regarding Menander – of the essential intrinsic and extrinsic theatrical properties which integrate and govern the extant text. It is often the case that scholars who keep these properties actively in mind restore or confirm the text in an appropriate manner, or rather illuminate clearly the expressive texture of an artistic conception which was originally integrated and governed by such properties.

For example, keeping to Aristophanes: anyone who, like Eduard Fraenkel 1936 (1964), simply observes that the scenic façade of *Clouds* constantly represents two houses, always pertaining to the same two people (quite exceptional in Aristophanes), adding that it is no less unusual that there should be talk of 'next-door neighbours' in the opening scene etc., will immediately understand that these are the solid, stylistic elements of an entire scene, effectively the embryo of a scene from new comedy; and anyone who, like Alexandre Marie Desrousseaux, has noted roughly the following in his translation of *Birds*: 'Euelpides and Peisetairos go into the air and ether through the forest, Peisetairos returns through the forest' (through the forest of the scenic façade, that is, not through the corridor leading out of the theatre) has done justice to the unitary artistic design of Aristophanes, a dramatist of verisimilitude, whose desire is to suggest concretely that behind the forest there do indeed stretch the limitless aerial worlds of the birds and of the gods, while the men from earth appear in the new city, and disappear, through the external corridor.

Although Jean Andrieu comes to the very realistic conclusion that: 'ce n'est que par un hasard de leur survie littéraire que les textes de théâtre sont devenus des textes lus', his polemical idols reason far less realistically when they interpret the circulation of the theatrical texts as tantamount to their definition as 'literature' (Aeschylus' tragedies were so little 'literature' that in the fifth century a State decree allowed for their performance in the theatre after the author's death). They add that only amidst ancient monuments need one concern oneself with the material execution of the dramas and that an evaluation of them as theatre, while undoubtedly useful (particularly in the case of comedy), is of secondary importance (particularly in the case of tragedy), since the critic must direct his energies towards the eternal values of a text, not its temporal ones. Here, too, lazily abdicating all responsibility, they confound the issue: with the means at our disposal (from the monumental ruins to how much we do not know in general regarding diction, music, dance, masks and costumes), ancient theatre is at most only partly, and secretly, re-evokable, and always in a somewhat hypothetical way. It is true that the material execution of the drama was a temporal, secondary fact, and today inspires the interest of a few prestigious archaeologists and refined *hommes de lettres* alone. Yet it is precisely the theatrical properties of ancient dramas with which we should be concerned, and obviously not as a marginal curiosity: a philological awareness of these properties helps one to recognize in an ever less anti-historical way a linguistic expression rendered complete and governed by a particular form of stagecraft, and by a theatrical civilization. Amongst the theatrical properties of a stage-work there are some which the analytic reader would consider improprieties (an insistence on, or an abandonment or re-adoption of certain themes, for instance), and one also encounters improprieties of expression. On-stage, however, these would have passed unobserved.

The more material stage-properties are also implicit in the letter of the text transmitted to us, a text transmitted more or less faithfully (albeit less so in the case of tragedy, which underwent readaptation in later epochs). These more material stage-properties may also be cautiously annotated at times on the basis of later erudite documentation concerning the theatrical civilization of Athens, and, in the case of tragedy, on the basis of figurative artwork. However, whereas erudite documentation, figurative artwork and monumental ruins are frequently either absent or mute, the theatrical texts have proved eloquent enough, particularly those of the comic dramatists: although they do not reveal everything, they do say and insinuate much. For example, the various external sources cannot, at least for the moment, tell us whether classical Greek theatre employed a curtain, whether Hellenistic theatrical machinery is valid for the fifth and fourth centuries as well, whether actors other than the first three belong to the same professional category, and whether they could utter short remarks made by characters previously portrayed by one of the first three actors, and so forth. Nor can these sources assure us, at least for the moment, that Sophocles, Euripides and Aristophanes wrote dramas for a theatre other than that of Dionysos Eleutherios – for the Lenaion, to be precise. However, the texts of the comic writers explicitly guarantee, through *Acharnians* 504 and a fragment of Sannyrion, that for the entire fifth century, at least, Athens' second theatre was the Lenaion. The dramaturgy of some of Aristophanes' Lenaian comedies also appears sensibly different from those of his comedies for the Dionysia. As regards the two tragedians, from an interpretation of later erudite testimony it emerges that Sophocles definitely took part in the Lenaian contest of 432 and those following, and that Euripides never participated in the contests frequented by the comic dramatists. This is discussed in the first section of chapter 10 on *Thesmophoriazusae*.

4 *Acharnians*: the Pnyx, the Attic countryside, Athens

The stage-technique of the most ancient extant comedy is remarkable for its mobility and extemporaneousness, whilst a greatly extended period of dramatic time is given up to the energetic and predominant role played by the protagonist. These are some of the reasons why the Lenaian *Acharnians*, from the year 425, appears to be, or rather is, the most instinctive and free of the extant comedies: for some scholars it is the most 'naïve', the most 'archaic', the work of a young dramatist cutting his teeth. Yet apart from the fact that this young chap had already presented three comedies in the years 427 and 426, assisted by expert didaskaloi, the structural action and stage-technique of *Acharnians* need only be reconstructed properly to receive just technical recognition.

The action begins in the deserted orchestra, which for the moment is a scenically neutral zone. From the corridor, not from the scenic façade, an old countryman has advanced into the orchestra. He wanders up and down gesticulating, and then 'lets loose at the top of his voice', complaining that 'this Pnyx here' (20) – the site of the morning reunion of the Athenian Popular Assembly – is still empty. He continues to hold forth until the latecomers arrive from the Agora: he has to wait for some time (cf. 20 and 40). This character is the protagonist of the comedy: if there is only one character active on-stage at the beginning of the comedy, then that character is undoubtedly its protagonist, the first actor; this is the case in *Clouds*, *Lysistrata* and *Assembly-women*, and perhaps in *Plutus* also. Here in *Acharnians*, as if to set up a relationship of solidarity with the audience, the protagonist does not immediately present himself as a citizen who has come to the Pnyx (that scenic value is not affirmed until line 20), but simply as a man who loves the theatre (1–4, 5–16), particularly as the admirer of a certain anti-Kleonine work (5–8), most probably Aristophanes' extremely recent *Babylonians*: further on, the protagonist, as the poet's mouthpiece, speaks explicitly of 'the comedy from last year' (378).

'This Pnyx here' is represented by the orchestral space: this is definitely the case in *Knights* 723–51 also, in which there is a movement from the scenic façade towards the orchestra-Pnyx; the parodic assemblies of *Thesmophor-iazusae* and *Assemblywomen* are also held in the orchestra. In *Acharnians*, in which there is an assembly in the fullest sense of the word, complete with a Herald, Prytanes, Archers, Ecclesiasts and Ambassadors, the scenic value might be reinforced, though not necessarily so, by material objects: a couple of wooden benches for the Prytanes, for example (cf. 42 and also 25). The Ecclesiasts and Prytanes are seated with their backs to the audience, in whose direction the various orators speak, so that the spectators, with the real Athenian Prytanes in the front row, are made to feel as though they were genuinely in the Pnyx, united with the Ecclesiasts in the orchestra. It is neither effective nor opportune to imagine, as has been proposed, the contrary arrangement (the orators speaking to the Prytanes and Ecclesiasts seated in front of the scenic façade), because the next stage-element, the houses, must be kept to the rear for the time being, and also because the speaking characters alone are assigned dramatic roles, not the extras representing the Prytanes and Ecclesiasts: the spokesman of the latter is the Herald, who gives an order on their behalf in 54. Besides, an arrangement of this kind is to be inferred by analogy to *Thesmophoriazusae* 536 and *Assemblywomen* 165–8, in which the women, united in assembly, address the audience in passing. The wooden benches, should they actually have been employed, would be removed silently after 173 either by stagehands or by the Ecclesiasts themselves: the silent clearing of the stage is a perfectly normal procedure.

In the 1930s it was ascertained that the structure of the Pnyx existed in the fifth century. It is possible to establish, therefore, that Dikaiopolis' allusions to the Pnyx are to the real Pnyx, since only from the raised hill on which it lay would one be able to see the Agora and the surrounding countryside (21, 32) and, in it, 'run down' towards the wooden seats of the Prytanes (25).

The Pnyx is the setting of the prologue, and of the prologue alone. In *Lysistrata* and *Thesmophoriazusae* also, the prologue has its own distinct setting: yet whereas the latter comedies suddenly shift from a bourgeois residence to install themselves permanently in the Acropolis, in front of the Thesmophorian temple, in *Acharnians* there is a gradual movement, during the irruption of the Acharnians, from the Athenian assembly to an ephemeral private setting in front of the country residence of Dikaiopolis. The progression orchestra → scenic façade is perfectly natural, in so far as the protagonist's plan has been realized during the prologue: a scandalous sitting of the Assembly has constrained Dikaiopolis to procure an extremely private truce with Sparta, using the services of a private messenger, a prodigious truce thanks to which he is free to transfer himself to his country residence. The elements which make the prologue a little drama in itself (certainly not an 'act'), of remarkable dramatic force, are the following:

a corps of characters for the prologue exclusively (six speaking and at least a dozen mute): a unique case in Aristophanes, if one excludes the different, innovatory prologue of *Assemblywomen*. The protagonist alone reappears after the prologue, to provide immediate stage-illustration of his private, family truce (foretold in 132 and 202), yet he too disappears from the stage at the end of the prologue. During the fundamental section of the prologue, Dikaiopolis makes his presence felt through 'asides' alone (64–98, 125–56), apart from 101–22 and 157–71 (111 does not imply that Dikaiopolis has a stick; cf. the relative scholion and that to 31);

an off-stage mission which, by means of an unusual technique, allows for the complete realization of the protagonist's plan: the envoy of Amphitheos to Sparta. The lightning speed of the Ambassador

Amphitheos, who exits at 133 and re-enters at 175, is perfectly natural, and not just because Amphitheos is a divine being (this is discussed in section 9 below): his lightning-fast, economical, concrete and energetically intoxicating off-stage envoy, 'a great and extraordinary undertaking' (129), is dramatically opposed to the plurennial, highly expensive, inconclusive and fraudulent on-stage delegation received with full honours by the mute Prytanes and Ecclesiasts. After the opening monologue, the delegations are the exclusive theme of the prologue: 45–60, 61–125, 125–33, 134–73, 175–200;

all of the characters, the protagonist included, appear gradually from without, and all, excepting the protagonist, gradually disappear without;

the orchestra creates the setting and the scenic façade is ignored. The latter becomes the object of visual attention only towards the end of the prologue, when the protagonist disappears into it (202). In all the other comedies – *Plutus* apparently excluded – the action of the prologue sooner or later has the façade as its visual point of reference;

at the end of the prologue the stage is void of characters (203), and remains so throughout the irruption of the Acharnians (204–40; the irruption is strongly predicted and motivated in 176–203).

The character appearing on-stage in 241 is Dikaiopolis, who had set off home in 202 to prepare for the celebration of the Rural Dionysia. Now he emerges from his home, celebrates the Rural Dionysia (250), invites his wife to admire the procession from the roof (262), and sings hymns to celebrate his return to the countryside after five years of war (266–70). During the subsequent clash with the Acharnians, Dikaiopolis goes indoors twice to fetch a charcoal basket and a kitchen chopping-block (327, cf. 330; 365, cf. 359). When his house is mentioned again, it is in the city, and a private Agora is temporarily installed in front of it (719), perceived none the less as being the Athenian Agora (cf., e.g., 729). There is a shift, therefore, from Dikaiopolis' country home to Athens, and it would be worth while to examine the much-discussed technique by which this shift occurs.

The Assembly has been dissolved and the Pnyx emptied (173): the orchestra no longer has any fixed scenic value; it is a neutral zone. We are naturally in Athens, but no longer in the Pnyx. Amphitheos returns from Sparta with the truce sealed for the countryman Dikaiopolis, who is tired of the city and wants to return to his farm (cf. 32f.). Dikaiopolis tastes the little bottle containing the truce, and the magic wine speaks into his mouth: 'go wherever you wish' (198). Already, there is a warning, a foretelling, if you wish, that whoever possesses this magic wine is free to go wherever he desires (cf. then 1027 and 1058). Indeed, Dikaiopolis, who had definitely entered the orchestra-Pnyx from the corridor (i.e. from the city: cf. also 28f.), does not exit by the corridor but moves joyously towards the scenic façade, until then opportunely ignored, paying no attention to the menacing Acharnians, whose arrival (in Athens) had been announced and re-announced by Amphitheos. With a remark presaging a scene set in the countryside, Dikaiopolis subtly accustoms the spectators to the idea of a country destination: 'free of war and other misfortunes I'm going home to celebrate the Rural Dionysia' (202), a feast which, needless to say, was not held in the city. However, attention is immediately distracted from the scenic façade towards the orchestra and the fleeing Amphitheos. The latter announces the arrival of the Acharnians, who immediately burst on to the scene (203, 204). Encountering no one, they decide to search for the traitor, 'to chase him from land to land, until we find him for good and all' (234f.). With these words, the stage-action abandons Athens (as seen in section 9 below, the dramatic time of the parodos probably 'lengthens', too), and at that very instant the Acharnians see Dikaiopolis emerging from his home. And it is now, during the celebration of the Rural Dionysia (250), that the foreseen rural scenic value both of the house and of the orchestra is explicitly affirmed (262, 266–70).

The house is moved from the countryside to Athens by means of a slow scenic and dramatic progression. In the mean time, however, the *character* is returned to Athens. 'I have to go to Euripides now', says Dikaiopolis in 394, moving significantly from the orchestra towards the façade. At this point the scholiast remarks: 'a change of place occurs'. Before his visit to Euripides, the dramatic status of the character Dikaiopolis is reduced, so to speak, from actor-poet to mere actor, in need of a costume-change in order to perform (cf. 377–84). After visiting Euripides, the new Dikaiopolis-Telephus is literally *in the theatre*, in the Lenaion (cf. 496–508). This is one possible reason why the return to the city of a countryman who had wished solely to remain in the countryside passes unobserved. Next, there appears the Athenian warrior Lamachus, who takes up position in the scenic façade alongside Dikaiopolis.

5 The parodos, the statue of Dionysos, the spectators

It was noted above that at the end of the prologue and during the parodos the stage is dominated by the Acharnians. In *Lysistrata* also, the parodos is void of characters (in *Wasps* they are asleep in front of the house); in their place, however, there appears a semi-chorus of Old Men pursued by a hostile semi-chorus of Old Women. The appearance of the chorus of Acharnians is amongst the most natural in Aristophanes: Acharnian coal-merchants, carrying sacks of coal over their shoulders (213, cf. scholion 211), enter with great violence like Erinnean Negroes, in pursuit of Amphitheos. Their objective is not a character or place directly or indirectly linked to the scenic façade, as in other comedies. The patriotic Acharnians, imagined as veterans of Marathon (the cretics and paeons of their songs are filled with ancient, furious energy), enter in pursuit of the 'bearer of the truce' (207), pass through the orchestra and attack Dikaiopolis, a person unknown to them: this shift in objective has disturbed many scholars, from the graduating Friedrich Leo onwards. In fact, however, it is quite simple to understand: by now, the Acharnians want to punish 'the man who sealed the truce with the enemies' (226). For the spectators, therefore, it is perfectly natural that the Acharnians should attack the man to whom they saw Amphitheos pass the wine of the truce, and for this reason there is no need to attribute to Dikaiopolis a costume and appearance resembling those of Amphitheos. Both of these factors are reinforced by the postponement of the attack, which is caused by the Acharnians' hiding (cf. the second scholion to 239), observing the character who 'has sealed the truce' (251, 268) and attacking only when he pronounces unequivocal words of peace: 'it's him, it's definitely him!' (280). The furious entry of the chorus on to a stage by now void of characters (204–40), the peaceful ceremony of Dikaiopolis and his family on a stage void of choreutai (241–79), the family's flight indoors and Dikaiopolis' clash with the Acharnians (280–346) are all elements of a unitary design. The phallus-bearing procession in miniature – which provides private and realistic stage-illustration of the private truce, during which the protagonist, like a chorus, sings a lyric hymn – is insinuated into the scene of the chorus' entrance by means of the ritual invitation pronounced by Dikaiopolis indoors in 237 and outdoors in 241, at which point he and his family have already emerged and the choreutai are in hiding: the 'internal' ritual invitation in 237 is in effect the chorus' cue, to cease talking and withdraw (cf. *Peace* 232–7, or rather *Peace* 60, if 60 pertains to Trygaeus etc., through to *Plutus* 639–41). The chorus withdraws to the zone of the house, hiding itself behind a 'little wall', mentioned and similarly employed in *Assemblywomen* 497. As it lies in wait, the chorus remains menacingly present: whilst it may be invisible to Dikaiopolis, it can still be glimpsed by a section of the audience. It does not disappear into the corridor, therefore, deserting the dramatic action. In other comedies also, the actors apparently hide behind the wall in the scenic façade: *Peace* 234, *Thesmophoriazusae* 36, *Frogs* 315; in *Assemblywomen* 28, the movement seems to be a different one, perhaps on the stage side of the wall.

The phallus-bearing procession, which is organized throughout by Dikaiopolis, takes place in stages: 242–3 and 244–6, preparations for the rite (it emerges from 245 that Dikaiopolis' wife has leant over); 247–52, sacrifice and prayer to Dionysos; 253–62, dispositions for the procession; 263–79, procession and phallic hymn.

Lines 257f., 'go ahead, my daughter, and watch out that no one in the throng gets the chance to nibble at your jewels', if it alludes to the spectators in the front row (cf. *Peace* 967–72), could imply that the sacrifice to Dionysos takes place in the proedria, in which there stood a statue of the god. In *Acharnians*, the presence of a statue of Dionysos in the proedria is undeniably hypothetical, but from *Knights* 536 it is evident that during the dramatic contests a statue of the god was positioned in the zone reserved for the important spectators, in the proedria, that is to say: in *Knights* 536, in fact, a wish is expressed that the old and glorious Kratinos should be maintained by the State in the Prytaneum, that he should abandon the stage and become a spectator παρὰ τῷ Διονύσῳ, the old and glorious Kratinos, who on that particular occasion happened to be competing with the neo-didaskalos Aristophanes. The reference to the statue is obviously valid for more than one theatre: indirect confirmation that the statue was positioned in the proedria (and not in the middle of the orchestra, as many scholars continue to maintain) is provided by the ruins of the theatre of Priene.

In any case, it seems definite to us that the sacrifice does not take place near Dikaiopolis' residence, i.e. beneath the scenic façade, but rather in the orchestra, and that the following procession, if it does not move along the proedria, moves instead around the orchestra, turning eventually towards the scenic façade (and not vice versa), close to which the Acharnians lie in hiding: Dikaiopolis, with his daughter, wife, two slaves and maybe other members of his family (see 132, 891, 1003), does not appear from the house in 241, but by 239 has already moved silently from the scenic façade into the depths of the deserted orchestra. Similarly, in *Thesmophoriazusae* Agathon's Servant appears with an absent air in 36, but does not call for silence until 39, whilst in the mean time Euripides hides with his relative in the area of the scenic façade and makes an 'aside' commenting on the Servant's appearance, as do the Acharnians in 239 and 240. Whereas the Servant in *Thesmophoriazusae* 58–60 does not stray far from the scenic façade, in *Acharnians*, because of the realism and complexity of the rural ceremony, there is undoubtedly a movement deep into the orchestra, which, as seen further on, assumes the value of the Attic countryside (267). At the end of the phallic hymn, 277–9, Dikaiopolis seems to move from the 'countryside' towards the house, into which his family apparently flee as soon as the Acharnians take up stoning (282). Dikaiopolis' wife, having taken part in the sacrifice, was invited to admire the procession from the 'roof' of the house (262).

Should Dikaiopolis be referring to the statue of Dionysos and to the throng of spectators, this would be the first clear example of Aristophanes' constant natural tendency to absorb the spectators and the zone reserved for them into the dramatic illusion, a tendency which, as seen further on, is extremely strong in the finale of *Acharnians*. In *Peace*, to give just one example, the protagonist actually consigns a lovely maiden-extra to the spectators seated in the proedria: it should be noted, moreover, that *Peace* is the comedy richest in speeches addressed explicitly to the spectators. All things considered, there-fore, the real Ecclesiasts in the prologue of *Acharnians* are clearly the citizens-spectators and Prytanes sitting in the proedria. In *Knights* 702–4 also, the Paphlagonian-Kleon is the double of the real Kleon sitting in front of him in the proedria, under threat of being transferred to the back row. The coryphaeus of Acharnians asks the audience for news of Amphitheos, and some of the spectators obviously tell him that he has fled by the corridor (cf. 204–7, 208). An active agreement between the dramatist and the didaskalos on the one hand and friends in the audience on the other is evident in the prologue of *Knights* 37–9, the comedy which puts most pressure on the audience (it was Aristophanes' first official appearance). Such an agreement is also to be found in the prologue of *Wasps* 73–86 and elsewhere. In *Clouds* 1322, *Peace* 79 and *Thesmophoriazusae* 241, the 'neighbours' mentioned are none other than the spectators – Lamachus aside, this is also the case in *Acharnians* 1045 – and so too the Heliasts invoked from the stage by the Paphlagonian in *Knights* 255.

The spectators are not alone in being drawn into the comedy: so too are the stagehands, the 'dressing rooms' of the choreutai, threatened by thieves, the choregos, the machine operators, the corridor leading to the theatre, and even the theatre itself: cf. *Peace* 729f., 731, 1022, 174 and *Daedalus* fr. 192, *Clouds* 326 and *Birds* 296, *Acharnians* 504 and *Thesmophoriazusae* 1060. Everything is freely and artistically absorbed into the comedy, and only the most modernistic of scholars could say anything about the stage-illusion being broken.

6 Dikaiopolis *chez* Euripides: the *ekkyklema*

The lengthy visit to the poet of *Telephus* in 393–479 (488) requires detailed comment, and also some brief clarification of a general kind. The visit is a diversion (the chorus makes this immediately clear in 385), a kind of 'aside' between Dikaiopolis and Euripides, but nevertheless it has its own dramatic and scenic genesis and consequences. The immediate motivation for the visit – the need for a pitiful costume to avoid the rigours of Kleon, this time at least (383f.) – has its genesis in Dikaiopolis' promise to speak in the name of justice, in favour of the enemy, even with his head on the block (318); the block he brings out in 366. He has promised, in effect, to speak as Euripides' Argive Telephus, who spoke before the Argives in the name of justice, in favour of the Trojan enemy: 'O Agamemnon, even should one brandishing an axe prepare to strike me on the neck, no, I would not keep silent, for the arguments I propose are just.'[6]

Just as this Euripidean metaphor is parodically staged (one has already had the paratragic *coup de théâtre* of the baby boy = charcoal basket: cf. 325–40), now one must also provide concrete evidence of Dikaiopolis' transformation from suppliant before the Acharnians into suppliant before the Athenians, and in the mean time, into suppliant before Euripides. Euripides, too, must appear on-stage dressed in beggar's rags (cf. 412f.). The visit to Euripides is a lengthy one, because the spectator has not as much time to reflect as a reader, but must principally see and hear, and also because it was presumably the first time that Aristophanes had presented the character of Euripides to his public. After the visit, Dikaiopolis not only has the pitiful costume he desired – that of the Euripidean beggar-king Telephus – but is also a new *character*, Telephus: his mode of expression is new, and so too his acting style. He is not the actor of a κωμῳδία, but of a τρυγῳδία ('the song of the must'), of a tragi. . .comedy

(499). So strong is the Euripidean element that the agon itself is not written in long lines, but rather in iambic trimeters, some of which are markedly tragic: many of them, indeed, are borrowed *en bloc* from *Telephus*. Telephus-Dikaiopolis ceases to quarrel with the Acharnians, but instead turns to the spectators to make the promised lengthy speech in defence of peace (cf. 416) to *them*, the Athenians (497f., 504, 513), since by now the furious coal-merchants have become 'numbskull choreutai', in the Euripidean manner (cf. 442). The chorus is mute during the visit, for the simple reason that it is *absent*: it had left Dikaiopolis free to go, disguise himself as he wished and then return (387–91). Dikaiopolis had subsequently abandoned the 'lists', leaving his block behind him (cf. 483), and moved towards the scenic façade-house of Euripides, delivering a remark as he went, intended less for the chorus (393f.) than for the spectators, which first established the tone of detached secrecy characterizing the entire scene. At the end of the visit, he returns to the orchestra, addressing his own heart, and after a pause returns to the lists (480–4, 485–8): at this point, the chorus becomes aware of him again, but says nothing about Euripides or his new costume. The chorus, let us say, has not the faintest idea that Dikaiopolis has been to see Euripides: 'since today', said the protagonist to Euripides, 'I must pass for a beggar, be exactly what I am, and not merely appear to be so. The audience already knows who I am, while the chorus just stand there like so many numbskulls allowing themselves to be mocked by my little phrases.' It is clear that one is dealing with an interlude. There is an evident parody of Euripidean disguise and recognition, comparable to that in which the chorus of *Thesmophoriazusae* knows nothing about the 'actor' Euripides-Menelaus-Echo-Perseus. The recognition of Dikaiopolis occurs during the scene with Lamachus: 'a ragamuffin, I?', exclaims Dikaiopolis-Telephus to Lamachus, who had rushed to aid the Acharnians. 'Who are you, then?' At this point 'Telephus' throws off his Euripidean rags, and on-stage once more stands the honest citizen Dikaiopolis (595).

Let us consider the encounter between Dikaiopolis and Euripides and the technique by which it is governed. The latter will be easier to understand if one keeps *Thesmophoriazusae* in mind. There, it is Euripides who is in trouble and set to entreat his colleague Agathon. The Servant tells him that it is not really necessary to 'call out' Agathon, since his master is just about to ἐξιέναι: he has to compose a lyric song and, since it is winter, it is difficult for him to mould the strophes unless he sits outdoors in the sun. Euripides, therefore, must wait (*Thesmophoriazusae* 65–70). And Agathon ἐξέρχεται (95), ἐκκυκλούμενος (96) in female clothes (98, 151f.). At the end of the episode, Agathon orders: εἴσω τις ὡς τάχιστά μ᾽εἰσκυκλησάτω (265). Just before, in 261, Agathon's κλινίς is indicated, his work-couch (his desk, in effect). Agathon, in fact, is *rolled* in and out on a couch by servants, and perhaps stays reclining for the duration of the scene. The female clothes required by Euripides all appear to be on the couch. However, Euripides does order a servant to bring out a torch from the house (ἐνεγκάτω τις ἔνδοθεν, 238).

51

According to the scholion on line 96, Agathon ἐπὶ ἐκκυκλήματος φαίνεται. The scholiast on *Acharnians* 408 describes the *ekkyklema* as a wooden machine with wheels, which as it moved revealed the interior of the house to the spectators. Other sources agree with this really not very clear description, while others, with no greater clarity, speak of a large platform on which the internal scene was rolled or pushed forward. The majority of modern interpreters maintain that for *Acharnians* and *Thesmophoriazusae*, and for some tragedies too, use was actually made of one of these two machines (the verbs ἐκκυκλεῖσθαι and εἰσ- are absent from tragedy and to be found in Aristophanes alone; the term ἐκκύκλημα can only be dated through Pollux IV.128).

Regarding the use of *ekkyklema* for Agathon in *Thesmophoriazusae*, it is not even necessary to refute the erudite sources, since with pristine clarity the text implies the use of a couch alone, on wheels certainly, which is pushed in and out through an opening corresponding to the doorway. Nothing obliges one to consider the opening as being any wider than normal: a couch is hardly a bedroom.

In the case of *Acharnians*, where there is no explicit talk of couches, the *ekkyklema* proposed by the erudite sources has met with greater success. Euripides' Servant informs Dikaiopolis, who has asked him whether Euripides is ἔνδον, 'his spirit is without collecting little lines', οὐκ ἔνδον, but that Euripides ἔνδον ἀναβάδην ποιεῖ τραγῳδίαν (398–400). Ἀναβάδην, which returns in 410, reveals a detail invisible to Euripides working indoors, and the adverb does not mean 'above, on the next floor', for example, since a gesture would have sufficed for that or a different mode of expression. The Servant would also stress the tone on ἔνδον opposed to οὐκ ἔνδον, as previously in 396. In *Plutus* 1123, Hermes recounts how his hunger has by now constrained him to ἀναπαύεσθαι ἀναβάδην, i.e. ἄνω ἔχων τοὺς πόδας as the relevant scholia remark: to lie down with his feet raised from the ground, to recline on a pallet or a bed, because he is too hungry to stand up. Only in this acceptation is the adverb employed, in union with καθῆσθαι, in Dio Chrysostom LXI.16, Plutarch, *Moralia* 336c and Athenaeus 528f.; in each case regarding Sardanapalus on a couch. One may also refer to Pollux III.90 and VI.175. The scholia on *Acharnians* interpret well once, and once badly: well on 399 with ἄνω τοὺς πόδας ἔχων ἐπὶ ὑψηλοῦ τόπου καθήμενος, badly on 410 with φαίνεται γὰρ ἐπὶ τῆς σκηνῆς μετέωρος; perhaps the second part of the scholion on 399 also gives this interpretation.

Dikaiopolis, nevertheless, wants to see Euripides, and orders his Servant to 'call him outdoors' (402). The Servant replies that this is 'impossible' and closes the door. Dikaiopolis knocks again, invokes Euripides as a god, and presents himself: 'I, "Righteous towards the city", am calling you, Χολλῄδης ἐγώ.' Χολλῄδης is effective demotic, exploited here since, recalling perfectly χωλός, Euripides might interpret it as 'Son of a cripple'. Euripides replies from within: ἀλλ'οὐ σχολή. This curt extra metre reply implies at least 'to hear you', 'to move', 'to come out'. Dikaiopolis proposes: ἀλλ'ἐκκυκλήθητι, implying 'if you don't have the time or the desire to inconvenience yourself personally'. Euripides, again from within: ἀλλ' ἀδύνατον. And Dikaiopolis: ἀλλ'ὅμως. And Euripides: ἀλλ' ἐκκυκλήσομαι· καταβαίνειν δ'οὐ σχολή. Immediately after this remark, Euripides becomes visible, and Dikaiopolis exclaims: ἀναβάδην ποεῖς, ἐξὸν καταβάδην, and goes on: 'no wonder your heroes are lame; but why are you wearing these rags of tragedy, miserable garb? No wonder your heroes are beggars' (410–13).

Euripides, in effect, behaves just like Agathon: Agathon writes about women, reclining on a couch-desk dressed as a woman, whereas Euripides writes about heroes who cannot stand up and about beggars, reclining on a couch-desk with his feet off the ground, dressed as a beggar. And Euripides, too, was rolled on to the stage. Directly after the καταβαίνειν δ'οὐ σχολή, when he becomes visible, he is immediately risible: the simple fact is that he did not want *to get off his couch*, to put his feet on the ground! All those excuses in 402–9 with all those 'buts' were intended to demonstrate that even when he is not working Euripides is ἀναβάδην and never καταβάδην, since he is a poet incapable of καταβαίνειν, hence his heroes cannot but be lame. One should note that καταβάδην is a unique formulation, and for that very reason all the more expressive, coined jokingly to contrast with ἀναβάδην. It is also quite certain that throughout the scene Euripides remains on his couch, not once putting his feet on the ground, just as he does when he is at home working. The couch on wheels and the idea of his being 'lame' go together perfectly, and the solution, a surprise one, comes immediately to Dikaiopolis, 'Son of a cripple'. The game is also based on Euripides' two ambiguous σχολή, 'I haven't the time', 'I don't want to', particularly on the second, since by now Euripides has the σχολή to be rolled out. The last ἀλλά in 409 is also 'strange', in so far as it would lead one to expect an ἀλλ' ἐκ. . .ποδῶν. For καταβαίνειν in the absolute sense as 'get out of bed', cf. *Thesmophoriazusae* 482, and also 483. Socrates in *Clouds* must instead καταβαίνειν from the 'sky' to the earth, where he is incapable of philosophical speculation, and it is the Student who advances the pretext οὐ γάρ μοι σχολή for calling his master. The families of Euripides, Socrates and Agathon each make life difficult for their visitors, and Euripides is the most difficult of all.

The scene between Euripides and Dikaiopolis – a genuinely secret exchange during which the spectators are not addressed – is conducted in such a way as to suggest that it is not taking place outdoors. At the end of the scene, for example, Euripides does not say, like Agathon, 'roll me in', but in tragic language orders the Servant to 'seal up the palace shutters' (479), thus providing cover for the transportation of the couch. However, it is also possible that the latter operation might also have been effected after 470, when Euripides had already bid farewell to his plundered tragedies and Dikaiopolis repeated in apparently definitive terms, 'that's enough, I'm going' (471).

Although Euripides might have kept his heroes' masks on his work-couch, amongst the tools of his trade (418; Bellerephon in line 427 could simply be *ille*), these could not have included the mask of Telephus, otherwise the fine ambiguity of the piece would have been cut drastically short. It is the extremely acute and now mute Servant, on the orders of the immobile Euripides, who offers the rags of Telephus to Dikaiopolis. But here again the language does not explicitly indicate that he goes indoors to fetch them (cf. scholion on 434), since there is a verb such as δός whose value is neutral (although in *Acharnians* 1125 and elsewhere it is used to indicate a movement from an interior to an exterior). In fact, the verbs of movement from 449 onwards are all verbs used elsewhere regarding visitors in open spaces (cf. *Acharnians* 564 with *Birds* 948 alone), but they can be adapted to interiors, given that ἄπειμι and the like are vague enough (cf. also 450, 456, 460, but also 402 and *Frogs* 748).

Materially, the technique is the same as that adopted for Agathon in *Thesmophoriazusae*, with the single difference that here the visit is perceived as being an *extremely private* one. Hence, the couch is left in front of the house itself, not in the orchestra, towards which Dikaiopolis moves in 483–7, once Euripides has disappeared. In the orchestra, moreover, there stands the chorus, which is meant to know nothing about Euripides (cf. again 440–4). The Aristophanic chorus always enters into contact with characters who appear between the prologue and the parabasis: Euripides is the only non-metaparabatic character to be ignored by the chorus. The perfectly designed stagecraft of the episode, which displays Euripides οὐκ ἔνδον καὶ ἔνδον, both explains and covers the blindness and inactivity of the chorus (only in *Frogs* does the chorus not enter into communication with the minor characters who appear between prologue and parabasis).

The scholars who prefer to assume use of the complicated *ekkyklema* and interpret ἀναβάδην as 'upstairs', imagining Euripides being rolled out in some way, since he has neither the time nor the desire to come downstairs, have never once asked themselves why Euripides and Dikaiopolis are on the same level throughout the scene, i.e. 'downstairs'. The scholars who interpret ἀναβάδην correctly, yet still assume use of the complicated *ekkyklema*, neglect the remark καταβαίνειν δ' οὐ σχολή, which seems to imply that, rather than being displayed in his study on a couch by means of a platform on wheels or some other rotating device, Euripides is simply transported out on his couch like an invalid. When agreeing to be rolled out passively – to be seen, in effect (which he had previously said was 'impossible') – he adds a strong reservation; a reservation, however, *not* an explanation: καταβαίνειν δ'οὐ σχολή. The dramatic transporting of the couch and the remarks following are intended to illustrate, and also to lend comic colour to, Euripides' reservations. One no longer laughs because Euripides has finally revealed himself to a human being (by means of an artifice, moreover), but because it neither was nor is an appealing idea for him, even when he has decided to give this mortal a hearing, to get down . . . from his desk-couch and put his feet on the ground.

The information which the Servant provides, that Euripides is composing a tragedy ἀναβάδην, is taken up and used comically to display Euripides ἀναβάδην even when he has stopped working. Whereas in the prologue of *Thesmophoriazusae* Agathon is rolled out of his own free will in order to work, Euripides is rolled out against his wishes, but still ἀναβάδην. The scholars who assume use of the *ekkyklema* for Euripides alone, not for Agathon, forget that ἐκκυκλεῖσθαι cannot but signify the same operation in *Acharnians* from the year 425 as it does in the later *Thesmophoriazusae*. The only thing is that the stagecraft of the *ekkyklema* interlude between parodos and parabasis differs for stylistic reasons.

The scholiasts on *Clouds* 184 and *Thesmophoriazusae* 277 put the contorted *ekkyklema* into action a third, fourth and last time for the Socratic reflectory and the Thesmophorium, in each case inappropriately. The presumption of the Aristophanic, and tragic, scholiasts derives from the usages proper to their own times, which they attribute also to the theatrical civilization of fifth-century Athens. The latter does allow for an *ekkyklema*, but only for one which is used moderately, employing a moving platform of moderate proportions.[7]

7 Aristophanic interiors: some notes on Aristophanes and the theatre of Euripides

To keep to Aristophanes and *Acharnians* (since the presumed use of the *ekkyklema* in *Clouds* and *Thesmophoriazusae* and in other comedies is discussed briefly in the relevant chapters), some interpreters would have the *ekkyklema* employed during the cooking scene in 1003–47 also. However, this is the only occasion in Aristophanes in which the operation of cooking is *not* displayed to the audience: in other cases, the oven and attendant utensils are dramatically transported into the orchestra: see *Peace* and *Birds*. In *Acharnians* 1003–47, however, all that can be seen is Dikaiopolis, not in the act of cooking, but rather yelling orders in the direction of the house and the kitchen staff and skewering thrushes under the envious eyes of the chorus, which he then passes to his servants to have cooked (see 1007 and 1047, 1011f.): the scene opens and closes with these two refined operations. The stagecraft of the comedy's secret cuisine lets off its first precursory spark in 987b, when Dikaiopolis, having run indoors from the orchestra to prepare the meal, starts throwing bird feathers through the door. Further on, he is to be seen handling casks of wine. At that point, however, he is in front of the house, as the two verbs in line 1067 demonstrate. So occupied is he with his work that he fails to notice a Messenger of the strategoi, whose arrival is announced instead by the chorus. Regarding the cooking operation, there is also an artistic motive for not displaying the hares, thrushes, giblets, cuttlefish and eel as they are actually being cooked: later on, all of these dainties, already cooked, are brought out on-stage to be shown to the starving Lamachus, a

Servant carrying them gradually from the house to the orchestra (1098). The dainties, bought from a Theban merchant in 873–80, are almost all made of papier mâché or wood (cf. *Thesmophoriazusae* 772–5), like the billy-goat in *Birds* 901–2, 'which is reduced to a state of horns and hair', or the thighs of mutton saved for the choregos in *Peace* 1022, in both cases during cooking scenes taking place in the orchestra (*Peace* 973–1126). There is another outdoor cooking scene in *Birds* 1579–1693. *Acharnians* 887–93 demonstrates in miniature how the ovens are set up: Dikaiopolis orders that a small oven and a bellows should be brought forth to cook some eel. In *Peace*, the projection of the kitchen into the orchestra is so marked that in 1050 a technical term typifying an interior is employed. It is not only in *Peace*, however, that the orchestra is perceived as a closed space, since terms proper to such a space are applied to it elsewhere: *Acharnians* 825, *Knights* 365, *Birds* 278 and 990–1 and also 1169, *Thesmophoriazusae* 657, *Plutus* 872 (cf. also *Wasps* 891; in *Acharnians* 1222 and *Knights* 1407 the complements are explicit in this respect).

In ancient Greek theatre, therefore, interiors are projected outwards, on rare occasions 'rolled out', and never, at least in Aristophanes, displayed through the openings in the scenic façade. The usual practice – when indoor environments or facts are neither described nor referred to – is that most obvious one of having a back-stage character emerge carrying accessories proper to the indoor environment, or simply of having these accessories brought forth. In the first case, the opening remarks of characters moving from the scenic façade to the orchestra – to affirm or confirm a scenic value there (explicit or not) – occasionally create the artistic impression that a dialogue initiated back-stage is being continued (cf. at least *Wasps* 1122, a scene which many scholars, beginning with Wilamowitz, maintain involves the *ekkyklema*). The orchestra, which assumes values distinct from those of the façade (particularly in Aristophanes' Lenaian comedies, and also in Aeschylus), tends normally to be the zone representing the essential values of interiors.

An example is provided by *Thesmophoriazusae*, the only Aristophanic comedy in which the scenic façade, from the prologue onwards, pertains to the chorus, not to the actor-protagonists: the scenic façade = the Thesmophorian temple remains purely decorative, whilst the interior of the temple is represented in practice by the orchestra. In *Birds*, the city of the birds is built outside the theatre between ether and sky, yet it is still the orchestra and the air above which represent the fabulous city in the theatre.

Lysistrata, *Peace* and *Plutus* are significant from a different point of view. In *Lysistrata*, the characters, invited by Lysistrata, pass from the orchestra into the façade = the Athenian Acropolis. However, the interior is not displayed to the audience, since the door closes on the character-actors' backs, and as they banquet unseen in the Acropolis, in the orchestra (neutral in value) the chorus entertains the spectators with a song. In *Peace* 1305, Trygaeus, who is banqueting indoors with his guests, advises 'those remaining here', or rather the choreutai, to eat of their own accord, while he goes back inside and the door closes behind him. During the crowded and secret domestic banquet, two of the guests' sons emerge to have a pee, and 'before they go back indoors' are begged to sing, a request which they satisfy at some length (cf. *Peace* 1265, 1296). In *Plutus*, datable to 388, Karion comes out into the orchestra and describes the indoor environment and the sacrifice which is being performed to the chorus. He tells them that the house has been completely transformed, that the furniture is full of gold and silver, that the pans have been turned into bronze, the plates into silver and the lanterns into ivory. He has come out, he explains, because the smoke of the sacrifice is burning his eyes (*Plutus* 802–23, cf. 791–9).

How is it that the lovers of the magnificent *ekkyklema* are never disappointed – they who confuse ancient theatre with the theatre of the opera – that so many spectacular indoor environments and events remain invisible to the spectators? How is it that they have never once paused to think that when a character goes to visit another living in the scenic façade he never crosses the threshold but either 'calls out' whoever lives inside, or sees him emerge spontaneously (cf. *Plutus* 1103 and 964f. alone), the door always closing behind him, the chorus and new characters keeping the show under way?

When the subject-matter of Greek comedy became altogether bourgeois and intimate, when the chorus lost its vitality and theatrical taste turned towards the technical, then perhaps machines were invented which might, in certain cases, have appropriately displayed the most secret aspects of that private subject-matter. Yet the subject-matter of fifth-century Greek theatre remains fundamentally 'public', or almost always 'publicable', at least. The works of Aristophanes, furthermore, in indubitable contrast to the inferior stagecraft of Latin comic theatre, never make public display of subjects which it would have been legitimate to see only through the scenic façade, with the breaching, so to speak, of the fourth wall. Undoubtedly, the modern analytic reader will notice slight instances of scenic unnaturalness in the works of the Greek theatre. But he or she should remember that the ancient spectator was struck only ephemerally by these, if at all, since the ancient spectator was not plunged into the pitch-black darkness of the modern theatre, but was actively accomplice to the properties and conventions of his theatrical civilization and of its particular stage-technique; a complicity which the work of Aristophanes explicitly solicits and often 'rewards' by including the spectator and the zone reserved for him within the expressive texture of the scenic illusion which, as the sun shone down brilliantly on to the orchestra, often affirmed on stage darkest night, sometimes by means of burning torches, sometimes not.

Indeed, in Aristophanes four comedies actually begin at night: *Clouds*, *Wasps*, *Lysistrata* and *Assemblywomen*. Others seem to finish at night: *Wasps*, for instance. The subject-matter and nocturnal atmosphere – if one is prepared to concede an apparent digression – probably allude to Euripides, in the pathetic parodoi of *Wasps* and *Assemblywomen* at least, since from Euripides' work Aristophanes borrows and reproposes critically – or rather puts to new ends – single theatrical or expressive effects alone, not conceptual material (in *Frogs*, the discussion is mainly concerned with form and stage-technique). Nor is it purely a coincidence that the only two scenes exploiting the *ekkyklema* in Aristophanes (*Acharnians* and *Thesmophoriazusae*) should involve Euripides, for Euripides availed himself too often of the moving platform considered above, and did so also for pathetic events (Phaidra, Alcestis). Indeed, by citing a line from *Bellerophon* κ υ λ ί ν δ ε τ' εἴσω in *Knights* 1249, Aristophanes attributes the platform parodically to Euripides, whilst according to the scholiasts Euripides had said κομίζετ' εἴσω, as in fragment 673 of *Stheneboia*. The moving platform, introduced apparently by Aeschylus, appears extremely rarely in extant Sophocles, in which there is also no evidence for the use of the flying-machine, so favoured by the miracle-loving Euripides parodied by Aristophanes in *Peace* (a beetle standing in for Pegasus and Trygaeus for Bellerophon). It is hardly casual either that in the second part of *Thesmophoriazusae*, Euripides should appear as a mannequin, a mechanical protean 'actor', who also imposes this particular taste on his Relative, a prisoner amongst the women.

The pathetic prisoners (the Relative-Andromeda-Helen and Philokleon), the heroes with the lives of a million perils (Dikaiopolis-Telephus, Lamachus-Telephus, lame at the end of *Acharnians*; Trygaeus-Bellerophon, limping too), the mad characters (the nymph Echo from *Helen* = the demented hag in *Thesmophoriazusae*), the prodigiously mature youths (*Wasps*, *Peace*), the exquisitely shrewd Servants (*Acharnians*, *Thesmophoriazusae*), the cretinous and blind choreutai (*Acharnians* and *Thesmophoriazusae*), and finally the plots with supernatural (*Knights*) or totally over-elaborate solutions (*Thesmophoriazusae*), all of these are pure Euripidaristophanery, as the albeit limited extant Euripides makes perfectly clear.

Aristophanes' own dramaturgical line seems, on the contrary, to be fundamentally that of a 'conservative', closer to the refined, rigorous and essential dramaturgy of Sophocles. In Aristophanes, even more than in Sophocles, the most salient features are: verisimilitude in the presentation of the characters (to which Euripides pays little attention) and in the treatment of dramatic time; the theatrical unity, in the Dionysian comedies, of the milieu of the protagonist and of nearly all the other characters' action (evident in Sophocles' later tragedies, for the protagonists alone, but not in the more ancient *Ajax* and *Antigone*); the almost constant on-stage presence of the protagonists in the Dionysian comedies; the back-stage and off-stage widening of the dramatic landscape (*Birds*); the constant presence of the chorus in the orchestra (in *Ajax* the chorus is absent in 815–65); and lastly the dissimulated use of the flying-machine, never for miracle-working ends (*Clouds*, *Birds*, apart from the parodic *Peace*). In the Lenaian comedies, the stagecraft true and proper is on the level, let us say, of that of Aeschylus, who worked for a technically backward theatre such as the theatre of Dionysos during the fifth century.

8 From Dikaiopolis' market to the allusive epilogue in the theatre of an off-stage contest

The second part of *Acharnians* is normally considered to be a fortuitous and sketchy piece. Whereas this may indeed be true of the second part of *Peace*, in the second part of *Acharnians* the structure and subject-matter are fairly well calculated and extremely varied: 719–970, trade with the foreigners but not with Lamachus; 971–99, comment and evocation, with personifications of War and Reconciliation; 1000–68, announcement of the off-stage Pitcher symposium (cf. 961); preparation of the banquet; the magic wine of the truce and the Athenians; 1069–1233, realistic and conclusive contrast – on-stage, off-stage, then on-stage again – between Dikaiopolis and Lamachus.

Dikaiopolis' private and symbolistic agora, which is installed then and there in the orchestra, by means of a technique which is also employed in *Wasps* for the private and symbolistic lawcourt, is an illustration of the public pro-clamation made in 623–5; similarly, the first scene with the Megarian Pig-dealer is along the lines envisioned by Telephus-Dikaiopolis in 520–3 and 535. Yet this is not all: the scenes with the Megarian Pig-dealer and the Theban, which are composed with great care and are also completely different from each other in terms of scenic make-up and the use made of the actors, allude implicitly to two different comic styles. The first scene, whose 'dialectal' protagonist is the coarse Megarian with his 'little piglettes' – Μεγαρικά τις μαχανά (738) – and whose willing Calandrinesque deuteragonist is the Attic Dikaiopolis, plays up indirectly the superficiality of 'buffoonery purloined at Megara' (cf. *Wasps* 57); the other scene, whose scoffing protagonist is a sophisticated and often paratragic Dikaiopolis, plays up the refinement of the Attic spirit. Here the chorus takes part in the action, and the coryphaeus converses with Dikaiopolis and the Theban.

The subsequent bulk of the comedy is naturally dedicated to the direct contrast between the two champions: their antagonism is particularly brilliant, and significant, in the finale, the acme of the structural action of the comedy, culminating in the public defeat-victory of the two characters. This climax is reached after a well-prepared and simultaneous exit, provoked by events occurring off-stage, an exit from which the characters move to antinomic destinations, so that the dispute is provided to all practical purposes with two external perspectives. In *Knights* the destinations of the two exiting antagonists are identical, but there are not the same concrete scenic consequences. One should note that Dikaiopolis' exit is delayed (cf. 1000), and in order to make this delay seem more natural the Messenger solicits him in the name of the priest of Dionysos (cf. 1088, 1093), thus drawing attention to his tardiness.

From the Messenger's order one may also glean a reason for the sudden conflict that breaks out over the preparations for the banquet: cf. 1086 with 1098 and 1133. Lamachus returns defeated and wounded, borne by two men, Dikaiopolis victorious and drunk, in the arms of two courtesans. The sung conflict between the two antagonists requires the most extreme bravura: verbal pastiche and correspondence of tone and rhythm produce sentiments, gestures and scenic games tragically and comically antithetical in their symmetry (1190–1225).

Dikaiopolis has made his way, pitcher in hand, to the sanctuary of Dionysos in the Marshes (cf. 1087), open that single day of the year, and then to the public banqueting contest of the Pitchers, which in reality took place in the Themothetaion a month after the comic contests. When he returns, an identification is established between the conclusion of the banqueting contest and that of the Lenaian comic contest (cf. 1224f.: both of which were governed by the archon basileus), since the wineskin, sign of victory in the revelry (cf. 1002), is consigned to Dikaiopolis directly in the orchestra (1230, by the Acharnian coryphaeus, portrayed certainly by Aristophanes). One should note that on reappearing in the theatre Dikaiopolis did not move towards his house, like Lamachus: the only reason for his return was to allow him to scoff at Lamachus and then to make his way towards the judges and the archon basileus in the proedria to claim his prize.

A victorious off-stage action has a realistic and allusive epilogue in the theatre: victory at the feast, victory over Lamachus and augury for victory in the comic contest.

9 The dramatic time of *Acharnians* and Aristophanes' synchronistic method

Acharnians is the comedy with the widest time-range in Aristophanes: immediately after the parodos Dikaiopolis celebrates the Rural Dionysia announced at the end of the prologue, and from the end of the parabasis to the end of the comedy the period of the Pitcher Feast is affirmed and reaffirmed on-stage and back-stage. The Rural Dionysia took place in Poseidon, the sixth Attic month (our December), the Pitchers on the twelfth day of Anthesterion, the eighth month. A realistic shift, prior to the parabasis, recalls both the ongoing and intermediate Lenaias.

The progression of months takes place during the pause formed by the parabasis: just before the parabasis Dikaiopolis launches a proclamation in Athens inviting foreign peoples to do commerce with him, not with Lamachus (on behalf of the entire people, the chorus agrees). As soon as the action resumes he founds a market, declaring it open to foreigners and closed to the sycophants. At the market, travellers arrive from Megara and Boeotian Thebes (cf. 750, 754, 862, 868), whilst entry is refused to the sycophants and to Lamachus' Messenger: the latter had wished to buy goods for the Pitcher

Feast. In short: 623–5, commercial proclamation; 626–718, parabasis; 719–28, foundation of market; 728–9, stage void for a moment of characters and chorus mute; 729–835, Megarian; 836–59, stage void of characters, exceedingly dramatic choral stasimon; 860–958, Thebans; 959–70, Lamachus' Messenger. This Messenger – like the Megarian before him and Paranymphos and the Priest of Dionysos' Messenger after him – knows the pacifist's name, whereas Dikaiopolis pretends to have forgotten who Lamachus is (748, 959, 1048, 1085; 963).

After a dramatic stasimon (cf. 971–8 and the beginning of the antistrophe), during which the stage is void of characters, a Crier announces the Feast of the Pitchers and the Banqueting Contest (1000–3). As Dikaiopolis is preparing himself (cf. 1068), a Messenger arrives and orders Lamachus to leave at once for the passes, 'since it has been heard that Boeotian predators are going to make an incursion during the period of the Pitchers and the Pots' (1073–7). The Pots, not as joyful a feast as the Pitchers, was celebrated on the thirteenth day of Anthesterion, its vigil coinciding with the evening conclusion of the Feast of the Pitchers. Hence, the Messenger's statement is extremely appropriate; Aristophanes himself in *Frogs* 217–19 speaks of the joyful ceremony of the Pitchers extending into the vigil of the Pots. Lamachus and Dikaiopolis leave in 1142, after Dikaiopolis has been urged once more to go to the Pitcher symposium (1085–94; cf. 1133, 1135). This is followed by the choral stasimon 1143–73, which, apart from 1143–9, is extra-dramatic. Then, a Messenger of Lamachus announces the return of the warrior, who has wounded himself leaping over a trench 'as he chased predators and harried them with his lance' (1188, 1174–88). Lamachus immediately appears, crying out that he has been wounded 'by the enemy's lance', and also afraid that Dikaiopolis will see him in such a pitiful condition (1192, 1196). At that precise moment, Dikaiopolis returns from the feast and demands the prize due to the victor of the Pitchers (cf. in particular 1202, 1211–13, 1227–9). On his way out, Lamachus once more complains that a lance has pierced him to the bone (1226).

This rather crude version of the facts tends to confirm the truth of a current opinion: that in *Acharnians*, as in other comedies, Aristophanes displays total indifference towards chronological verisimilitude. It is claimed that in this particular comedy he puts a lengthy and a brief time-period on the same chronological plane: Lamachus at war against the Boeotians and Dikaiopolis at the Pitcher Feast. This inverisimilitude, however, were it actually to exist, would be neither so important nor so indicative: this is the only time in Aristophanes that two characters perform synchronous off-stage actions with conflicting aims (not so in *Knights*, *Wasps*, *Assembly-women* and *Plutus*). It is also the end of the comedy, when dramatic time may with a certain legitimacy be accelerated, even at the cost of disharmonious coincidences.[8]

However, the latter does not appear to be the case with Aristophanes. He has concentrated exclusively on the day of the Pitchers, not out of chronological indifference or by virtue of 'poetic licence', but because the licentious duration of the Pitcher Feast, extending into the nocturnal vigil of the Pots, was perfectly adapted to Lamachus' mission, which took place 'during the period of the Pitchers and the Pots'. Furthermore, it is hardly as if Lamachus actually goes to Boeotia: during the Peloponnesian war, if not in the winter of 426 itself, it was quite common for the Boeotian militia to make incursions just a few miles away from Athens, as indicated by *Acharnians* 1023 (Phyle, needless to say, is extremely close to Athens), and noted also by the scholiast on 1077. What more does one require? If anyone still disdains the verisimilitude of the piece, one might add that the returning Lamachus is presented as a boasting soldier: when he appears, and when he disappears, he cries that he was wounded by an enemy's lance, although the Messenger has already attributed to him a pedestrian mishap in pursuit of unspecified 'predators'. The Messenger's final line, 1188, moreover, should the entire public have picked it up or not, is a remark pertaining to Euripides' Telephus, most probably when the feigned mendicant with leg wounds falsely informs the Achaeans that he has been wounded or has wounded himself 'while pursuing predators and harrying them with [his] lance'.

The public, of course, would have had no problem in understanding the situation, helped as they were by the bands and bandages that Lamachus' servants, on the orders of the Messenger, had brought out on-stage after 1189 in order to tend their master, who in 1222 asks instead to be taken to hospital. The genesis of a Euripidean invention.

Hence, the more or less accelerated off-stage time periods of the comedy are absorbed into the parabasis and into an extra-dramatic choral stasimon, during both of which the chorus is active and there are no characters on-stage. It is very likely that there is time-acceleration during the parodos also, since it is void of characters and contains a movement from Athens into the countryside. All perfectly legitimate procedures. Time is similarly accelerated or absorbed in other comedies: most perceptibly in *Peace*, *Lysistrata* and *Plutus*, less so in *Knights*, *Wasps*, *Birds* and *Assemblywomen*. Scenic time, however, is always homogeneous in Aristophanes, concrete and possessed of an explicit rigour: during the parabasis of *Thesmophoriazusae*, in which two characters quite exceptionally remain on-stage, time passes homogeneously (cf. *Thesmophoriazusae* 654 with 854, 783–4 with 846–8). When two secondary characters in the prologues of *Acharnians* and *Peace* make long off-stage journeys yet return swiftly to join the ranks of the other characters, the prodigious voyagers are *deities* (*Acharnians* 129–78, *Peace* 262–8 and 275–80). In *Lysistrata*, a human delegation is seemingly given the time necessary to journey from Sparta to Athens, since during that wait the action involves two semi-choruses alone.

Aristophanes with his eye on the clock? Certainly not, but neither is he indifferent to on-stage chronological verisimilitude; and he is most concerned with harmonizing accelerated off-stage events, a verisimilitude and harmony which contemporary tragedy apparently did not profess (although tragedy is less licentious than is commonly affirmed). Jean Andrieu, however, concerned with refuting ancient and modern 'act' theories, even for fifth- and fourth-century dramas, was induced by *Acharnians* to deny that Aristophanes paid any attention to chronological verisimilitude and harmony.[9]

Aristophanes' method in dealing with non-scenic action pauses involving time-acceleration would not have implied, and does not imply, a latent division into 'acts'. Quite the contrary: Aristophanes demonstrates a clear concern to attenuate the lengthy interval of the parabasis, and not only because it is the interval during which these accelerations of various intensities actually occur (*Acharnians, Knights, Peace, Lysistrata* and *Plutus*). After the parabasis – other artistic and technical insights apart (cf., for instance, *Knights* 611–25, *Wasps* 1010 and *Peace* 729) – Aristophanes never assigns the opening remarks to new characters, but always to those already active prior to that enormous pause which more than any other might have been inclined to generate 'acts' (who knows how things stood in the most ancient Greek comedy? Regarding *Plutus* the reference is naturally to the point which is recognizably 'parabatic'). After the effective minor parabases of *Knights*, *Wasps, Peace* and *Birds* also, time-accelerated or not, the dialogue is opened by established characters (cf. also *Clouds* 1131).

Who knows, the hypothetical rhythm of music apart, whether time-acceleration during the parabasis was indicated in some way at the resumption of the stage-action? It is certainly true that after the major parabases in which time is accelerated a single character appears on-stage (Dikaiopolis, the Sausage-seller, Trygaeus, Lysistrata and Karion), and sooner or later a second, in most cases new or long-absent (*Acharnians, Lysistrata, Plutus, Knights* and *Peace*). After the major parabases in which time is homogeneous, two characters immediately appear, both already known to the audience: Socrates and Strepsiades (the latter is at once indirectly present in line 628), Philokleon and Bdelykleon, Peisetairos and Euelpides, Aiakos and Xanthias, not to mention Euripides' Relative and the Second Woman (*Assemblywomen* is examined in turn). All of this might, of course, be fortuitous, a consequence of the intrigue in progress in each comedy: a rather significant consequence, however, considering that the solitary metaparabatic character immediately provides an account of the protracted off-stage events, or else initiates the *new* scene announced directly prior to the parabasis (*Knights* 615 and 624–82, *Peace* 819–41, *Lysistrata* 708–27 and following lines, *Plutus* 626–759, *Acharnians* 719–28).

The metaparabatic couple, by contrast, frankly continues the previous stage-action, which either did not progress at all back-stage or did so quite normally. The previously examined case of *Thesmophoriazusae* is remarkable, a comedy in which time is always homogeneous because the protagonist is always on-stage (apart from 947–1000); so too *Clouds*, which compromises itself after the parabasis with expressive time-adverbs of concrete value. One need hardly mention, of course, that in Latin comedy *iam* and *dudum* did not always mean *iam* and *dudum*.

Aristophanic comedy, therefore, does not neglect chronological veri-similitude, artistically fills out accelerated off-stage pauses in the action, attenuates the fracture caused by the parabasis, and at least implicitly conveys to the spectators the quality of the comedy's metaparabatic time. Even in *Assemblywomen* and *Plutus*, whose dramaturgy was new and of a diverse tendency (especially *Assemblywomen*), Aristophanes did not abandon his method. The comic parabasis might easily have led to the creation of 'acts' true and proper, but it did not. Nor did it favour the opening of a distinct rift between the prologue and the parodos: at the end of the prologue the scene never clearly changes, not even in *Acharnians*, *Lysistrata* and *Thesmophor-iazusae*. The only fifth-century theatrical work to divide its material effec-tively into 'acts' is Aeschylus' *Orestes*, a four-'act' work: the fourth begins with *Eumenides* 235. Aristophanes' *Assemblywomen* demonstrates a tendency towards 'acts' when the chorus exits at the end of the prologue, and the protagonist for good in line 729, the comedy proceeding from 730 onwards as though it were a theatrical 'revue'. The second part of *Frogs* develops naturally and is introduced by a second prologue performed by two characters from the first part of the comedy, subsequently inactive.

One might perhaps add that in the case of *Acharnians*, which ends at night (like *Wasps* and *Assemblywomen* at least), the metaparabatic resumption of the comedy is perceived as occurring during the morning, since shortly after-wards the Herald opens the feast-day of the Pitchers. The first part of *Acharnians* also begins early in the morning, with Dikaiopolis alone in the Pnyx. When the latecomers arrive, much time has passed. This is typical of certain monologues and retrospective expositions in Aristophanes: a factor to be discussed regarding the prologue of *Wasps*.

10 The scenic façade

Three different characters are lodged in the scenic façade of *Acharnians*: Dikaiopolis, Euripides and Lamachus. However, the existence of three tenants does not imply the existence of three separate houses or of three separate doors. The only doors, or houses, to be used distinctly and con-temporaneously are those of Dikaiopolis and Lamachus: cf. 1071–1133, and before that 622–5 and 959–70. There is no reason why one should not assume that the temporary house of Euripides in 395–479 is in fact the future house of Lamachus, or rather that in order to represent Euripides' house use is made of the door that from a certain point onwards is assigned permanently to Lamachus. In *Assemblywomen*, the rotation of tenants in the façade is beyond all doubt. In that comedy also, as in *Clouds* and *Thesmophoriazusae*, there are inarguably two contemporaneously distinct entrances.

In Aristophanic comedy there is no case for arguing that there are definitely three distinct entrances in the scenic façade: they are very likely in *Peace* alone (house of Trygaeus, house of Zeus, cave), and perhaps in *Lysistrata* (house of Lysistrata, house of Kalonike, entrance to the Acropolis). In support of a theory postulating three distinct doors, fragment 48 of Eupolis' *Autolycus* from the year 420 is normally cited, a comedy whose contest is unknown. Who can judge the truth of this, as long as the fragment remains isolated from its context?[10]

The scenic façade apparently employs, partially at least, a level, usable roof, inasmuch as Dikaiopolis' wife at one point is invited to climb on to it (262). In *Clouds*, *Wasps* and *Lysistrata*, the roof of the façade is a fully fledged acting zone.

In 1072, when Lamachus comes out and asks, 'who is pounding around my bronze-glittering abode?', it is by no means certain that the phrase refers to the exterior of the façade.

Regarding Lamachus, it is normally maintained that on his first appearance in 572–4, invoked by an Acharnian semi-chorus, he emerges from the scenic façade, given that he is subsequently to lodge there. It would seem more natural, however, should he rush to provide succour from the exterior: the most warlike of the Acharnians cry out for the warrior to come, and the 'historical' personality, having rushed from the city, is drawn realistically into the dramatic game. The tragic/epic hero takes his place in the door previously assigned to Euripides, and beside him, further on, is lodged Dikaiopolis. It has previously been remarked that with his visit to Euripides Dikaiopolis moves from the countryside to Athens. Just as Euripides was not conceived as being the next-door neighbour of Dikaiopolis, so Lamachus and Dikaiopolis from the outset are not perceived as being next-door neighbours. Their polemical cohabitation within the scenic façade begins just before the parabasis, a novelty to which Dikaiopolis twice draws explicit attention (625, 719). The parabasis, in short, allows for the belated assignation of an element of the façade to a character who has appeared from the exterior. The only other comedy in which this occurs is *Assemblywomen*.

Technically, it is impossible to compare Lamachus' appearance from the exterior with those of the choruses of *Knights*, *Clouds* and *Peace*, all invoked by characters in need of help. However, on a stylistic level there is some contact between Trygaeus' appeal in *Peace* 296–8 and that of the Acharnian semi-chorus. It should also be noted that were Lamachus conceived as lodging already within the scenic façade, the semi-chorus would not have invoked him as it does (cf. 566–74).

As mentioned previously, the house of Euripides is a temporary one. In other comedies, apart from *Assemblywomen*, episodic characters are lodged in the façade during the prologue alone: Agathon in *Thesmophoriazusae* and Herakles in *Frogs*, themselves visited – by characters coming from the exterior – for help and advice. As already seen, an adroit piece of stagecraft limits Euripides' visit to the space between parodos and parabasis. The two

Arguments in *Clouds* are a case apart, since they are conceived as being within the Socratic school from the very beginning of the comedy.

11 Notes on certain properties of the orchestra, the scenic façade, the chorus and the actors

Acharnians 173–5 and 203–4 and *Birds* 1034–50 imply that the theatre contained two corridors. The existence and use of two corridors is evident in Sophocles' *Ajax* 805–74. *Thesmophoriazusae* 1222, 'which of the two paths?', is also fairly clear. But which corridor, respectively the right or the left, signified for the public of tragedy and Aristophanic comedy an entrance 'from the Agora' or 'from the countryside' has never come to light, not even from the text of *Assemblywomen*, whilst *Birds* 1034–50 at least excludes any differentiated use.

Perhaps it was more normal to use a particular corridor for the entrance of the chorus: when in *Clouds* 326 Socrates indicates to Strepsiades that the Clouds, which he expects to appear from on high, are παρὰ τὴν εἴσοδον, Strepsiades, and the public, immediately look in a particular direction, where the Clouds finally appear. In *Birds* 296, after Peisetairos claims to have seen a flock of birds, Euelpides immediately looks to one side and cries out that the wings of the birds are making it impossible to see τὴν εἴσοδον.[11]

The area most typically frequented by the chorus is the orchestra. The Clouds, for example, are there in line 328, well in view. The comic chorus also remains constantly present and visible (or at least partly visible) for the duration of the comedy. This is true even of *Peace* 427, in which the choreutai are invited to enter an opening in the scenic façade = the cavern of the goddess Peace. In *Assemblywomen*, whose choreutic dramaturgy is entirely original, the chorus absents itself to take part in off-stage action. When special ὀρχησταί (*Peace* 789) are invited to dance in the orchestra, the choreutai yield up their position and retire, probably towards the scenic façade: see *Wasps* 1515–16. On that occasion, it appears that the chorus is again perceived as εἴσοδος: 'if some τραγῳδός pretends to dance, ἐνθάδ' εἰσίτω' (*Wasps* 1499). Expressions such as those in *Clouds* 1510, ἡγεῖσθ' ἔξω, and *Wasps* 1535, ἐξάγετε . . . θύραζε, are effectively suited to the chorus, of whom extra-scenic provenance is more in character than any relationship to the scenic façade. In the case of the mystic chorus of *Frogs*, however, which lives near the residence of Pluton (*Frogs* 163), it is quite fitting that whoever leads the chorus out should ἐξάγειν it from the façade into the orchestra (*Frogs* 352). In *Thesmophoriazusae*, the only comedy in which the scenic façade is lastingly assigned to the chorus rather than to the actor-protagonists (before the end of the prologue, apparently: cf. *Thesmophoriazusae* 278), the chorus most probably enters the orchestra and at the end exits from it through the façade = the gates of the Thesmophorium temple. Elsewhere, the scenic façade is assigned sooner or later to the character-actors and is never entered by the chorus, except perhaps in the finale of *Birds*, in which the façade represents a copse.

The uses, almost uniformly eloquent, to which the character-actors put the openings in the façade possessing scenic value – for their own exits and entrances or to bring people and things in or out – are marked by verbs such as ἐξέρχεσθαι, ἐξιέναι, ἐκφέρειν and the like, and by the respective opposites εἰσ-, and so forth.

Only a couple of times are such terms employed to indicate the use of openings which are apparently neutral in value: *Knights* 998 and 1110 and *Thesmophoriazusae* 930 and 1011. Apart from the two cases listed, which can be explained with reference to the particular *mise-en-scène* of the comedies concerned (in *Knights* the scenic façade is a house = Athens), it is beyond doubt that characters of extra-scenic provenance always make use of the corridors to enter or exit from the orchestra, and never employ neutral openings in the façade. Indeed, since the entrances of characters coming *certainly* from extra-scenic locations into the orchestra are indicated by terms such as προσέρχεσθαι and the like (cf., for example, *Acharnians* 865, *Lysistrata* 65 and 77, *Thesmophoriazusae* 571 and 923), this necessarily implies that all the other characters announced on the point of προσέρχεσθαι or anything similar (προσιέναι) employ the other corridor: this is true not only of the two characters who have returned from their off-stage mission in *Knights* 891 and *Wasps* 1324, but also of characters who arrive for the first time in the orchestra, and naturally of any other characters who enter from the exterior without having been announced. The dancers in *Wasps*, although they are invited to εἰσιέναι, when they gradually appear προσέρχονται and ἔρχονται like the character-actors (*Wasps* 1505, 1508, 1531). Only when the scenic façade represents an open space, such as the copse in *Birds*, for instance, is it possible for characters to traverse it as they variously appear and disappear. In *Peace*, characters arrive at the scenic façade = the house of Trygaeus directly from the city, and two of them later emerge from the house and enter the orchestra (cf. *Peace* 1192, 1265f.). Similarly, in *Lysistrata* the women occupy the scenic façade = the Acropolis from the rear. However, there is not a single instance of a character who has already entered his base in the scenic façade sub-sequently appearing from the orchestra. Trygaeus in *Peace*, in order to return from sky to earth on foot, enters the scenic façade = the cavern in *Peace*, and after the parabasis appears from the corridor.[12]

The performance of *Acharnians* is opened by a character of extra-scenic provenance: the same is true of *Birds*, *Thesmophoriazusae*, *Frogs* (a couple of characters) and *Plutus*. In the other comedies, the opening characters are strictly related to the scenic façade. The opening characters of extra-scenic provenance are either close to the façade or indicate it: *Acharnians* 202, *Birds* 52, *Thesmophoriazusae* 25, *Frogs* 35 and *Plutus* 231 (cf. 43). The other opening characters immediately draw attention to the façade, and at times are clearly performing in more or less direct proximity to it (*Wasps, Clouds, Peace* and *Assemblywomen*). Regarding the chorus: in the parodoi of *Acharnians, Wasps* and *Lysistrata*, and particularly in those of *Acharnians* and *Lysistrata*, it appears that after its opening march the chorus is either close, or extremely close to the façade; as noted previously, in these three comedies the chorus enters a stage void of actors. In certain prologues, and also throughout each comedy, the characters definitely seem to be active in the orchestra, or rather in the same zone as the chorus and in close contact with it, even when the chorus is neither in nor near the façade: i.e. when it is in the orchestra. *Acharnians* 564–5 provides the first sure example of the chorus having close contact with characters in the orchestra, since the scenes preceding and succeeding the visit to Euripides demonstrate that Dikaiopolis has moved from the orchestra/lists/chopping-block towards the façade-Euripides' door, and then from the façade back to the orchestra (cf. 366, 394, 480, 483–9). After *Acharnians* 280 the dispute is already supposed to be taking place in the orchestra. And, if the interpretation given in section 5 above is correct, the phallus-bearing procession entails a movement from the façade to the orchestra and back again. Occasionally, the characters even seem to be in contact with the spectators in the front row: *Peace* 905 and 962–72 and *Frogs* 297, apart from the previously discussed position in *Acharnians* 257–8, are examples.

The characters also perform in the depths of the orchestra, therefore, and since the orchestra – see section 7 above – can at times represent the essential scenic values of the interior of the façade (to such an extent that it can even be perceived *as* an interior), so the characters move freely from the façade to the orchestra, wherever and whenever they desire. When the characters withdraw, the choreutai who remain in the orchestra are 'those who remain here' (*Peace* 1305), the chorus advises the characters not to re-enter but to 'remain outside' (*Peace* 1023), and the characters are those left inactive within the scenic façade waiting for a signal inviting them to emerge into the orchestra (cf. *Lysistrata* 1105f. and *Plutus* 641–3 and 964f. alone). And so on. Again: the Clouds advance from the corridor in 326 and in 328 πάντα ἤδη κατέχουσιν, whereas in the prologue of *Knights* 99 the Servant spreads the word on πάντα ταυτί. In each case, one is dealing with the orchestra, and perhaps in *Peace* 319 also, in which the monstrous Polemos might throw into confusion with his feet πάντα ταυτί, the place where Trygaeus and the choreutai are situated, that is.

Hence, it seems that there was no particular zone of the theatre reserved exclusively for the actors. They perform freely in the choreutai's terrain, while the choreutai themselves are often to be found in close proximity to the façade.

The free movement of the actors (and of the choreutai) from the scenic façade to the orchestra and vice versa is never singled out by verbs or movements which might indicate a difference in level between the orchestra and the area immediately in front of the façade, even in those scenes containing expressive movements in close proximity to the openings in the façade (cf.

Birds 639–75), *Assemblywomen* 976–1111, *Plutus* 1088–95 alone). In *Lysistrata*, however, the semi-chorus of Old Men, trudging from the corridor to the orchestra (254) and then towards the façade-Acropolis (266), complain of the climb they have to face just before reaching the Acropolis (286–8, 294), where they eventually arrive in 302 and 306. If it is effectively mounted, this ramp, ignored throughout the rest of the comedy, is a stage-feature specific to *Lysistrata*, alluding by means of a slightly inclined plane to the slope that led to the real Acropolis. Also in Sophocles' *Philoctetes* a sloping path would be required in the staging of the cavern. It is less probable, however, that the verbs in *Thesmophoriazusae* 261, 585, 623, 893 and 1046 allude to an actual difference in level (they reflect the elevated position of the real Thesmophorium); likewise *Peace* 725. In *Birds* 50 and 51, there is simply an allusion to the lofty spur on which Hoopoe's nest is perched. Other presumable or presumed characteristics of the terrain of the orchestra are discussed in relation to *Peace* and *Frogs*.

In some of the comedies, characters are to be seen above the scenic space in the flying-machine (*Clouds*, *Peace*, *Birds* and *Daedalus*). They also perform on the roof of the façade (*Wasps*, *Lysistrata*), at windows (*Wasps*, *Assemblywomen*) and behind the façade. The most extensive lines delivered back-stage in a comedy, *Birds* 209–22 and 227–62, are lyrical. The choruses of *Clouds* 274–90 and 299–313 and *Frogs* 323–36 and 340–53 sing invisibly, and the small chorus of Frogs also seems invisible.

The interior of the scenic façade, as mentioned previously, is never displayed through the doorway-opening. The door has two wings like a real fifth-century door. The scenes in *Acharnians* and *Thesmophoriazusae* involving the *ekkyklema* do not imply that there is a stage-opening any larger than normal, as seen in section 6 above. In the invisible interior of the façade, in practice, are located the actors' dressing rooms. The actors enter from the corridor or the façade and, in case of necessity, reappear from the corridor or the façade as new characters. The choreutai in *Peace* 729–31 talk of σκηναί threatened by thieves who are lurking in the vicinity and implore their assistants, ἀκόλουθοι, to be on the alert. Stage-hands such as these are always available; their duties include clearing the orchestra of any surplus properties employed in the course of the action. Whenever the choreutai take off their cloaks, the stage-hands silently appear: see *Acharnians* 627, *Lysistrata* 622 and 686 and *Thesmophoriazusae* 656. In *Wasps* 409 the cloaks are carried off by the youths who accompany the chorus. *Wasps*, in fact, is the first example in Aristophanes of a chorus being temporarily enlarged by personnel not pertaining to it (cf. then *Birds* and *Frogs*, and probably *Peace* also).

The Aristophanic chorus, which provides the title for seven of the extant dramas, is never called upon to affirm the value of the scenic milieu, except in *Thesmophoriazusae*. It is related to the milieu in *Frogs* alone, and less intensely in *Clouds* and *Birds*. *Thesmophoriazusae* and *Frogs* apart, it is a corps typically extraneous to the scenic milieu, composed of the façade and orchestra and affirmed by the actors, a milieu which it is either encouraged to enter or to which it is attracted (*Knights, Clouds, Peace, Birds, Plutus, Acharnians, Wasps* and *Lysistrata*). Even when it is not actually on the attack, this extraneous corps is always a cause of slight anxiety to the characters within the scenic milieu (*Clouds* 267f., *Birds* 294f. and 308f., cf. *Peace* 309–23). Otherwise, it is in a bad mood (*Plutus* 275–82, cf. *Wasps* 251–4), or after expressing itself in neutral or solemn tones passes to a tone of warning (*Thesmophoriazusae* and *Frogs*). The non-aggressive parodoi are consistently governed by appropriate stage-techniques: the most significant examples, apart from the off-stage or back-stage parodoi of *Clouds* and *Frogs*, are those of *Wasps* and *Peace*. A method is even found to animate the peaceful appearance of the choreutai of *Peace*.

The chorus of *Assemblywomen* is on a radically innovative level, symptoms of which are to be found in *Thesmophoriazusae*. These are the only two comedies in which the two female character-actors mingle with the choreutai, and vice versa: hence the title embraces both. In *Lysistrata*, the semi-chorus of Old Women becomes confused with the Women of the Acropolis (in chapter 9 on *Lysistrata*, the actors and choreutai's costumes are discussed). Apart from *Clouds, First* and *Second, Thesmophoriazusae, First* and *Second*, and *Assembly-women*, at least a couple of the comedies not preserved must have had choruses of a typically female kind.

Of the chorus functioning as a 'curtain', mention is made in chapter 6 on *Wasps*, where the whole question of the existence of curtains in fifth- and fourth-century theatre is discussed.

12 Distribution of the parts and notes on Aristophanes' use of the first three actors and of the extras

In *Acharnians*, there are *twenty-one characters* and a large and varied crowd of extras. In the prologue six characters appear; of the four new characters active between prologue and parabasis Lamachus is the only one to reappear from among the eleven new metaparabatic characters, and of the latter only Lamachus' Messenger appears a second time.

For all of these parts three actors and two amateur actors are required:

The *first actor* is naturally assigned the part of Dikaiopolis, delivering altogether around 550 lines in 1–202, 237–625, 719–28, 750–833, 864–970, 1003–1142 and 1198–1231: this last passage, 1198–1231, includes sung parts, also to be found throughout 263–79. For the other twenty characters one might envisage a distribution such as the following:

second actor, delivering around 250 lines with sung passages in 1190–1226: Ambassador, 65–108, Theoros, 134–66, Euripides, 407–79, Lamachus, 572–622, Megarian, 729–835, Theban, 860–954, Farmer called Dercetes, 1018–36, Paranymphos, 1048–57, Lamachus, 1072–1141 and 1190–1226;

third actor, delivering around 100 lines: Amphitheos, 45–55 (mute in 56–128, but certainly on-stage), 129, 176–203, Dikaiopolis' Daughter, 245–6, Euripides' Servant, 395–402, Sycophant, 818–27, Messenger of Lamachus, 959–65, Herald of the Pitchers, 1000–2, Messenger of the Generals, 1071–7, Messenger of the Priest of Dionysos, 1085–94, Messenger of Lamachus, 1174–89;

first amateur actor: Herald of the Assembly, 43–173 (around twelve lines), the Megarian's Daughter, 735, Nikarchos, 910–58 (with around ten lines in the passage 910–26 alone: see section 13 below);

second amateur actor: Pseudartabas, or rather False Money, 100, 104.

One has already had the opportunity to appreciate the value of the sigla in the Byzantine and pre-Byzantine manuscripts: here in *Acharnians* the Megarian might better be given the siglum of the 'Megarian Pig-dealer', since that is how he actually describes himself in 818; the Theban is Theban certainly, but is also apostrophized as 'Boeotian' in 953 (cf. 872).

The distribution of some roles between the second and third actors here, as in other comedies, is purely empirical: Dikaiopolis' Daughter, Euripides, the Herald of the Pitchers, the Peasant and Paranymphos, for example, are attributable *en bloc* to the second or third actors. And some parts may obviously be inverted: the Ambassador and Theoros with Amphitheos, for example.

The essential thing is that it should be taken for granted, here as elsewhere, that the second actor dedicates himself to the character most active on-stage after the protagonist, in this case Lamachus. It is also legitimate to infer that this actor might possibly have been employed for other more active or important characters, such as the Megarian, who in terms purely of the number of lines delivered slightly exceeds Lamachus, the Theban and Euripides. The third actor of *Acharnians*, therefore, would be given parts of meagre proportion and slight characterization (even the Peasant and Paranymphos, if you wish), given that the second actor is not too busy with Lamachus: the latter's late appearance and subsequent long absence make it possible for the second actor to deal with the difficult roles of Euripides, the Megarian and the Theban.

Only in comedies in which the economy governing the characters is limited is the third actor definitely employed for larger and more important roles, as in *Knights*, *Thesmophoriazusae* and *Plutus*, or for very important roles, as in *Frogs*. If the distribution of roles adopted here for *Knights* is correct – it is the current one, in any case – then the third actor is assigned larger roles than the second and also has a sung part. He also interprets the most important character in the prologue, in which the first actor appears unusually late (*Knights* 150). Needless to say, this late appearance depends on the comedy's intrigue. But one must bear in mind that all the other comedies are opened by the first actor, or by the first and second (or third) together: *Acharnians*, *Clouds*, *Lysistrata*, *Assemblywomen*, *Plutus*, *Wasps*, *Peace*, *Birds*, *Thesmophoriazusae* and *Frogs*. It is hardly necessary to mention that, besides such reasons of intrigue, the dramatist would have been instinctively interested in seeing his comedy open with acting at the very highest levels. He would also have been concerned that for important episodic roles expedients should even have been adopted to free the first actor temporarily, as, for example, in the finale of *Lysistrata*.[13]

From the uses to which the actors are put here (sometimes definite, sometimes highly likely), or rather from these uses *also*, it follows that a fourth and fifth actor would not have been calculated for roles even equivalent to the larger and more significant ones assigned to the third: Aristophanes' practice regarding the fourth and fifth actors is discussed in section 3 of chapter 5 on *Clouds*. *Acharnians* needs a fourth actor for a dozen lines in the prologue, and also a fifth for two others. The fourth actor is required again for two words in 735 – would not an extra have been enough? – and perhaps for the small role of Nikarchos, which is dealt with in the following section.

However, nothing would have prevented the didaskalos from making use in these instances of two of the twenty-four choreutai, whom he himself instructed and directed along with the actors on the State payroll: the choregos, who paid the expensive choreutai, would have given a free hand to the didaskalos, whom he paid as well. In any other part of the comedy other than the prologue it would clearly have been impossible to employ one of the choreutai as a fourth actor, except in certain appropriate cases discussed further on (a fifth proves necessary in *Clouds* alone). The interesting thing is not who furnished the fourth and fifth actors, if the State itself furnished only three, but rather their artistic function: this is discussed in chapter 5 on *Clouds*.

As mentioned previously, the *extras* in *Acharnians* are numerous and varied, even in the prologue. Some of them are extremely colourful and indeed unique. In order, they are:

Prytanes (40), Ecclesiasts (cf. 56 and 173), Archers (54), a second Persian Ambassador at least (65), two Eunuchs (117), Odomantian soldiers (156). After the prologue: Xanthias, Dikaiopolis' Servant (243, 259), other Servants (259, 805, 887, 926, etc., perhaps a Servant with Dikaiopolis in the exodos), Dikaiopolis' Wife (245, 262, 1003, cf. 132), Dikaiopolis' Children (891, cf. 132 and, in general, 249), Megarian's Second Daughter (731), Ismenia, the Theban's Servant (861, 954), Theban Pipers (862), Matron of Honour (1056), Lamachus' Attendant (1091, see further on), Lamachus' Servants (1174, cf. 1189), two Soldiers with the wounded Lamachus (1214), two Courtesans with Dikaiopolis (1216).

This review of the *extras* is probably not complete. For example, the two extravagant legations from Persia and Thrace might have a far larger retinue than the letter of the text suggests. It is important to point out that certain extras are artistically superior to others: for example, the Matron of Honour, the two Soldiers with Lamachus and, to an even greater extent, the two Courtesans with Dikaiopolis. When the two Courtesans appear the text suggests movement and dance, which implies that the extras would have been dancer-flautists. Neither would Lamachus' Attendant in 1097–1141 nor the Servant of Dikaiopolis in the same passage (Xanthias from the phallus-bearing procession?) have been of excessively humble rank: there is a strong possibility that the former wears the mask of Lamachus' Messenger-third actor in 959–65 also. Here in 1097–1141, he is an extra, since it is unlikely that the third actor could have been assigned this role as early as line 1097: the Attendant, probably an extra still, exits with Lamachus, to return as the third actor in 1174. His mutism in 1097–1141 is perfectly natural, since at that point the scenic game requires a dispute between Lamachus and Dikaiopolis alone, assisted by a pair of mute Servants: Euripides' Servant, although he is the third actor, utters not a single word during the scene with Euripides and Dikaiopolis. The role of the Messenger, third actor → extra → third actor, is an example of the practice: character-actor → extra, character-extra → actor, employed to significant effect in *Lysistrata*, *Thesmophoriazusae* and *Plutus*. In *Acharnians*, and this is discussed in the next section, a character-actor is probably replaced by a puppet.

The on-stage presentation of characters in *Acharnians*, and in the other comedies as well, is thoroughly motivated, or rather thoroughly motivated and prepared. It is fair to say that Aristophanes worked to the same principles as Sophocles, not Euripides. Only in *Assemblywomen* and *Plutus* does one encounter casual appearances, and on a single occasion in *Lysistrata*. There are also a few forced passages in the second part of *Peace*.

In *Acharnians*, the appearance of the countrymen-coal-merchants is thoroughly prepared, and still more thoroughly motivated. That of Dikaiopolis' family is already insinuated into the action half-way through the prologue (132), although Dikaiopolis' house has yet to be assigned any scenic value. In Aristophanes, all the characters ascribed significant back-stage or off-stage vital force during the prologue never fail to appear on-stage (this is discussed in section 3b of chapter 5 on *Clouds*). Lamachus' appearance is not prepared, since he is invoked as a god; but Dikaiopolis does refer to the warlike character in 270 when he declares himself to be 'free of troubles, battles and Lamachuses'. The appearance of the Herald of the Pitchers is thoroughly motivated and poorly prepared (961). And so forth.

The chorus always enters into communication with the characters who appear before the parabasis. With Euripides in *Acharnians*, however, it does not, and we have seen why. In the case of the metaparabatic characters, the chorus enters into communication with the most noteworthy alone, particularly if they happen to be many. This is not the case with the Megarian, however, because the merchant must prepare the trick of the little tarts 'in secret'. Demos, the only new metaparabatic character in *Knights*, is ignored by the chorus until 1111, despite the fact that in 973–96 he is the only character on-stage, and has already been there since 727. In this case, however, the chorus wishes to sing for the spectators alone, and to reveal to them alone who is lurking beneath the nickname of the Paphlagonian. In *Lysistrata* and *Thesmophoriazusae*, the chorus enters into communication with all the characters: in *Lysistrata* there is one exception, in the *one* scene which is also technically imperfect as far as character presentation is concerned (cf. *Lysistrata* 980–1013 and section 4 of chapter 9 on *Lysistrata*). In Aristophanes, the chorus announces the arrival of the characters in fewer than about ten cases. Sometimes, it must do so; in others its involvement is intended to make the announcement seem tragic (e.g. *Acharnians* 1069, *Knights* 611–15).

Whereas the appearance of characters is always prepared or motivated, their disappearance is normally silent. There is nothing unnatural about this, since when a character has finished performing, there is no reason why he should not silently depart. Even the reader remains interested in a character only as long as he is speaking: this is why the Aristophanic scholiasts rarely endeavour to distinguish the characters' exits, and concern themselves with silent appearances alone. Let us repeat that the latter are hardly ever casual.

13 Nikarchos: actor first, then actor no longer

As already mentioned, *Thesmophoriazusae* promotes a character-extra to the rank of character-actor: the mute Archer in 924–46 (an amateur is also employed in this passage) is no longer mute during the subsequent action, and is portrayed most certainly by the third actor, available after line 946. In order to effect the substitution, rather strangely an Archer is ordered to enter the scenic façade and to bind up a prisoner. The Archer carries out his orders and reappears in 1001, all of a sudden becoming extremely loquacious. His importance as a character is to increase steadily.

As far as we are concerned, the actor in *Acharnians* is replaced by an extra or puppet. The nature of the manœuvre, which allows for an erstwhile character-actor, now sycophant, to be presented nicely wrapped up quite naturally, can be gleaned from certain remarks made in 926–53.

In the private market in front of his home, Dikaiopolis has been arguing since line 916 with Nikarchos the sycophant in the presence of the Theban and his slave: Dikaiopolis has convinced the Theban to accept as merchandise a sycophant wrapped up as though he were a piece of earthenware. Now, Dikaiopolis attacks Nikarchos (942b–925), the latter protests (926a) and Dikaiopolis yells out two orders: 'stop his mouth; give me some straw, so that I can wrap him up and carry him like a piece of earthenware. In that way he won't get broken in transit' (926b–928). The singular desire to render Nikarchos mute is expressed at once, and a movement foreseen towards the Theban on Dikaiopolis' part after the packaging operation: ἵν' αὐτὸν ἐνδήσας φέρω (927b). It is quite clear that: (a) Dikaiopolis is no longer near the

Theban who, silent since 914, is to remain inactive until 954; (b) Dikaiopolis has attacked and seized Nikarchos, that invaluable piece of merchandise; (c) two different anonymous orders have been given to slaves, those invoked close above by Dikaiopolis, during the same scene; (d) the slaves have come running, immediately as usual; one of them has silenced Nikarchos (who says nothing after 926a), and the other has brought some straw.

It appears that the packaging operation takes place on-stage, and maybe has already begun, when the coryphaeus suddenly initiates an expressive dialogue in iambic monometers and dimeters, inciting Dikaiopolis: 'Wrap up well, my dearest man, the stranger's purchase, lest he should break it in transit' (929–31). And Dikaiopolis: 'I'll see to that (ἐμοὶ μελήσει ταῦτα), and all the more since, listen, can you hear the noise it makes, chattering, cracked, altogether in god's disdain' (932–4). It is during this passage that Dikaiopolis disappears indoors to wrap the vase up 'well', particularly as it is so 'cracked' (the groaning Nikarchos). This lively dialogue between the coryphaeus and Dikaiopolis keeps the show under way during the brief absence of the protagonist and Nikarchos, in the course of which Nikarchos continues to groan (after 939 his groans are heard from within, and are commented upon by the coryphaeus in 940–3). In 945, Dikaiopolis appears at his doorway and displays the packaged 'Nikarchos' held upside down by his feet. Addressing himself to the Theban, the coryphaeus rejoices at the positive outcome of the affair and wishes him good luck with his business (946–51). During this last exchange, Dikaiopolis silently transports the package into the orchestra and leaves it on the ground. In 952, when the iambic trimeters take up again, he says to the Theban: 'It was heavy work wrapping up this swine [a remark intended as an account of the difficult indoor packaging of Nikarchos, seen neither by the Theban nor by the spectators]! Boeotian, lift up the earthenware and bear it away.'

One should note that during the packaging no pronouns are heard which might typically imply the stage-presence of the packager, discussed so much by Dikaiopolis and the coryphaeus; indeed Dikaiopolis' ἐμοὶ μελήσει ταῦτα, in response to the coryphaeus' solicitation to bind up the merchandise 'well', is typical of characters who either will act or are already acting in conformity with the wishes, but *not beneath the gaze*, of their solicitors: cf. *Peace* 149 and 1041 and also 1311, *Thesmophoriazusae* 1064 and 1207 (yet cf. 1208 and previously 1172), *Plutus* 229. In 1008–17 and 1037–46 also, when Dikaiopolis is either indoors or at his doorway, iambic dimeters delivered by him and the chorus together convey to the spectators what is happening within.

Regarding Nikarchos, apart from the fact that it would have been quite simple for one to miss this particular on-stage and back-stage action, it has always been thought that he, and not the Messenger of Lamachus who appears later, was portrayed by an amateur actor, cut to measure, so to speak, since in line 909 Nikarchos is referred to as being 'little'. This particular description is made in a context charged with meaning. Satisfied with the large gains he is going to make from the sycophant, the Theban says: 'A sycophant is like a monkey brimming with slyness', Dikaiopolis: 'And here comes Nikarchos!', Theban: 'He's little, though', and Dikaiopolis: 'But he's a swine right through.' Roles of reduced stature are discussed in regard to *Peace*. Naturally, those who contemplate a dwarf-sycophant can still attribute the part to an amateur actor. However, as far as we are concerned, the back-stage manœuvre allowing a puppet or completely packaged extra to appear on-stage seems perfectly clear.

Argument I.25-7, in its brief summary of Dikaiopolis' action with Nikarchos, reads: 'Having seized a sycophant and shoved him into the sack, Dikaiopolis consigns him to the Boeotian.' This may be conjecture, although it could imply a back-stage manœuvre, assuming, of course, that the scholiast has not simply forgotten that the Megarian's sack was no longer on-stage, but rather in Dikaiopolis's house (cf. 830-5, 745, 822).

Regarding the Messenger who enters in 1084, there is every reason to think of the third actor, who has exited after 1077. As usual, there would be no difficulty in employing an amateur actor. But the third actor does have all the time necessary to change costume, even should the intermediate passage 1078-83 be performed at normal pace.

14 The unlocked door and the serried ranks

The Messenger of the strategoi has ordered Lamachus to leave immediately for the war, and the priest of Dionysos' Messenger has ordered Dikaiopolis to go immediately to the banquet. Lamachus complains, and Dikaiopolis observes: 'It happens sometimes, when one adopts the insignia of the great Gorgon (σύγκλειε, καὶ δεῖπνόν τις ἐνσκευαζέτω).' In the original, the line quoted was 1096. In 1097, Lamachus orders his Servant to bring his shield out of the house; in 1098 Dikaiopolis orders his Slave to fetch a basket for the banquet. Things go on in this way for a good while. Now: σύγκλειε in 1096 is normally interpreted as an order from Dikaiopolis, telling his Slave to 'shut the door'. Rather than closing the door, however, the Servant makes use of it continually as he comes and goes from the house with provisions for Dikaiopolis. Lamachus' Servant behaves in the same way. Some scholars are inclined to think, then, that σύγκλειε has the same value as συσκεύαζε το δεῖπνον in *Wasps* 1251: linguistically, stylistically and logically this interpretation is an arbitrary one. It would seem, therefore, that there is no alternative to judging the text corrupt.

I think that one is dealing here with the military συγκλείειν, with a teasing invitation to Lamachus, who is pained at having to go to war, to 'serry ranks', so to speak. Lamachus' sword is mentioned in 1095 (the Gorgon), and σύγκλειε might be meant to imply τὴν Γοργόνα (i.e. τὴν ἀσπίδα, cf. συγκλείειν τὰς ἀσπίδας in *Cyropaedia* VII.1.33), or the latter might even be said directly as in Thucydides IV.35.

The second invitation is a command to the Servant. For instances of two or more orders in which gesture renders the use of pronouns superfluous, cf. at least *Birds* 1580 and *Thesmophoriazusae* 238–9. The unusual δεῖπνον ἐνσκευαζέτω, instead of σκευαζέτω or συσκευαζέτω, is intended solemnly as *pendant* to σύγκλειε: 'equip you the lunch!'. Here too there is a military overtone: ἐνσκευάζειν frequently has a military connotation. This teasing play on military terms is continued in 1135, θωρήξομαι, in 1139, ἐξέρχομαι, and in 1143, στρατιάν.

4

KNIGHTS

1 'Escort the poet with propitious Lenaite clamour'

Ἐδιδάχθη τὸ δρᾶμα ἐπὶ Στρατοκλέους ἄρχοντος †δημοσίᾳ εἰς Λήναια δι' αὐτοῦ <τοῦ> Ἀριστοφάνους, thus Argument I.64f., which goes on to provide the place-list: first Aristophanes, second Kratinos, third Aristomenes. It is known that with *Knights* Aristophanes πρῶτον ἦρξε διδάσκειν (*Wasps* 1029). The significance of the official début and the tasks of a poet-didaskalos were discussed in section 6 of chapter 2, where it is also maintained that Aristophanes was victorious at the Dionysia of 425, at the contest immediately preceding the Lenaian *Knights* of 424.

As he was presenting himself officially to the spectators for the first time, Aristophanes was particularly anxious that *Knights*, which he had heralded personally in his capacity as coryphaeus in *Acharnians* 291–300, should have been awarded first prize. The chorus invokes the goddess Victory, 'today, O goddess, as never before must you ensure in every way that victory goes to our men', 'join us against our adversaries' (*Knights* 589–94). The coryphaeus, moreover, having provided a history of the theatrical fortune of the old poets and lauded the prudence of the new poet, who only today after a shrewd three-year apprenticeship has decided to pilot the ship on his own account, says to the spectators: 'since he did not leap haphazardly on to the boat, for him raise a great wave of applause, escort him to the beat of eleven oars with propitious Lenaite clamour, such that the poet may depart joyful at the outcome he desired, radiant, his forehead blazing' (*Knights* 545–50). The spectators have already been requested their approval at the beginning of the prologue, lines 37–9, and towards the end will be asked to sing a paean (1318). The Knights keep extremely close to the captain, Odysseus, and celebrate the first canto of the *Iliad*: this is discussed in chapter 1 in regard to the dawn of comedy.

'Propitious Lenaite clamour', θόρυβον χρηστὸν ληναΐτην: the neologism ληναΐτης, probably formed from the toponimical Λήναιον, is highly expressive. And the function of the suffix might indeed be toponimical, 'the clamour *of the Lenaion*', although ληναΐτης could also be a mock-noble variant on ληναῖος. Should the first interpretation prove correct, one would

78

then be provided with direct evidence of *Knights* having been performed at the Lenaion, as in the case of *Acharnians*. According to Pollux VIII.133, the comic poets spoke of θόρυβον πυκνίτην, i.e. ἐν τῇ πυκνί. The personified Athenian Demos in *Knights* is πυκνίτης in so far as his home is the precinct of the Pnyx (cf. *Knights* 42 and 750). Ληναΐτης, in the *Suda* ἐξ ἀμαξῆς and in the scholia on Demosthenes XVIII.122, is an attribute of the χορός: the suffix -ιτης, as we know, was later to lose its original toponimical value.[1]

2 The economy of *Knights* and its prologue

'He imagines the polis as a household', 'the household is the polis, the master Demos, the servants the strategoi', states the scholiast on *Knights* 40 and Argument I.68. A commentator from the second half of the nineteenth century has also observed that the small cast of *Knights* is intentional. As it was his first official appearance, Aristophanes preferred not to distract the audience with too large a crowd of characters.[2]

It is undoubtedly true that the comedy of Aristophanes' official début, which was certainly not written with today's poetry critics in mind, is vigorous and effective, in so far as it is an elemental comedy. However, its small cast (the smallest in Aristophanes) and essential economy reflect in reality a conception founded in metaphorical realism, governed by a deterministic oracle of tragic hue: the constituents are a household-Athens, an Athenian Master-Demos, three Servants-Strategoi (the oracle has predicted that the most ignoble of these shall lose) and a single new Servant-Strategos (a still more ignoble external character foreseen by the oracle) with his allies the Knights. The oracle's fulfilment is succeeded by an exodos in which the surviving characters appear in a state of metamorphosis: the new Servant as the marvellous and noble redeemer of Athens and of the Master-Demos from the good old days, the deposed Servant as the mute reincarnation of the ignoble character foreseen by the oracle.

The microcosmic and fatalistic conception of the comedy is foreshadowed in the prologue. Two Servant-Strategoi, though already suffering through the high-handedness of the ignoble third Servant-Strategos, abdicate in favour of an outsider. *Knights* is thus swiftly identified as being an agonistic representation of the catastrophic downfall of one character – a downfall which that character alone does not foresee – and the advent of another still more ignoble one. The metamorphosis during the exodos is the appropriate surprise, or rather the appropriate comic 'correction' of an oracular paratragedy.

From the very first lines uttered by two doleful Servants, the real significance of the household and of the characters on-stage and back-stage can already be well enough understood. The two express their wish that the gods will do away with the Paphlagonian, acquired recently to work in the house, where he beats and slanders the other servants (1–7). They are not, in other words, the traditionally coarse pair encountered again in *Peace* 743–7 (where one servant mocks and questions his companion, who has been beaten, but certainly not by another servant). Moreover, should these two strictly anonymous Servants be wearing masks more or less resembling the strategoi Demosthenes and Nikias, then the other pseudonymous Servant back-stage – who appears at 235 without a portrait mask – is already more or less identifiable as the new strategos, Kleon, before lines 44–60 and 74–9. Also the title of the comedy, which alludes necessarily to anti-Kleonine figures soon to arrive, adumbrates no less clearly its range and scope: 'Kleon, whose hide I'll have to make shoes for the knights', announced *Acharnians* 299–302 a year previously. However, the Paphlagonian is certainly not to be skinned by whoever keeps him in service, or by his two desperate victims. This is implicit in the first lines of the comedy, and is made clear in the negative attitudes the two Servants express in 71–84. These are merely a restatement – after Demosthenes' brusque and rather flat explanation to the audience – of the attitudes displayed in 11–35 (it should be noted that, apart from the search 'for some sort of safety for us two' in line 12, by 20 the two were already planning to run away 'from the master', the dreaded master of lines 69–70).

The decisive character, a Sausage-seller, is drawn miraculously into the dramatic action in 150 and charged with the mission of liberation. The latter has been laid down for him, an ignoble character, by an obscure oracle, stolen on the spot from the sleeping Paphlagonian by Nikias, acting on the initiative of Demosthenes. 'The serpent' – the Sausage-seller, as Demosthenes explains – 'will triumph over the leathery eagle, provided he doesn't allow himself to be softened up by long speeches', 209f.; but cf. previously 127, 143, 197–201 (regarding the oracles, cf. 61; the gods of liberation, previously in line 3, in paratragic style). In 71–2, the phrase 'now then, let's think of which way to turn, and *to whom*', seems to suggest that the thought of resorting to an outsider has arisen: it is with the expression 'now then' that in other Aristophanic prologues individual plans of action are hinted at (*Acharnians* 37, *Clouds* 75; cf. *Peace* 292). In this case, however, the two Servants neither have nor ever had such a plan. Quite the contrary, the first real initiative of Demosthenes – the theft of the oracle under the inspiration of the Pramnian Genius (108) – leads effectively to his abdication, whereas Nikias disappears for good (inevitably, since from line 235 the second actor must assume the role of the Paphlagonian; although Nikias has already withdrawn at 154). Their abdication does not take place for typological reasons, i.e. that Servants from a prologue cannot take part in the action of liberation: the two Servants procrastinate selfishly and abdicate precisely because they are caricatures of Demosthenes and Nikias, delighted that the ignoble third 'Servant' is to be defeated by an even more ignoble newcomer, by an outsider. The allusive conception of the piece conspires to govern their procrastinating uncertainty in such a way that it coincides with the fated arrival of an external liberator: it should be noted that this is the only time the main character comes on-stage so late. It is also the only time that an Aristophanic comedy entrusts the role of liberator to a character external to the scenic milieu (here representing the official political world of Athens), or rather this occurs again only in *Plutus*, there too as determined by an oracle. Appropriately, not this externally recruited protagonist, but Demosthenes himself invokes the Knights (seen always as trustworthy and realistic allies: cf. 225f., 242f., etc.), and appropriately the Knights, unaware of the oracle, reinvest with authority the stranger they find struggling with the Paphlagonian, encouraging him to be louder and more insolent than the other (276f., 322–4, and cf. previously 252).[3]

The Paphlagonian, sleeping and snoring drunkenly indoors, had been the dominant back-stage character for almost the entire prologue. He appears at 235, and feigns intimacy with the conspiracy. He fails to imagine, however, that the frightened character apostrophized as a 'sausage-seller' by Demosthenes in 241 could be on terms with his oracle, even when he wonders at the boldness of his adversary (342, cf. 903f., 949f.). His recognition of the extremely peculiar Sausage-seller takes place much later, at the close of the comedy, the oracle in his hand. As mentioned previously, the condition preliminary to the oracle's fulfilment is that the Serpent should not allow himself to be softened up by the long speeches of the leathery Eagle. The speeches made by the two mythical colossi of the oracle occupy the entire section between the prologue and second parabasis.

3 Notes on the agons and exodos of *Knights*

Between prologue and second parabasis there are characters on-stage for around nine hundred lines: of these, almost six hundred are delivered by the two relentless antagonists, the Sausage-seller in the ascendant by about a hundred and fifty (the Knights 140, Demosthenes 60, Demos 110). These oratorical floods, without a single lyrical interruption (even the chorus, that ever consistent 'character', does not have many) are relieved and made more colourful generally by strong metaphorical language, whereas the truly dialectical disputes are organized into systems which rarely cover or exceed ten long lines, a measure nowhere to be found in the agon-debates of *Clouds* and *Wasps*. The agons of *Knights* are also remarkable for a series of rapid and graduated 'tight' systems, which hold the spectator at corresponding levels of tension and emotion: 284–302, 367–81, 443–56, 824–35, 911–40. In no other comedy are these systems so numerous or so extended, apart from those of the two Arguments in *Clouds* 889–948.[4]

The management of the off-stage duel also demonstrates how vital and well contrived are the agons of *Knights*. The exit of the two main characters, which in *Acharnians* and *Wasps* takes place during the demonstrative section of the comedy, here fills the lengthy interval of the first parabasis, when the characters must in any case withdraw. Their exit is conceived as, and technically designed to be, a natural way out for the Paphlagonian, in the role of denouncer, whom the Sausage-seller at Demosthenes' instigation follows at speed (cf. 363, 395, 475, 485–502, 611–14, 625f., 682, 722). In contrast to *Acharnians* and *Wasps*, the account of the exit involves one of the main characters, the Sausage-seller, and involves him in an uninterrupted report which is here and there paratragic and also paratragically introduced (624–82). This extended passage, appearing in the middle of the comedy (only in *Plutus* 653–763 can anything apparently similar be found), describes in a lively and varied narrative style the conflict which has taken place before the Boulē.

By means of the exit, the on-stage presentation of a second duel is avoided. The first took place before the Knights and Demosthenes, while the third, decisive one is to be acted out before Demos in the Pnyx, following the real procedure, let us say, of the Bouleuterion → Pnyx. Hence, the delayed appearance of Demos-third actor in 756 is perfectly natural ('at home this old fellow is extremely intelligent, but when he sits in the Pnyx he is an idiot', 752), whereas the fact that Demosthenes-third actor is already absent in 611 might be conceived as being inopportune, in so far as it was he who had encouraged the Sausage-seller in the first place and had seemed to be awaiting his return (the disappearance of Demosthenes is discussed in section 5 below).

The dispute which takes place before Demos is divided into two clearly distinct phases, each with its own clearly distinct significance. First, there is an authentic duel in the orchestra-Athenian Pnyx, containing some rather austere political discussion (765–940). The Knights award victory to the Sausage-seller and Demos agrees (941, 942–8). However, the Paphlagonian pesters his aged master for two more demonstrative rounds, which Demos alone must judge: on this occasion, too, Demos awards victory to the Sausage-seller (960–72, 997–1110, 1151–1227). This adjunct to the agon is 'episodic' in structure and written in iambic trimeters. It seems to take place no longer in the Pnyx, but rather in the area of the house-Athens, to which the protagonists twice withdraw to prepare for the tests. These two ultimate encounters are no longer dialectical in character, but professional: the Paphlagonian versus the Sausage-seller as interpreter of oracles, the Paphlagonian versus the Sausage-seller as cook. In short, now that the tripartite oral and dialectical agon is complete, there follow two comic epilogues of a demonstrative kind. Here, the iambic trimeters are particularly rich in resolutions: *Knights* is the comedy with the highest number of resolutions in this metre (more than 72 per cent).

During the first and second absences of the champions, a stasimon delivered by the Knights and then a lyrical dialogue between the Knights and Demos – only here do the Knights become aware of Demos – fill the pause, revealing the comedy's scope and raising its tone. The stasimon of the Knights, 973–96, is dedicated in particular to the audience, or rather to the citizens of Athens and their absent allies. It also contains the only mention of Kleon by name in this entire anti-Kleonian comedy. Why is his name mentioned here? One scholar has observed that:

little choral songs like this, if they happened to catch the fancy of the town, were likely to come into vogue as popular melodies (cf. *Knights* 529); and the song would obviously be made more telling by the introduction of Cleon's actual name. For the same reason, the little lyrical dialogue infra 1111–50 altogether drops the fiction of Demus the householder and Paphlagonian the slave, and deals only with the real Athenian People and the real Athenian demagogues. (Rogers)

These two comic epilogues are followed – the Knights and Demos mute – by a markedly paratragic one, in which the Pythian oracle is confirmed. Only now does the Paphlagonian admit defeat, and agree to surrender the ruler's crown (1228–52). Have we reached the end of the comedy? Yes and no. Certainly, we have reached the end of the grotesque oracular paratragedy – the victory over the ignoble of one who is even more ignoble. At this juncture, however, the expectation of a new drama is delicately introduced, the *personal* drama of a character who, having been drawn miraculously into the action as protagonist, has become 'a public figure'. One is also led inadvertently to assume that the Paphlagonian is about to be punished and some therapy administered to Demos by a character who, when asked his name, replies as Agoracritos (cf. 1257–63, and for the name Agoracritos, chapter 3, section 2); with respect to the magic Agoracritos, see chapter 1. Demos and Agoracritos withdraw, while the Paphlagonian seems to be left alone on the orchestra floor (cf. then 1407f.). A short parabasis follows: 'what finer thing at the beginning or *at the end* than to sing?'. While the chorus suggests the conclusion of one drama, the parabatic interlude foreshadows another. Something similar occurs shortly before the great parabasis in *Birds*: the two earthbound pilgrims are finally asked their names and allowed admission to Hoopoe's nest, where after the parabasis a wonderful life begins – one previously foreseen. In *Knights*, however, the audience is left in suspense. So much the more intense shall be their wonder at the vision of Agoracritos and Demos radically renewed, wearing costumes and masks which have also most certainly been renewed.

The marvellous exodos of *Knights*, which upsets the plain logic of so many scholars, is the comic 'correction' of the grotesque σωτηρία τῆς πόλεως required by the paratragic oracle. An allusion to Euripidean tragedy nevertheless remains: the now solemn and magical Agoracritos behaves like a miraculous *deus ex machina*, like an Apollo, liberator from evil, and to Apollo the Knights refer twice during the parabatic interlude (1270–3, 1307).

Nor has the conclusion of the comedy, in iambic trimeters, received a good press from scholars, many of whom consider it to be mutilated. They claim that it is too silent, that it lacks a lyrical interjection on the part of the chorus, or something of that kind. Max Pohlenz has 'integrated' the extant conclusion with the spectacle of thirty nude dancing-girls, and his hypothesis has enjoyed a certain degree of success. The idea of dancing-girls is an ancient one: the scholiasts on *Knights* 1388 and 1390 speak of πόρναι and of ἑταῖραι ὡραῖαι, which would be represented by the Σπονδαὶ τριακουντίδες discovered by Agoracritos in the household-Athens and offered to the rejuvenated Demos (*Knights* 1388–95). However, the term σπονδαί, defective in the singular, is to find physical expression in *one* maiden alone, beautiful maybe, but not nude. In *Wasps* 1361, the defective αἱ δεταί is represented by a single torch, as shown in lines 1330 and 1372. Also, the erotic comment 'is it possible to belt them thirty times?', made by Demos as he runs his hand over the Σπονδαὶ τριακουντίδες, 'Thirty-Year-Truce', clearly alludes to a single maiden. Hence, the rejuvenated Demos, 'smelling sweetly of peace' (1332), gets one girl and no more: likewise the Spartans and Athenians in *Lysistrata* 1114–21 are awarded the maiden 'Reconciliation' alone. Besides, the presence of Max Pohlenz's thirty *danseuses nues* would necessitate a closing lyrical passage, since a troupe composed of 30 dancing girls and 24 young choreutai obviously requires a dance.[5]

The conclusion of *Knights*, in iambic trimeters, is one that is indeed tempting to 'integrate'. Yet, apart from the fact that the comedy obviously continues along its pungent way after the final iambic trimeter (1408), with the Paphlagonian being dressed up as the Sausage-seller and then escorted out of the orchestra 'to be seen by the foreigners whom he used to oppress' (the foreigners did not form part of the Lenaian public; cf. also *Knights* 975), would not some final demonstration in favour of the neo-didaskalos have been enough in itself to render the comedy complete? One should not forget that *Knights* was Aristophanes' official début, or the unusual appeal made by the coryphaeus to the audience. 'For the poet, raise a great wave of applause, escort him to the beat of eleven oars with propitious Lenaite clamour, such that he may depart joyful at the outcome he desired, radiant, his forehead blazing' (*Knights* 546–50). When else, if not at the end of the comedy, as the Paphlagonian-Kleon was being led ignominiously through the orchestra, could the invitation have been taken up to applaud in a 'propitious' manner the neo-didaskalos of the influential and allied Knights (cf. amongst others, lines 507–11) and also to flaunt publicly the secret comedies of his apprenticeship? In chapter 1, it was remarked that the reference to ancient Athens in the finale of *Knights* is intended as a celebration of old comedy, legitimized in the times of Miltiades and Aristides, and hence as praise for its astute celebrator, the young playwright, faithful to his origins.

Aristophanes would certainly have prepared his official theatrical début in a particular way, since it was to take place in the theatre where the neo-strategos, Kleon, would be sitting in the proedria for the very first time (*Knights* 702–4): the very personage at whom this entire début comedy is aimed, and by whom the poet himself had been persecuted.[6]

4 The façade-Athens and the orchestra-Pnyx

'He imagines the polis as a household' was quoted at the beginning of section 2 above. In the light of this statement, it is hardly unnatural that the Sausage-seller, although still alien to the scenic façade, should go into competition with the Paphlagonian in the household-Athens, where he can fetch his oracles and prepare his dainties. Naturally, he uses a different door to Demos' 'house', one which extemporaneously and temporarily suggests some dwelling of his. Commentators generally have him emerge from the corridor, thus demonstrating their inattentiveness to, or unawareness of, the indications of the text, which point instead to an interior.[7]

Equally common is the opinion that, in *Knights*, the orchestra is the scenic equivalent of the Agora, apart from one intermediate passage in which it undoubtedly assumes the value of the Athenian Pnyx. This theory is based on inaccurate textual interpretation.

The oracle, as we know, has foreseen the arrival of a Sausage-seller. 'But, where will we find this fellow?', Nikias asks Demosthenes. 'Let's look for him', replies Demosthenes, and the two plainly begin the search. Nikias: ἀλλ'ὁδὶ προσέρχεται ὥσπερ κατὰ θεὸν εἰς ἀγοράν. Demosthenes (or Demosthenes and Nikias together, while the Sausage-seller is still invisible to the audience): ὦ μακάριε ἀλλαντοπῶλα, δεῦρο δεῦρ', ὦ φίλτατε, ἀνάβαινε σωτὴρ τῇ πόλει καὶ νῷν φανείς. Finally, the Sausage-seller, coming up into the orchestra: τί ἔστι; τί με καλεῖτε; and Demosthenes: δεῦρ'ἐλθέ (146–50).

Now, προσέρχεται εἰς ἀγοράν does not mean 'going towards the orchestra-Agora', but 'going towards the Agora', the real Agora. In fact, Demosthenes and Nikias loudly distract the merchant from his path (cf. 160f.), which they naturally believe leads to the Agora (as we discover later, he plies his trade at the gates of the city: cf. 1245–7). Were the Sausage-seller's destination to have been the orchestra, his appearance would have been remarked by a δεῦρο προσέρχεται, or something similar (cf. *Birds* 1414). He would also have reacted differently to their call, and not have asked: 'Why are you calling me?'

Προσέρχεσθαι, one of the verbs which in Aristophanes marks an entrance from the corridor (see section 11 of chapter 3), is here uncharacteristically accompanied by a complement – precisely because it does not have its normal technical value. In conclusion, the Sausage-seller had not been directing his steps spontaneously towards the orchestra, and in order to catch him the two Servants had glanced out into the corridor. Only in that way could they have hoped to find him. Fate required that the Sausage-seller should have been passing nearby (that much the oracle had ensured), whereas the task of drawing the innocent into the game fell to the Servants. Demosthenes appears at the corridor once more to appeal for support from the Knights (cf. in particular 244f.).

The orchestra, a neutral zone in front of Demos' house, assumes the value of the Pnyx through the simple phrase 'let's go to the Pnyx', accompanying a movement from the scenic façade towards the open space of the orchestra (cf. 723–51). There, an assembly is held in which the entire Athenian people is represented by Δῆμος πυκνίτης (42, 746). The latter sits first on a pile of stones, and later on a cushion offered by the Sausage-seller (783, see also 754; 784). After the political debate, this correspondence with the Pnyx begins to fade away, and eventually disappears, in so far as the comic action which follows has Demos' house as a frequent point of reference (970, 1110). From the house, the Paphlagonian has brought not only his dainties, but also a bench for Demos (1164), while the Sausage-seller offers his stand as a table (1165, cf. 152 and 169). It seems, therefore, that we are no longer in the rocky Pnyx, despite 1028. We may be in the orchestra, but we are not in the Pnyx. The question is in any case irrelevant. During the exodos, the orchestra is undoubtedly a neutral zone, and the contemporary household-Athens assumes the value of the ancient household-Athens – a value verbally affirmed and visually manifested by the appearance of a rejuvenated Demos wearing a different mask, robed in a sumptuous costume and with a cicada in his hair (cf. 1323–9, 1330–2).

5 Characters, actors and choreutai

The comedy's five characters are played by three actors. A likely distribution of the parts could be the following:

first actor (delivering 435 lines): the Agoracritan Sausage-seller, 150–495, 615–972, 998–1110, 1151–1263, 1316–1401;

second actor (delivering altogether 280 lines): Second Servant, or rather Nikias, 6–154, 234 from within (see following section), Paphlagonian 235–481, 694–972, 997–1110, 1151–1252;

third actor (delivering altogether 370 lines): First Servant, or rather Demosthenes, 1–497, Demos 728–1260, 1335–1408 and the sung passages in 1121–50.

Many modern commentators, Victor Coulon included, adopt for lines 1254–6 the conjectural siglum found in the Byzantine manuscripts R²A, the siglum of Demosthenes, that is. The other manuscripts and the Venetus scholia attribute these three lines to the chorus, or more precisely to the coryphaeus; this is obviously conjecture, too. Certainly, lines 1254–5, addressed to the victorious Sausage-seller, 'remember you've become an important figure thanks to me', would tend to make the reader think of Demosthenes, since during the prologue it was he who had assured the Sausage-seller, 'as this oracle declares, you will become an extremely important figure' (174f.). Nevertheless, one should not forget that, having supported the Sausage-seller up to the parabasis, Demosthenes-third actor subsequently does not appear, although the third actor is still free and although Demosthenes had been waiting for the Sausage-seller to return from the Boulē, where he himself had encouraged him to go. In *Birds*, the involvement of Hoopoe-third actor ends at the parabasis: although the third actor is free immediately after the parabasis, and at other times, Hoopoe never returns to congratulate Peisetairos on his foundation of the city or to remind him of the help which he gave. Hoopoe, let us say, is cancelled out by the Birds that Hoopoe himself has invoked. In *Knights*, the chorus, which Demosthenes has invoked, begins to cancel out Demosthenes in 498–502 (cf. 485–97), and after the parabasis he is forgotten completely by the Knights and the Sausage-seller (cf. 611–14, 627 with 487, etc.). The Knights declare themselves the long-time allies of the Sausage-seller and acknowledge him as their champion (689f.; 276f.; 328–34, etc.). It would be extremely strange were Demosthenes to return to deliver 1254–6 alone. His reappearance would also have to be accompanied by an explicit reappearance on the part of Nikias, who originally stole the oracle, and Demosthenes would be obliged to reappear during the exodos as Agoracritos' assistant: the characters of Aristophanes, even the minor ones, are not puppets. One should also note that any possible resurrection of Demosthenes could not involve the third actor, now playing Demos, but would necessitate the introduction of a fourth. In Aristophanes, however, a fourth actor is never introduced to play the part of a character already taken by one of the first three actors. This is discussed in section 3 of chapter 5 on *Clouds*.

The comment made in lines 1254–6 must therefore pertain to the coryphaeus of the Knights, to the faithful allies of the Sausage-seller. That they, at all times treated in a dignified manner, should ask the victorious Sausage-seller for 'a small favour' is not in the least inappropriate in the context of the burlesque conclusion to the oracular paratragedy. Besides, they must certainly say something at the moment of the definitive triumph of their champion. It is also true that anticipation of the Archilochean ὦ χαῖρε καλλίνικε in 1254 was provided by the coryphaeus in 276 with the equally Archilochean τήνελλα. What more does one require?

In section 12 of chapter 3, discussing Aristophanes' use of actors, I said that *Knights* is the only comedy opened by the third actor, and also the only one in which the first actor comes so late to the stage. One should note, moreover, that whereas the participation of the third actor in *Knights* is remarkable for its extent and quality (the part of Demosthenes alone is equal, purely in terms of the number of lines delivered, to that of the Paphlagonian-second actor, and Demos also has a sung passage), a more demanding and extremely important role is reserved for the second actor, who also remains longer on-stage. The idea that Aristophanes himself might have taken the part of the Paphlagonian is a fantasy disseminated by the ancient grammarians, led astray by *Knights* 231–2 (and also by *Wasps* 1021b and the relevant scholion, *Wasps* 1029–36 and Argument I.65 of *Knights*).

Extras: a maiden – 'Thirty-Year-Truce', discussed at the end of section 3. Some commentators think that the extra is a boy who appears on-stage at line 1385. The text does not provide sufficient evidence for this.

The chorus: the famous Berlin black-figure amphora n. 1697, dating from the years 560–540, has generally led commentators to believe that the twenty-four choreutai enter one as horse, the other as rider (cf. in miniature, *Acharnians* 1206); hence, twelve 'horses' wearing equine masks and tails (θηρία, 273) and twelve young-looking, long-haired horsemen (731; 580, 1121). The Berlin amphora pre-dates the comedy by more than a hundred years, but an arrangement of this type seems justified by the laudatory phrases addressed to the 'horses' in 595–610, and is already more or less implicit in line 245 when Demosthenes, glancing out into the corridor, announces the arrival of the Knights amid clouds of dust. The Knights descend from 'horseback' having first charged the Paphlagonian (cf. 266, 273), since prior to 257, rather than attacking him, they circle in the orchestra, urging on the Sausage-seller (247–54): cf. ἐπικείμενος in 252 with ξυνεπίκεισθε in 266.

When the coryphaeus, in the parabasis, invokes the 'beat of eleven oars' for the finale, the ten fingers and tongue are not intended (one claps with the hands, not with the fingers), but rather a resounding display on the part of the eleven (+ 11 + 1 + 1) choreutai, envisioned as oarsmen on an equal footing with Aristophanes, who had himself been an oarsman-choreutes during his apprenticeship (542).[8]

6 Fearful Nikias and the frightened Sausage-seller

Line 234 has been attributed to the Sausage-seller, and removed from Nikias, to whom it was assigned by the Byzantine editors. Yet the line must pertain to Nikias. Having gone indoors at 154, while Demosthenes remained behind to conspire with the Sausage-seller, he now warns his friends that the Paphlagonian is about to emerge: οἴμοι κακοδαίμων, ὁ Παφλαγὼν ἐξέρχεται. All told, he does what is expected of him, since he had gone indoors in the first place to keep an eye on the Paphlagonian. Οἴμοι κακοδαίμων is fitting on the lips of this timid, whining character: οἴμοι 97, οἴμοι δείλαιος 139, and cf. 112. The Byzantine siglum is undoubtedly astute, since it would have seemed more obvious to ascribe the comment to Demosthenes or the Sausage-seller. But it certainly cannot fall to the newly arrived Sausage-seller to announce the appearance of a character who, apart from being unknown to him, is also not wearing a portrait mask (cf. 230–2), while this fearful announcement is unthinkable on the lips of the fearless Demosthenes. Yet someone *must* announce the menacing arrival of this new character, *lupus in fabula* since 230–3 (and particularly 232 and 233), and this someone must obviously be Nikias, since it was he who had been spying on him.

It would be more practical, perhaps, to enquire whether Nikias gives his warning on-stage or from the house, which he had undoubtedly entered at 154. Here, also, the answer leaves no room for doubt: Nikias remains indoors, since the Paphlagonian, made suspicious by his warning, directs his threats immediately at the only *two* characters he encounters on-stage, Demosthenes and the Sausage-seller (235–9). On hearing these menacing roars, the Sausage-seller does not behave as an oracular hero should, but instead runs away in fear. Demosthenes calls after him: οὗτος, τί φεύγεις; οὐ μενεῖς; ὦ γεννάδα ἀλλαντοπῶλα μὴ προδῷς τὰ πράγματα (240f., cf. *Thesmophoriazusae* 228f.). Many think that οὗτος . . . μενεῖς is addressed to Nikias, fleeing for good into the house, from which he would have appeared at 234 or which he would never have entered. But, in Aristophanes, οὐ μενεῖς; = μένε, 'why won't you stop? Stop', is directed at characters who on the spur of the moment flee, but eventually *remain on-stage*: cf. *Acharnians* 564, *Birds* 354, *Lysistrata* 757, *Thesmophoriazusae* 689, *Plutus* 417 and 440 (single exception: *Birds* 1055). In this passage the tone of the command is raised by a grave μὴ προδῷς τὰ πράγματα, preceded appropriately by a solemn apostrophe, as in *Birds* 1466–7 and *Plutus* 439.

The fact that all attention is focused on the fleeing Sausage-seller, pursued by the Paphlagonian, is subsequently demonstrated by Demosthenes' appeal to the Knights – promised as allies to the Sausage-seller in 225–6 – and by the recommendations in 244 and 246.

Thus, 234 is spoken by Nikias from within, the last words of this fearful character, by the actor who from line 235 onwards is to play the Paphlagonian.[9]

5

CLOUDS

1 The two versions of *Clouds*, both for contest at the Dionysia

The text of *Clouds* as it was staged at the Dionysia of 423 has not been preserved. The extant text is one to which the author added a new parabasis around the year 419–417: lines 520–35 of this parabasis reveal that his intention had been to re-enter into the competition the comedy which had been defeated in 423 by Kratinos and Ameipsias. However, this version of *Clouds*, commonly described as the *Second*, was not subsequently performed: this is attested to rigorously by ancient sources as reported by the scholia on *Clouds* 549 and 552.

Clouds is known to have been staged at the Dionysia. The version known as the *Second* was also devised for the Dionysia, for the audience of the Dionysia: the poet, who salutes 'the Athenians and their *allies*' (609), in lines 520–35 of the *new* parabasis turns with reproach to the spectators 'first' to have been offered the *Clouds* of 423. This was discussed in section 3 of chapter 2, 'Chronology of an apprenticeship'.

2 Aristophanes, the didaskalos of *Clouds*

The highly personal style of the well-known parabasis of the *Second Clouds* might lead one to think that Aristophanes himself had planned to be its didaskalos. Be that as it may, he was undoubtedly the didaskalos of the *Clouds* of 423.

Αἱ πρῶται Νεφέλαι ἐν ἄστει ἐδιδάχθησαν ἐπὶ ἄρχοντος Ἰσάρχου, ὅτε Κρατῖνος μὲν ἐνίκα Πυτίνῃ, Ἀμειψίας δὲ Κόννῳ: the first lines of Argument VI. Contest, archon, place-list of poets and titles of comedies – solid and extensive information, from an unimpeachable Aristotelian source. If this information includes no reference to the didaskalos, it follows that the didaskalos of *Clouds* was Aristophanes himself.

Mention of a didaskalos other than Aristophanes, an administrative datum of major importance, has also been preserved, amidst a body of information regarding the dramatic contests only part of which survives: with respect to *Lysistrata*, there is no record of the contest or of the place-list, yet of the archon and of the didaskalos Kallistratos, there is; in regard to the Dionysian *Birds*, in Argument II.39, independently of Argument I.9–11, a record is provided of the archon, the contest and the didaskalos Kallistratos, and it is added that in the Lenaia of that same year Aristophanes' *Amphiaraus* had Philonides as its didaskalos. In the case of *Peace*, however, as in that of *Clouds*, the didaskalos is not named, for no other reason than that the didaskalos of *Peace* was Aristophanes himself. In regard to *Knights* and *Plutus*, the official boundaries to the theatrical career of Aristophanes, it is instead appropriately emphasized that the didaskalos was the author (although for *Plutus* there is no record of the outcome of the competition).

In contrast to *Peace*, however, when one comes to deal with *Clouds*, this most obvious of deductions has generally been disregarded in favour of the certainty, or the doubt, that the didaskalos might have been Philonides, since full credence has been lent to Anonymous, *De comoedia* III: 'it is said that Aristophanes entrusted the political comedies to Kallistratos, and those against Euripides and Socrates to Philonides.' The value of this hearsay passed on by the Anonymous was discussed in section 6 of chapter 2. The scholiast on *Clouds* 510, however, whilst affirming without the minimum of doubt that Aristophanes was the didaskalos of *Clouds*, does no more in fact than to interpret superficially the opening lines of the parabasis of the *Second Clouds*.

That the *Clouds* of 423 also constitutes Aristophanes' official début at the Dionysia, following his Lenaian début with *Knights* in 424, cannot be established with any certainty, for if fragments of *Farmers* and *Merchantships* must indeed be assigned separately to the two intervening competitions, the Dionysia of 424 and the Lenaia of 423, then Aristophanes might already have made his début as a Dionysian poet-didaskalos in the competition of 424 won by Eupolis.

One celebrated passage from the Lenaian *Wasps* of 422 is commonly perceived today, and with great certainty, as an allusion to the *Clouds* of 423 alone. However, the passage permits such certainty only to those – such as Wilamowitz, for instance – who prefer to exclude any reference to other comedies of 423 and then to suggest that it contains an extremely subtle, tendentious description of *Clouds*. Yet, *Wasps* 1037–42 μετ' α ὐ τ ο ῦ κτλ., 'together with the monster the poet attacked the demons last year . . .', as to the *Clouds* of 423 alone, might equally refer to the *Merchantships* of 423 alone, or to *Merchantships* ('together with the monster') and to *Clouds* ('the demons . . .'), or confusedly to both comedies. It is by no means true that the πέρυσιν, thought to refer to *Clouds* in *Wasps* 1044, implies the anterior dedication exclusively to *Clouds* of the πέρυσιν found in line 1038. Quite the contrary, the second πέρυσιν itself, standing at the beginning of one line and after another such as 1043, could express with emphasis, and without any particular vocal inflexion on the part of the coryphaeus, 'yes, last year, precisely last year'. One cannot seriously pretend that the author, in order to avoid posthumous skirmishes between his chronologers, would have referred to separate contests of the previous 'season' simply by saying 'twelve months ago' and 'ten months ago'. Likewise, the correction μετ' αὐτόν, 'after the monster', or rather after *Knights*, makes a reference exclusively to *Clouds* no more probable: αὐτόν, moreover, is not suited to the neuter τέρας of *Wasps* 1036, whilst αὐτό, stylistically speaking, hardly amounts to a gem. The exceedingly vague scholiasts of *Wasps* did indeed relate the passage to *Clouds*, but it is possible that they were aware only of *Clouds* as a comedy of 423.

3a A regimen for the performance of *Clouds* and Aristophanes' normal practice in dealing with the actors

The performance of the debate between the two Arguments in *Clouds* 889–1104 and 1105–12 cannot be ordered in conformity with Aristophanes' normal practice in dealing with the actors. The unitarian critics either overlook this phenomenon or deem it entirely normal: for them, the unperformed *Clouds* handed down to us is identical – apart from the parabasis, of course – to the *Clouds* performed in 423. Yet, if it is really so abnormal, this phenomenon might reveal a certain imperfection, or difference, in the unper-formed text with far greater objectivity than the textual, structural and metrical indications – indications, in short, of a 'literary' nature – pointed out by those, influenced above all by Argument VII to *Clouds*, who have attempted to demonstrate, or at the very least to make it seem, that the *Clouds* of 423 was completely retouched, and partially revised by the author. For instance, the χοροῦ between lines 888 and 889 neither indicates nor proves in itself that a change, and an imperfect one, was made in the agon of the two Arguments, in so far as the author, by way of exception, might have struck out this choral song. The artistic and dramatic perfection of this particular agon is the war-horse of the advocates of the unity of the *First* and *Second Clouds*, a war-horse which they deny might be as treacherous as the horse of Troy.

The singularity of the regimen for the performance of the agon of the two Arguments was first brought to light more than a century ago: Carl Beer observed that the extant text would have required the presence in theatre not of three, but four actors. With a certain amount of documentary evidence – and much success – the objection was subsequently raised that it was quite normal for Aristophanes to use a fourth and a fifth actor. Hence, the most recent unitarian critics find reasonable, if not comforting, the idea that on the stage of the theatre of Dionysos in the year 423 the agon of the two Arguments would have involved not three or four but five actors.[1]

And they are right: on-stage there are five actors, since judging from lines 1105–11 it emerges that the two protagonists, Strepsiades and Socrates, together with the tritagonist, Pheidippides, have assisted at the debate between the two Arguments, between the two new Socratic characters who appeared at 889 with the specific purpose of being heard by Pheidippides. Hence:

fourth actor: Weak (or Strong) Argument, with more than a hundred lines during the agon 889–1104, and mute, or rather inactive, in 1105–12;

fifth actor: Strong (or Weak) Argument, with more than eighty lines during the agon, and mute in 1105–12;

first actor: Strepsiades, mute during the agon, with the four lines 1107–10;

second actor: Socrates, mute during the agon, with the three lines 1105, 1106 and 1111;

third actor: Pheidippides, mute during the agon, with line 1112.

The scholars, beginning in practice with the grammarian of Argument I.21, who attribute lines 1105–6 and 1111 to the Strong Argument rather than to Socrates in this way obviously free the second actor. There are others, however, who are undoubtedly correct in objecting that lines such as 'would you like to take this son of yours away, or shall I teach him to speak for you?' and 'don't worry, you'll get him back a skilled sophist' cannot but pertain to Socrates. In line 1149, Strepsiades knocks on the door of the reflectory and enquires of Socrates: 'that son of mine, whom you showed indoors just a while ago, ὅν ἀρτίως εἰσήγαγες, has he learned that argument, then?'. To adopt the εἰσήγαγον of one manuscript does little to resolve the dilemma, since 'that son of mine, whom I showed into your house just a while ago, εἰσήγαγον' fails to take into account that it was obviously the character of 1105–6 and 1111, *whoever he might be*, who took Strepsiades' son with him and showed him into his own house. After these remarks the reluctant Pheidippides protests (1112), at which the coryphaeus in 1113–14 says: 'go away then [to Pheidippides and his master]; I think you are going to regret this [to Strepsiades, moving towards his own house]'. Εἰσήγαγον, moreover, to a greater degree implies, 'that son whom just a while ago I showed into the house, *into my house*' (for the use of this verb cf. solely *Clouds* 1212 and *Peace* 73). Εἰσήγαγον, then, is either a false variant provoked by the λόγον directly above it, or derives from the corrupt tradition of an εἰσηγάγου. Equally, a pedant could observe that the character of 1106 knows who Strepsiades is and who his son is, whereas the Arguments were aware only of a 'young lad' (990, 1000, 1071). Hence, a fifth actor is required for the part of the Strong Argument, in so far as Socrates is undoubtedly present.

Now, what exactly is Aristophanes' normal practice in dealing with actors other than the first three? This is quickly explained. From *Acharnians* to *Frogs*, he employs a fourth actor in one or more scenes of the same comedy; once, in the prologue of *Acharnians*, he employs simultaneously a fourth and a fifth. To the fifth actor of *Acharnians* two lines are attributed; the fourth actors of *Acharnians*, *Wasps*, *Birds*, *Lysistrata*, *Thesmophoriazusae* and *Frogs*, employed for one or more characters of little importance, utter all told respectively 20, 8, 3, 34, 8 and 28 lines (the 34 lines in *Lysistrata* take in the 27 delivered by Lampito in the prologue, although these might be assigned to one of the choreutai). In these six comedies taken as a whole, the fourth actor utters 121 lines altogether.

In *Clouds* the fourth actor has more than *a hundred* lines, and the fifth around *eighty*. *The number of lines assigned to the fourth actor is very much larger than normal, whereas the number assigned to the fifth is a sensational innovation.* One should also note that from *Acharnians* to *Frogs* the fourth actor is called in when the other three are delivering dialogue or else are engaged in some concrete action or other stage-exigency. In *Clouds*, however, besides the sensational use which is made of a fourth and of a fifth actor, there is the simultaneous waste of at least two front-ranking actors, who are kept on-stage simply to remain in silence for over two hundred lines wearing the masks of Strepsiades and Socrates, and then to utter one or two remarks. In Aristophanic comedy the protagonists do remain off-stage, sometimes for long periods of time (Lysistrata, for example, withdraws to the Acropolis for around two hundred and fifty lines), but when they are present their extremely rare silences are moderated and given artistic balance (lyrical finale of *Lysistrata* 1247–1321, parodoi of *Thesmophoriazusae* and of *Frogs*, *Thesmophoriazusae* 381–465).

It could be objected, however, that in *Clouds* there is a magnificent agon involving new characters, episodic and intermediate, not the long-term protagonists, and hence that one should not be surprised to see the latter remain on-stage, mute, for over two hundred lines, all the more so when dialogues between four 'majors' are unknown in Aristophanes. Obviously they are unknown, for Aristophanic comedy does not employ a fourth actor at the same level as the first three and, even if it did, would have little idea what to do with him. Although he may not be enamoured of them, however, Aristophanes does not exclude four-part dialogues between three 'majors' and one 'minor' (the coryphaeus eloquently mute). The agon in *Frogs* is important in this respect: it is held between two important new characters in the extremely active presence of the long-term protagonist of the comedy, whereas the householder, Pluton, utters only about twenty lines. In *Clouds*, with five major actors on-stage, the entire weight of the dialogue would fall instead on to the shoulders of the fourth and fifth actors. For artistic reasons one can understand the silence of the third actor-Pheidippides, since he is conceived as a listener, but it is quite impossible to understand the silence of the first two actors, of the two long-term protagonists of the comedy, one of whom is Socrates, the master of the two Arguments. If *Clouds* had been so pointlessly extravagant, in 423 it would never have found impresarios.

One is therefore compelled to assume that in 423 the regimen governing the performance of the comedy would have been of a different, less extravagant kind. Let us suppose that Socrates and Strepsiades withdraw at 888 and reappear after the choral song interpreted by a fourth and fifth actor (it is also possible that Socrates might reappear only at 1105, or towards the end of the agon). In this way, the first two actors could portray the Arguments, and the mute absenteeism of Socrates and Strepsiades, whilst remaining artistically abnormal, would at least be provided with a technical motive. Certainly, the momentary withdrawal of Strepsiades to his own house is scenically both artificial and unnatural: by leaving Strepsiades on-stage at 888, one could allow that Pheidippides, interpreted in the prologue and elsewhere by the third actor, from 816 to the second parabasis should be portrayed instead by a fourth actor, delivering twenty lines altogether. Hence, the third actor would be free for one of the Arguments, and the second for the other; the first actor would not discard the mask of the none the less silent Strepsiades, and the fifth actor would take up that of Socrates. These two procedures, while certainly not entirely felicitous in artistic terms, would still conform to the hitherto customary practice in dealing with actors other than the first three.

Besides, apparent or presumable financial motives apart, there is yet another aspect of Aristophanes' normal practice regarding the actors which would favour these two procedures, confirming the absurdity of the other more extravagant regimen discussed above. The fact is that for important episodic characters he always resorts to one of the first three actors. This is by no means a 'truism', but the interpretation of a rare and significant phenomenon. In some comedies one of the long-term characters reappears *mute* on-stage, and in the mean time, in the presence of two other speaking characters, either a *new* character begins to speak or an already-established one, silent in his turn before the character who has now been rendered mute. In both cases, that is to say, the mask of the silenced long-term character is passed to an *extra*, whereas in the former, that of the main character of *Lysistrata*, the first actor is freed to play a new character (the Spartan Singer in the finale of the comedy), and in the latter the part of an already-established character is taken over by a different actor: this is the case of *Plutus* (Plutus restored). This practice is one which does not lead to artistic improbabilities and clearly implies that *for important episodic roles, either new or already established, the dramatist employed one of the first three actors.*

A phenomenon to be observed in *Thesmophoriazusae* is also significant, this time in relation to the fifth actor: a remarkable new character, the Archer, is mute on his first appearance, as long as the action still involves a fourth actor (*Thesmophoriazusae* 924–46); yet the tongue of this mute character is loosened by means of a back-stage manœuvre, once the third actor is substituted for the extra. In all of these cases, it could be said that the silent, or silenced characters, in the words of Hippocrates *Laws* II.5, σχῆμα μὲν καὶ στολὴν καὶ πρόσωπον ὑποκριτοῦ ἔχουσιν οὐκ εἰσὶν δὲ ὑποκριταί.

This practice undoubtedly confirms that for the episodic and in addition intermediate Arguments of *Clouds*, Aristophanes thought of freeing two of the first three actors. There remains one major difficulty, however: not so much that of a fifth actor for Socrates (three lines), or that of a fourth for

Pheidippides (twenty lines), but that Aristophanes *never grants to the fourth actor the mask and lines of characters already portrayed by the first three actors.* He does pass the masks of already-established characters to the extras, but is extremely careful that they should not utter even a single word. The only time he entrusts a character to another actor, having previously assigned him to the third, that character is completely transformed: Plutus is no longer blind and sick, but can see and is invigorated. The only case to which one might appeal, that of Demosthenes-fourth actor in *Knights* 1254–6, third actor up to the parabasis, lacks foundation, as seen in section 5 of chapter 4.

Before resolving the question of the performance regimen in *Clouds*, it would be best to conclude on Aristophanes' normal practice in dealing with the actors. Involving three basic actors and an optional one – modest and occasional, his functions clearly distinct from those of the first three – and also some extras, masked where required as former speaking characters, Aristophanes' practice in this regard was fruit of a historical process, whose origins pre-date him. His performance regimens, rigorous and consistent as indeed they are, were the end-product of a sustained process of refinement, stimulated to no insignificant degree by the regulations of the contests themselves, under which it was considered feasible to sanction officially a fundamental artistic and technical syntax of acting-types developed gradually by the dramatists. This code of regulations would certainly not have deemed it necessary to contemplate as genuine any actor other than the first three. This 'fourth actor', whom Aristophanes sometimes employs, sometimes not, never for demanding roles or short remarks made by characters previously played by one of the first three actors, bears all the signs of being an actor without any permanent State role. It is of little importance knowing who provided him, or by whom he was paid, if indeed he was paid, or his technical denomination. What are important, rather, are his intrinsic characteristics – to be precise, those of an *amateur* actor, maybe of a volunteer or a novice. Nor would it be possible to adapt to him lines certified to be those of the first three actors, hence qualifying him as a μισθωσάμενος τὰ τέταρτα τῶν ἐπῶν λέγειν, one engaged for the 'fourth parts', since fixed and developed 'fourth parts' do not exist in Aristophanes. In some comedies the 'third parts' are already of modest proportions, or rather in Aristophanes even the third actor is not used extensively.

The later aesthetic theory of performance structures involving three characters and no more was drawn from tragedy, but with fair reason might equally have been drawn from Aristophanic comedy. Clearly, it was drawn from tragedy, conceived as a literary form, that is, not as stage drama subject to the economic law of a theatrical civilization – although this economic law, prescribing three actors, was itself derived from an interpretation of performance structures which in purely artistic terms also were fundamental and sufficient. Nevertheless, that Aristophanes was occasionally impatient with this law – an impatience more than natural in a comic dramatist – hardly implies the use of a fourth and of a fifth actor, as is so often claimed, without a minimum of discriminative rigour.[2]

That one is not dealing simply with a play on words is demonstrated by all the performance regimens in Aristophanes. Only the agon of the two Arguments in *Clouds* would involve the use of a fourth and of a fifth actor at the same level as the first three, or the use of a fourth and of a fifth actor with the masks and lines of two characters already played by two of the first three actors: on the one hand, an uneconomical, indeed illegitimate regimen, on the other, one which is graceless and anti-artistic.

3b *Clouds* unperformed and *Clouds* performed

The gravely abnormal regimen for the performance of *Clouds* 889–1112 betrays the text's inadequacy for the theatre and suitability for the reader alone: to facilitate a reading, for example, a choral song between lines 888 and 889 would not have been required. Such imperfect choral dramaturgy apart, the abnormal performance regime of the extant text could on no account have been a feature of the *Clouds* staged at the Dionysia of 423, but of *Clouds* at any rate retouched, subsequently left unpolished for the theatre and obviously circulated in that form: what is known for certain is that the author never brought the *Second Clouds* on to the stage. This unperformed text reveals, at least, *the abandonment of a plan to free two of the three normal actors for the sizeable parts of the new autonomous, episodic and intermediate characters of 889–1104.*

This plan for the disposition of the actors, coupled with a scenic and artistic one, is evidenced:

1 by 886–8, which free the second and first actor: ΣΩ. Αὐτὸς μαθήσεται παρ'αὐτοῖν τοῖν Λόγοιν. Ἐγὼ δ'ἀπέσομαι (886–887a). ΣΤ. Τοῦτό νυν μέμνησ', ὅπως πρὸς πάντα τά δίκαι' ἀντιλέγειν δυνήσεται (887b–888: in place of νυν, tradition has νῦν, or γοῦν). Line 886 heralds the appearance in the open air of the two Arguments as masters of the character present on-stage: 'he in person will be taught by the two Arguments in person'. Line 887a heralds the simultaneous absence of Socrates during the lesson given by his assistants: 'I will not be here: I will have gone away.' It is this fact, already vaguely implicit in line 886, that Socrates with curt indifference wishes to emphasize. Ἄπειμι, 'I'm going', although metrically possible, would not have been so precise: it might have indicated a simple standing-apart on-stage, the intention to abandon the stage or even some definitive detachment, but not a complete absence imminently to coincide with the lesson given by the two special masters of Pheidippides. Strepsiades well understands the meaning of this warning, since to Socrates, about to move towards the reflectory, he replies: 'Remember this, then, that he should be able to refute any weak argument.' Technically, this last petulant entreaty

97

also tends to suggest that in the mean time Socrates gives instructions to his two vice-masters. Indeed, when they appear, not only do the Arguments seem to be continuing a dispute begun indoors (cf. 889–92), but, as if they had been warned in advance, they also contend knowingly for the privilege of gaining as a pupil the character whom they encounter on-stage (929–33). Apparently, the grammarian of Argument I.19 analysed the matter well when he said: 'Socrates has the two Arguments come out for Pheidippides.' In the case of Strepsiades, there is obviously no need for an explicit remark distancing him from the stage: he had reappeared with the sole purpose of bringing his son to Socrates (cf. 803, 866–8) and had already settled everything (877–85). Not even the novelty of Socrates' absence or the spectacle about to be offered by the two vice-masters, never seen before, induces him to remain on-stage, but merely to recommend to the departing master of the Arguments that the lesson should be planned in such a way as to allow his son to gain the maximum benefit. In effect, the petulant and self-interested Strepsiades, despite himself, may not remain on-stage in some way to oversee the lesson. Besides, it is hardly as if Socrates invites him to remain and take part with his son in the great novelty of the lesson, when in his brief remark of a line and a half Socrates so clearly provides the stage-directions: 'Pheidippides, stay here; the two Arguments will come; I will have gone away.' The withdrawal of the two characters hitherto the protagonists of the comedy, one as desperate master, the other as impossible pupil, is perfectly natural: on-stage, from 816 onwards, stands the new pupil Pheidippides-third actor; two new masters are expected to appear for him alone; and the old master and old pupil, having nothing left to teach and being incapable of learning anything else, withdraw (the general propae-deutic required was imparted to Pheidippides by his father in 814–55). It is also appropriate that Strepsiades should not hear the reasoning of the Strong Argument, which at the end of the comedy, on the lips of his Socratized son, is to take him by surprise. The chorus, which has made no comment on the appearance of Pheidippides, may during the wait extend him its greetings (χοροῦ, between 888 and 889). Only in *Frogs* does one again encounter the simultaneous introduction of two important new characters, Aeschylus and Euripides, and this is effected by recourse to the second and third actors and through the elimination of the slave Xanthias-second actor, while the first actor continues to play the still important role of Dionysos and the new secondary part of Pluton is taken up by an amateur actor. In *Clouds*, since the third actor was engaged for the disciple, Pheidippides, and the introduction of amateur actors would have proved entirely inadequate, no alternative remains other than resorting to the first two actors, hence establishing all the artistic and technical premises for an intermediate withdrawal of the erstwhile protagonists, Strepsiades and Socrates. In *Lysistrata* 864–954 also, the protagonist is absent during the remarkable Kinesias-Myrrhine episode, and not for reasons of economy regarding the actors, since Lysistrata a moment before has held a conversation with the newcomer Kinesias. In *Clouds*, it is the use of the actors reserved principally for the two long-term protagonists of the comedy which demonstrates that the Arguments are conceived as an autonomous and episodic pair destined to make no simultaneous contact with the two protagonists, only with the third actor-Pheidippides (see 3, 4 and 6 below): until Strepsiades and Socrates withdraw, this new Socratic pair cannot appear and hence, on this occasion at least, Strepsiades makes the acquaintance neither of one nor of the other Argument;

2 by the χοροῦ, a choral song between 888 and 889 which would have given the two actors time to reappear as the Arguments;

3 by the remarks made by the two Arguments, who present themselves to the audience in a purely autonomous manner (889–95), without the slightest introduction from either the chorus or other characters;

4 by the remarks of the two Arguments, of the coryphaeus and of the chorus, which presuppose at all times that there is only one character on-stage (929–33, 937f., 990–1023, 1043f., 1071–86), a character whom the two Arguments address as a 'young lad' (990, 1000, 1071);

5 by the freedom of discriminating attention (886), judgement and choice (937f., 990) allowed to the youth, hence considered not to be under the tutelage of other characters;

6 by the choral song not even projected between 1104 and 1105, in contrast to that projected between 888 and 889; this might imply that the first two actors were intended to portray the Arguments during the epilogue 1105–12 also, or that there was no thought of re-employing them there for other characters, Strepsiades and Socrates in particular.

The abandonment of the plan to free the first two actors for the Arguments emerges:

1 from the fact that the necessary choral song was never drafted between 888 and 889;

2 from the entire conception – scenic, artistic and concerning the actor's roles – of the extremely brief epilogue 1105–12 (iambic trimeters) which is damaging to the outstandingly effective conception of the extended passage 886–8 and χοροῦ 889–1104. Damaging, in that:

(a) it re-employs the first and second actors between 1104 and 1105, without even a choral song, for the two former protagonists Socrates and Strepsiades, or else necessitates the abnormal use of amateur actors for these parts;

(b) it reintroduces the characters of Socrates and Strepsiades, hitherto absent, or at any rate ignored, with unusual scenic and stylistic abruptness (see the interrogative τί δῆτα at the beginning of line 1105);

(c) it ignores the presence on stage of a character such as the victorious

Strong Argument, who is not, even for an instant, put into direct contact with the youth whom he has done everything to gain;

(d) it deprives Pheidippides of the freedom of choice conceded to him, when he has already been perhaps excessively mute during the debate between the two Arguments, but at this point is unusually silent and immobile. A judgement or choice of his could by now have been expressed by means of an exclamation and a movement, given that the Weak Argument has admitted defeat and abandoned the field. Instead, his only reaction, an anti-Socratic one (provoked by the remarks of Strepsiades and Socrates), overlooks the fact that the Weak Argument himself has been converted;

(e) it restores to Socrates and Strepsiades positions of mastery and tutelage, by now anachronistic after the agreements of 874–88.

NB: The continuation of the comedy depends on this extremely brief epilogue, 1105–12. In 1144–50, Strepsiades knocks on the door of the reflectory and enquires of Socrates whether his son, whom Socrates had taken in as a pupil a while before, has learned the Strong Argument. Those who maintain that lines 1105–6 and 1111 pertain to the Strong Argument should remain impressed by the fact that Strepsiades does not ask *at least* if his son has learned the lesson *from* the Strong Argument.

The improprieties existing at all levels of the proagon-agon of the two Arguments, χοροῦ lines 889–1104, scenic, artistic, and concerning the distribution of roles, indicate that it is an exclusive or partial novelty of the unperformed *Second Clouds*. If partial, this novelty could be the fruit of a development and of a transformation on the thematic level, or in respect of the actors. The thought of a structural novelty pure and simple – fruit of a transposition pure and simple – is excluded by the very imperfection of the proagon-agon itself, bereft at the beginning of a choral song and also of any coherent conclusion, and by the incongruities provoked by the epilogue. Yet this will be dealt with further on in the attempt, through internal means, to appraise the problematic novelty of the agon, internal means which obviously cannot be those of Wilamowitz, who stated that 'the agon of the two Arguments [is] simply poetry for the reader': are there not other Aristophanic agons perhaps less 'theatrical' than this? In the mean time, let us turn to the external means, in case they might help us to decide on the nature of this novelty.

The celebrated passages from the *Apology* 18b and 19bc are undoubtedly inadequate: whether they allude to the performed *Clouds*, as the Platonic text encourages one to think, or whether they allude to the unperformed *Clouds*, nothing can be inferred in relation to the two Arguments as *characters*, or to the fact that alongside Socrates the Strong Argument functions as a character. Likewise, the famous Argument VII to *Clouds*, having discussed the nature of the general revisions (διόρθωσις), gives little help when it goes on to list some more evident examples of radical re-elaboration (ὁλοσχεροῦς τῆς διασκευῆς): ἡ παράβασις τοῦ χοροῦ ἤμειπται, καὶ ὅπου ὁ δίκαιος λόγος πρὸς τὸν ἄδικον λαλεῖ, καὶ τελευταῖον ὅπου καίεται ἡ διατριβὴ Σωκράτους. The parabasis 518–62, in its content and character, and also in its metre, is entirely new, we are informed by the scholion on *Clouds* 520. The ambiguous ἤμειπται *might perhaps* indicate substitution, in that the parabasis is a fixed part of comedy, easy to single out and substitute, limited to the brief duration of about forty lines in the same metre (whereas in *Clouds* the absolute novelty of the parabasis is evident in itself). Yet in the case of those parts of the comedy which are non-canonical and so unequal in terms of length, 'in which the Weak Argument speaks to the Strong' and 'in which the school of Socrates is set on fire', ἤμειπται *might also* indicate the partial novelty of transformation. Regarding the phrase 'in which the Weak Argument speaks to [or indeed 'against'] the Strong', one should note that in the extant text the Weak Argument is the first character to speak during the proagon and agon (889f., 961ff.), that he intervenes systematically and with ever-increasing frequency in the second iambic part of the agon dedicated to his adversary and that it is he who utters the final remark. In the quantity and quality of his lines he stands out the most: to him pertain the first and last remarks. The phrase from Argument VII undoubtedly takes in *all* of the debate, but does not enable one to decide whether it was entirely or partially new. It is indeed possible that the grammarian might have made intentional use of an imprecise and unclear term such as ἤμειπται, thus rapidly indicating both entire and partial novelties in greatly differing zones. Our 'change, alter' would be just as ambiguous, in reference to a composition made up both of brief fixed parts and of free ones.

Regarding the final part of the comedy, 'in which the school of Socrates is set on fire' by Strepsiades with the help of the slave Xanthias (1483–1510; in practice, this part does not begin until line 1483, where the pretence is made that the god Hermes has advised the devout Strepsiades, rather than denouncing the philosophers, to set fire to their house at once), it can be established that near the end of the *First Clouds*, also, Strepsiades made clear his intention to punish the philosophers. Clearly of no validity in deciding whether the punishment afterwards took place or in what form, in itself this verification of the facts is not so idle, and moreover has the merit of bringing the two Arguments into play as *characters*. When Strepsiades exhorts his son, Pheidippides, to come with him and 'deal with' their swindlers '*Chaerephon* and Socrates', and his son retorts that he has no intention of harming 'the masters' (1464b–1467; he is to abandon to his own devices the father who has called him to the respect for Zeus denied by the Socratics, 1468–75, whence Strepsiades is to embrace the idea of a lawsuit), at this point the extant text undoubtedly coincides with that of the *First Clouds*: it coincides, since in the *First Clouds* Chaerephon definitely functioned as a *character* of importance, as a second master.

In the extant *Clouds*, lacking the final touches, one is impressed from the prologue onwards by the frequent affirmation of the vital *back-stage* presence of Chaerephon; particularly so, since in other Aristophanic prologues in which the physical presence and vital force of characters behind the scenic façade are emphasized, their names divulged and perhaps some comment made on their masks, *sooner or later these characters appear from the façade and take up parts of very great, or at least of great importance*. In short, back-stage characters evoked and characterized in the prologue *never* miss their appointment with the audience. And this could on no account be otherwise, since physical and nominal references which strive to provide a dramatic forecast cannot then be wasted: it is enough to look at the case of Demos, who finally appears in the second part of *Knights*, or at that of the four characters in the second part of *Frogs*, all heralded in an authentic second prologue. In the prologue of *Clouds*, whereas Strepsiades' wife, who never appears on-stage, is given no real vital force back-stage, Socrates and Chaerephon are, and in the strongest terms; it is also insinuated that with the philosophers in the reflectory stand two opposed Arguments (112), and care is even taken to give precise off-stage vital force to the two future Creditors of Strepsiades. Pheidippides knows that the reflectory is inhabited by charlatans 'with pale faces and bare feet, including Socrates and Chaerephon' (103f.), and the anonymous Socratic Disciple recounts to Strepsiades the conversation which 'just a while before' took place between the thick-eyebrowed Chaerephon and Socrates in the reflectory (144–7, 156–8). Chaerephon's name is mentioned four times in the prologue and is also the only one to be heard along with that of Socrates, yet Chaerephon never appears, although he is to be heard of again, as a vital force, before the previously cited 1465. Showing Strepsiades into the reflectory, Socrates guarantees that amongst all his disciples he will end up resembling the cadaverous Chaerephon (502–4), and Strepsiades, back from the reflectory, talks to Pheidippides about the masters Socrates and Chaerephon, sketching out for him the physical appearance of the Socratics (830–3, 836f.). Ancient and modern editors alike, surprised that Chaerephon never allows himself to be seen, make him a gift of line 1505 in the finale (others lines 1497 and 1499a also): a little gift which amounts to a gigantic gaffe. Another gaffe would be that of saying that Chaerephon never comes out into the sunlight for the intensely refined reason that, notoriously, he shunned the light. Yet in Aristophanic comedy everything comes to light, Chaerephon included: exactly ten months after the *First Clouds*, the cadaverous Chaerephon appears on-stage in *Wasps* 1388–1414 as witness for a baking-girl appealing for justice in face of the unjust Philokleon. But Chaerephon is mute: perhaps he had done too much chattering in the *First Clouds*. . . .[3]

Why has Chaerephon disappeared from the unperformed *Clouds*? Evidently because the circle of Socratic characters came to be altered: in the extant *Clouds*, besides the anonymous Disciples in the prologue and finale, there also appear Socrates-second actor as the master of Strepsiades-first actor and the two Arguments as vice-masters of Pheidippides-third actor during the planned, yet not perfected, absence of Socrates and Strepsiades. In the *First Clouds*, would another *two* vice-masters hence have appeared alongside the vice-master Chaerephon? This is highly improbable, if only for reasons of economy in the use of actors. The *First Clouds* also, governed as it was by an itinerary lying between the two enduring internal milieux of the protagonists, had little chance to manœuvre and exploit its actors (in *Clouds* 222–814, the third actor remains inactive for about six hundred lines; in *Peace*, during the on-stage voyage from the house of Trygaeus to that of Zeus, the third actor remains inactive for more than seven hundred lines). Besides, the *First Clouds* kept the first two actors almost constantly engaged for Strepsiades and Socrates, and the presence of a fixed deuteragonist, as we learn from *Knights* and *Wasps*, necessitates strict economies, even in respect to episodic characters (in the extant *Clouds*, the second actor, other than for Socrates, is used in practice only for one of the two Creditors). In *Birds*, for example, the elimination of the deuteragonist Euelpides opens the door at once to a flood of new characters; *Frogs*, in order to put Aeschylus and Euripides on-stage in the presence of the long-term protagonist, sacrifices the complementary protagonist of its entire first section.

The two characters of the Arguments, conceived as they are to be autonomous vice-masters and complementary antagonists, either appear as a pair, or not at all. In the *Second Clouds*, from which the vice-master Chaerephon has disappeared, they appear as a pair. It becomes increasingly difficult to accept that they would also have appeared in the *First Clouds*, in minor tone and form, alongside a Chaerephon of more or less reduced dimensions, and that in the *Second Clouds* Chaerephon would have fallen victim to a mere expansion – thematic and concerning the actor's roles – of the debate between his two old comrades. This may be possible, but it is extremely unlikely.

If indeed such a distinctive pair of characters were to have belonged to the overall texture of the *First Clouds*, as Chaerephon certainly did, thus influencing both its role distribution and scenic design, they would have left behind, at the very least, clear traces of indirect vital force both before and after their appearance, and for better reasons than Chaerephon. There is a vaguely concrete reference to the two in the prologue, line 112, and substantial mention of the Strong Argument in 1451 (in a context, however, which is better read from line 1444, bearing in mind 1336f.): a touch too little, and a touch too little for the *Second Clouds* also. There is, however, frequent mention of the Strong Argument, and double reference to both arguments, as dialectic images, before and after the debate: 116, 657, 882–4, 885; 1148f., 1228f., 1336f., 1444. It has been observed that in Plato, too, Logos is a person one moment, a dialectic image the next. True enough, but a comedy is not a dialogue: a comedy involves the physical. Indeed, the metaphorical references to the two arguments are rather disconcerting when Arguments in flesh and blood have already been seen on-stage. Personified images either leave or do not leave physical traces, but it is rather strange that they should leave behind metaphorical language, and, in addition, almost exclusively metaphorical language. An Aristophanic comedy, let us repeat, is not a Platonic dialogue: on every occasion, it tends instinctively to translate the language of metaphor into that of the stage. Nor are speaking personifications so easily forgotten: before he appears from the scenic façade, Athenian Demos in *Knights* is ascribed remarkable vital force; in *Peace* the ephemeral Polemos retains a physical dimension back-stage (cf. *Peace* 310, 319–21), and in *Plutus* the audience is constantly reminded of Plutus, even through the use of an extra, where no actors are available. Here, in *Clouds*, nothing, nothing at all, not even an extra, or at the very least adequately concrete language: immediately after the debate the Arguments evaporate, and two or three minutes later Strepsiades, who is supposed to have been present, arrives at the reflectory to fetch back his son from his presumed back-stage master, the Strong Argument, and as noted previously, it does not even cross his mind to ask Socrates whether his son has learned the lesson *from* that Argument, but instead whether he has learned 'that argument'. From the door of the reflectory, Socrates replies, 'he has learned it', and not even he refers in any concrete terms to his worthy vice-master, who is there inside the reflectory, just a step away, where he has been since the beginning of the comedy together with the Weak Argument (112; cf. 886, 889–92, and perhaps 916f. also).

Can one then conclude that the two Arguments, as *characters*, are an exclusive novelty of the *Second Clouds*? It seems so to me. For this new pair, Chaerephon was sacrificed and an actor required for the character in excess – the first, let us say, for the Weak Argument – which obviously led to the artistic revision of the material of the *First Clouds*.

The revised comedy was even more unfortunate than that defeated by Kratinos and Ameipsias, in so far as it never found its way on to the stage: the author's plan to present *Clouds* once more, this time as the *Second Clouds*, was abandoned for some reason. From the 'novelty' of the two Arguments the final touches, scenic and as regards the actors at least, came to be omitted when the ensuing artistic revision of the old text must already have been at an advanced stage: a new parabasis had been written which referred in its final part to events both topical and specific regarding the theatrical and political history of Athens; its target, as we have already seen, was the Dionysian contest of March–April 423 BC in which *Clouds* had met defeat. Written in Eupolideans, the new parabasis, too, lacks the final structural adjustments: entirely in the first person and without the minimum reference to the mask of the chorus, it appears abruptly after the short piece in anapaests, 510–17, and contains no final 'climax' (a proem and an epilogue are also missing from the debate between the two Arguments).

The drafting of the forty-five Eupolideans – which are exclusively theatrical in character (cf., for example, 520, 523, 528, 534–62) – took place not earlier than the second half of the year 420 and not later than the spring of 417, the dates bounding the events described in the final Eupolideans. It took place, let us say, in 419–417. This parabasis reveals that for his plan to enter *Clouds* into a competition once more, as the *Second Clouds*, Aristophanes had as an approximate aim one of the several Dionysia succeeding his defeat. It is naturally possible, although the reflection is obvious to a fault, that this belligerent design, complete with an adequate parabasis, might also have been aimed at the contests of preceding years, Dionysian contests in particular (cf. *Clouds* 609), excluding that of 421, of course, in which it is known that Aristophanes was accepted to participate with *Peace*, a comedy with an extremely well-realized parabasis. In the summer of 423, after the defeat of *Clouds*, the new archon, Ameinias, had accepted *Wasps* for the Lenaia of 422, and the outcome of the competition had been positive, albeit the first prize had gone to Philonides, to whom Aristophanes had unusually ceded one of his own comedies, *Proagon*, and had also entrusted the staging of *Wasps*, as if he had wished to devote his time to something else. Afterwards, however, at the Dionysia of 422 and at the Lenaia of 421, it seems that no Aristophanic comedies were performed. In the parabasis of *Wasps* Aristophanes had naturally protested in favour of *Clouds* and admonished the spectators that 'in future' they should understand 'immediately' new ideas such as those the comedy had contained (cf. *Wasps* 1048, 1051–4). Regarding·the year 420 and those immediately following nothing is known, apart from this parabasis in Eupolideans from around 419–417: a parabasis, let us repeat, of exclusively theatrical character. Only a new performance in the theatre would have been enough to satisfy the defeated poet. From the reader, Aristophanes could have expected no more than the most slender satisfaction, if ever a fifth-century dramatist would have regarded a 'book' as an effective expedient, or at the very least a way to ensure the wide diffusion of a text after its performance; better the theatre of Piraeus or that of some other city, or an unofficial contest in Athens.

Clearly the *Second Clouds* was allowed to circulate, and just as the author had left it after abandoning his plans for the theatre. The circulation of an unperformed comedy in a version lacking the final touches was a quite natural thing, but the restricted circles in which it was read were more exacting than the wider circles of today, which find the χοροῦ between lines 888 and 889 superfluous. The edition was clearly successful, in so far as the *Second Clouds* dispersed the *First* defeated by Kratinos and Ameipsias, which must *also* have been in circulation. Naturally, for Eratosthenes – who observed that the *Second Clouds* was not 'among the plays performed' but 'among those subsequently revised', and who sternly corrected Kallimachos (scholion *Clouds* 552) – the tools we possess could, strictly speaking, have been enough: the archon of the only performance and the text of *Clouds* complete with line 553. Also, the scholion on *Clouds* 520 does not necessarily imply the existence of a reader's edition of the *First Clouds*, merely direct or indirect knowledge of the metre of the old parabasis alone. The grammarian of Argument VII, however, in order to have identified the variations existing in the *Second Clouds*, must have used some special supporting text. True enough, it has been suspected that this grammarian, with treacherous analytic zeal and swayed by Eratosthenes, presumed to indicate as novelties the clash between the Weak and the Strong Arguments due to the χοροῦ in a text characterized by normal choral interludes and because of the mutilated second parabasis (cf. scholion *Clouds* 1115), and the fire in the finale on account of *Clouds* 543 and 1090–4. Yet the minor novelties introduced by the revision, to which the grammarian with tranquil detachment dedicates the central part of his most prudent considerations, could not have been singled out without some adequate means of collation. That he did not give examples is entirely natural: he had far better, chosen examples of radical novelty to relate, and did not feel pressed to go to great lengths in the mechanical description of suppressions, additions, structural transpositions and changes in the sequence of characters: τὰ μὲν γὰρ περιήρηται, τὰ δὲ παραπέπλεκται καὶ ἐν τῇ τάξει καί ἐν τῇ τῶν προσώπων διαλλαγῇ μετεσχημάτισται.

The fact that the *First Clouds*, directly or indirectly known to the grammarian of Argument VII, was therefore put into circulation despite the *Second*, or vice versa, could also mean that the variations between the two texts were not limited simply to the parabasis. The posthumous 'success' of the *Second Clouds* could not have been the exclusive merit of the forty-five Eupolideans of the new parabasis alone. One can understand that for the later scholiastic editors the unperformed, yet revised text would have been of greater interest than the text performed.[4]

Here is a hypothesis on the *First Clouds*, governed none the less by the presumption that the greatest novelty in the *Second Clouds* is the two Arguments.

In the *First Clouds*, the champion of the most important Strong Argument might perhaps have been the shrill and squalid Chaerephon, Χαιρεφῶν. 'Choose which of the two arguments you wish to uphold' (1336), the Socratized Pheidippides proposes hostilely to his father: in like manner, Chaerephon, in the *First Clouds*, would have challenged one of the non-Socratic characters who survived into the *Second*. The character challenged with such hostility would have been Pheidippides. In the *Second Clouds* also, Pheidippides is established with full vital force – from as early as the prologue, and again in 814–85 – as a traditionalist who is socially and physically anti-Socratic in type – as potentially 'weak' and 'virtuous', in short. He wears the flowing tresses of the knights, is a horseman (cf. κρόνιππος in 1070), undoubtedly well-heeled, half-noble, his mummy's darling (cf. 1001), robust and highly coloured (see 1012–18); although antagonistic to the Socratics, who are πονηροί and gossipy, in the end he obeys his father (cf. 994); he is καλὸς κἀγαθός, ἀρχαιικός (cf. 915, 984), not trained in the use of words (cf. 1401 with 963, 1013, 1017, 1058f.), and so on. Pheidippides is the antithesis of the 'strong', both as a character and in his mask (cf. 88); yet in the *First Clouds* he was later to become 'strong', in his mask as well. Strepsiades must have been present at the clash between the two 'Arguments', during which Pheidippides stood his ground (apart from 1112 and 1105f., cf. κόλαζε in 1107), since in 1337, rather than ignorance of the two Arguments, he manifests disgust and rejection. The character of 1105–6 and of 1111 was not Socrates, but Chaerephon.

Chaerephon could have been portrayed by the same actor as Socrates, Socrates dedicating himself more to Strepsiades, Chaerephon to Pheidippides (cf. 1465f.). Through the elimination of the debate or dialogue between Pheidippides the 'weak' and Chaerephon the 'strong', substituted by the analogous scene 'in which the Weak Argument speaks to the Strong', or in which α ὐ τ ὸ ς [Pheidippides] μαθήσεται παρ' α ὐ τ ο ῖ ν τοιν Λόγοιν (886), the *Second Clouds* avoided the twin roles: Socrates and Chaerephon, masters – Strepsiades and Pheidippides, pupils; Chaerephon and Pheidippides, the 'strong' – Pheidippides and Strepsiades, the 'weak'. It was also possible for artistic motives to justify the freeing of the first actor for the Weak Argument, since Strepsiades' absence during the debate between the two Arguments rendered more genuine the curiosity and eventual surprise of a 'weak' man when confronted by his 'strong' son. For Pheidippides, however, the consequences were damaging: during the new debate between the two Arguments his predisposition to a polemical vitality could not even begin to emerge, since on-stage there stood the Weak Argument. As a result, he was assigned the role of critical listener, impartial judge, although he would not have been left entirely mute. Directly after the debate, when lines from the *First Clouds* reappear, he is suddenly polemical once more, loathing the Socratic mask and community (1112). With the elimination of Chaerephon, the attack on Socrates, as master of the two Arguments also, became more direct. When Plato's *Apology* relates that there was a Socrates τὸν ἥττω λόγον κρείττω ποιῶν, this naturally does not exclude the possibility that in the *First Clouds* it fell to the extremely Socratic Chaerephon to τὸν ἥττω λόγον κρείττω ποιεῖν.

If this is how things stand, all told the two *Clouds* were not so very different in substance and significance: in the *Second* Pheidippides retained his definition as a 'weak' man, which he could not bring to fruition afterwards, the 'strong' Chaerephon preserved a certain back-stage vital force, Strepsiades punished the Socratics, whom he had at least threatened to punish in the *First Clouds*, and the new Strong Argument, not to mention the Weak, did not succeed very well in inserting himself into the pre-existing texture. In practice, the *Second Clouds* was quite similar to its predecessor: it was the *First Clouds* partially revised.

It might indeed have been the plan to enter a defeated comedy into competition once more without a radical and general transformation which prevented the *Second Clouds* from being performed: to the author, who must have protested that the comedy he himself so much appreciated had been revised enough, a chorus was never granted. It is conceivable that certain lines of the new parabasis – 546 in particular – allude specifically to the disregarded 'novelty' of the *Second Clouds*. Aristophanes must clearly have experienced some distress; it was the first time he had found himself compelled to revise a comedy. These considerations, like those above on his absence from the Dionysia of 422, are not intended voluntarily to add grist to the mill of Argument VI.7, which apparently concludes with the information that the *Second Clouds* fell under the archontate of Ameinias, in 422: αἱ δὲ δεύτεραι Νεφέλαι ἐπὶ ᾽Αμεινίου ἄρχοντος. This phrase gives no record of the period of the performance, since it lacks the verb ἐδιδάχθησαν and all other information relative to the contest. Argument VI, from the beginning to the end, is stylistically based on the theatrical misfortune of the *Clouds* of 423 and on the greater misfortune of the consequent plan and attempt to enter *Clouds* into competition once more as the *Second Clouds*. Its concluding line creates a singular impression, in so far as it records the period of a singular event – one with which we are not familiar. The name of the archon must either be incorrect or corrupt, if one prefers not to think that in 423 Aristophanes had already attempted to propose the *Second Clouds* to the then archon, Ameinias, for the Dionysia of 422. What would be wrong with that? Regrettable, perhaps, a touch of administrative misfortune for the only Athenian comic poet who has had the good fortune to survive? The archon, at any rate, refused at least once the project for the *Second Clouds* (probably the archon of 419–418, whose name was Archias: ἐπιαρχιουαρχοντος, that is), and faced as he was by the opposition of comic poets of outstanding merit, Aristophanes would certainly not have reproposed the *Clouds* of 423 complete with the single novelty of the forty-five Eupolideans, as modern believers in the textual virginity of the *Second Clouds* maintain. If the *Second Thesmophoriazusae* is really the *Second*, and not a new comedy, then in respect to the *First* the surviving fragments, from the prologue onwards, bear witness to a profound upheaval both in substance and performance regimen.

Here are a few imprudent words on the finale also, yet not overly imprudent, in so far as they are merely descriptive. In the finale, apart from the emphasis on the fire's taking place 'as soon as possible' and the punishment's being inflicted 'today' (1484, 1491), there is a tendency to recall the direct Socratic experience of the only non-Socratic character on-stage, Strepsiades: precisely, his experience with Socrates and with the anonymous Disciple from the prologue (cf. 1498/497, 1502/224, 1503 = 225, 1505 and 1509/247f. and 367f., 1507/171f.). That the Strong Argument, for example, is not explicitly recalled is perfectly natural. Besides, no names are heard at all during the finale: the characters reappear recalling some of their past adventures. And on the finale there is nothing more to be said.

Those who have used fragment 393 'that the two of them are bedding like two coupling mosquitoes', in an attempt to 'reconstruct' the finale of the *First Clouds*, have forgotten first to consider five 'ifs': if the fragment really heralds a stage event, if that event is translated scenically, if the fragment pertains to Strepsiades, if it refers to Socrates and to Chaerephon and if it falls close to, or in the finale, if so, then . . . . And those, furthermore, who have observed that the operations of demolishing and setting fire to the reflectory are too complex and technical for the Athenian theatre, and hence did not belong to the *First Clouds*, but to the *Second* in a version meant only to be read, have forgotten the parodos of *Lysistrata* and, above all, not reflected on the fact that the demolition and fire are to a large extent verbal – a ladder, two or three bangs on the roof and a torch, would be sufficient.

It is possible that this text of *Clouds*, complete with its two new Arguments – subsequently not perfected by the author to conform to contemporary norms regarding the use of actors – might have been staged in later periods. A scholion on line 889, to be found in the Venetus manuscript, yet not in the Ravenna, states: 'the Arguments are brought on to the stage in cages like fighting cocks'. If not just the fancy of a commentator, the latter might reflect some polemical image once contained in the missing choral song. However, the text legitimizes Arguments in human shape and bourgeois dress alone: the Strong Argument has 'hands', the Weak Argument a 'cloak' (933, 1103). A scholion on 1033, found in both the Venetus and the Ravenna, comments in the following manner on the ἀνήρ with which the Chorus – in 1035 also – refers to the Weak Argument: 'the Arguments are introduced as human figures, ἐν σχήματι ἀνδρῶν'. This scholion clearly proves no coincidence between the unperformed and performed *Clouds*. It simply contains a correct deduction from the text, and leads perhaps to a reflection, that these abstract arguments are portrayed by human beings.

Another scholion, on line 344, found only in the Venetus, asserts that the masks of the Clouds 'have big noses and other ridiculous and deformed features'. Yet the text neither suggests nor tolerates caricature or absurdity in the female dress of the choreutai: the comic invention resides in the *human* and female transfiguration of these natural phenomena, a fact emphasized by the dialogue between Strepsiades and Socrates in lines 340–55: the choreutai are cloud-women who enter from the 'corridor' like the island-women in fragment 403 of the pseudo-Aristophanic *Islands*.

4 The enduring coexistence of two milieux. The scenic framework and substance of *Clouds*

The principal scenic feature of *Clouds* is the *two* houses in the back-drop, present *from the beginning to the end* of the comedy as the dwelling-places of its two main characters, Strepsiades and Socrates. In other comedies, the coexistence within the scenic façade of two or more milieux is either extemporaneous or temporary: in *Assemblywomen*, in which apart from the final part of the comedy this coexistence endures, the two houses are attributed to a series of new characters, one in immediate succession to the other. In *Clouds*, the coexistence of the two milieux – governed from the prologue onwards by an equally distinct coexistence of markedly different major characters, antagonistic only in the finale – comes to be permanent, in so far as the school of Socrates re-emerges after line 1169 as the renewed and ultimate destination of Strepsiades, who sets it on fire (1483–1510, and previously 1464–7).

Whereas in *Clouds* the enduring scenic coexistence of two milieux is an unusual feature, in Menander it is entirely normal; and, as frequently in Menander, in *Clouds* the two close-lying milieux in the reality of Athens lie far apart, since the characters, in a word, are hardly conceived as being neighbours. Pheidippides, for example, is ignorant of the fact that the building indicated by his father, Strepsiades, is the 'reflectory of wise spirits' (91–4), and his countryman father, although constrained to live in Athens by the war (5–7, 43), presents himself at the Athenian reflectory as a certain Strepsiades 'who lives far off in the countryside' (134–8).

When the house of the Socratics first comes into view, through the remark, 'look over here; can you see that little door and that little house?' (91f.; οἰκίδιον only here in Aristophanes), it is not intended that the two diminutives should delimit a dwelling any smaller than normal, rather present affectionately to the sullen youth the building which immediately afterwards is sonorously described as φροντιστήριον, 'reflectory'. The building is clearly solid, since it has a proper roof which is climbed at the end of the comedy, in the attempt to demolish it (1486f.). Apart from the door, Socrates' house, as seen further on, at least has an opening serving as a window. Close to Strepsiades' door there stands a statue or effigy of Hermes (1478ff.; cf. *Plutus* 1153). Not of Poseidon, however: Pheidippides' exclamation in 83 could perfectly well mean *per Neptunum illum equestrem*, since the pronoun οὑτοσί, like οὗτος and ὅδε, does not necessarily imply visual presence: cf., at least, *Knights* 203, *Clouds* 1427 and 1473, *Wasps* 215, *Lysistrata* 1168, *Thesmophoriazusae* 748.

Clouds, like *Wasps* and *Peace*, opens on a pre-staged, animated tableau: characters wrapped up in blankets are stretched out in front of a house. The character who first begins to speak provides, in a few remarks, an indirect account of this tableau – this is also the case in *Peace*, whereas in *Wasps* a direct retrospective account is provided – and immediately declares that it has been night for some time (2f., 4, 9): the illusion of night is reinforced for a certain period by means of a burning lamp (18–56). When, however, with a 'now then', the prologuist refers for the first time to his plan of action (cf. *Acharnians* 37, *Knights* 71), 'the entire night' has already passed (75). The presentation of characters sleeping in the open air is not in the least unnatural

– is it really necessary to recall attention to the fact that it is the beginning of spring and that the spoiled Pheidippides is carefully wrapped up in half a dozen blankets? – and in any case is the only technically feasible alternative. Besides, the text itself expressly excludes an interior: Strepsiades orders a slave – probably also stretched out in the open air with other slaves (5) – to light a lantern and bring *out* his account book (19); Strepsiades begs Pheidippides, hitherto dreaming and talking, evidently in the zone in which his father had delivered his monologue, to turn his eyes towards the Socratic reflectory (91f.); at the end of the scene, Pheidippides *goes indoors*, and Strepsiades directs his steps towards the reflectory (125, 126–32). The moment he separates himself from his own milieu, it is probable that household slaves, silently as usual, clear away what are most likely pallets (in 10 and 37, there is explicit mention only of blankets).

In the context of this pre-staged, nocturnal tableau depicting the domestic intimacy of the protagonist, the latter's muddled and sobbing monologue, interspersed with the remarks and movements of his somniloquist son, provides an intimate account most unusual in an 'old comedy', judging at least from the material which has come down to us, an account which could be the germ-cell of an entire 'new comedy':[5] the *past years* of the marriage between a countryman and an aristocrat, recounted in a newslike and factual style, the disastrous diary or résumé, so to speak, social, mundane and financial, of a family whose spoiled young mummy's boy has left his father deeply in debt (1–74; the mother is again indirectly present in lines 1441–6). Having spent the entire night in thought, however, the father has at last found a path to salvation (75–7: notice the ironic language) – in contrast to *Acharnians* and *Knights*, the genesis of his plan of action is intimate, not scenic – and thus wakes up his son, pointing out to him the dwelling-place of the philosophers, whom the pair discuss as one discusses 'neighbours', another passage which would be unusual in an 'old comedy'. The father entreats his son to go to the reflectory and learn the Strong Argument, hence ensuring that not even a single penny need be repaid to their creditors (78–90, 91–115, 116–18). From as early as line 91, the contact linking the milieu of Strepsiades, through his scheme, to the Socratic milieu is quite plain to see, in scenic terms also – and this contact is to endure. In *Peace*, although the milieu and destination of the protagonist lie, physically at least, within the same stage-context, prior to the parabasis the protagonist returns to his own house for good (*Peace* 182–729; house of Trygaeus → house of Zeus → cavern of the goddess → house of Trygaeus). In *Clouds*, the Socratic milieu, destination first of Strepsiades and then of his son, Pheidippides (126–790, 866–1169), becomes the *main scenic station* of the comedy, and the milieu of Strepsiades regains importance only in 1214–1464.

From midway through the prologue to the parabasis, the Socratic milieu is defined scenically for the visitor with unusual diligence by means of the Socratic Disciples, the reflectory, Socrates and the Clouds; after the parabasis it is embodied by the two Arguments, and then, after the apparent second parabasis, by the Socratized Pheidippides wearing a changed mask. Whereas in *Frogs* the visited milieu, defined scenically with no less breadth and variety, remains a simple pastoral and folkloristic proem to the more elevated section of the comedy, in *Clouds* it spreads to such a degree that it establishes itself as the principal scenic and ideal element within the setting of the private milieu of the indebted Strepsiades: a private, domestic setting – of exemplary value, none the less – which prolonged contact with the Socratic milieu alters radically (*Clouds* is the first comedy to have a well-developed plot). Two contrasting, yet analogous stage-movements complete the framework of the proem and of the finale: the son, who has been spoiled by his mother, refuses to go to Socrates' school and returns indoors as his father directs his steps towards the reflectory to learn how to swindle his creditors (125–32); the son, at this point Socratized and hostile even towards his mother, refuses to go to the school in order to destroy Socrates and returns indoors, whilst his now anti-Socratic father makes his way towards the pernicious reflectory (1464f.). From the scenic conception alone, it is clear that Strepsiades and Pheidippides are elements of a framework, the two instrumental protagonists – Pheidippides in an extremely mechanical way – of an affair in which the energy of the performance is focused exclusively on the Socratic milieu, the active scenic and ideal centre of the comedy.

Marked parodic references back to this scenic and ideal centre lend comic relief to the 'Aeschylean' and moralistic *fabula docet* concluding the comedy, 1452, which with a certain heaviness explains how intentionally negative had been the unusual itinerary of the comedy and how perfectly instrumental Strepsiades (cf. 1456–7 with 42–4): the comic hero of faint-hearted wickedness (cf. 129f.), the declared enemy of justice, hence also 'Strepsiades' (cf. 434, 1455), and now, no less instrumentally, the enemy of the wicked (significant in this respect is the involvement of the new counsellor Hermes in 1481–5). Strepsiades' transformation of the reflectory into a suffocating oven, from a position on the roof, amounts to a stage-translation of his own first description of the reflectory: 'there, in the reflectory, live people who when they speak of the sky persuade you it is an oven lying all around us and that we are the coals' (95–7); better still, the final dialogue between Socrates and Strepsiades, 1502–3, returns to the first between Strepsiades and Socrates, 224–5. In the latter, Strepsiades had enquired of the meteorological sophist hovering in the air, 'tell me, I pray, what are you doing up there?', and Socrates had replied: 'in the air I proceed and descry the sun'. Here, besieged indoors, Socrates demands from a window of the incendiary, 'what are you doing on the roof?', and Strepsiades replies: 'in the air I proceed and descry the sun'. A well-calculated gesticulation and an allusive delivery of these lines would not only form a comment upon the triumphal reversal of roles, but also focus ironic attention upon these two furthermost stations along the abnormal scenic and dramatic itinerary of the comedy.

5 The Socratic milieu. Pauses and progressions in the structural action

After the account given by Strepsiades and Pheidippides in 91–115, the direct presentation of the Socratic milieu is got under way by means of two dialogues between an anonymous Disciple and Strepsiades, 133–84 and 185–217, governed by markedly distinct forms of stage-technique: the first, on the secrets and most recent thoughts of the master of the reflectory, takes place with the door closed, and it appears that the two interlocutors can see each other only through an opening at the level of the door (cf. 141 and 181); the second is held with the door finally open (183), through which at once a group of strange Disciples, all mute, run out – the fact that the Disciples come outdoors is clearly demonstrated by the invitation in line 195 and also by lines 196–9 (no *ekkyklema*, therefore). Some of these extras set themselves to studying the ground (186); others bend over so much that they seem to be examining the sky rearwards, so to speak (191–3). When the Disciples go back indoors, they leave outside instruments of study, objects symbolizing Astronomy and Geometry and a map of the world (cf. 200–6).

As Strepsiades is studying the map of the world, Socrates suddenly swings into view, miraculously suspended in mid-air (the technique and significance of his entrance are discussed in section 6 below). Between the two a brief dialogue follows on the super-terrestrial speculations which explain Socrates' aerial position, and when he comes down to earth once more, Strepsiades explains to him the practical motive for his visit, swearing by the gods to pay him a fee. On hearing this oath, Socrates replies, 'do you require clear knowledge of things divine as they really are, and do you wish to enter into discussion with the Clouds, our divinities?' (250–3). We have reached the end of the prologue, which is 'extremely well contrived and composed with great ability' (Argument V.6), and the protagonist's scheme has taken one small structural step ahead: Strepsiades has finally made contact with Socrates (cf. 182), whose intention is to introduce him to his Clouds.

The prologue, concentrated from line 91 onwards on the Socratic circle as one which is principally naturalistic and meteorsophistic, creates the premises for a theological propaedeutic on the part of the patron divinities and delays the practical dialogue between Socrates and Strepsiades. In simpler terms, the exposition of the Socratic 'marvels' is allowed to get under way, this time from the point of view of Socrates himself, whilst the tone of the comedy becomes almost solemn for some time. The simple elements serving to define the reflectory are lost from view (already from line 221, in fact, and the disappearance of the Disciple into the school). Instead, the invocation and the songs of the invisible Clouds and their silent apparition create the 'setting', first off-stage and naturalistic, then on-stage and symbolic. In the mean time, the structural action goes almost completely into repose: the promised colloquy between Strepsiades and the Clouds does not take place until 427–75, and then on solicitation of the Clouds themselves (cf. 359), who subsequently do no more than to entrust Strepsiades to their minister, Socrates (476, cf. 436). When the parabasis begins in line 510, nothing has yet taken place between the two protagonists. Hence, this parabasis may truly be described as being premature, and not merely because the piece between prologue and parabasis, 263–509, is the shortest in Aristophanes; *Knights* 242–497 is almost as short, but, in that case, much has already taken place. The pedagogic dialogue between Strepsiades and Socrates gets under way, with little pertinent zeal, only once the parabasis is complete, and swiftly fails. Therefore, the still-sullen Pheidippides is brought out on-stage in 814 to go to school in Strepsiades' place. The third actor, inactive between prologue and parabasis only in *Clouds* and *Peace*, is thus re-employed in line 814 (he has been inactive since 221) and the structural action is resumed, apparently at least, with a new pupil and new masters.

The stage-technique of the parodos, which extends from 263 to 363 in solemn anapaestic tetrameters and lyric metres untypical of comedy, is unusual – a few similar passages can be found in *Frogs*. When the twice-invoked Clouds are still invisible, their songs can be heard (the first in 275–90 to the beat of the thunder machine, the second in 298–313, louder certainly, and as dictated probably by the 'directions' given in 297, 'a great swarm of goddesses move forward *singing*'), yet from the moment they have actually appeared in 326–8, they are left mute until 357: while they are still invisible, one is led to assume that these divinities will appear from the sky as natural phenomena (266, 276, 286–90), but when they are really set to appear, they are heralded instead as divinities of eloquence and, with the spectators' anxious anticipation teasingly distracted in lines 323–5 towards the invisible mount Parnes, the side corridor is suddenly indicated as the site of their epiphany (326). In *Birds* also, where there is as much reason to assume that the winged choreutai will appear in the theatre from the sky, in line 296 the corridor is indicated. Now visible to the spectators, the Clouds parade in the orchestra, forming the physical and symbolic 'setting' for the dialogue between Strepsiades and Socrates in 329–55, which underlines the inventive-ness of the personification assumed by these sophistic, protean goddesses, and also that of their female masks. As goddesses of eloquence they salute Strepsiades and Socrates in 358–63, then, mute, create the 'setting' for Socrates' meteorological propaedeutic in 364–411, and in 412–77 speak with Strepsiades as goddesses of eloquence once more (at this stage, Socrates is completely mute, apart from 423f.).[6]

In 509, Socrates introduces Strepsiades as his pupil to the reflectory. After the parabasis, 510–626, the lesson which has taken place in the mean time, without the slightest profit on the disciple's part, is delivered once more before the spectators (636–790) as though the failed indoor version had never occurred (cf. 510–17, 627–31): '*however*, I'll call Strepsiades outdoors into the light . . . . O Strepsiades, what *first* do you wish to learn?. . .' (631f., 636); after the on-stage lesson, Socrates repeats in almost exactly the same terms the negative judgement previously expressed (785–90: 627–31). Yet during this fruitless lesson – the comic show-piece, 658–93, is resumed and illustrated scenically by Strepsiades in 847–51 and 1247–58 – the rejected disciple had devised a means of avoiding paying debts of which Socrates had approved (747–57), since on Strepsiades' insistence (657, 'I only want to learn the strongest argument', 693, 738–9, 'you've heard a thousand times what it is I want; it's a matter of interest, how to avoid paying it') Socrates had at a certain point abandoned the general propaedeutic – cf. 658 – ongoing since the end of the prologue, and encouraged Strepsiades to speculate alone on the way to avoid paying debts. To Strepsiades, moreover, stretched out on a pallet he himself had removed from the reflectory (cf. 633, 709; the pallet from 254–62 is either there already, or else is brought out silently and then removed), this suggestion had again been endorsed by the eloquent Clouds (659, 735, 737, 740–3; 700–5, 727–9). The sudden desire to be done with Strepsiades is not so much evident, as evident in the extreme – albeit the approval Socrates gave to his idea in 749–73 might have indicated ironic paedagogical indifference. To sum up, Strepsiades' Socratic experience has served above all to invest the propaedeutic with comic effect, introducing to the Socratic milieu a slow-witted and forgetful old man (cf. 129f.). Now, space must be made for the young Pheidippides. The fact that one has entered a zone of open and eventful structural transition is demonstrated by Strepsiades' intensely gauche invitation to Socrates, mute since line 790 and apparently absent, 'go back indoors and wait for me a moment' (803). The presence of the resigning and more than pessimistic master is here explicitly restored, or at the very least affirmed, in so far as the rather strange choral song 804–13 is addressed to him (strange even should 804–8 be addressed to Strepsiades and dedicated to Strepsiades and Socrates) and his subsequent absence must be explicitly provoked: in 814–55 it is Strepsiades in person who is to impart to his son Pheidippides a summary 'Socratic' propaedeutic. In this manner, Pheidippides, consigned to his master in lines 866–85, is able, without analogous delay, to learn the oratorical art of debt-evasion. Indeed, Socrates sets out at once on the subject of legal eloquence (874–6), and places at the disposition of the youth the Weak and Strong Arguments in person: through this play within the play, in the charge of two physical personifications of an allegorical type, the technique of direct instruction is varied.[7]

The two Arguments, in debate before the mute Pheidippides, provide an on-stage demonstration of the sophistic dialectic favoured by the new generation, vanquisher of the old: the comedy's real objective (cf. 1321–1451). Then Pheidippides, back-stage, is finally taught the verbal artifice for the evasion of debts (cf. 1142): the comedy's ephemeral structural goal. Socratized even in appearance (1171, 1176), he communicates this verbal artifice to his father on-stage (1178–1200), and Strepsiades becomes first the solitary and fitting protagonist of the structural goal (1214–1302, cf. the significant lines 1201–12), then the doleful and surprised victim of the dialectic of his son, mouthpiece of the Strong Argument and of Socrates (1321–1451, and then 1467–75): a victim the more forewarned (865, 1112, 1114, 1242; and indirectly in 934–8, 949–60, 1024–33) the more he is instrumentally demonstrative (cf. 1303–20, 1338–41, 1403–7), a character who remains instrumental even when he reveals himself to be a 'weak' man, a stalwart of traditional pedagogy (cf. 1352–8, 1361 etc.). In conclusion, regarding Strepsiades as the solitary protagonist of the scenes with the Creditors (1214–1302), one should note that for the absence of Pheidippides-third actor reasons of economy in the disposition of the actors need not necessarily have been pre-eminent: a short pause between one scene and another, for example, would have made it possible for the second actor to be employed for the Second Creditor also.

The demonstrative adventure of Strepsiades is contained within the space of a *single* day. At first light, Strepsiades goes to the reflectory, is received and then rejected (cf. 853), brings Pheidippides to Socrates, a short while later returns to fetch his newly Socratized son and goes home to feast (cf. 1149, 1213): during the feast, his dreaded creditors arrive (1214–1302) and a quarrel breaks out between father and son (cf. 1307, 1354, 1361; πάλαι in 1313 is related to αὐτίκα in 1312). Strepsiades sets fire to the reflectory 'today' (1491).

Some scholars instead maintain that the time-scale of *Clouds* takes in more than one day, that the comedy begins on the 20th and finishes on the 25th–26th of the month, the 'second parabasis' marking the passage of time, or else that it begins on the 25th–26th and finishes at the end of the month, the passage of time taking place instead between 1213 and 1214. The comedy actually begins in the last *ten days* of a given month, and also close to its end (17), at the monthly deadline for the payment of interest and debts (cf. 754–6). The precise day, however, is never mentioned. After the 'second parabasis' (1115–30), which Pheidippides spends with Socrates, Strepsiades again reveals his dread of the final day of the month – when creditors may denounce a debtor who is in default (1135–6, 1180) – and confirms that the date is the 25th–26th of the month (1131–4). The action began, therefore, on that particular day, and Pheidippides' internment in the reflectory proves to have been as brief as it was fruitful: the sophists, it should be remembered, had promised to finish teaching 'shortly'. It has also been observed that Strepsiades' creditors arrive on the same day as the feast, on the 25th–26th of the month, that is. They do not desire immediate repayment, merely to establish whether Strepsiades intends to return them their money or not: if not, they are going to denounce him (cf. 1243, 1252; 1255, 1277f.). Strepsiades had not so much been dreading a visit from his creditors at the end of the month as that they might have denounced him at the end of the month without agreeing to a private settlement (cf. 1135–42). Now, obviously, he no longer fears either denouncements or lawsuits (cf. 1256).

6 The aerial appearance of Socrates

Towards the end of the prologue, Socrates suddenly appears outdoors, suspended in mid-air. Socrates' appearance is undoubtedly an external one, since the use of a technique displaying him to the spectators through the open door as he studies the sun from inside the reflectory would be highly improbable. In 509, Socrates and Strepsiades enter the reflectory, imagined as a shadow cave of Trophonius (508, 632): the interior as usual is never displayed. It has already been shown how the strange Socratic Disciples swarm into the orchestra, rushing out of the reflectory. Strepsiades is completely absorbed in seeking explanations from the Disciple and inspecting a map of the world (206–14). When his attention is distracted from the map (215b–217, uttered in the direction of the audience), a man suddenly swings into view, suspended in mid-air. Strepsiades enquires of the Disciple: 'Hey! Who is οὗτος οὑπὶ τῆς κρεμάθρας ἀνήρ;' (218). It is Socrates. Strepsiades calls him by name, and begs the Disciple in vain to shout out loudly to his master. Twice more invoked, Socrates finally speaks, as might a god to a mortal (223b), and explains to the awestruck countryman: ἀεροβατῶ καὶ περιφρονῶ τὸν ἥλιον, 'in the air I proceed and descry the sun' (225). By 239, Socrates is on the ground.

Socrates' appearance has at least one clear technical characteristic: that of being unexpected. Having remained explicitly invisible until line 199, Socrates becomes visible all at once, a few seconds earlier for the spectators than for Strepsiades. It would have been the spectators' reaction, in fact, that provoked Strepsiades' glance upwards towards the sky and the question he poses in line 218. Socrates' aerial position seems moreover to be a mobile one (ἀεροβατῶ). As to what the κρεμάθρα in 218, in which he is situated, is exactly, it is quite impossible to be sure: undoubtedly a piece of equipment or a device capable of suspending or of being suspended. But neither from the κρεμάθρα nor, even less, from the ταρρός in 226 (without the article) can one deduce the technique of the apparition.[8]

The scholars who exclude the use of the flying-machine think that the philosopher is either in a basket or on a hurdle hanging by a rope from a beam positioned outside the house; his descent would involve the use of a ladder. Socrates is portrayed by the second actor, who, having portrayed Strepsiades' Servant until line 59, would then position himself in the basket or hurdle and remain concealed, by a curtain, evidently, until the moment for his appearance arrived.

I am not convinced by this solution, and not merely because of the curtain, which would have to be a miniature drop-curtain, and drop-curtains were unknown in the theatre of the fifth century (this is discussed in chapter 6 on *Wasps*). Yet it is impossible also, to provide rigorous proof for the use of the flying-machine. The text of *Clouds* does not reward examination as generously as that of *Birds*, or as obviously as that of *Peace*, also because Socrates' aerial appearance in *Clouds* was intended as an unheralded surprise. Whereas it seems that this Socrates is never going to appear (cf. 182), in the end he does, up there, suddenly, through the air: on the flying-machine, in my opinion. In Plato's *Apology* 19c, which refers to *Clouds*, the most vivid image is that regarding the airborne Socrates: ταῦτα γὰρ ἑωρᾶτε καὶ αὐτοὶ ἐν τ̂ Ἀριστοφάνους κωμῳδίᾳ, Σωκράτη τινὰ ἐκεῖ περιφερόμενον, φάσκοντά τε ἀεροβατεῖν καὶ ἄλλην πολλὴν φλυαρίαν φλυαροῦντα. A verb such as περιφέρεσθαι could allude to the evolutions of the machine.

Not only would this technique parody certain divine apparitions in tragedy, but it would also provide satisfying stage-translation of the metaphorical language typical of philosophers: the spirit of the thinker drifting through the air, above the heads of ordinary mortals. This is explained by Socrates himself in lines 227–33 and had already been mentioned by Pindar, as quoted in *Theaetetus* 173e. Indeed, it would principally have been this metaphor which led Aristophanes to make of Socrates a meteorological sophist, the minister of Air, Ether and the Clouds.

As mentioned in the previous section, at the end of the comedy there is a verbal and scenic parody of the aerial apparition of Socrates.

We come to the so-called thunder-machine. When the chorus of Clouds is still invisible the βροντεῖον goes into function back stage (scholia on *Clouds* 292 and 294). According to Pollux IV.130 the latter would have consisted of 'leather bags full of stones, which were beaten against metal plates', while the scholion on *Clouds* 294 (Dübner, p. 428) reports that the sound of thunder was created by rolling a bronze amphora full of stones. This 'machine', employed in *Birds* 1748–52 and perhaps in *Peace* 233–5, is heard rumbling once more in *Prometheus* 1082 and *Oedipus Coloneus* 1456.

7 The closing lines. Characters and actors

The dialogue at 1493–1509 has engaged the interest of scholars since the time of the ancient grammarians. As no names appear at all in these lines, remarks and stage-movements may not clearly be assigned, particularly in the case of the non-Socratic characters. From an interpretation of 1493–1509 based on 1485–1490 it follows that the slave Xanthias, not Strepsiades, should be assigned the outstanding remarks and actions found in lines 1495b–1496 (thus the RV manuscripts), 1499b–1501 and 1503 (thus RV): Xanthias, the slave-demolisher, on the roof and Strepsiades, the incendiary, on the ground with lines 1494, 1498 and 1506–9. Those who have actually proposed this 'logical' ordering of the dialogue – induced to do so, perhaps, by the lack of any sufficient illustration for the none the less correct conventional ordering – have apparently not taken into account that although Xanthias is mute with his master, he converses allusively with the Socratics and Socrates, whose company he has never kept.[9]

It would be worth while, therefore, to examine the text line by line, leaving aside this artistic and stylistic consideration. Having received advice to burn down the charlatans' house, Strepsiades gives his slaves two orders: Xanthias should fetch a ladder and a mattock, climb on to the roof of the reflectory and demolish it, making it cave in on its inhabitants; Strepsiades himself should be brought a burning torch with which to punish those who have swindled him (1485–8, 1489; 1490, 1491f.). Orders given to slaves are always executed on the spot, in silence normally. The execution of the second anonymous order is verbally manifested at once, since it regards the protagonist directly: Strepsiades incites the torch to do its duty (1494; it should be noted that the exclamation ἰοὺ ἰού in 1493 might pertain to Strepsiades when he receives the flaming torch with joy: this would explain the ἰοὺ ἰού). A Socratic pupil appears at a window – better a window than the door – and demands: ἄνθρωπε, τί ποεῖς; (1495a). This question is obviously addressed to the only speaking character present on-stage, a character whom the questioner also appears to know: one is perhaps dealing with the disciple who had engaged in subtle dialogue with Strepsiades during the prologue (ἄνθρωπε is addressed to a slave only in *Frogs* 299). From Strepsiades' retort – 'I am engaged in subtle dialogue with ταῖς δοκοῖς τῆς οἰκίας' (1495f.) – one cannot infer that he is actually on the roof, not so much because δοκοῖς might be followed by a pause alluding ironically to δοκός and similar in value to 'meteor in the form of a rafter, meteor', but because the remark might also be made by Strepsiades as he brandishes his torch in the direction of the 'rafters of the house', or of the roof, if you wish. At this point, a Socratic voice – emanating apparently from the interior of the reflectory – cries out and demands to be informed as to the identity of the incendiary (1497): 'he whose cloak you stole', replies Strepsiades in line 1498 with just as much impersonality. The worried Socratic voice reacts with ἀπολεῖς ἀπολεῖς (1499a), and whoever then responds in lines 1499b– 1501 must be the character whose cloak has been stolen, Strepsiades. He is in a dangerous position. If he were to fall, he would break his neck (1501): he is either on the roof or in the act of climbing on to it. Until now, therefore, he could have been on the ground, on the ladder or on the roof. The ladder, in any case, has been on-stage for some time: the slave, Xanthias, had immediately carried out his orders and after 1489 climbed on to the roof, mattock in hand. He must still be there, since to emphasize his own position Strepsiades recalls attention to the mattock, and not as an anti-Socratic instrument in his own personal control (1500; one indirect scenic repercussion of Xanthias' actions would be fragments of wood, which Strepsiades, wherever he happens to be, sets alight and brandishes at the Disciple). There was obviously no need for Strepsiades' ascent on to the roof to be announced in advance. At this point, Socrates appears at a window and addresses himself exclusively to Strepsiades, to the protagonist of the comedy (1502). When the spoken performance of the comedy is about to end, Strepsiades at least is still on the roof. He orders a slave to pursue the Socratics as they flee out of the house and of the theatre (1508). Were Strepsiades already to have reached the ground, or always to have been there, his reaction to the fleeing Socratics would have been of a different kind.

The Socratic voice in line 1505 could originate from within, like that of 1497 and 1499a. The first actor, therefore, is employed for Strepsiades, the second for Socrates, the third for the Disciple in line 1495a (as in the prologue) and the second or third, or an amateur actor if preferred, for the other Disciple in 1497, 1499a and 1505. As in the prologue, extras would be employed for any other fleeing Socratic disciples and for the two slaves of Strepsiades. The attribution of line 1505 to Chaerephon and the technique of the 'demolition' and 'fire' were considered briefly in section 3b. The RV manuscripts are again so artlessly logical in their treatment of this passage, attributing 1508–9 to the inanimate Hermes and not to Strepsiades.

The comedy involves ten characters, and they are portrayed by three actors. In the distribution of parts no calculation is made regarding the two Arguments, who in the extant text would necessitate the use of a fourth and a fifth actor. Unlike in the other comedies, we have also omitted to provide the overall diction of the three actors, and limited ourselves to quantifying the number of lines uttered by Pheidippides.

first actor: Strepsiades 1–508, 634–803, 814–88, 1107–10, 1131–1213, 1221–1302, 1321–1509: lyric parts in 1154–70;

second actor: Strepsiades' Servant, 56–8, Socrates, 223–509, 627–790, 868–87, 1105–11, 1145–69, First Creditor (referred to as Pasias in the prologue), 1214–55, Socrates, 1502 and 1504: Socrates also has a couple of lyric lines;

third actor: Pheidippides, 25–125 (around twenty lines), Socratic Disciple, 133–221, Pheidippides, 816–1112 (around twenty lines, mute in 871–1111), 1178–1200 (around fifteen lines), Second Creditor (called Amynias in the prologue), 1259–99, Pheidippides, 1325–1475 (around fifty lines), Socratic Disciple, 1495, Second Socratic Disciple, 1497, 1499, 1505.

Extras are required for Socratic Disciples in the prologue and probably in the finale also, for a Witness of the First Creditor, for Strepsiades' slave, Xanthias, and for other Servants (cf. 1297–1490).

6

WASPS

1 *Proagon* and *Wasps*

Argument I.37–8 reports that *Wasps* was produced at the Lenaia of 422 by Philonides, and that Philonides himself took part in that same Lenaia with *Proagon*.

Today it is unanimously agreed that *Proagon* is an Aristophanic comedy: on the one hand, there is no further mention of a *Proagon* by Philonides, and on the other it has since emerged, directly and indirectly, that Aristophanes himself indeed wrote a *Proagon*. This conclusion is not entirely convincing, as few – only three – Philonidean titles are actually known to us. Yet one must also consider how improbable it is that Aristophanes would have entrusted the theatrical fortune of *Wasps* – in immediate succession to the failure of *Clouds* – to a colleague such as Philonides competing with a comedy of his own. Moreover, his absence from the consecutive Dionysia of 422 and Lenaia of 421 – the Dionysian *Peace* of 421, as seen further on, was staged directly after *Wasps* – could be perceived as supporting evidence in favour of a second Aristophanic comedy at the Lenaia of 422.

Whilst it is therefore unanimously maintained that Aristophanes chose to cede *Proagon* to Philonides, clearly to avoid the norm prescribing one comedy per author, it is also unanimously overlooked that although copyright and the public responsibility for *Wasps* in such a case would have remained Aristophanes' (cf. *Wasps* 1016–59 and 1284–91, and *Peace* – whose didaskalos was Aristophanes and which frequently refers to *Wasps*, and see also the end of section 6 of chapter 2), Philonides would have borne a double responsibility in competition and would also have found himself involved with two choregoi. Other technical or administrative considerations apart, his position with regard to the two individual choregoi would have been irregular enough in itself. It is true that in the Lenaia of 288 second and third places went to the same dramatist, Diodorus (*IG* II².2319, 61–3), but there one is in an age of State choregy with five poets competing in the contests; in 422, moreover, it had only been a few years since the number had been reduced from five to three.

121

Hence, the text of Argument I.37–8 to *Wasps*, for this precise reason retained interpolated by many nineteenth-century critics (some, for example, excluded Philonides as the didaskalos of *Wasps*), needs to be interpreted in a more appropriate way. The Arguments prefacing the individual Aristophanic comedies are concerned – as naturally they ought to be – with providing the most complete theatrical information possible as regards *Aristophanes*: for example, it emerges from these Arguments that he alone made use of didaskaloi, whereas his fellow-competitors *at all times* took part in person. Effectively, the Argument to *Wasps* was in no way bound to report that Philonides, 'author' of *Proagon* and didaskalos of *Wasps*, entered *Proagon* into competition through a didaskalos.

The author of *Proagon* cannot have remained unknown for long: if Pollux, Athenaeus and others cite *Proagon* as an Aristophanic comedy, this implies that the Alexandrian philologists had at hand the tools necessary to define it as non-Philonidean, and thus to include it in their edition of the comedies of Aristophanes. However, how might the Argument to *Proagon* have reached its conclusions? Evidently in the same way as the Argument to *Wasps*: that is to say, *Proagon*, whilst already collected in the Aristophanic edition, might perfectly well have remained under the name of Philonides (and the Argument, in addition, may have furnished the name of Philonides' didaskalos). So, Philonides, on this as perhaps on other occasions, is 'the poet recorded in the plays of Aristophanes', τὸν ποιητὴν τὸν ἐν τοῖς ’Αριστοφανείοις ἐγγεγραμμένον δράμασιν (scholion *Plutus* 179). This definition, plainly originating from the editors, not from the contests themselves (like Argument I.38 to *Frogs* in the Ambrosianus L 39 and the Aldine), is suited, not to Philonides, the didaskalos of Aristophanes, but to the poet Philonides = Aristophanes.

On the subject of *Proagon* nothing is known, except, from the scholiast on *Wasps* 61, that Euripides was one of its characters. This notion and, still more, the feasible paratragic interpretation currently preferred for the rather strange title, *Proagon*, have given birth to the idea that *Proagon* was not a politico-civil comedy. Be that as it may, after the failure of a comedy such as *Clouds* – to which the polemical parabasis of *Wasps* is entirely given up – Aristophanes thought it best to re-encounter his public with *Wasps*: with a politico-civil comedy like *Knights*, that is to say, characterized even more profoundly than *Knights* by a concentration of the greater weight of performance on two antagonistic characters alone, each of a clear and elementary type. In the parabasis, moreover, after the lengthy anti-Kleonine spectacle occupying the first part, the poet actually suggests a relationship between *Knights* and the comedy in hand (cf. 1029–37).

The preamble of *Wasps* is also significant:

> spectators, don't expect anything too lofty from us, or buffoonery purloined at Megara either. For we don't have a pair of slaves to throw

nuts to the spectators from a basket, or a Herakles swindled out of his lunch, or even Euripides, outraged again [the Euripides of *Proagon*?]; nor, allowing that Kleon truly shone, would we beat that character to pulp again, relying on such good fortune. Instead, we have a little story full of good sense, not superior to your intelligence, certainly, but more refined than a trivial comedy.

(lines 56–66)

Wasps, therefore, whilst mischievously vaunting its intention no longer to insist on the subject of Kleon from the fortunate *Knights* (here, as lines 133–4 announce, the protagonists are called Philokleon and Bdelykleon!), still declares itself to be a comedy which is neither 'too lofty' – like *Clouds* (cf. also lines 1043–59) – nor 'trivial' – like the comedies which defeated *Clouds* (cf. *Clouds* 524–5) – preferring instead to describe itself as one which is moderate and accessible. Even Bdelykleon, who wishes to cure his old father, Philokleon, of the Athenian mania for the law, feigns modesty: 'it is a difficult undertaking, requiring great intelligence, more than the comic poets possess, that of curing a chronic disease congenital to the city' (650–1).

To this 'difficult undertaking' is dedicated the extremely long opening section of the comedy, which is so long that the parabasis too begins unusually late. The second part, little more than four hundred lines, deals with a subject typical of the theatre of entertainment: the conversion of the old dicast to a worldly and sensual life. The calculation governing the theme and structure employed – which the failure of *Clouds* might partially explain – is so absolutely plain that in this second part of the comedy the chorus is anxious to call to mind the lessons of the first and to cast doubt on the real possibility of the austere dicast espousing a new way of life. By so doing, it mischievously recognizes the levity of the second section of the comedy, in which the problematic father–son relationship, unlike that in *Clouds*, becomes merely playful and in which, at the end, 'the old father gives himself up to the flute and the dance and the play turns to laughter' (Argument I.28–9). The choral song is as follows:

how I envy the good fortune of this old fellow: how he's changed his severe character and his way of life! Now he's learned other things, he'll abandon himself to pleasure and indulgence. Yet who can tell if this is really what he wants, since it's hard to detach oneself from the nature one's always had? Many have done it, though: in contact with other people's ideas, they've changed their habits. Much praise, in my judgement, and in that of all sensible people, should go to the son of Philokleon for his filial love and his wisdom. I have never known such a lovable person, or once gone so wild for the manners of others or brimmed over thus with joy. When was he less than superior in countering his father [in the antepirrhema of the debate, 526–724], desiring to adorn him with more fitting habits?

(lines 1450–73)

This eulogy for the young and anti-Kleonine son of Philokleon is a eulogy which the young and anti-Kleonine Aristophanes, in practice, intended for himself: 'we are devoted to you' – said the wasp-dicasts to Bdelykleon in 887–90 – 'since we have discovered that you love the people more than all the other young men'. Two years previously, the young Knights had said of the young poet, in anapaests 507–11 of the parabasis:

> if one of the old comic poets had tried to force us Knights to address the public in the parabasis he wouldn't have got away with it so lightly. But this time the poet is worthy, because he hates the same people as we do, and because he dares to tell the truth and marches generously against Typhon and Hurricane [Kleon, that is].

Who knows if the portrait mask worn by the young and proud Bdelykleon, in Philonides' production of *Wasps*, might not have been that of Aristophanes himself?

Wasps came second in the place-list, and was defeated by *Proagon*, ceded to Philonides (Leukon came third with *Ambassadors*): this has emerged from the still slightly corrupt textual tradition of Argument I.37–8, from which others have instead deduced that *Wasps* won the first prize. From *Peace* come the following lines: 'but, O Muse, if Karkinos comes begging you to dance with his sons, pay him no heed, don't enter into their company, but hold them all farmyard quail, little dwarfs, relics of goat's pills, charlatans' (*Peace* 781–90, see also *Peace* 864). It was in precisely this way that *Wasps* had closed, with an explicit theatrical novelty, the dance of the three minuscule dancer 'sons of Karkinos' (and Karkinos himself had appeared on-stage). This new type of ending, or its interpretation at least, evidently failed to gain approval, and *Peace* puts the blame on Karkinos and his three dancer sons. The incomplete success of *Wasps* seems, therefore, to have an echo here, if not a justification, and in the parabasis of the comedy where Aristophanes makes his personal return to competition directly after his appearance with *Wasps*.[1]

2 The prologue and parodos

The nocturnal prologue of *Wasps* opens and closes with two drowsy sentinels half asleep before a house-prison. This scenic symmetry is a reflection of the prologue's particular character. In contrast to the other Aristophanic prologues, all of which start from zero, or almost from zero, the prologue of *Wasps* rests on a fundamental event, fully concluded, whose scenic consequences are likewise of a fundamental nature: the imprisonment of the old dicast Philokleon at the hands of his son, Bdelykleon. After an allusive introduction (1–53) and a preamble dedicated to artistic polemic (54–66), the prologue provides a highly extended account both of the imprisonment and of the conditions which have provoked it (67–135). This is followed by three lively scenic illustrations of the prisoner's craving for escape (136–213; then, near the end, Bdelykleon gives warning of the perhaps imminent arrival of his father's wasp-colleagues (214–29).

Largely retrospective, the prologue is typified by the sequence in trimeters uttered by the prologuist Xanthias (54–135), the longest in Aristophanes: of a total of 82 trimeters almost 70 provide information regarding the scene, and only in 73–86 does an apparent dialogue with the public – which might imply some previous agreement with friends in the audience – vary the expository tone. In the formally similar prologues of *Knights* and *Peace* the accounts of the slave-prologuists occupy respectively around 30 and 20 lines.

At the beginning of the comedy, as at the key-points of the account (69, 112, 132), the motif of the watch is introduced: 'a night watch', 'we're guarding a monster' (2, 4). Then, the two drowsy sentinels recount their dreams (9–53) in a dialogue pertinent to the theme of the comedy, in so far as the second dream 'regards the whole vessel of the State' (29) and both dreams, in accordance with the initial mysterious reference to a 'monster' made in front of a house resembling a cage, are filled with wild beasts and monsters (15, 32–9, 43–51; the bestial image of Kleon is developed in the parabasis). The opening dialogue, moreover, through these dreams which recede in time to the somnolent vigil, symbolically conveys the latter's extended duration (the retrospective monologue delivered by Dikaiopolis in the prologue of *Acharnians* similarly both covers and conveys the extended duration of his wait in the deserted Pnyx).

The fact that the prologue is a species of 'interlude' is confirmed, as previously mentioned, by the symmetry existing between its conclusion and its opening: although having already foreseen that the prisoner's friends might arrive, the sentinels still give in to sleep, and awake only when Philokleon, incited and reassured by his friends, is set to escape (395). The dramatic action begins, therefore, with the parodos, with the placid arrival of the unknowing friends of Philokleon. When his friends learn from the prisoner what has befallen him, when they are vexed by the sentinels who arise and put an end to his escape, it is then that their wasplike nature emerges and they become aggressive (404–14, cf. 223–7). To claim, as has Wilamowitz, that 'the parodos of *Wasps* is an interlude that has nothing to do with the action of the comedy or with the wasplike nature of the choreutai' is unconvincing, for the simple reason that the closing lines of the prologue make no preparations for an aggressive expedition on the part of the wasp-dicasts (or for any hostile initiative on that of the sentinels: cf. 222–4), but rather for a normal night-time visit to Philokleon, lit up by lanterns and gladdened by old tunes (cf. 218–21).

It is instead the kernel of the retrospective account provided in the prologue that has nothing to do with the ensuing action of the comedy: the spectators are informed that for some time prior to his imprisonment, only now secured, the dicast Philokleon had endured the cruel and sensational persecution of his son, whose aim was to prevent him from going to the lawcourts (115–30; this motif makes a fleeting return in 719, and perhaps in 479 also). Afterwards, however, they learn that his day-to-day colleagues know nothing of the severe professional and family problems besetting their friend, Philokleon, albeit until yesterday he had accompanied them tranquilly to the lawcourts (266–81, 317–41). The prologue, therefore, perhaps as it is constrained to dramatic inaction, lets loose with an unduly sensational retrospective account, such that one ancient grammarian – led astray possibly by line 197 – felt induced to describe the relationship between the prologue and the following scene of *Wasps* in this way: 'Philokleon, unable to escape, cries out; and his colleagues appear camouflaged as wasps to bear away their companion, concealed by this artifice' (Argument I.5–8).

Instead, the closing lines of the prologue, as one has already seen, prepare the ground for a peaceful parodos, and douse the flames of the retrospective account and of the prisoner's craving for escape: it is taken for granted that there is no risk of Philokleon trying to slip off again, that the Servant is about to fall asleep and that it would also be better not to irritate Philokleon's wasp companions (cf. 212–29). At 229 the prologue ends, and all attention shifts from the scenic façade to the orchestra, which the choreutai begin to enter from 230 onwards preceded by elements extraneous to the chorus (the lantern-bearing youths). The house, the prisoner and his guardians are by now out of the dramatic game: in fact, the guardians fall asleep and remain so for a good while (up to 395). Philokleon, on the other hand, puts in an appearance at 317, although he had been called up prior to that by his companions in 273–89: but here there is good reason to suspect that the text has not been handed down in correct order, since it would be more natural were lines 230–65 to be followed by lines 290–316 and then, close to Philokleon's house, by lines 266–89 + 317 and those following.[2]

Scenically and as far as its cast is concerned, the nocturnal parodos of *Wasps* is unusual in one particular respect. 'The choreutai are accompanied by lantern-bearing youths; in all probability, since the result is that the orchestra is full', says the scholion on 248. In truth, the presence of these elements extraneous to the chorus can be interpreted, on the text of the parodos, in a more appropriate way. These youths, who would number at least three, have the technical function of animating the unaggressive parodos of the aged choreutai. In *Peace*, *Birds* and *Frogs* also, elements extraneous to the chorus appear along with the unaggressive choreutai. In *Wasps*, one of the lantern-bearers is a *singer*: in 248–57, the latter holds a dialogue with the coryphaeus in Euripidean asynarteta, and in 291–316 sings an amoibaion with him, a song which establishes the human background to the comedy (the social situation of the aged Athenian dicasts). The lantern-bearing youths are then dismissed with the pretext of their going to call up Kleon – the lanterns are no longer required, since day-break has already occurred (cf. 366) – and henceforth, rather than pathetic fathers of families, the choreutai are *wasps*: the youths load themselves up with the paternal mantles, and *now* the stings of the choreutai come into view (cf. 404–20). This is why the parodos of *Wasps* was opened by elements extraneous to the chorus, by youths passing ahead of the choreutai to light up their path, while the choreutai themselves, in contrast to those of *Acharnians* and *Knights*, appear, not immediately *en bloc*, but slowly and in groups (cf. 230–4).

3 The exodos and structural action

The final exit is just as odd, and in the chorus' parting lines its novelty is proclaimed: 'come, if you wish, lead us out swiftly as you dance, for no one's ever done that before in dismissing a comedy's dancing chorus'. The invitation is addressed to three tragic dancers who, having entered the theatre not long before in response to a challenge made by Philokleon, have just this moment won the orchestic agon proposed by their challenger. The novelty consists in the fact that specialized dancers, and not simple actors, lead the dancing choreutai out of the theatre to the rhythm of a dance. One arrives at this new genre of exodos after the orchestic agon between Philokleon and the three minuscule dancer sons of Karkinos, which itself is preceded by the solo-dances of the agile Philokleon (1484–96, 1518–37). Both of these spectacles are apparently 'theatrical' in character (the three dancers, for instance, seem to be engaged on the spot from amongst the public: see 1497–1500), but, in reality, result from the drunkenness and sensual frenzy of Philokleon, a delirium which governs the final section of the comedy: the Servant of 1474–81 heralds the two spectacles, to the chorus and to the public, as an effusion of Philokleon's drunkenness ('some madness is beginning', says the Servant later in 1486), while the two antagonistic dances – a veiled attack on the orchestics then current in tragedy (cf. 1490, 1524) – are nothing less than a caricature of the dances of the hetairai at the symposia. The exodos of *Wasps*, lines 1474–1537, represents, in short, the paroxysmic acme of the theme of worldliness, established on-stage with ever-increasing intensity since the end of the parabasis.[3]

The introduction of the metaparabatic theme of worldliness is not, as is customary to repeat, sudden and arbitrary. The alternative proposed by Bdelykleon to his dicast father was precisely that of a sweet and sensual life, and this alternative had been brought into play at the outset of the real dramatic action, just after the song of the coryphaeus and the lantern-bearing youth had exposed the frugality of the dicasts' table: 'my son' – the prisoner reveals at 341 to his colleagues – 'doesn't allow me to be a dicast, or commit any wrong, but is ready to make me live well; I don't want this, however.' This, so to speak, is the germ-cell of the agonistic section of the comedy: the young, anti-dicast son, champion of the good life; his aged, philo-dicast father, its opponent. The alternative is repeated in 504–6, 709–11, 719–23 and 737–41. Faced by Philokleon's most recent refusal, the son proposes a compromise: his father may continue to be a dicast, but only at home and before the members of his household.

Thus, in 760–1008, there follows the scene of the private lawcourt, a sort of play within a play, which adds variety to the conflict between the two antagonists by introducing new characters and a new style. The lawcourt is installed on a conception founded in symbolic realism, similar to that of the private market in *Acharnians*: the accused dog Labes = Lakhes (a defendant found there on the spot perfectly naturally: cf. 826–93, and for Lakhes cf. 240–4), the prosecuting dog from Kydathenaion = Kleon (cf. *Knights* 1017–34), the chamber-pot = the waterclock, and so on (the vitality of this scene can be found after more than twenty centuries in Ben Jonson's *The Staple of News* and Racine's *Les Plaideurs*, which emulate *Wasps* thoroughly). When Labes comes involuntarily to be acquitted by Philokleon thanks to the trickery of Bdelykleon, Philokleon is distraught: 'it's all up with me! How will I ever convince myself of having absolved a defendant? What on earth is going to happen to me [cf. 159–60]? Pardon me, O most venerated gods, for I acted despite myself and not in accordance with my character.' And his son: 'yes, but don't get so upset about it, since I, my father, shall nourish you well. I'll bring you everywhere with me, to dinner, to the symposia, to the shows, and thus you'll live in happiness for the rest of your days, and Hyperbolus won't laugh because he's defrauded you. But let's go indoors.' And Philokleon: 'let it be so, if this is how it must be' (1003–8).

Technically, these lines form a prelude to the parabasis. The polemical parabasis of *Wasps* begins at an unusually late stage, and the delay, as mentioned in section 1 above, might be a calculated one, calculated polemic-ally, so to speak, as a testament to the zeal the dramatist had brought to bear in his elaboration of the comedy's most extended section. After the parabasis the comic action continues for four hundred lines or more. The theme is naturally that which had again been repeated at the end of the private lawcourt scene: the introduction to a sweet and wealthy life of an old dicast, led astray and impoverished by the demagogues. The absolutory conclusion to the extemporaneous private trial has left Philokleon stunned – although he has for some time been shaken by his own unaccustomed clemency (cf. 973–4, 982–4) – and has had the effect of weakening his resistance, thus rendering inevitable his acceptance of the social and worldly alternative. The intro-duction of the new theme proceeds gradually in accordance with an appro-priate scenic technique.

After the long pause formed by the parabasis, Philokleon and Bdelykleon appear on-stage: even this simple reappearance is well regulated, since the two characters seem to be continuing a discussion on social and worldly themes begun at home (cf. 1122–4). Philokleon, although he has already entrusted himself to the care of his son, does not as yet appear transformed – like Demos after the second parabasis of *Knights* – but is still trying to resist. Hence, his new costume is put on him on-stage: he is forced to abandon his miserable old dicast's mantelet, and to don in its place a fine woollen tunic and luxurious Laconian shoes (1131–69, cf. 116). The putting on of this new costume on-stage is an expression of the forced worldliness to which Philokleon is made subject (something analogous can be found in the prologues of *Thesmophor-iazusae* and *Assemblywomen*), whereas the following scene, 1170–1207, demonstrates how much fine manners and brilliant conversation are indeed extraneous to him. In the course of the imaginary political symposium, however, Philokleon all at once reveals himself to be a fine man of the world. Yet here one is dealing with a hazardous inclination, since his brilliant and convivial retorts are offensive to Kleon and to other imaginary guests (1208–48). Bdelykleon, content with these convivial onslaughts, invites his father to a banquet in the house of a friend, at which the two exit in the company of a slave, yet not before Philokleon has expressed his intense fear of the lawsuits and fines which could be provoked by the drunkenness to which his son is inciting him (1249–64). The conversion of the old dicast into a reveller – or rather into a lusty and offensive drunk – takes place appropriately in the course of the off-stage banquet, while the chorus sings on-stage (here the chorus sings lines 1450–73 and not 1265–91: lines 1450–73 constitute an excellent commentary on the scenes in 1122–64; where they have been erroneously handed down in place of lines 1265–91, they appear too late).[4]

An account of Philokleon's bravado at the banquet is given in 1292–7 and 1299–1325 by the groaning Servant who has preceded him on the turbulent path home, whereupon a series of scenic repercussions and progressions which ensues from their outing presents a lascivious and anti-dicast Philokleon menaced by lawsuits and a Bdelykleon devastated by such a prospect, a scourge antithetical to that which had so recently raged through the house: 1326–41, the anti-dicast Philokleon and one of his pursuers, 1342–63, Philokleon and the flute-girl from the banquet, 1364–87, Philokleon scorns Bdelykleon, 1388–1414, Philokleon and the Baking-girl, 1415–49, Philokleon, Bdelykleon and the Man pelted by stones. Then, empty stage and minor parabasis (the current lines 1265–91), and after an appropriate account from the Servant of the inebriated Philokleon's increased sensual frenzy back-stage, we have Philokleon's wild dancing exodos along with the dancers he has challenged, a representation of another aspect of his new-born mania. During the exodos, Bdelykleon is not only present, but also holds a dialogue with his father in 1496–1511.

Wasps ends at night: '*tonight* Philokleon just won't stop dancing', announces the Servant in 1478. The comedy had begun during the previous night (2) and the darkness lingered on beyond the prologue: at 366 there is mention of 'day-break', whereas at 216, at the end of the prologue, one was at 'the heart of dawn' (dawn, obviously, is the third and final part of the night). One section of the parodos of the choreutai is lit up by lanterns (246, cf. 219). The temporal acceleration which bears the comedy into the following night takes place during the choral stasimon 1450–73 (between 1264 and 1292), when Bdelykleon and Philokleon go to an evening banquet in town (δεῖπνον, 1250)

– whence Philokleon returns with a torch (1331) – and during the minor parabasis 1265–91 (between 1449 and 1476). This synchronistic method of Aristophanes was discussed in section 9 of chapter 3 on *Acharnians*.

4 The house and scenic organization

Wasps, like *Clouds*, opens on an animated tableau: two characters sleeping in front of the house and another on the roof. In *Wasps*, the house, which provides the scenic focus for nearly all the dramatic action, is very solid and pre-arranged in a rather unusual way.

The house and the roof are covered by a net (131–2, cf. 164, 208, 368; in 131 αὐλή = οἰκία), all its openings are blocked (126–8, cf. 352) and the door is bolted from without (more on this subject further on). The net does not cover the door – this can be deduced from 177–96 – but can be manœuvred from below using slender cords (cf. 208–9). The house possesses *one* window (ἡ θυρίς, 379, ἡ ὀπή, 317) and a level tiled roof (68; 206). There are also olive boughs at its door (339); near the door stands a stone dedicated to Apollo Agyieus (875). Mention is made of an oven with a chimney-opening equipped with a cover (139, 143, 147) and of a sink with a drain (141). Both the oven and the sink communicate with the house (cf. 139–41 and 837), or rather are unquestionably internal to the house; they are not located, that is to say, in some adjacent hut situated at a lower level (Wilamowitz, Pickard-Cambridge), since Bdelykleon, on the roof, does not examine the chimney-opening from a more elevated position (cf. 143–8).

The drain is situated at the rear of the house, and hence is invisible to the spectators: the slave, Sosias, when asked to survey it, abandons his watch at the door and disappears from sight for good (138–41). In fact, the actor assumes the new role of Philokleon, roaring in the oven and attempting to escape on to the roof through the chimney. Bdelykleon, who is on the roof, drives Philokleon back and replaces the chimney-cover which the prisoner has displaced (143–7). At 153, Bdelykleon announces that he, too, is coming down to guard the door, and by 168, if not previously, is in front of the door of the house-prison. Clearly, he descends from the roof by an external ladder positioned at the rear, and appears in the orchestra after circling the house. In *Wasps*, the house bears all the signs of being a massive block: cf. previously ἐν κύκλῳ φυλάττομεν at 132 and περιδραμεῖται at 138.

The house-prison of *Wasps* has one door, which is naturally barred (113). When the prisoner begins to stir, the sentinel, Xanthias, receives orders to lean against the door (142). When the door, opened for a moment between 177 and 196, is closed again, Bdelykleon gives orders to Xanthias to pile up stones against it and to put a large cylinder on the bar (199, 201–2). These two orders – executed between 206 and 210 (cf. 211) – imply, as did that of 142, that the shutters open outwards (cf. 152 as well), in contrast to those of *Antigone* 1186 and *Orestes* 1561–2 and to the shutters typical of the fifth century. But this is perfectly natural, since in *Wasps* the house functions as a prison, where the lock too is external (cf. 154–5 and 200).

Once the door is bolted and barricaded, Bdelykleon and Xanthias stretch out in front of it and fall asleep (337, 362, cf. 319 and 382). They wake up as Philokleon is climbing down from the window on a rope (cf. 380–1). Bdelykleon orders Xanthias to climb up, making use, or so it seems, of the other end of the rope (398), and to force Philokleon back through the window (399, 402); this is exactly what the prisoner had feared (382–3). In the mean time, Bdelykleon appears to go indoors to capture Philokleon, and then re-emerges with his father (415–16; according to Wilamowitz, Philokleon slides gingerly down in front of the door and is captured there by his son). The wasps attack. Philokleon tries to slip away. At 433, Bdelykleon calls to other slaves for help, and two of these take hold of the old man (cf. 442, 452). Bdelykleon, who had run indoors at 436 (cf. 452), reappears at 455 with a torch and a stick: the stick he gives to Xanthias (456, 458), the torch to another slave (457, 459).

When is the door unlocked? Perhaps when the private lawcourt is installed before the house, or maybe previously. The private lawcourt is improvised before the door, and not in some fronting portico: ἐν τοῖς προθύροις in 802 is the same thing as πρὸ τῶν θυρῶν in 804 and ἔμπροσθεν τῶν θυρῶν in 871. Prior to the parabasis, the lawcourt is silently cleared by servants; after the parabasis, the conversation and imaginary symposium of Bdelykleon and Philokleon take place in the orchestra, not in an interior visible through the open door or by means of the *ekkyklema* (Wilamowitz). The text clearly indicates that one is outdoors: cf., amongst others, line 1154, where a servant is sent back into the house, and 1251, where an order is given to a servant indoors.

Philokleon's house is not situated at the periphery of Athens (Wilamowitz), because his colleagues' march at the end of the night to fetch Philokleon and then to go directly to the lawcourts indicates that Philokleon lives in town (cf. also 120). Returning home from the banquet Philokleon passes through the zone of the Agora (see 1389–91). During the scene at 1326–1441, the orchestra does not represent a stretch of the road between the house of Philoctemon and that of Philokleon or, in particular, the Agora and the Altar of the Twelve Divinities (Wilamowitz): we are in front of the house of Philokleon, by now returned from the banquet (cf. 1322, 1324; at 1325 the Servant goes indoors).[5]

5 Characters and actors

Wasps, like *Knights*, employs the first two actors for the two main characters alone (in *Wasps* the first actor is initially employed for an ephemeral minor character), and to an even greater extent than *Knights* relies almost exclusively on these two protagonists and hence has no 'third parts' of any importance comparable to Demosthenes and Demos. It is enough to think that of the approximately one thousand one hundred lines spoken by actors, no fewer than 440 pertain to Philokleon and 400 to Bdelykleon.

The characters number nine altogether (or ten, if one holds that the Servant of 835–43, 1292–1325 and 1474–93 is not Xanthias), and they are played by three actors, a young male singer and an amateur actor:

first actor: Sosias, First Servant, 1–137 (around thirty trimeters), Philokleon, 144–73 from within, 184–97, 317–833, 844–1008, 1122–1263, 1326–1448, 1482–1515 (all told about 440 lines, of which around 20 are lyrical);

second actor, with around four hundred lines, of which half a dozen are lyrical: Bdelykleon (I), 136–55, 168–227, (228)395–436, 456–1008, 1125–1264, 1364–1449, 1496–1511;

third actor, with almost 215 lines: Xanthias, Second Servant, 2–229, (230)395–502, 835–43 (still anonymous), Dog from Kydathenaion, 903–30, Xanthias (still anonymous), 1292–1325, Myrtia, the Baking-girl, 1388–1412, Xanthias (still anonymous), 1474–93;

boy singer: Lantern-bearing Youth (230) 248–316 (414), with fewer than 20 lines, of which 10 are lyrical;

amateur actor, with eight trimeters altogether: Mistreated Man, 1332–4, Man with Witness, 1417–41.

three dwarfed dancers, the sons of Karkinos, are active with Philokleon during the orchestic agon in the finale. Their father Karkinos, who appears at 1531, is not a dancer. Some scholars maintain that these dancing dwarfs are three of the Lantern-bearing *Youths* from the parodos: the latter, who indeed total at least three, must also be able to dance. As regards the only Youth to sing, see section 5 of chapter 7 on *Peace*.

Extras: Midas, Phryx, Masyntias (433), Chrysus (1251) and other servants of Bdelykleon, the Dog Labes (899), Labes' Cubs (976), Cheese-grater (963; the other Kitchen Instruments in 937–9 are not interrogated, the Grater being the most important witness: cf. 964), Flute-player from the banquet (1341, cf. also 1368–9), Philokleon's Pursuers (cf. 1327–8), Chaerephon (1408), Witness (1416), Karkinos (1531).

For a brief period during the prologue a donkey appears (179) and, in the private lawcourt scene, a caged cock (815, 817, 934).

The Wasps have stings positioned at the base of their spines beneath the waist (225, 1075, 1072) which, when they attack, they manœuvre forward between their legs. They also have sticks (727).

7

PEACE

1 *Peace* after *Wasps*

'No longer shall you find in me a sour and intractable dicast, or naturally the same rough grit as before. Instead you'll see me mild and so young again, once I am liberated from the troubles of war': the chorus of *Peace* 348–52, in clear allusion to the dicasts of *Wasps* 277 and 1105. Similarly, lines 781–90 of *Peace* allude to the closing scene of *Wasps*, as if that particular scene had met with the spectators' disapproval: this was discussed in section 1 of chapter 6 on *Wasps*.

These two passages demonstrate that after the Lenaian *Wasps* of 422 Aristophanes made his return to the stage with *Peace*. It is also known that *Peace* competed at the Dionysia of 421. Aristophanes, therefore, although present with two comedies at the Lenaia of 422, took part neither in the Dionysia of 422 won by Kantharos (cf. *IG* II.²2318, 115), nor in the Lenaia of 421, in which Eupolis presented *Marikas* (cf. scholion *Clouds* 552). As previously observed, it is not clear whether Argument VI.7 to *Clouds* implies that Aristophanes was denied permission to participate at the Dionysia of 422 with the *Second Clouds*.

It was with *Peace*, therefore, that Aristophanes returned to the Dionysia, two years after his defeat with *Clouds*. This time, too, he competed officially, and this time came second in the place-list: first place went to Eupolis with *Flatterers*, third to Leukon with *Clansmen*. This has emerged from Argument III.48–50.

A number of lines in the parabasis of *Peace* are identical, or extremely similar, to lines from the parabasis of *Wasps*: cf. *Peace* 752 and 754–60 with *Wasps* 1029–37. One variant is significant: 'but all along I stood up to the monster, fighting for you and *for the islands*'. In the Dionysian *Peace*, the poet adds 'and for the islands', since his public this time includes the allies from the islands, not the Athenians alone (an 'ionic' spectator at 46).

The repetition of lines from the parabasis of a Lenaian comedy in a comedy appearing consecutively at the Dionysia – a repetition which surprises many modern readers, for they indeed judge by the criteria of *readers* – is in itself perfectly natural, and one must also consider that in *Wasps* these lines had formed a portrait of Kleon, and that in the mean time Kleon had died. In the light of such an event, this fine allegorical portrait from *Wasps*, before the assembled public of Athenians, allies and foreigners, assumes the value of an epigraph, a political valediction of monumental proportions, in a comedy whose whole intention is to bid farewell to Kleon (cf. *Peace* 647–56). To the existing lines the poet adds one more, 753, which clearly refers to the demagogic leather-merchant, 'marching through the dreadful stench of leather and foul-mouthed threats'. Today, the spectators should recall the poet's long anti-Kleonine struggle, and for that very reason award the prize to him (759–61)!

Aristophanes had clearly intuited that Kleon's death and the peace then imminent between Athens and Sparta had brought to an end one phase of his career, until then pursued amidst the noise of arms, which had been in-augurated officially with the attack on Kleon in *Knights*: an intuition voiced by the joyful choreutai lacking 'the same rough grit *as before*' (349, cf. also 1312). The final parabatic anapaests of *Peace* are apparently designed to recollect that bitter anti-Kleonine chapter, in a comedy 'lacking rough grit'. It is all the more natural, therefore, that the anapaests from *Wasps* should have been repeated.

Besides, the parabasis of *Peace* taken as a whole is a species of résumé. The first part is a résumé of the poet's artistic merits, and one which is also extremely euphoric: the recent double affirmation with *Proagon* and *Wasps* must have helped him forget, for the moment at least, the mortification he suffered with *Clouds*. Better: his competitors this time included Eupolis, who at the Lenaia two months previously had presented the Aristophanized *Marikas* (cf. *Clouds* 553–4). For this reason too he felt the need to subject the public to a résumé of his own artistic and political originality, and to conclude, indeed, with an invitation to award the prize to him, Aristophanes, for the added motive that after his victories in the past he had never gone by the gyms to seduce young boys (762–4). This, too, the poet had said before in the parabasis of *Wasps* 1023–5, and there the scholiast had indicated that the gibe was aimed at Eupolis. He must have been correct, since here one finds it repeated in a contest where Eupolis, with his aggressive and satirical *Flatterers*, is the competition Aristophanes fears the most.

2 'Lacking the same rough grit as before.' The economy of *Peace* and its prologue

The repetition, in *Peace*, of a group of lines from *Wasps* has been listed by many scholars amongst the signs of its author's artistic weariness.

Although this repetition, as one has just seen, may quite naturally be reconciled with the contemporary theatrical and political history of Athens, *Peace* undoubtedly bears the signs of being a minor comedy: after the prologue its dramatic intensity and scenic force diminish, and at times it resembles a historical poem; after the parabasis, notwithstanding its inarguable vitality, the action is marred here and there by a sporadic loss of organic unity and is bereft of structural progressions. Even the parodos depends on an expedient: it is a well-known fact that the chorus of *Peace* is not aggressive, but in excellent humour and most obliging (*Peace* is the only extant comedy not to take its title from the chorus). Hence, in order to enliven its appearance it is made to dance for joy, to the rage of the pacifist Trygaeus, who has asked its help in disinterring the goddess Peace: the parodos goes on like this to the end, the countrymen dancing and shouting for joy, and Trygaeus trying in vain to keep them quiet, scared that the god Polemos, by whom Peace has been buried away, will burst from the house of Zeus (cf. 309–45). The monstrous Polemos, active at the end of the prologue along with his minister, Riot, never reappears, although he lives there, a step away from the noisy mob of countrymen (cf. 310, 318–20 and also 204–6), and although the actor by whom he was played in 236–88 is now free of any other commitments. This in itself is a sign of how the prologue's intense dramatic energy and the commitment it requires of the actors are never brought to fruition in the following scenes. The only adversary to emerge for Trygaeus and the peasants is Hermes, who reappears at 362 (if in a somewhat mechanical way). Yet he is swiftly deprived of all agonistic force, forgetful of the punishment threatened by Zeus (cf. 371–2). Hence, prior even to the hyperbolic toil involved in the disinterment of the goddess, *Peace* relaxes into placid conversation, and thereafter into idyll and symbology (*Peace* is the comedy richest in extras of symbolic value).

The peace sealed between Athens and Sparta in April 421 'immediately after the Dionysia', as reported in Thucydides V.20, had been in the air for a number of months, and it was in such an atmosphere that Aristophanes had been working, one quite distinct from the atmosphere he had evoked a few years earlier in *Acharnians*, where the truce sealed had been polemical, private and original. The powerful and accelerated rhythm of the prologue of *Peace* – conceived, perhaps, immediately after the death of the two warmongers Kleon and Brasidas in October 422 (cf. *Peace* 259–321) – proved not easy to sustain when, on the threshold of peace, Aristophanes found himself presenting for the first time characters 'lacking the same rough grit *as before*' (*Peace* 349).

The performance structure of the section between prologue and parabasis is indicative in itself: of the no fewer than seven characters active during the prologue, only Trygaeus and Hermes survive, and Hermes disappears with the parabasis. In *Clouds* also, Strepsiades and Socrates are the only characters to be left active between the prologue and the parabasis (in the prologue, these actors are accompanied by two other characters, one of whom is in all respects secondary). Yet after the parabasis Socrates remains active, and the Pheidippides of the prologue re-emerges. In *Birds*, where similarly no new characters appear between prologue and parabasis, the performance of the section is carried on by three of the four characters who had appeared during the prologue. Moreover, it is hardly as if the chorus of *Peace* has any of the dramatic force or stage-presence of that of *Birds*. Not even in *Acharnians* does one encounter the disproportion characterizing the performance structure of *Peace*: of the six characters from the prologue, only Dikaiopolis survives, whereas a total of four new characters are introduced. One should also note that the third actor of *Peace* is left idle between 288 and 1052: something similar was observed in regard to *Clouds* 222–814, the only other comedy in which the third actor remains inactive between prologue and parabasis (throughout the whole of *Peace* the third actor utters only 60 lines, while Trygaeus alone speaks 600!).

In *Peace*, the Servant of lines 1–113 – in a weak attempt to link the second part of the comedy to the first – re-emerges after the parabasis to become the intensely modest chief interlocutor of Trygaeus from 824 to 1126, after which the two withdraw into the house (yet without any adequate motivation). Promoted to the rank of tritagonist, the Servant is again portrayed by the second actor, who had played Hermes between 180 and 728. The five other characters active after the parabasis are all new, with the exception of the extras, Harvesthome and Holiday, who had come to light with Peace: the latter – a statue, as will be seen – comes to be forgotten almost completely, while the marriage of Trygaeus and Harvesthome, apparently imminent in 868–70 (cf. 842–4 and 859), takes place instead at the end of the comedy and hence loses its dramatic value, becoming simply a joyful singing parade. The only characters of any note in the final part of the comedy are the two small antinomic sons of Lamachus and Kleonymos: these, along with the daughter of Trygaeus in the prologue, form a trio of original and well-developed child characters.

The two Children appear at the wedding feast at the house of Trygaeus (1192), of which no announcement is ever made and at which the guests, as we shall see further on, arrive without having passed through the orchestra. The appearance of this innovative pair of Children is preceded, separately, by those of a Sicklemaker and an Arms-dealer (1197–1208, 1209–64), two appearances which in a highly conventional way dramatize the conflicting reactions gathered by Trygaeus and Hermes amongst the spectators after the disinterment of the goddess Peace (cf. 545–9). In this respect, it should be noted that *Peace*, more than any other Aristophanic comedy, constantly addresses itself to the audience. Indeed, the zone made up of seats reserved for the members of the Boulē and the Prytaneis is regarded as an authentic scenic station within the dramatic game (817–98, cf. 846).

The prologue of *Peace* is lengthy, varied in metre – out of 300 lines, 50 are in metres other than iambic trimeters – and also remarkable for its dramatic force: enough to say that, apart from the protagonist, another six characters appear (three in the terrestrial section 1–148, three in the celestial, 180–300) and that midway through the prologue there is a spectacular flight from earth to sky astride a beetle. This paratragic valour evinced in the prologue – 'more tragic' had the flight involved a Pegasus (135–6) – is recalled to the minds of the spectators after the parabasis, when the comedy starts to wane: 'I mounted a beetle and saved the Hellenes', exclaims Trygaeus in 865–7.

The prologue is opened by a pair of Servants, but in respect to *Knights* and *Wasps* the variations and refinements are outstanding, whilst in the parabasis the poet justly takes pride in having developed the comic typology of the Servants (742–7; 742 should be read after 743). The opening dialogue 1–19 and the speech in 20–41, for instance, at once discuss and sustain a contemporary scenic action by which all attention and expectation are focused on the gigantic, revolting beetle lurking behind the doorway (30). And when the only Servant left on-stage begins a mimetic account of his master's extravagance, his account is confirmed by the exclamations and remarks of his master, who is inside the house (60, 63–4, cf. *Clouds* 25–7). As the Servant talks and imitates his master, therefore, the latter is already active back-stage: this implies that the protagonist's action begins, not after the account, but during it. One can already deduce that this prologue is an unconventional one when the Servant announces his subject, not 'to the spectators' (*Knights* 36, *Wasps* 54), 'but instead to children, to young men, to men, to supermen, even to super-supermen' (50–3).[1]

3 The celestial residence of Zeus and the cavern of Peace

Scholars are in disagreement, and always will be, as to the stage-technique of *Peace*: whether the sky and the cavern of Peace are at the same level as the earthly home of Trygaeus or not.

The Servant spies through the doorway (78) and cries out: 'my master is rising into the air astride a beetle' (80–1). Here, the iambic trimeters end and the anapaestic dimeters begin: Trygaeus, who has appeared suspended in mid-air astride the beetle, asks the beast to slow down and, for the moment, just beat its wings (82–6). The anapaestic dimeters, apparently a comment on the beat of the wings, continue until 101. From 102 to 153 the metre is once again iambic trimeters (apart from the Alcmanians of 114–17 and dactylic hexameters of 118–23). At 154, when the anapaestic dimeters are resumed, Trygaeus urges the beetle to move faster (154–6), but the loathsome beast directs its nostrils at once towards the smells of the earth, and a freshly laid piece of terrestrial dung compromises the ascent (157–72). Trygaeus had made this clear, addressing the spectators: 'as for you, neither fart nor shit for three days, for if the beetle gets that smell from above, he'll come to eat, throwing me down headlong' (150–3).

When at 173 the iambic trimeters are taken up once more, it seems appropriate to assume that the beetle, abruptly, draws within range of the ground = orchestra floor. Trygaeus ceases to speak as if he were in character, but instead appeals to the operator of the flying-machine, apparently to provide comic relief during the operation of landing in the sky = ground:

oh, what an awful thought [that of ending violently on the ground like Euripides' Bellerophon], *I'm no longer saying this as a joke*. Operator, take care. I can already feel a touch of colic around my belly-button. Be careful, or I'll end up fattening the beetle.

(173–6)

Having landed safely, Trygaeus introduces another element of comedy to the scenic game: 'but, I seem to be close to the gods. There, I can see quite distinctly the house of Zeus! Who's that in the porter's lodge? Why don't you open up?' (177–9). 'I can see quite distinctly', καθορῶ (cf. *Clouds* 326 and also *Lysistrata* 319), is given emphasis by 'there', καὶ δή (cf. *Lysistrata* 925): the flying-machine has deposited Trygaeus miraculously before the house of Zeus himself, 'in the sky', and the celestial Διὸς αὐλαί of 161 are now, realistically, 'the house of Zeus'.

Did Trygaeus pass through the air from one side of the stage to the other? Did he land, that is, at the level from which he had taken off? It would seem so, although to date we lack the proof to establish with absolute certainty that such a technique was actually employed.

Hermes comes to open the door of Zeus' residence and shouts menacingly at Trygaeus: 'how did you get up here?' (ἀνῆλθες, 184). The use of this verb, which indicates difference in level, is perfectly natural. The deity could express himself in no other way when addressing the terrestrial Trygaeus (180): by now the scene is imagined to be in the sky. But it is significant that Hermes, threatening Trygaeus with death in the name of the goddess Earth (188), should not have said: 'mind, I'm going to hurl you down', or something of that kind. Were the sky indeed at a higher level, such a remark would have been not only effective, but also necessary (cf. 146–7). None the less, such a degree of silence excludes decision.

The scene 'in the sky' continues. Trygaeus desires to discover the whereabouts of the goddess Peace: EP. Ὁ Πόλεμος αὐτὴν ἐνέβαλ' εἰς ἄντρον βαθύ. TP. Εἰς ποῖον; EP. Εἰς τουτὶ τὸ κάτω. Κἄπειθ' ὁρᾷς ὅσους ἄνωθεν ἐπεφόρησε τῶν λίθων, ἵνα μὴ λάβητε μηδέποτ' αὐτήν (223–6). Those who maintain that the scene is divided into two levels, or into three (I, earth, II, cave, III, sky), invoke at first line 224, which they interpret as 'down there, in that cavern there'. But εἰς τουτὶ τὸ κάτω (sc. ἄντρον) has to mean '(he's thrown her) into this deep ἄντρον here'. Hermes' account, which continues with 'furthermore, as you can see, above he's accumulated a mass of stones', tends to make one imagine a profound *cavity* lying beneath the heap of stones visible at the mouth of the cavern. In 223, Hermes had already vaguely mentioned the ἄντρον which was βαθύ and now, indicating it, casts it into relief and gives a sense of its profundity. One should note that the poetic term ἄντρον does not denote the exterior of the cavern but its interior (cf., for instance, *Odyssey* IX.216). At the bottom of the cavern lies Peace: to recover her it is first necessary to remove all the stones (ἀφέλκειν τοὺς λίθους, 361,

138

427) and then to haul out the goddess (ἐξελκύσαι, 294, 315, 417, 506), in effect, to disinter her (ἀνορύττειν, 372), to draw her up towards the light (εἰς τὸ φῶς ἀνελκύσαι, 307, 445). Similarly, the god of wealth, Plutus, imagines that the parsimonious man will inter him deep in the hidden depths of the earth (κατώρυξέν με κατὰ τῆς γῆς κάτω, *Plutus* 238). The τουτὶ τὸ κάτω ἄντρον of *Peace*, therefore, is a cavern containing an 'underground' cavity, comparable to the πετρώδης κατῶρυξ in which Kreon buries Antigone alive, and whence he is ordered to restore her to the light (*Antigone* 774, 1100), and to the μυχοὶ ἀνήλιοι ἄντρων in which, prior to Prometheus, man once lived deep underground (κατώρυχες, *Prometheus* 452–3).

In conclusion: τουτὶ τὸ κάτω ἄντρον, in *Peace*, does not denote a cavern to be found at a level set lower than that from which Hermes speaks: the pronoun τουτί in itself implies that the cavern is within the same spatial circle and on the same plane as Hermes. The cavern, in fact, must be situated between the house of Trygaeus – by now removed from all scenic attention – and the house of Zeus: the cavern is the central element of the façade. The scholars who, on the other hand, locate the cavern on the level below, on the level of the orchestra, that is, and Hermes and the sky on that above, fail to consider that the cavern is imagined as being *in the sky*: the two ministresses of Peace who emerge from the cavern 'descend' from sky to earth along with Trygaeus (cf. 725–8, 847). If these scholars were consistent, they would also have to place the cavern on the level above.

The following scene at last gives proof of the representation of the sky and of the cavern at the level of the orchestra. Trygaeus appeals to the chorus to come and, along with him, disinter the goddess (ἡμῖν, 300, 315, 417): δ ε υ ρ' ἴτε, (298), 'come here', or rather into the sky. And the twenty-four choreutai rush to his aid. The scene at this point is set in the sky, which one approaches by means of the general corridor. The choreutai begin to dance wildly, and continue to do so for some time; in the orchestra, evidently. Trygaeus implores them not to shout too much, or else the god Polemos will emerge from the house of Zeus (ἐκδραμών, 319).

The house of Zeus, the cavern and the site of the chorus' dance are all, as can be seen, on the same level, and this could certainly not be raised, since it would be impossible for twenty-four choreutai to dance in a small elevated zone: the poet would not have omitted to draw attention to such a daring innovation. Nor is it legitimate to assume again that Hermes and Trygaeus are standing at a higher level than that of the chorus and the cavern: apart from the fact that the cavern is imagined as being in the sky, the text explicitly affirms that Trygaeus, if not Hermes too, actually participates in the disinterment of the goddess. And, as usual, there are no remarks such as 'you two up there', or 'you down there'.

Let us see how the operation of disinterment proceeds. The cavern, as mentioned previously, must be the central element of the façade. This implies that the cavern's central opening corresponds to its mouth, while its recesses fade imaginatively behind the scene: within it, and at its mouth, stones are piled up, and beneath these stones, deeply entombed, lies the goddess Peace (see 223–5). The object is to 'remove' the stones, by shovel and lever, and then to 'haul out' the goddess, to 'disinter her', to 'restore her to the light'. The two operations are thus distinct. The first is left exclusively to the chorus (and to the extras who accompany it). Equipped with shovels, levers and ropes (299, cf. 307), the chorus is advised to *enter the cavern* with its shovels and to remove the stones (426–7; the much-discussed εἰσιόντες of 427 has to mean 'entering' an opening in the scenic façade, or rather the cavern). In 431–57, while the chorus is silently at work in the recesses of the cavern (and hence is only partially visible), Hermes and Trygaeus make a toast to peace before the eyes of the spectators. In 458, a new order is presented: the coryphaeus (or Hermes) invites everyone to 'pull hard and heave ashore with the ropes' (ὑπότεινε δὴ πᾶς καὶ κάταγε τοῖσιν κάλῳς), that is, to stretch the ropes across their shoulders and, with tautened back and lowered head, heave ashore as they might a boat. Evidently, in so far as there is talk of ropes, the issue is no longer that of removing stones or – as is commonly maintained – of raising a tombstone, but of restoring to the light the disinterred *goddess* lying at the bottom of the pit (cf. τ ή ν δ ε ἐξελκύσαι at 506).

And this, in fact, is the second and final operation: evidently some of the choreutai, once all the stones were removed (there is no further mention of stones from this point onwards), had wound their ropes around the goddess (the latter, as we shall see, is a statue). The task now is to ἕλκειν (470, 475, 478, 481, 504), ἀνέλκειν (469), τείνειν, σπᾶν (492, 498, cf. 514), ἐξελκεῖν (506, 511). Hermes and Trygaeus are invited to collaborate in this final operation (the extras, however, are not made to pull). Trygaeus pulls on one of the ropes, and Hermes perhaps does likewise (cf. 469–71, 484 ποιοῦμεν, 485 ἅπασιν ἡμῖν). Hermes, in any case, oversees the work (maybe from inside the cavern) and keeps the choreutai informed of its progress (509, 513, 516). It appears, indeed, that the choreutai cannot fully appreciate the results of their efforts (see 510): most probably they are in the orchestra and their ropes, which must be extremely long, extend from there. At 520, the statue of the goddess finally emerges into the light, and with her appear Harvesthome and Holiday (strictly speaking, there is no need to assume that they, too, were imagined as having been entombed along with the goddess). Further on, Hermes invites Trygaeus to bring Harvesthome and Holiday back with him to the earth (706–8, 713–14).

But where is the beetle for the trip home? It is not here, replies Hermes: 'yoked to the chariot of Zeus it bears the lightning bolts' (722 = Euripides fr. 314, *Bellerephon*!). 'But how am I supposed to *descend*?' 'Relax, it's easy: this way, near the goddess herself' (τῃδὶ παρ'αὐτὴν τὴν θεόν). And Trygaeus parts with the two girls. What path does he choose? Evidently, while Hermes disappears into Zeus' residence, he *enters the cavern* (τῃδί indicates a place which is very close by, and also clearly delineated), in front of or near to which stands the statue of the goddess. After the parabasis – during which the orchestra and stage-edifice are ascribed a neutral value (see 729–31) – Trygaeus reappears *on the earth* through the corridor complaining of aching legs from the long trip home (824–6, cf. 819–20). Through these simple means, the illusion is created of a journey on foot from sky to earth through the recesses of the celestial cavern.

After the parabasis, naturally, the house of Trygaeus from the prologue comes back into the picture. The Dionysian *Peace*, therefore, implies the existence of three doors within the scenic façade (the door from which Polemos appears at 236 must be the same as that by which Hermes re-enters at 233, the sole entrance to the house of Zeus). As regards the conjectural median positioning of the cavern, for confirmation of a general type one may refer in this case to Pollux IV.124: 'of the three stage-doors the central one was a palace, a cavern or a noble residence'.[2]

In the second part of the comedy characters extraneous to the scenic façade appear in the orchestra *through the door* of Trygaeus' house, which, by means of a most unusual technique, they had apparently entered during the second parabasis from without or, more precisely, through the rear entrance. In fact, after the second parabasis, Trygaeus comes outdoors to announce that, at his home, 'a great crowd of guests have arrived for the marriage feast' (1192). Amongst these are the children the spectators see entering the orchestra at line 1265.

The lightning trips of the divine Riot in the course of the prologue (sky–Athens–sky–Sparta–sky) pass, not through the corridor, but through the scenic façade: that is to say, from the orchestra, Riot re-enters the scenic façade = the celestial home of Zeus and then, from the wings, 'descends' to earth, reappearing in the sky from the scenic façade once more (not from the corridor). In *Birds* too, Peisetairos' lightning voyage from Cloud-cuckoo-land to the sky traverses the scenic façade.

4 Harvesthome, Holiday and Peace. The Greek cities

Harvesthome and Holiday – an English rendering of Ὀπώρα and Θεωρία – are two flesh-and-blood young girls, and are treated as light-hearted and extremely forward (709–11, 848–55, 868–70, etc.; but it is not true that in 886 Holiday is invited to take her clothes off. As noted by the scholiast, there she lays down her symbols of peace). Harvesthome and Holiday are both mute, as are the carnal Thirty-Year-Truce of *Knights*, Regina of *Birds* and Reconciliation of *Lysistrata*.

The goddess Peace is also mute, but in every other respect is treated in a wholly different manner. Peace is an untouchable and immobile being, devoid of carnal attributes. Brought out into the light of day from within the chamber of the cavern, there she stands in front of the cavern, stiff as a pole, to such an extent that Hermes, showing Trygaeus his path, makes use of her as a point of reference (726). During the parabasis the goddess remains in front of the cavern, and is there still when Trygaeus, back to earth after the parabasis, holds a ceremony to install her (923): close to Peace an altar and a table are brought, and a sacrifice is performed (923, 938, etc.). Once installed, the goddess is no longer addressed (the final references are in 1062, 1073 and 1108): there she stands, immobile at the centre of the stage, the solid trophy of the pacifist Trygaeus, by whom she has been restored for the sake of the Athenians and of the Hellenes. 'You, my lady, we shall never forsake', said Trygaeus in the sky (705, cf. 1108).

Obviously, as the technique by which she was removed from the cavern gave one reason to suspect, Peace is not a human being, but a *statue*. At a certain point, the coryphaeus exclaims meaningfully, 'now I understand why she's so beautiful: she's a relative of Phidias!' (617–18). And Trygaeus' Servant, on seeing her for the first time, is reminded of a 'little statue of Hermes' (924). In 682, Trygaeus asks Peace: 'what are you doing? Where are you turning your head?' From this remark, one should not conclude that Peace is a living being, or a statue with a mobile head. By means of this question, Trygaeus mischievously attributes to the goddess a gesture of disgust, as Strepsiades in *Clouds* 1478–83 attributes expressiveness and a voice to the statue or effigy of Hermes ('but, my dear Hermes, don't get angry with me'). Besides, from a distance, any such movement of Peace's head would have been imperceptible to the spectators: what is essential is its verbal affirmation. Similarly, in *Lysistrata* 127, to give just one example, the women are ascribed physical reactions which their masks make it impossible to see: 'why are you changing colour? what is this tear that falls?'. The 'dialogue' between Peace and Hermes takes place in 661–3 on the model of that between the simulacrum of Hermes and Strepsiades. Yet the questions the goddess poses through the mouth of Hermes no longer imply any feigned colloquy in whispered undertones (cf. 670, 679, 688, 695): Hermes is no longer a spokesman, but an autonomous interpreter of the thoughts of the goddess.

A statue, therefore, but not a colossal statue, as some scholars who imagine a scenic arrangement at two levels would prefer to believe: the feet of Peace on the earth and her head in the sky, close to her spokesman Hermes. In the extant text there is absolutely nothing to justify an interpretation such as this (the 'greatest of all the goddesses' in 308 is metaphorical; besides, at that point, the goddess is still entombed). Equally, the choreutai's task in extracting the goddess proves to be a difficult one, not because she is a colossus, but because there are so many stones piled over her and since, when they move to the ropes, there are those who sabotage their work; and because one must also show just how hard it is to recover peace. The idea of the colossus comes from the scholion on Plato, *Apology* 19c: (Aristophanes) κωμῳδεῖται δὲ καὶ <ὅτι> τὸ τῆς Εἰρήνης κολοσσικὸν ἐξῆρεν ἄγαλμα· Εὔπολις Αὐτολύκῳ, Πλάτων Νίκαις. Plato's *Victories* cannot be dated, but the *First Autolycus* of Eupolis is from 420, and it is therefore highly probable that in that comedy Eupolis made reference to the Aristophanic *Peace* of 421. However, let us repeat, in the text of *Peace* there is absolutely nothing to suggest that on-stage there stands a colossal statue of Peace. The proclaimer of oracles Hierokles, for instance, is not even aware the goddess is there (see 1052, 1054). It is possible that the Platonic scholiast might have paraphrased a κολοσσός from Eupolis and Plato, and it is an established fact that in the fifth century κολοσσός did not denote a gigantic statue.

Trygaeus, the Attic countryman, risen to the skies for the sake of all the Hellenes (cf. 93, 150), on seeing Tumult and Polemos disappear from the stage, exclaims almost directly to the Hellenic public seated before him in the theatre (cf. 244 and 276), 'the propitious moment has come, O Hellenes, for us to bring forth Peace, so dear to us all', and then continues in a louder voice: 'come, O countrymen, merchants, artisans, workers, metics, foreigners and islanders, come all of you here, the whole people together, swiftly as you can, with shovels, levers and ropes' (291–300). In response to this invocation the coryphaeus and the chorus enter: 'from here, let each of us march with fervour, directly to liberation. All Hellenes, lend your aid, now or never!' Then, the coryphaeus begs Trygaeus to give the orders necessary to restore to the light 'the goddess who *more than any other loves the vineyards*' (308; cf. also 520, 557–9). From the latter, it would seem that the coryphaeus is speaking for the countrymen alone, seen as Attics, naturally (cf. 348, 356, 395) and ready and willing for the toil (305–36, cf. also 428–30). But when the operation of restoring the goddess to the light is actually underway, Trygaeus observes that not all are pulling equally (464) and, with Hermes, accuses successively the Boeotians, Argives, Laconians and Megarians, and the Athenians also, of being the saboteurs of the disinterment (466; 475–7, 493; 478–80; 500–2; 503–7). The chorus remarks: 'what slackers we have amongst us!'. And Trygaeus in retort: 'but you at least, you who yearn for peace, pull hard!' (496–8). In the end, the coryphaeus makes a decision: 'come, my friends, let us alone get down to work, us countrymen' (508); and, indeed, 'only the countrymen are pulling on the ropes and no one else' (511). From this point onwards, there is no further mention of 'others', only, throughout, of countrymen, Attics (cf. in particular 557–63, 571–600, 603).

It seems, therefore, that along with the twenty-four countrymen-choreutai there have also appeared a number of extras, which implies that to Trygaeus' appeal in 296–300 there responded as choreutai the first category invoked – the countrymen – and as extras representatives of the other categories, or at least of the Greek cities either at war or neutral (Boeotians, Laconians, Megarians, Athenians, Argives). Urged on by the coryphaeus' exhortation ('All Hellenes, lend your aid', 302), these extras probably stand aside in the orchestra between 508 and 511 and exit silently after 511 or 581, or maybe at the parabasis. One is given reason to suspect that they do not withdraw immediately after 511 by lines 538–42, which Trygaeus and Hermes dedicate to the Greek cities, by now reconciled and serene, albeit 'terribly disfigured in the face and filled with cupping-glasses' (these cities must obviously include Athens, and hence it is reasonable to assume that lines 503–7 are addressed to the Athenian extras, not to the Athenians in the theatre, or to the Athenians in general). Lines 543–9 are then quite clearly addressed to the warmongers and pacifists seated in the theatre; lines 550–5 to the countrymen-spectators seated in the theatre (and not to the countrymen-choreutai, for whom Trygaeus afterwards has a special appeal in 560–3); and lines 564–81 to the countrymen-choreutai, at this point drawn up in fine array, having broken rank for the operation of disinterment. That the extras withdraw at the beginning of the parabasis one might perhaps infer from the invitation which the chorus extends to its 'attendants': 'we in the mean time will entrust the tools [the shovels, ropes and levers] to the care of our attendants since around the theatres a crowd of thieves are normally in wait, ready to do their business. Look after them then, like good fellows' (729–31). Might not these 'attendants' (οἱ ἀκόλουθοι) be the Greek cities extraneous to the chorus? In *Wasps*, the Youths extraneous to the chorus, although one of them has already been active along with the coryphaeus, are ignored for around a hundred lines, until the choreutai have consigned them their mantles, that is, and then dismissed them with a pretext (*Wasps* 408–14).

Many scholars deny that other supplementary elements appear along with the countrymen-choreutai, and instead maintain that the apostrophized Boeotians etc. are purely imaginary, or that the twenty-four countrymen-choreutai are freely treated first as Attics, then as Hellenes, then as Attics again. These scholars also observe that Trygaeus apostrophizes Lamachus directly in 473, and that Lamachus is definitely not on-stage. However, this nominal apostrophe, a speaking name which is so generic, could be addressed as a joke to some unwilling choreutes or extra, whereas the entire series of other apostrophes and remarks made relative to the sabotage cannot but be aimed at real, quite clearly distinguished targets present on-stage. The remarks in 508–11 are decisive in this respect.[3]

Elements extraneous to the chorus in Aristophanes also accompany the choruses of *Wasps* and *Frogs*, while in *Birds* the appearance of the chorus is preceded by the parade of four birds.

5 Characters and actors. The child parts

In *Peace*, there are twelve characters, and the subdivision of the parts might be as follows:

first actor: First Servant of Trygaeus, 1, 4–8, 11–12, 15–18, 41–9 (altogether seventeen trimeters), Trygaeus, 60 and 62–3 from within, 82–728, 819–1126, 1191–1310, 1316–59, uttering all-told 600 lines, of which around 30 are lyrical;

second actor, uttering around 330 lines, of which half pertain to Hermes:

Second Servant of Trygaeus, 2–113, Hermes, 180–233, Riot, 255–62, 268–75, 280–4, Hermes, 362–726 with a couple of lyrical lines, Second Servant of Trygaeus, 824–1123, Arms-dealer, 1210–64;

third actor, uttering around sixty lines: Polemos, 236–88, Hierokles, 1052–1119, Sickle-maker, 1197–1206;

two boy singers: these two are employed for the three child parts, which will be discussed shortly.

Strictly speaking, the third actor could be given the part of the First Servant, yet it would be preferable to opt for the first actor since in *Peace* Aristophanes employs the third actor only when absolutely necessary: there is no other Aristophanic comedy in which the third actor is so rarely employed.

There remain the three child parts to assign: around twenty lines for the Little Daughter of Trygaeus in 114–48 (four Alcmanians, one dactylic hexameter and fourteen trimeters), about ten dactylic hexameters for the Little Son of Lamachus in 1270–91, and an elegiac couplet and half dactylic hexameter for the Little Son of Kleonymos in 1298–1301. Child parts such as those in *Peace* are encountered elsewhere only in *Wasps*, in which a youth utters six lines in fourteen-syllable Euripidean metre and about ten lyric lines; in other comedies children and youths utter no more than a few words (*Acharnians* 735, *Lysistrata* 879; the daughter of Dikaiopolis in *Acharnians* 245–6 is not a child, despite *Acharnians* 132). In the extant Euripides, authentic child parts are to be found in *Alcestis* 392–415 (approximately twenty lines), *Suppliants* 1123–62 (approximately twenty lines), *Andromache* 504–36 (approximately ten lines); in *Medea*, four iambic trimeters intended for a child are to be found in 1271–8, but are delivered back-stage; in other Euripidean tragedies children do appear, but they are left mute, as in the case of the youths of *Ajax*, *Antigone* and *Oedipus Rex*.

To whom were these child parts assigned? Were they actually entrusted to children, or were amateur adult actors, very short in stature, employed? The normal actors are out of the question, since in *Suppliants*, *Andromache* and *Wasps* in the first place they are unavailable.

The lines uttered by these Euripidean and Aristophanic children and youths are unusual, quite distinct from those reserved for amateur actors in Aristophanes. Whilst the latter always speak in iambic trimeters, the Euripidean and Aristophanic youths appear in parts which are purely lyrical (Euripides), partially lyrical (*Wasps*, the Little Daughter of Trygaeus), or noble in style, and in any case sung (the Little Sons of Lamachus and Kleonymos, see *Peace* 1267, 1268, 1271, 1279, 1285, 1289, 1294, 1297, 1300). The sheer persistence of this phenomenon excludes the idea that these parts were intended for amateur actors, and leads one instead to assume that the dramatist employed children trained in song. This can already be deduced from *Peace* 1265–9: 'There, the guests' children are coming out for a pee, as a prelude, it would seem, to the songs they're going to sing. You, little fellow, repeat first what you intend to sing, here beside me.' If child-singers were present at the banquets, there is no reason to assume that they would not also have been available for theatrical use. It is conceivable that the dramatist employed some of the many παῖδες forming the dithyrambic choruses. In *Peace* he needed two. Even the scholion on *Peace* 114, albeit lacking in rigour and precision, does conceive of a category apart for these children.[4]

Extras: the other Daughter, or Daughters of Trygaeus (119), 'The Greek Cities' (539), Harvesthome (523), Holiday (523), Pot-maker (1202), Helmet-maker (1255, cf. 1213), Lance-maker (1213, 1260), other Children of the guests (1265). The 'attendants' of line 729 were discussed in the previous section, as was the statue of Peace.

6 'The victor was [not] the actor Hermon'

Argument III 20–3 Zacher to *Peace* reports the following: ἐνίκησε δὲ τῷ δράματι ὁ ποιητὴς ἐπὶ ἄρχοντος 'Αλκαίου, ἐν ἄστει. πρῶτος Εὔπολις Κόλαξι, δεύτερος 'Αριστοφάνης Εἰρήνῃ, τρίτος Λεύκων Φράτορσι. τὸ δὲ δρᾶμα ὑπεκρίνατο 'Απολλόδωρος, †ἡνίκα ἑρμῆν λοιοκρότης.†

The last two words 'manu revisoris exarata sunt in *V* unde fortasse colligas haec in exemplari non perspicue scripta fuisse' (Zacher). The Venetus provides our sole extant witness to the entire second part of Argument III, and this is blemished to a remarkable degree by corruptions and omissions. To the hand of the reviser must also be ascribed the whole of Argument IV, to be found in the final part of folio 123[V], left blank by the first copyist. Argument IV, at more than one point, is a desperately corrupt text. No less desperately corrupt are the final words of Argument III, or at least the final two: the vulgate and current ἐνίκα ''Ερμων ὑποκριτής is unacceptable, simply because ὑποκριτής would constitute unnecessary specification after the name ''Ερμων and the information provided on the actor Apollodorus. The amendment, evidently provoked by the single fact that an actor named Hermon, active in the age of Aristophanes, is mentioned in the scholia on *Clouds* 542, would further imply that in the year 421 a contest between the comic actors was already taking place at the Dionysia, whereas from *IG* II.[2]2318 col. XIII and *IG* II.[2]2323a it emerges that this contest, in force at the Lenaia since 445–442, was introduced at the Dionysia only between 329 and 312 (besides, in respect to the Dionysia of 421, the spaces of the fifth column of *IG* II.[2]2318 would have been insufficient to accommodate the name of the victorious comic actor).

Thus, the Apollodorus named by the Argument, of whom no other mention is made, was the first actor of *Peace*. Information of this kind is exceptional in the dramatic Arguments, and is to be found elsewhere in two Arguments to Menander alone (*Dyskolos* and *Imbrioi*). After the mention of the first actor, the Argument continues with the information of a different kind, relative to *Dyskolos* alone, however.[5]

8

BIRDS

1 *Birds* and the Dionysia

The Dionysian *Peace* dates from 421, the Dionysian *Birds* from 414. Of the presumable output of Aristophanes during the years 420–415 all that unquestionably remains is the forty-five Eupolideans drafted by the spring of 417, destined to form the parabasis of the unperformed *Second Clouds*. *Birds*, produced by Kallistratos, gained second place; first went to Ameipsias, third to Phrynichos. At the Lenaia two months previously, the other didaskalos, Philonides, had entered Aristophanes' *Amphiaraus* (cf. Argument I.9–11 and Argument II.39–40). The staging of *Birds*, for Kallistratos and the choregos, must have entailed an effort more intense than normal, since this unusually expansive comedy requires masks, costumes and make-up adequate in quantity and variety, and striking enough in style, to meet the demands of around thirty or more different birds and approximately twenty characters; in addition, a flautist of exceptional ability and a choral group chosen with care.

The Dionysian *Birds* mirrors two ceremonies held in the theatre itself prior to the contests of the Dionysia (yet not to those of the Lenaia). In the scene involving the Unnatural Son, the remark 'I'll fit you out with the wings of an orphan bird' (1361) – the youth is given a shield, a sword and a helmet (1364–6) – alludes to an intensely solemn State ceremony celebrated previously in the theatre of Dionysos: during this ceremony the orphan-epheboi of the fallen were presented in panoply to the Hellenic public and called into the proedria (Aeschines, *Ctesiphon* 154). Hence, as the Unnatural Son of *Birds* is being rigged out in panoply like an orphan and counselled to go to war in Thrace, the orphans of the fallen are seated before him in the front rows.

Furthermore, as one of the many proclamations made in the theatre before the Dionysian contests (cf. Aeschines, *Ctesiphon* 41), the names used to be announced of Athenian and foreign citizens on whom particular honours had been conferred (Demosthenes, *On the Crown* 120). On this occasion – or rather on this occasion, too – the names must also have been proclaimed of outlawed citizens with a price on their heads, since *Birds* pronounces the death-sentence for the bird-catcher Philocrates in such a context:

more than ever one hears proclaimed these days [those of the Dionysia]
'whosoever of you kills Diagoras the Melian will receive one talent . . .';
we, therefore, *we in this place too* (χἠμεῖς ἐνθάδε) wish to proclaim:
'whoever among you kills Philocrates . . .', and if any of you keep birds
as prisoners in your homes, we invite you now to set them free.

(1071–85)

The invitation to liberate the imprisoned birds might reflect an Athenian
custom by which prisoners were set free on bail during the Dionysia and the
Panathenea to allow them to attend the festivals (scholion on Demosthenes,
Against Androtion 68).[1]

Birds must have been performed in the afternoon, since when Prometheus
reaches Cloud-cuckoo-land the *actual* time of day is late afternoon (cf.
1498–1500). A number of tragedies had been performed during the morning
(cf. 786–9). At the Dionysia – though this was not the case at the Lenaia – the
tragedies were the main element of the programme.

2 The prologue and structural action of *Birds*

From the scenic landscape of *Birds* all bourgeois elements are absent. In other
comedies involving an escape from the earth, or from the environment of
everyday life, there is always a terrestrial or bourgeois preamble: house of
Trygaeus → the sky, houses of Lysistrata and Kalonike → the Acropolis,
house of Agathon → the Thesmophorium, house of Herakles → the under-
world. In *Birds*, the land of Hoopoe and the birds is the comedy's initial (and
long-term) setting, the two Athenian wayfarers by whom the comedy is
opened having all but reached this destination after an extremely long journey
begun prior to the dramatic action.

These circumstances lend immediacy to the comedy's opening, an immediacy enhanced by the fact that the two prologuists of *Birds* are markedly
distinct from any other Aristophanic prologuists: in *Knights*, *Wasps* and *Peace*
there are two passive and purely functional characters, while in *Thesmophoriazusae*, *Frogs* and *Plutus* one of the two is the innocent victim of the schemes
excogitated by his fellow. In *Birds*, the two characters in the opening scene are
responsible and like-minded. Hence, the comedy's initial stages need not be
abruptly interrupted to allow for a formal account similar to those of its
predecessors. The account to the spectators unfolds naturally from the
dialogue preceding it (cf. γάρ in 30), while information is already provided in
13–22, although on a stylistic level its target is not the spectators (after *Birds*,
the account to the spectators disappears altogether).

After *Peace*, the superior quality of the couples in the opening scenes leads
also to an improvement in the comedies' general structural design. While in
Wasps and *Peace* one of the two Servant-prologuists disappeared during the
prologue itself, and the other gradually faded away to re-emerge after the

parabasis, possibly as an interlocutor employed out of pure convenience, Euelpides in *Birds* and Xanthias in *Frogs* remain vital presences on-stage up to the parabasis, and for a good while afterwards (until *Birds* 846 and *Frogs* 813), Euripides re-emerges as the main character throughout the second part of *Thesmophoriazusae* (as in many respects did Pheidippides in *Clouds*), and Karion in *Plutus*, along with his master, Chremylos, is established as the comedy's long-term character.

The protagonist of *Birds* is Peisetairos, but he announces himself as such when the prologue is already at an advanced stage. It is only at 162 that he makes his dramatic leap to the foreground, propounding a revolutionary scheme in defiance of all expectations (see 44–8; although it is he, not Euelpides, who poses the question to Hoopoe in 155–6 from which this scheme ensues). Prior to that, the more loquacious character is Euelpides, who delivers the account to the spectators in lines 30–48, as Peisetairos prowls about looking for the birds. The performance structure of the prologue is eloquent in this regard: 1–59, dialogue between Euelpides and Peisetairos, with almost fifty lines given up to Euelpides; 60–84, dialogue between Euelpides and Hoopoe's Servant, Peisetairos' single remark provoked by a question (67; 61 quite certainly belongs to Euelpides); 85–91, dialogue between Euelpides and Peisetairos; 92–161, dialogue between Euelpides and Hoopoe, with two interventions on the part of Peisetairos, 136–42 and 155–6a (the first provoked by a question); 162–208, dialogue between Peisetairos and Hoopoe, Euelpides mute. Nevertheless, from the comedy's opening lines, and from 49–58, one can already deduce that the leader of the expedition is Peisetairos, not Euelpides (cf. 255 and 340).

However, it remains perfectly fitting that Euelpides, not Peisetairos, should provide the spectators with an account of the 'mania' which has led them to abandon Athens in search of the land of Hoopoe (whenever Euelpides expounds the purpose of the voyage, Peisetairos is either at a distance from him or absorbed in something else: cf. 12–22, 27–49, 114–22): the comic hero must never appear mad, abnormal or extravagant, but act in the most complete and optimistic conviction of his own wisdom, take himself seriously, in short, as when he vents his discontent directly through a monologue (Dikaiopolis, Strepsiades). Euelpides, therefore, although attributing to himself, too, the mania afflicting Peisetairos (31), fulfils a function assigned in precedence to the Servants of *Wasps* and *Peace*, who also provide accounts of their keepers' mania (*Wasps* 71, *Peace* 54, 65, 90, 95; cf. *Plutus* 2).[2]

The prologue is followed by two grand events, artistically distinct yet counterbalanced (an analysis is provided in section 4 below): first, back-stage, a lyrical and instrumental performance given by Hoopoe (here most probably played by a singer and no longer by the third actor) and his bride Procne, an exceptionally gifted flautist, who remains invisible to the spectators until the parabasis; then, on-stage (where Hoopoe, henceforth Tereus, reappears in the panoply of King Tereus), a purely visual display, commented upon by

Hoopoe-Tereus and the two wayfarers – the mute parade of the four + twenty-four birds, each one different from the other (cf. 209–67, 268–309). Once, through the intercession of Hoopoe, the twenty-four birds (the chorus of the comedy) have agreed to hear the plans and teaching of Peisetairos, and have been left enchanted by them (the birds, thanks to Hoopoe, both understand and speak the language of man: cf. 198–200), the scene in iambics 639–57 and a remark made by the coryphaeus in 658–60 prelude a suspension of activities on the part of the three character-actors and the entrance of Procne, the nightingale-flautist: the execution of Peisetairos' scheme takes place after the parabasis (cf. 640 and also 809), but in its course the orders are already given for the construction of the aerial walls of the city of the birds (cf. 837–8).

The parabasis, 676–800, is the first in Aristophanes uniformly consistent with the mask of the chorus, and in addition an invitation made by the chorus to the spectators provokes authentic dramatic repercussions (753–9 → 1337–71). Moreover, the chorus of *Birds*, as has been noted, is not composed of human beings who occasionally compare themselves to animals, and act accordingly, but of animals, at times behaving like human or divine beings, yet throughout conceived coherently as animals: everything the chorus says remains, in almost all cases, intrinsically pertinent to birds. But this is the only time an Aristophanic coryphaeus – and in a context other than the parabasis – swears loyalty to his agreements with a character, 'provided that all the judges and all the spectators award the victory to me . . . and should I prove unfaithful, may I win by one vote alone' (445–7).

As soon as the parabasis ends, Hoopoe's guests reappear furnished with wings which have grown in the mean time through the agency of a certain root (cf. 654–5), and a ready remark of Peisetairos brings to an end one section of the comedy (801): this conclusion is reinforced by the non-reappearance of Hoopoe himself. At this stage, Hoopoe has fulfilled his task and Peisetairos' direct collaborators are the birds (cf. previously the conclusive lines 636–7, bearing in mind the disappearance of Demosthenes after the parabasis of *Knights*). 'What should be done now?', the coryphaeus asks Peisetairos. 'First of all, the city should be given a name, a grand and illustrious name; then, once that is done, a sacrifice should be performed to the gods' (809–11). As one can see, the city is conceived as already being born (cf., in fact, 922–3). 'Who will hold the pelargic walls of the city?' (832), asks the ever-impatient coryphaeus. The question reminds Peisetairos of the aerial walls meant to block out the Olympian gods. Hence, he dispatches Euelpides: 'go up to the air and lend a hand to the wall-makers . . . go where I'm sending you, my dear; without you, nothing I say will ever be done' (837–47).

In this manner, the deuteragonist is sent away – for good – for an excellent technical and civic motive (cf. *Lysistrata* 242–4), and until the walls are complete the comedy proceeds through scenes of anticipation which, step-by-step, interrupt and postpone Peisetairos' sacrifice to the new gods until, at a certain point, he decides to perform it indoors. This is followed by the second parabasis, in immediate succession to which Peisetairos announces the favourable outcome of the sacrifice and reveals his impatience for news regarding the walls. During the wait there appear, one by one, five earthly characters whom Peisetairos drives away: these characters bear little relation to the drama of the sovereignty of the birds, which might in part explain Peisetairos' astonishment at their untimeliness (cf. 922–3, 957, 1033–4). Yet, these characters, who appear in 904–1057, do serve to recall attention to the fact that in the comedy's background lie the earth and, in particular, Athens. In the words of Argument II.28–31: 'nor are the jestful scenes involving the Inspector, the Decree-scribe and the others in the least superficial: they lay bare a general determination to enrich oneself without scruple'.

After the second parabasis, 1058–1117, the basic plot is taken up again. From the walls arrives a Messenger-bird with an account in Herodotean style of the colossal structure's fabulous completion and on its heels a Sentinel-bird, come to sound the alarm: a winged Olympian deity has penetrated the kingdom of the birds, passing through its fortifications! This deity is Iris, in unknowing flight from Olympus to the earth to bid mankind make sacrifice to the gods (clearly, in Olympus, notice has at once been taken that things no longer function as they should): Peisetairos arrests the goddess, and sends her back with the news that now the birds are the lone sovereigns of the upper world, and to the birds alone must man make sacrifice (1122–69, 1170–1261).

The scene involving Iris is of interest from a dramaturgical point of view: Peisetairos' plan, once the walls had been completed, was to dispatch a herald to Olympus to reclaim the empire of Zeus (534–61, cf. 843). Now, obviously, it is Iris, the messenger of the gods in person, who will refer to Zeus the great novelty of a kingdom of divine birds and of the herald: in effect, nothing more is heard. Once, by means of this particular scene, an alternative zone of dramatic repercussion is installed – Olympus – it is from the earth, or rather Athens, that news arrives: a Messenger-bird presents himself to Peisetairos, sent down to earth from the walls (cf. 844, and previously, 561), and is followed soon afterwards by three earthbound ornithomaniac characters whom Peisetairos drives away (1271–1307, 1337–1469).

At this juncture, it would be natural to expect some reaction from the Olympians and Zeus (cf. 1259), but instead Prometheus appears. Prometheus does arrive from Olympus, yet only as the enemy of Zeus, to lend good counsel to Peisetairos in view of the fact that the gods, impeded by the walls, are set to dispatch a legation to Cloud-cuckoo-land (1494–1552).

With this scene – bearing all the characteristics of a *prologue* – the plot takes a new and exciting turn. The comic action regains its energy and henceforth extends exclusively towards Olympus: Peisetairos, who has emerged victorious from his dispute with the divine legation, is invited by the ambassadors to make his way skyward, so that Zeus may consign to him the ruler's sceptre for the birds and bestow on him as his wife an exquisite maiden, symbol of the royalty of Zeus, whose name is Regina. So, Peisetairos ascends to the sky carrying with him a wedding robe, and is accompanied, naturally, by a few servants (1565–93). Regina (Βασίλεια, cf. 1537 and 1753), cause of such distress to the scholars, is an *Aristophanic* deity, brought into being for theatrical ends (a simple appearance of Peisetairos, sceptre in hand, would have seemed inadequate in scenic terms; indeed, when Peisetairos appears beside Regina, the sceptre goes entirely unremarked) and to indicate that the marriage of the victor Peisetairos to his bride, Regina, is a replica of that of the one-time victor, Zeus (see 1731–42). Regina, in short, is a rejuvenated Hera.

The comedy, of exceptional length so far (almost 1,700 lines), now moves swiftly towards the exodos, the wedding feast. Following an extremely brief choral song, a Herald announces the couple's arrival at the city of the birds and goes on to direct the feast (cf. 1718–19, 1728b–1730, 1744–7). After the hymeneal, and the celebration of thunder and lightning, Peisetairos-Zeus invites the birds to follow him to Olympus, where lies his nuptial thalamus, and begs Regina to dance with him. The Utopian city of the birds has become the non-Utopian Olympus, the comedy's ultimate scenic destination.

The grandiose chief undertaking of *Birds* is contained within the space of a single day, and Peisetairos himself, quite stupefied, draws attention to its fabulous speed. The foundation of Cloud-cuckoo-land, the construction of the walls in the air and the visit of the earthly characters, etc. all take place within the same day: 'you're stunned that the walls have been built so quickly?' the coryphaeus enquires of Peisetairos, who has passed the time performing a sacrifice in honour of the new gods (cf. 848–1118). 'Yes, by the gods, and with good reason: to me it seems too good to be true!' (1164–7). Peisetairos had been just as stunned when confronted by the more than lightning speed with which the characters from earth had arrived in Cloud-cuckoo-land (cf. 957, 1033–4 and 922–3, which do not imply that nine days have passed by), yet he remains anxious to be informed of such prodigious novelties (cf. 1119–20, 1269–70). This paradoxical comedy unfolds, quite naturally, in accordance with an equally paradoxical suspension of time and distance. Scarcely have they been visited by the Messenger when the men arrive at once in Cloud-cuckoo-land, at such a speed that Peisetairos is afraid the wings intended for these immigrants might not be ready in time (cf. 1305–36).

The main action of *Birds*, therefore, encompasses a single day. Yet, during the stasimon 1470–94, a certain number of days pass by: during his visit to Cloud-cuckoo-land, Prometheus informs Peisetairos: '*since first* you colon-ized the air, mortals no longer sacrifice to the gods and *since that time* the thigh-smoke no longer rises towards us; instead we fast as at the Thesmophorian festivals . . . the barbarian gods, half-starved, threaten to come down in arms against Zeus' (1515–22, yet cf. 1230–3 immediately after the construction of the walls). As the gods must yield after a lengthy fast (cf. 186), the comedy's temporal rhythm assumes a realistic pace.

3 The land of Hoopoe and the city of the birds

The scenic façade of *Birds* is wooded and, at least in part, rocky: it is made up of a large copse and a steep cliff (ἡ λόχμη, 202, 207, 224, 265, ἡ ὕλη, 92; ἡ πέτρα, 54). Hoopoe's nest is imagined as lying behind the copse, at the point where the cliff is located (ἡ νεοττία, 642). The cliff is undoubtedly tall: the two compass-birds, for instance, lift their heads upwards to indicate to their masters the whereabouts of the land of Hoopoe (ἄνω τι φράζει, 50, ἄνω κέχηνεν, 51) and Euelpides beats a stone against the rock (53–9). 'The hoopoe', we are told by Aelianus, *De natura animalium* III.26, 'builds its nest in deserted zones, on rocky peaks.'

It is only after some time that the two wayfarers reach the scenic façade (cf. 49–52), since at the beginning they are struggling over rocky, impassable terrain: when the comedy opens they are climbing over a group of rocks, beyond which it is difficult to find a direct path (cf. 1–29). This can be inferred from lines 20–2, in which Euelpides says to his compass-chough: 'are you still searching for a place to lead us down there beyond the rocks? Here there's not the shadow of a path.' Climbing over the rocks at the very beginning of the comedy, Euelpides had enquired of his companion, following directly after him: 'straight on, you're saying, there where you can see that tree?'. And Peisetairos, coming into view himself, had displayed his compass-crow and exclaimed, 'but now, this one here is croaking to turn back!'. So they wander back and forth complaining (cf. 3, 20–3), and as Euelpides provides the spectators with the account, Peisetairos draws close to the copse and to the cliff in the background. The 'tree' mentioned at the beginning would definitely be positioned on the opposite side or, more precisely, near the other corridor; it would also be an isolated tree, distinct from the copse in the scenic façade, since in any case the moment is not yet ripe to focus attention on the façade.

The corridors, therefore, typically non-scenic elements of the theatre, are this time included in the landscape of the comedy, to render the scenic illusion complete. The fact that the entrance from which the two wayfarers appear is a rocky one was noted in his time, or so it seems, by Ioannes Tzetzes in his Argument to *Birds*, handed down by the Ambrosianus C 222 inf.: 'guided by a chough and a crow, amongst precipitous and rocky mountains they make their way to Tereus'. Argument III.15 to *Birds* implies, perhaps, an analogous interpretation: 'the scene is set *amongst the rocks*, amid the birds'. And Tzetzes again: 'the drama is set in Athens [= Argument I.6–7]; though others would have it amongst mountains and rocks, amid the birds: with this Tzetzes, too, concurs, distancing himself from the others'. This interpretation is probably based on line 20 of *Birds*.

The rough and deserted territory at which the two wayfarers arrive in their search for Hoopoe is imagined as a terrestrial zone outside Greece (409), over a thousand stades from Athens, to which it would be impossible to retrace one's steps (6, 9–11): a truly Utopian zone, then. To this territory Hoopoe calls all bird species, summoning them down from the most distant regions of the earth (cf. 230–54). Hence, this meeting place becomes *the* kingdom of the birds (cf. 326, 411, 418), while the scenic façade retains its value as the residence of Hoopoe (cf. 434–6, 642, 656–9). With the parabasis, Hoopoe's residence becomes that of his guests Peisetairos and Euelpides, and of Hoopoe nothing more is heard.

We come to the city of the birds. During the prologue, Peisetairos presents Hoopoe with his plan for a city of the birds, entailing the colonization and fortification of the air: the zone dividing the ether of the gods from the earth of mankind (172–93). Similarly, he expounds his plan to the birds: to secure a city for the birds alone, he explains, first all the air and space lying between ether and earth should be ringed with walls (550–2). After the parabasis, Peisetairos' first acts are to give the city a name – this name is Cloud-cuckoo-land (809–20) – and then to sacrifice to the new winged gods (810–11, cf. 848–1118). This implies that the city is *already* founded (cf. 922–3). Prior to the sacrifice, Peisetairos dispatches Euelpides into the air to be of help to the wall-makers (837–47, cf. also 1119–67). Hence, it is the orchestra (and the air above) which acquires the value of Cloud-cuckoo-land, while the walls themselves are constructed outside the theatre, in the air, authentic castles in the air. And on no account could this be otherwise.

Gradually, the characters from the earth-Athens and from the walls and sky begin to arrive in the orchestra = Cloud-cuckoo-land, and the space in which Peisetairos and the chorus are to be found comes to be defined as a 'city', the city of the birds, Cloud-cuckoo-land (cf. 921–3, 949–51, 957, 964–5, 1014, ἄστυ, 1022–4, 1034, 1169, 1277, 1280, 1313, 1316, 1351, 1565–6, 1708; with regard to the air above the orchestra, cf. 970, 995). The rocky and wooded environment left intact since the comedy's beginning easily acquires the scenic value of the city of the birds, since in a city meant for birds streets, houses and temples are hardly necessary (cf. 612–18, and also 181–4). Besides, should one desire to be pedantic, the city of the birds, in reality, is still located *on the earth*, as the land of Hoopoe: the poet Kinesias, for instance, arrives in search of wings which will allow him to fly amongst the clouds of the air (1382–5, 1409). It is only in the scene involving Iris that one has the sensation of an aerial city (cf. 1172–1268): but in that case the goddess is astride the flying-machine; better still, she is the comedy's only airborne presence. Yet Iris penetrates the airspace of Cloud-cuckoo-land without even noticing its fabulous walls!

With the parabasis, Peisetairos, as previously mentioned, takes possession of Hoopoe's residence. The scenic façade, rocky only in part, is without doubt uniformly decorated as a copse (cf., in particular, line 224): Hoopoe's rocky nest clearly occupies only one of the entrances to the stage. Immediately after the parabasis, Peisetairos finds himself in need of a priest for the sacrifice to the winged gods: 'to make sacrifice to the new gods, I'm going to call the priest to lead the procession. Slave! Slave! Bring the basket and the lustral water' (848–50). These lines are followed by a choral song (851–8). Then, Peisetairos reappears in the company of a priest (862), whilst on-stage a slave with the basket (864) and, silently, another bearing the lustral water also appear.

Where exactly did Peisetairos go to look for the priest? While the two slaves made their way to Hoopoe's nest – the abode of Peisetairos – to fetch the basket and lustral water (regarding the basket and water-pot cf. 43, and then 657), Peisetairos, whilst certainly entering the copse in the scenic façade also, used an entrance scenically neutral in value, other than that corresponding to Hoopoe's nest, and there found his priestly bird. The boundless kingdoms of the birds are therefore imagined to extend behind the copse (the raven-flautist, mocked in 859–61, undoubtedly appears from the copse). Not long before, Euelpides too had certainly vanished into the copse, proceeding through it to the air to direct the construction of the walls. And shortly afterwards it is significant that Peisetairos, on seeing two characters appear, may confidently announce that they have arrived from the walls (1119–21, 1168–9): clearly, they have appeared in the orchestra from the copse.

In the final part of the comedy it is through the copse that one arrives from Olympus and through the copse that one goes to Olympus. Prometheus and the divine legation certainly arrive from the copse, and Peisetairos enters it to make his way to the sky: δεῦρο in 1693 indicates the wooded zone to which Peisetairos is directing his steps behind Poseidon and Triballian, as Herakles goes to Peisetairos' residence to eat some little birds cooked previously in a kitchen improvised in the orchestra at 1579 (cf. 1689–92). Back from the sky, Peisetairos reappears in the orchestra-Cloud-cuckoo-land from the copse (see 1708), whilst it is natural that from within this forest, too, the Nuptial Herald should make his appearance in the orchestra. At the end of the comedy, the characters move in group towards the sky (cf. 1757), choosing as their path, naturally, the forest in the scenic façade. Hence, extending behind the 'open' scenic façade of *Birds*, one should imagine the aerial and etherial worlds of the birds and of the gods.

The characters coming from the earth-Athens appear, on the other hand, from the corridors: it is only in the case of characters arriving from Athens that the technical term προσέρχεσθαι is employed (1341, 1414), which elsewhere denotes a simultaneous appearance from the corridor (*Knights* 691, *Wasps* 1324 and 1508, *Peace* 1044 and 1209, *Lysistrata* 65 and 77, *Thesmophoriazusae* 923, *Plutus* 861 and 1038). The προσέρχεται in 1709, however, uttered by the Herald in relation to Peisetairos' return from Athens, is not intended to announce his *simultaneous* appearance (Peisetairos is still invisible: cf. 1718), but rather to announce an appearance of the winged Peisetairos *on foot*, not through the air.[3]

4 Hoopoe-Tereus and the parade of the twenty-eight birds

'How are you going to convoke the birds?', Peisetairos asks Hoopoe. 'Easy. I'll enter the copse at once, then wake up my little nightingale, and we'll call them together. The moment they hear our voices, they'll come running.' And Peisetairos: 'O most dear bird, I beseech you, don't delay! Enter the copse at once and wake the little nightingale' (201–8, iambic trimeters). Hoopoe enters the copse, and exhorts his bride to wake up and sing (209–22, anapaestic dimeters). Hoopoe's serenade is answered, from within the copse, by the sustained warbling of the nightingale (the playing of a flute). Euelpides cries out: 'O Zeus king, the voice of that little bird! How it's spread its sweetness throughout the copse!' And Peisetairos to Euelpides: 'Hey, you!' 'What's the matter?' 'Why don't you keep quiet?' 'Why?' 'The Hoopoe is about to sing again' (223–6, iambic trimeters). Clearly, Peisetairos has heard the nightingale start to warble again, and in fact Hoopoe's monody takes up just afterwards (227–63), accompanied undoubtedly by the nightingale. This implies that Hoopoe's programme has been respected to the word: 'then [I'll] wake up my little nightingale, and we'll call them together. The moment they hear our voices, they'll come running.' When the monody ends, Peisetairos asks Euelpides: 'can you see any birds?'. 'No, I can't, by Apollo, though I'm watching the sky with my mouth wide open'; 'in vain, therefore, or so it seems, did Hoopoe enter the copse to sing, imitating the plover' (264–6, iambic trimeters). Then, there follows a τοροτιξ τοροτιξ (267), which the scholia and manuscripts attribute either to Hoopoe or to the first of the birds to appear in the orchestra. This is followed by a dialogue between Peisetairos, Euelpides and Hoopoe commenting on the arrival of the birds, and the dialogue is then sustained by the coryphaeus of the birds and Hoopoe (268–309, 310–26, trochaic tetrameter catalectic).

Thus, having entered the copse at 208, Hoopoe has appeared in the orchestral space again between 267 and 269: this implies that after entering the copse to wake his little nightingale, he has sung his monody from within the copse as well, that monody in which he invites all the birds 'to assemble in this place here', 'to come here', 'here, here, here, here' (253, 229, 252, 259). 'Here': or, strictly speaking, into the copse, from which the spectators can hear him sing; while the birds, naturally, appear and assemble in the orchestral space in front of the copse. The motive for this slight incongruity resides in the fact that Hoopoe-third actor, even after waking his little nightingale, was still unable to leave the copse: in fact, Hoopoe's demanding virtuoso monody – the interpretative capacities which certain virtuoso passages required did not escape the notice of the scholiasts on *Birds* 228 and 237 – would not have been delivered by the third actor, but by a professional singer. The final remark of Peisetairos, on failing to see even one of the many birds that Hoopoe has invoked, mischievously conveys his astonishment at the fact that Hoopoe has summoned the birds while, strangely, remaining hidden inside the copse: 'in vain, therefore, or so it seems, did Hoopoe enter the copse to sing, imitating the plover'. The plover is a bird which hides itself away by day, to emerge exclusively at night. Naturally, the serenade to the little nightingale would have been entrusted to this singer as well: a future choreutes, perhaps. The difference in voice between Hoopoe-third actor and Hoopoe-the singer was calculated to pass unobserved. What was essential was that these songs, precisely because they were performed back-stage, should have been performed perfectly, in order to leave the public all ears. In other comedies, the delivery of back-stage lyrical passages is assigned to the chorus (*Clouds*, *Frogs*). In 406–30, however, when it falls to Hoopoe to sustain a sung stichomythia with the coryphaeus, the third actor will suffice, since the rhythms are simple and the actor, as the song progressed, could have taken his cue from the coryphaeus. The third actor of *Birds* will have other short passages to sing further on.

As regards the invisible nightingale, the bride of Hoopoe-Tereus, it has previously been mentioned that her far from brief solo between 222 and 223 is performed by a flute (cf. καλλιβόας αὐλός, 682–3; the flute employed is not the modern one, but closer to our clarinet or oboe). The style of this solo would not have been 'free', but adapted presumably to the vocal style of the preceding serenade of Hoopoe, just as the style of the new instrumental solo between 224 and 225 (and between 226 and 227 also?) would have pre-figured that of the succeeding monody of Hoopoe. It is certain that the monody itself would have been accompanied throughout by the nightingale-flute: not only was this accompaniment on the programme (cf. 204), but it can also be deduced from line 253, in which Hoopoe sings: '*we shall assemble* in this place all the races of the birds'. The vocal combinations in the course of the monody, τιοτιοτιοτιοτιοτιοτιοτιο in 237, τριοτο τριοτο τοτοβριξ, and others similar in 243, 260 and 262 (cf. also 267), are particularly suited to the accompaniment of the nightingale-flute. During the strophe and antistrophe of the parabasis, there recur the combinations τιοτιοτιοτιοτιοτιοτιοτιγξ (738, 741, 743, 752, 770, 773, 775, 784) and τοτοτοτοτοτοτοτοτοτιγξ (747, 779). Hence, there is every reason to assume that the Nightingale, made to emerge from Hoopoe's nest close to the parabasis to sound a prelude to the anapaests (684), accompanies the strophe and antistrophe as well: the nightingale, says the chorus, is 'the companion of all my songs'. At the end of the parabasis, the Nightingale perhaps disappears again, since in the choral songs which follow there are none of those combinations so suited to the accompaniment of a nightingale-flute. The Nightingale is a beautiful female adorned with golden jewellery (668–70). Euelpides would most willingly give her a kiss, were it not that the Nightingale, obviously, is wearing a beaked mask. This Euelpides peels off (cf. 671–4), permitting the beautiful flautist to play her instrument with greater ease. The Nightingale is no longer the back-stage 'character' of the serenade and monody, but a flautist in flesh and blood.

As we have already seen, Peisetairos is disappointed at the non-appearance of the birds invoked by Hoopoe; and, at this precise juncture, as if to demonstrate his goodwill, Hoopoe lets loose a τοροτιξ τοροτιξ (267), a final high-pitched call to the birds in their own language: cf. previously ἐποποποῖ κτλ. in 227, ἰὼ ἰώ in 228, τιοτιο κτλ. in 237, τριοτο τριοτο τοτοβριξ in 243, τοροτοροτοροτοροτιξ in 260 and τοροτορολιλιλιξ at the end of the monody. The τοροτιξ τοροτιξ in 267 has to be attributed to Hoopoe, still buried in the copse, since it repeats in a simplified manner the calls of 260 and 262; and this final call, one can be sure, would have been accompanied also by the nightingale-flute. The τοροτιξ τοροτιξ, therefore, is the final vocal and instrumental display on the part of the invisible couple, in immediate response to which a bird at last appears in the orchestra (268). To the latter, a number of manuscripts and the majority of modern editors attribute the τοροτιξ τοροτιξ of 267, an attribution made additionally improper by the fact that it would seem more appropriate were this bird, and the three which follow it, to remain silent, and so too the remaining twenty-four. The parade of the birds is a purely visual display, made up of colour and movement, designed to succeed the purely aural display of the serenade, the monody and the Nightingale's warbling. This will be discussed at a later stage.

Hoopoe's lengthy sojourn in the copse can also be justified for a technical reason, since on his reappearance in the orchestra he is wearing a new costume. Hoopoe, at this point Tereus, appears rigged out in the panoply of the warlike King Tereus (cf. *Lysistrata* 563) and, like the kings of tragedy, is probably accompanied by a bodyguard: the introduction of the panoply becomes evident to the reader when Hoopoe, confident of a peaceful resolution of the agon between the chorus and the two wayfarers, gives orders to his bodyguard to return his armour to the nest, and later bids his hoplites lay down their arms and return to their homes (434–6, 448–50; the bodyguard and the hoplites are discussed further on). Hoopoe-Tereus had been woken up by his servant in the course of a snooze (cf. 81–4) and had appeared before the two wayfarers at breakneck speed, in his dressing-gown, as it were. Now, as a solemn assembly of all the birds is set to begin, Hoopoe – in a sense, the king of the birds (cf. 385) – takes advantage of his sojourn in the nest to don his solemn panoply, and from this moment onwards Hoopoe-Tereus acts and speaks with unusual gravity. Now he is truly the 'daring rupestrian bird attired in panoply' from the tragic fragment attributed by ancient sources to Aeschylus and by the moderns to Sophocles or Philocles. In Aristophanes, in effect, there is a kind of inverse metamorphosis relative to that of myth and tragedy: here, it is Hoopoe who becomes Tereus. When Hoopoe reappears attired in panoply, Peisetairos and Euelpides have no time to comment on his new dress, since they are distracted by the first marvellous bird to appear. From the apostrophe οὗτος αὐτός in 270 alone, however, it is clear that they are addressing a Hoopoe newly invested with dignity. In the second part of the comedy, Peisetairos has a panoply already at hand (cf. 1363–9), and as to where these arms so suddenly appear from, the scholars are in a state of persistent enquiry. One is dealing with the panoply Hoopoe-Tereus ordered returned to his nest, which at this stage has become the residence of Peisetairos.[4]

The purely vocal display given back-stage by Hoopoe and the Nightingale is followed on-stage by an exclusively visual display: the mute parade of the twenty-eight different birds listed in 268–304.

The entrance of the twenty-eight birds takes place in two clearly distinct phases: first there appear *four* birds, then *twenty-four*. The first four appear one at a time, each at a distance from the other, drawing comments made in blithe stupor (268–73, 274–8, 279–86, 287–90; in 291–3, a general comment on the entire four). The others appear *en bloc* at the entrance to the orchestral space, and first are remarked on apprehensively as a group (294–6), then individually listed: the first four are identified and listed one by one by Peisetairos and Euelpides (297a, 297b, 298a, 298b); the next two are announced by Hoopoe (299b, 301a); while the names of the remaining eighteen are given by Hoopoe once more in lines 302–4. Each line makes mention of six birds: in 305–9 there follows a general comment on the entire group, delivered by Peisetairos and Euelpides (on the supposed 'blackbirds' of 306, see section 6 below).

'With the partridge [the bird mentioned in 297a] begins the enumeration of the twenty-four elements going to make up the chorus, leaving out the birds mentioned previously. The tragic chorus is composed of fifteen elements. Counting from there you will find the twenty-four elements forming the comic chorus': the scholiast on *Birds* 297. It is certain that the four birds mentioned in 268–93 are indeed excluded from the count: not only has it emerged from other sources that the comic chorus is always composed of twenty-four elements (Pollux IV.109 and scholion on *Acharnians* 211; cf. scholion on *Knights* 589), but when the twenty-four birds of 294–304 appear in the orchestra they alone display characteristics typical of the comic chorus: (1) the twenty-four birds inspire fear in the actors (294–6, cf. also 308–9), a typical feature to which attention was drawn at the end of section 11 of chapter 3; (2) when they appear, there is mention of the εἴσοδος (296), brought up in other comedies only in relation to the chorus, a factor discussed at the beginning of section 11 of chapter 3; (3) the twenty-four birds make their appearance *en bloc*, in accordance with the norms regarding the tragic and comic choruses: cf. *Birds* 294–5 with, at least, *Thesmophoriazusae* 280–1, given that in that comedy, too, the chorus appears silently.

The scholars who exclude from the count the four birds of 268–93 generally maintain that they are either flautists or dancers. Yet, the text of the comedy neither implies nor explicitly requests music or a dance. And if these birds are indeed flautists, why are there absolutely no remarks pertaining to flautists, as in the case of the Nightingale-flautist of 658–84 and the Raven-flautist of 859–61? The scholars favourable to the idea of the four flautist-birds cite the τοροτιξ τοροτιξ in 267, and also line 307: but the τοροτιξ τοροτιξ, as we have already seen, belongs to Hoopoe (and to Nightingale), while 307, 'how they chirrup and run around squawking', does not imply that the chirrups and squawks of the twenty-four choreutai-birds are produced by musical instruments or, more precisely, by the instruments of the four supposed flautist-birds of 268–93. Besides, is it really necessary to consider that instrumentalists might have been necessary during the prologue to imitate the sound of the crow (cf. 2, 24)? And would it really be appropriate to put four flautist-birds on-stage, when in the previous scene one has continually exalted a Nightingale-flautist positioned back-stage?

The basic function of these four birds is probably that most obvious one of providing spectacle on-stage in anticipation of the appearance of the chorus. The chorus of *Birds*, like that of *Clouds*, is one which hails from afar and must first assemble, a chorus whose sudden appearance would seem incongruous (when it appears, Hoopoe says that he has been there 'for some time': 313); it is not found directly at hand, like the choruses of *Knights* and *Peace* the very moment they are called upon for succour. In his monody, Hoopoe has called together the birds of the fields and gardens, of the mountain peaks, marshy vales and humid Marathonian plain, the birds of the seas, and separately the quail and little owl (cf. 230–7, 238–9, 240–3, 244–7, 250–4; 248–9 and 261): as this variety of common species is assembling, four of a more distinctive kind parade through the orchestra, drawing cries and incredulous remarks from Euelpides and Peisetairos. The first two are 'barbarians', the Crimson Flamingo and the Median, while the other two invite comparison with figures of Athenian fame: Hoopoe-the nephew with Kallias-the nephew, the Crimson Glutton with Kleonimus. All four (or the second, third and fourth at least) have in common a tuft on their heads resembling the helmet worn by the hoplites (291–3): Hoopoe, one should remember, has three of them (94). Might not these four birds, who without explicitly being invoked appear at once and remain in silence, be the bodyguard of Hoopoe-Tereus, now rigged out in panoply, the bodyguard dwelling close to his nest? One should not forget that one of them is Hoopoe's nephew. Might they not be the hoplites whom Hoopoe-Tereus invites to return home in 448–50, to return, that is, into the copse (nowhere is it actually stated that they appear from the corridor), close to which the second and third at least – the Median and Hoopoe-the nephew – apparently arrange themselves on the rocks (275–6, 279), perhaps on the rocks lying close to Hoopoe's rocky nest?

That the four birds are the bodyguard of Hoopoe-Tereus is naturally a hypothesis (although, at this stage, Hoopoe has two servants, as demonstrated by 434), but one thing remains certain: the four birds do not form part of the chorus; they also bear none of the characteristics typical of flautists and dancers, and throughout the rest of the comedy are never heard of again. Thus, it is not in the least over-hasty to affirm that their function is that of providing spectacle on-stage until the chorus has assembled and appeared, and that they have the additional function, thrilling as indeed they are, of balancing an upcoming parodos on the part of the choreutai which is bereft of verbal emotion, yet offers in recompense the parade of twenty-four choreutai-birds, each one different from the other (Eupolis, for one, had already presented the choreutai of *Cities* each as a single and distinct city). Aristophanes' unaggressive parodoi are always governed by an appropriate dramaturgical or scenic technique: in *Wasps*, *Peace* and *Frogs*, for instance, the choreutai are temporarily accompanied by elements extraneous to the chorus.[5]

5 Iris' flight

In *Birds*, neither a single bird nor the winged Peisetairos ever takes to flight: this implies that the flying-machine never comes into operation, either for Peisetairos or for the birds. Some scholars would deny its services to the goddess, Iris, too: otherwise, they claim, Aristophanes' splendid fantasy of the birds would be shattered, since one would discover that his birds are unable to fly. But this is precisely one of the episode's aims: to present Iris, the Olympian deity, in tranquil flight through the celebrated walls – which she, for one, has failed to notice – while the mythomaniac birds, the new gods, are unable to lift themselves upwards from the ground. Other scholars observe that the text, in contrast to that of *Peace*, provides no explicit evidence for the use of the flying-machine. But Iris' airborne appearance is a natural phenomenon, and in flight she relies on independent means (cf. also *Birds* 575): a goddess such as she cannot but appear in flight. Hence, to draw explicit attention to the use of a machine, in this context, would seem inappropriate: in *Peace* the light-hearted mention of the machine-operator is intended as a parody of Euripides' *Bellerophon*. However, the text does contain more than one implicit warning to the operator and, above all, clear indications regarding the mid-air flight of Iris. Let us examine it in more detail.

Iris appears at 1118, and the preparations are gradually made for her appearance. 'A short time ago a god flew through the gates of our airspace ... we don't know who he is, but that he had wings, of this at least we are sure' (1172–7). Again, in implicit warning to the operator to stand prepared: 'the god can't be far away; in fact, he must be around the place somewhere already ... take up your slings and bows ... keep a watch on the air, so that a god may not pass through unobserved' (1184–5, 1193–5). The spectators are obviously being prepared for an exceptional aerial appearance, not for an appearance on foot from within the forest (whence the other Olympian deities are to appear further on). The warning grows ever more explicit, and the language increasingly tragic in tone: 'each of you glance around with vigilant eye, since by now, close at hand, can be heard the winged and whirling hum of an aerial god' (1196–8). The moment these words are uttered, Iris appears in mid-air. Peisetairos' reaction contains fresh instructions for the operator, this time to arrest the machine: 'hey, you, where, oh where are you flying, where? Stay still, don't move, stop right there, hold up your course! Who are you? From what land do you come? You must tell us from where you've come' (1199–1201). This is followed by an·alteration between the goddess suspended in mid-air – speaking frequently in the tragic manner – and Peisetairos. The fact that the goddess is suspended above the ground, and is also inaccessible, is confirmed by lines 1205–6: 'why doesn't one of the birds go up there and catch her with a stroke of its wings (ἀναπτόμενος)?'. Other expressions relative to the flight are to be found in lines 1229–30: ναυστολεῖς, for example, is a term employed elsewhere solely in relation to the flight of Trygaeus and of Perseus in *Peace* 126 and *Thesmophoriazusae* 1101 respectively. In 1258, when the dialogue is about to end, Peisetairos gives the operator an implicit warning to put the machine into action again: 'Why don't you just run off? And quickly! εὐράξ, πατάξ'. These two sonorous exclamations are effectively the operator's cue, and at 1260–1 Iris disappears in flight behind the scenic façade.

> In εὐράξ there is εὖρος, or 'get away'; in πατάξ, rather than πατάσσω, as has been repeated following the example of one ancient commentator, there is πάτος, and consequently the idea of using one's legs. The fact that Iris is in the air and equipped with wings adds a note of drollery to the exclamation, which the airborne Iris takes as a grave offence (cf. 1259).

In relation to the question πλοῖον ἢ κυνῆ, which Peisetairos puts to Iris in lines 1203, the same scholar has noted the following:

> it is quite possible that the species of sail boat in which the actor is located, perhaps on foot, suspended on the ropes of the flying-winch, is being compared to an unclassifiable ship. And since κυνῆ, etymologically, is a dog-skin, it is not in the least improbable that the term is being used ironically to indicate an undefinable object tossed upon air or water.

The use of the thunder and lightning machines in *Birds* 1748–52 is just as natural as that of the thunder-machine in *Clouds*. The two machines are put into action at line 1748, after an implicit warning given to the operator in lines 1744–7.[6]

6 Characters, actors and extras

The action of *Birds* involves 22 characters: nowhere else in Aristophanes are so many characters to be found (*Acharnians*, 21, *Lysistrata*, 19), and nowhere else are the three main actors so constantly employed. For one of the characters, an amateur actor is required, although an extra would be sufficient, too:

first actor, uttering around 570 lines, of which a couple are lyrical: Peisetairos, 2–675, 801–50, 859–1057, 1118–1469, 1495–1552, 1579–1693, 1755–62;

second actor, uttering around 435 lines, of which about 40 are lyrical in 904–53, 1372–1409 and 1706–47: Euelpides, 1–674, 801–46, Priest, 863–88 (one trimeter, the rest in prose), Poet, 904–53, Meton, 992–1019, Decree-seller, 1035–54, Messenger from the Walls, 1122–63, Iris, 1202–59, Kinesias, 1372–1409, Prometheus, 1494–1551, Poseidon, 1565–1692, Nuptial Herald, 1706–47;

third actor, uttering around 305 lines, of which around 70 are lyrical (although the 50 or so lyrical lines given over to Hoopoe's serenade and monody are most probably entrusted to a singer: cf. section 4 above): Hoopoe's Servant, 60–84, Hoopoe, 92–205, 209–67 back-stage, 271–675 (with around ten lyric lines), Oracle-monger, 959–90, Inspector, 1021–31, 1046–52, Sentinel, 1170–85, Herald from Earth, 1271–1307, Unnatural Son, 1337–71 (with a few lyrical lines), Sycophant, 1410–66 (with a few lyrical lines), Herakles, 1574–1692;

amateur actor, Triballian, 1615b, 1628b–1629a, 1678–1679a.

Naturally, the distribution of parts between the second and third actors here, as in other comedies, is purely empirical. Yet it is not in the least improbable that a character such as Euelpides, who opens the comedy with the first actor, remains active after the parabasis and, all told, utters 180 lines, would have been entrusted to the second actor rather than to the third. To the latter, therefore, is assigned the part of Hoopoe, who – including the roughly 50 lines of the serenade and monody – utters almost 150 lines. The third actor might also have been given the role of the Priest in 863–88, and that of the Nuptial Herald in the exodos. Besides the trimeters 1706–19, the Herald also delivers the lyrical lines 1726–30 and 1743–7; as mentioned in section 2 above, he directs the first section of the exodos.[7]

Flautists: the activity of the exceptional nightingale-flautist, Procne (cf. section 4 above), emerges explicitly from the text, and also that of the raven-flautist, 'Chaeris' (cf. 858–61).

Extras: the most important include the four birds of lines 268–93, and in the exodos the very beautiful Regina. Peisetairos frequently gives commands, to Servant-birds, obviously: 463, 464, 656–7 (Xanthias and Manodorus?), 850 (cf. also 864), 933–47 (this Servant, wearing a tunic and a cassock, might be the human Servant from the prologue: cf. 71–5), 1186 (πᾶς ὑπηρέτης, or rather the servants), 1187, 1311–29 (Manes), 1579–80 (at least four), 1637 (cook), 1693. Regarding the order Hoopoe gives his two servants in lines 434–6, see section 4 above. In the list of Servant-birds, I have included Xanthias and Manodorus, invoked by Peisetairos in 656–7: these two are unquestionably birds (in the service of Hoopoe), not a pair of slaves who might have appeared at the beginning of the comedy with the two protagonists; like Manes in 1311–29, they are playfully ascribed the common names borne by terrestrial slaves (cf. *Birds* 523). During the exodos there probably appears a Torch-

163

bearer at least (cf. 1716–17), and also a number of Servants, to whom Peisetairos entrusts the insignia of thunder and lightning (in 1760 Peisetairos' arms, or wings, are free).

After the listing of the twenty-four different birds in lines 297–304, Peisetairos exclaims, 'Oh, the birds! Oh, the blackbirds! (. . . τῶν ὀρνέων . . . τῶν κοψίχων'). It is important to clarify that the latter are not extras appearing behind the chorus: here, 'blackbirds' is intended as generically as ὄρνεα itself. The term κόψιχος is used in relation to the birds' razor-sharp beaks, in so far as it makes one think of κόπτειν (cf. 342, 365), just as γαμψώνυχες in 359 is not intended to distinguish a group of choreutai-birds furnished particularly with claws, but to all the birds, this time feared for their claws.

The choreutai-birds, and the others, wear beaked masks (99, ῥάμφος for Hoopoe; 348, ῥύγχος for the choreutai), and their arms are made up as wings (cf. 1760–1; cf. the famous London black-figure jug B 509, from the end of the sixth century). They probably give the impression of being rather bald, the imperfection of their make-up justified by the fact that, in winter, birds tend to moult (cf. 105–6; although the action of the comedy might easily be imagined as taking place at the beginning of spring: cf. 683). The Messenger from the Walls is also a bird: cf. 1123, 'where's our leader Peisetairos?'.

9

LYSISTRATA

1 The contest of *Lysistrata*

Lysistrata was performed under the Kallias who succeeded Kleocritus as archon – in the year 411, that is to say – and was produced by Kallistratos: Argument I.34–5. No information has survived regarding the place-list and contest. However, the dramaturgy and setting of *Lysistrata* are those of a comedy intended for the Dionysian theatre, as observed in chapter 1. Similarly, its panhellenic propaganda, which is conveyed amongst other means by an abundance of non-Athenian characters and extras (from prologue to exodos more than a hundred lines are in the Laconian dialect), is better suited to the contests of the Dionysia than to those of the Lenaia, which were attended by the Athenians alone.[1]

Thesmophoriazusae must also have been entered into competition at the Dionysia of 411: this is discussed in section 2 of the following chapter.

2 *Lysistrata*'s two-edged and co-ordinated plot

'As here we contrive to withhold ourselves from our husbands, in order to constrain them to make peace', says Lysistrata to her young Athenian and foreign companions in the prologue, 'the older women, under the pretence of making a sacrifice, will seize the Acropolis to prevent our men from sustaining the war with the treasure of the Parthenon. They've already received their orders' (cf. 170–9). 'What's all this din?', demands the Spartan Lampito of Lysistrata towards the end of the prologue. 'As I told you, the women have already occupied the Acropolis. Go on, Lampito, go to Sparta and arrange things well in your own land ... and we'll join the other women in the Acropolis to help them post the bars', commands Lysistrata in 240–6. For these motives of solidarity, Lysistrata suddenly elects the Acropolis – which has been occupied in the mean time by the older Athenian women in a back-stage action aimed at blockading the treasure – the fixed scenic base of the younger women she has assembled at her home and, not without effort, induced to go on a pacifist sex-strike.

The permanent base of the ensuing action of the comedy is established, therefore, by back-stage characters, and accepted by the women of the prologue through the agency of Lysistrata. This reflects the complex nature of the double-edged plot devised, prior to the outset of the dramatic action, by Lysistrata (cf. 26–7): to restore the Greeks to a state of peace, Lysistrata must not only deny the men access to the State treasure, but also combat the weakness and incomprehension of the women. With the supposed aim, therefore, of bringing help to the women occupying the zone containing the State treasure, she simultaneously makes the Acropolis a place of enclosure for the younger women, recalcitrant in the face of the sex-strike (cf. also 706–80). Naturally, on-stage the incongruity of a sex-strike aimed at men at war far from Athens would have passed unobserved (cf. 99–110 with 149–54, and also 763–4 and 880–1).

Whilst the Acropolis, which clearly formed part of the opening scenery (cf. section 5 below), in this way becomes the scenic base of the characters who, earlier in the prologue, were to be found in the ephemeral residence of Lysistrata, it is the back-stage manœuvre involving the blockading of the treasure which occupies the scenes leading to the parabasis. The theme of the prologue, the sex-strike which Lysistrata imposes then and there on her companions, re-emerges and begins to function dramatically in the second part of the comedy (during the parabasis a number of days pass by): some time obviously had to pass before the sex-strike might have produced any real effect on the men of Athens, who in any case are left in the dark about it, as the only news which reaches them is that the women have occupied and barred up the Acropolis.

Hence, the two co-ordinated pacifist initiatives promoted by Lysistrata lead also to co-ordinated dramatic repercussions: while awaiting the outcome of the secret sexual obstructionism established on-stage during the prologue, the drama gives way to the overt political obstructionism begun with the occupation of the Acropolis, an event organized prior to the dramatic action by Lysistrata which occurs back-stage during the prologue.

'Don't you think the men will come back against us immediately?', Kalonike asks Lysistrata as the striking women are making their way towards the Acropolis, to which Lysistrata replies, 'little do I care for them; they will come neither with all their threats nor all their fire to make us open the gates of the Acropolis, if not on the terms we have imposed' (247–51). Henceforth, the comedy's title-character is only moderately present on-stage: suffice to say that, although Lysistrata is the comedy's one main character, after the prologue she delivers no more than 230 lines. She is bound, let us say, above all else, to remain in the Acropolis at the side of the women of Greece until the men of Greece have decided in favour of peace.

The location of the protagonist and her companions is fundamental to the comedy and hence governs the stage-action, which is in large part sustained: at times by the chorus (subdivided for this precise reason into a semi-chorus of

Old Athenian Men hostile to Lysistrata and a semi-chorus of Old Athenian Women favourable to her; the parodos 254–386 is left entirely to these two semi-choruses), and at times by male Athenian and Spartan characters of extra-scenic provenance. Both the appearance and the subsequent action of the metaparabatic characters have as their origin the strategy of the sex-strike, whereas the immediate appearance of the hostile semi-chorus – opposed soon afterwards by the semi-chorus of Old Women – and that, subsequently, of the Proboulos are provoked by the pre-dramatic initiative of Lysistrata whereby the Acropolis has been occupied in order to blockade the State treasure.

Hence, the Old Men appear, with two olive trunks on their shoulders and in their hands pans filled with burning coals and a branch serving as a torch, for in the city they have heard it said that the Acropolis is in the hands of the women (254–318). Then the Old Women come flocking to the scene bearing amphoras filled with water, for in the city they have heard it said that certain old men would like to put the women on the Acropolis to the torch (319–49). Then the Old Men and Old Women collide and the Old Men come off the worse (350–86), and in the end there appears a Proboulos with his archers to draw money from the State treasure (387–430). The motivation of the Proboulos is belated and weary (423), and no less belated and weary, and scenically ill-conceived, his appearance as a whole; and for the Old Men, who would have been twelve in number like the Old Women following them, what might the spectators have thought when they saw only twelve choreutai, not twenty-four? While they would undoubtedly have expected another semi-chorus to appear eventually, they would perhaps not have thought of a female one, for the liberated women of Athens, young and old alike, at that point were imagined enclosed within the Acropolis. One should note that on first seeing the Old Women, the Old Men exclaim: 'what an unexpected sight for us, a swarm of women coming from the city in relief!'. And the Old Women: 'What is it that makes you fart at seeing us? Do we really seem so many to you? And yet what you see here is no more than the ten-thousandth part of us!' (352–5).

Lysistrata, who had not emerged from the Acropolis to face the Old Men (cf. 247–51; the action of the semi-chorus of Old Men is conceived exclusively as a function of that of the semi-chorus of Old Women), emerges instead to face the Proboulos when, with the help of his archers, he attempts to force the gates (here, the semi-chorus of Old Women keeps still, since the character of the Proboulos is conceived as a function of that of Lysistrata and of her companions in the Acropolis and it is not from the semi-chorus of Old Women but rather from the women of the Acropolis that Lysistrata, further on, is to appeal for support). The Old Men and the Proboulos alike are ignorant of the ultimate objective behind the women's occupation of the Acropolis (the Old Women, on the other hand, are not: cf. 342–5), and so Lysistrata is given the chance to expound polemically the women's designs and motives: they have occupied the Acropolis in order to secure the State treasure, claiming that in any case it is entirely unnecessary to make war and that were the men finally to listen to the women's most sensible ideas, the city's problems would be resolved, those women who are the Athenian soldiers' mothers and wives and whom the men, busy with their wars, leave alone too much (486–607). The old Proboulos retires, humiliated and exposed to ridicule, perhaps, yet still not convinced, and Lysistrata re-enters the Acropolis not having said a word about the sex-strike (608–13).

The agonistic parabasis of the two semi-choruses, which begins directly afterwards (lines 614–705), takes up from, and is also profoundly influenced by, the political and feminist arguments aired by Lysistrata during her exposition of the motives for the occupation of the Acropolis. Towards the end of the parabasis, however, the coryphaea makes animated mention of the Spartan Lampito, who on-stage during the prologue had been Lysistrata's sole ally in her contrivance of the sex-strike. The mention of Lampito might, on a well-nigh technical level, be read as a suggestion to the spectators that the dramatic thread established with the seizing of the Acropolis and the blockading of the State treasure has come to an end. And so it has: of the seizing of the Acropolis and of the State treasure throughout what remains of the comedy nothing more is heard, and when Lysistrata appears on-stage immediately after the parabasis, she reinstates at once the comic motif of the sex-strike.

During the parabasis, as we shall see further on, five days pass by (881, cf. 725, 758–66, 865–9, 894–9). Hence, the sex-strike may begin to function dramatically, first on the women of the Acropolis, who themselves have promoted it (706–80), then on the unknowing men of Athens (829–979; in 839–41 there is a reference back to the oath made during the prologue), and prior to that on the knowing men of Sparta (980–1013; in 998, the mention of Lampito): in the course of this last scene, which is analysed in section 4 below, the representatives of the two cities also decide to elect delegations to negotiate a truce with the women. The two semi-choruses had soon adapted themselves to the erotic motif (781–828), and at once the Old Men, like the men of Athens and Sparta, yield to the graces of the Old Women and invite them to form a single group (1014–42), at which point this reconciled chorus, its cares set aside, turns playfully towards the spectators, men and women alike (1043–71; in 1043–7 the chorus gives warning that it will provide no political satire).

In erotic anticipation of a truce the delegations from Athens and Sparta arrive (1072–1107), and Lysistrata reappears in the orchestra to direct the culminating scene, the end for which she had originally promoted the sex-strike: since the parabasis, she has been present only in 708–80 and 828–64. She orders Reconciliation – an intensely lovely girl, who has to be found in the Acropolis, evidently, as a living personification of the conciliatory desires of the women of Athens and Sparta – to treat the Spartans and Athenians gracefully, reminds the men of their past fraternity-in-arms and lends them counsel for peace in a political language rendered comic by the persistent sexual and erotic allusions of the delegates. Now that the Athenians and Spartans are reconciled, they should come to feast in the Acropolis, and there exchange oaths, retake their women and then return to their homes (1108–88). It is from this invitation made by Lysistrata that the exodos of the comedy is to take its form.

3 The characters in the exodos

Now, then, since all the rest has been carried out well, O Spartans, lead you off these women here, and you others, these here. Let man stand by woman and woman by man, and having danced in honour of the gods for these happy events, let us seek in the future not to err again (. . . ὀρχησάμενοι θεοῖσιν εὐλαβώμετα τὸ λοιπὸν αὖθις μὴ 'ξαμαρτάνειν ἔτι).

Before these six trimeters, 1273–8, in the Ravenna and Parisian manuscripts stands the siglum of Lysistrata; Argument I.33 and the scholiast on 1274 think of Lysistrata too. Wilamowitz, in his 1927 commentary, assigns the six trimeters to a male character whom he defines as a Prytanis (and whom I – as explained further on – define as an Ambassador). To this Prytanis Wilamowitz also assigns 1295, 'Come, O Spartan, let's hear a song . . . [the clausula is corrupt]', a line which the Parisian manuscript assigns to the chorus (in the Ravenna the siglum of Lysistrata takes in 1279–95 also). Since in 1245–6 a male character had said, 'yes, take up the flute, by the gods, it's a joy for me to watch you dance', Wilamowitz deduced that the invitations and instructions in 1273–8 and in 1295 must also pertain to this character, the closing ceremony's sole director. This implies that Lysistrata herself is set aside, albeit her presence may be required. However, since it is not she who has the Spartans and Athenians take their oaths, at this point there are no further orders for her to give. This, in any case, is the opinion of Wilamowitz.

In 1928, Victor Coulon accepted the sigla proposed by Wilamowitz, but in 1956 recommended that 1273–8 and 1295 should be left to Lysistrata, since in 1273–8 she would effectively repeat what she had said in 1186–1187a (you have spoken well, Spartans and Athenians; go now and purify yourselves to allow us women to entertain you in the Acropolis; there should you exchange oaths and guarantees) 'and then each of you, having retaken his woman, is free to leave'.

Certainly, to have the protagonist of the comedy speak at least once during the exodos might seem a temptation to many, one which the indications provided by Wilamowitz in favour of a male voice have been insufficient to remove. Yet in order to facilitate this temptation one would be obliged to correct the text, to correct εὐλαβώμεθα, that is, in line 1277, as did at least two nineteenth-century translators without comment: 'habet Acht' (Droysen), 'habt Acht, dass ihr' (Seeger). And this is the problem: all the rest might even be assigned to Lysistrata, were it not that '*let us seek* in the future not to err again' is apt only on the lips of men who are guilty and now aware of their transgression, or more precisely on those of the Athenians and Spartans. The exhortation does not lend itself to being interpreted as that of a blameless woman meekly including herself and all the other Athenian and Spartan women amongst those who are in the wrong. Shortly before, a Spartan, singing in the Laconian dialect for the Athenians and at once for his fellow-Spartans (cf. 1244), had said:

> O Huntress, come here, virgin goddess, here to this truce, and keep us united for a long time: let there reign a fertile friendship between us thanks to our pacts, and *let us cease* to play the cunning foxes. Come here, come here, O virgin Huntress.
>
> (1262–72)

Let us cease – Spartans and Athenians – to play the cunning foxes. And the other: let us try, Athenians and Spartans, not to fall into the same errors in the time to come. At the moment of the two Athenian semi-choruses' reconciliation, the coryphaeus of the Old Men, admitting defeat, had said to the coryphaea of the Old Women: 'all right, now will I make peace with you, and in the future do you no harm, or from you receive any harm. Come, let's form a single group and together intone a song' (1040–3). As they yielded to the female graces, the men in that case had promised the women that they would put an end to their discourtesy, yet expected as much from them (and the women had been invited to form a group with the men); here, having already yielded to the women and agreed to a truce, they exhort each other in turns to abandon cunning and to avoid the same errors in future (and the women are invited to come to the side of the men).

'There, in the Acropolis, exchange oaths and guarantees, and then each of you, having retaken his woman, is free to leave', Lysistrata had told the delegations from Sparta and Athens as she led them into the Acropolis: in the Acropolis, therefore, the Athenians and Spartans had exchanged oaths and guarantees, and in effect sealed a pact of friendship (cf. 1264, 1269). Men of Athens are already on-stage at 1216; the men of Sparta do not appear until 1241 (and with them most probably the women of Athens and Sparta, and some other Athenians). The spectators, who have seen nothing of the secret ceremony in the Acropolis, now that the Spartans have also appeared on-stage, must be allowed to hear from the men's concordant voices that the truce has indeed been sealed, and to relive the atmosphere surrounding their exchange of oaths. Up stands a Spartan, then, to invite a flautist to accompany his song and dance for the Athenians and Spartans (1242–4), and an Athenian character renews the invitation to the flautist, because he likes watching the Spartans dance (1245–6); and then the Spartan dances and celebrates the exploits-in-arms of the Athenians and Spartans against the Persians (cf. Lysistrata's anti-Persian admonition in 1133–5), invokes the protection of the Huntress for the truce (the Huntress is a name the Athenians gave Artemis) and appeals for an end to cunning (1247–72; cf. Lysistrata in 1160: 'Athenians and Spartans, why not be done with this wickedness?'). At this point, an Athenian voice intervenes: 'Now then, since all the rest has been carried out well, O Spartans, lead you off these women here, and you Athenians, these here.'

'Since all the rest has been carried out well', ἐπειδὴ τἄλλα πεπόηται καλῶς: this positive conclusion, which appears immediately after the Spartan song solicited with such enthusiasm by the Athenian, is suited to a character who has *already* expressed his opinion and sense of satisfaction regarding the back-stage ceremony comprising the banquet and truce ('all the rest'), the ceremony in the Acropolis whose protagonists were the men, not the women, their hostesses. Rather than to Lysistrata, it is suited to a character who has been establishing himself on-stage, for some time now, as a spokesman for the peaceful banqueters. Emerging from the banquet in the company of one of his fellow-citizens, a male Athenian character had thought at once to drive a crowd of troublemakers from the gates of the Acropolis in order to allow the Spartans to come out in peace (cf. 1216–24). He had then expressed his personal satisfaction as regards the Athenians' loyalty towards the Spartans (cf. 1231–5), concluding that during the banquet 'all had gone as it should' (1236), and then driven off the troublemakers from the gates once more, as the Spartans at that point were set to emerge (1239–41).

This euphoric and extremely active Athenian character had, in effect, gradually assumed responsibility for doing the final honours of the house on-stage, excelling in courtesy towards the Spartans (cf. Lysistrata's admonition in 1116–17). As soon as the Spartan takes the initiative in dancing and singing, he spurs him on with all the enthusiasm of one whose only remaining desire is to enjoy the party to the full: 'since it's a joy for me to watch you dance'. After the song and dance of the Spartan, when a character turns first to the Spartans and then to the Athenians inviting them to retake their women, yet immediately directs the party towards a dance for two, following the solo dance of the Spartan, might not that character be this Athenian too, present on-stage since 1216?

'Let man stand by woman and woman by man, and having danced in honour of the gods for these happy events let us seek. . .': the Athenian's invitation is apparently addressed to the male (and female) characters from Sparta and Athens, but is intended above all for the corps of singers and dancers present in the theatre, for the twenty-four Athenian choreutai, twelve costumed as men, twelve as women; since in 1279–90 it is the chorus that sings and dances 'in honour of the gods' and invokes as chief divinity Artemis, the only divinity to have been invoked by the Spartan in lines 1262–72 (while in the Athenian chorus's song there appear here and there Alcmanians in homage to the Spartans). It is certain, however, that along with the Spartan couples the Athenians also take part in the dance, inasmuch as the Athenian character mentioned previously is one of the dancers (this can be deduced from 1277: cf. *Peace* 1319).

'Spartan, come on, let's hear a song' (1295): first, the Spartan, acting on his own initiative, had begun a song dedicated to the Athenians, and also to his fellow-Spartans, which as it came to an end had made direct reference to the ceremony of the truce, just that moment concluded; then, the song of the chorus, it too as it came to an end, had celebrated 'this gracious calm, work of the goddess of Cyprus' (1289–90). The Athenian, therefore, in the first case had associated himself with the initiative of the Spartan, in the second invited the couples to dance (and sing) and now, undoubtedly, is extending an invitation to the Spartan: the progress he is making in directing the feast is quite plain to see. The Spartan's song requested by the Athenian is a song for Sparta (1296–1320) which ends with an invitation from the Spartan 'to celebrate the mighty goddess, warrior throughout, of the temple of bronze' (1320, cf. previously 1300). The comedy ends, therefore, with the mention on Spartan lips of the goddess Athena, to whom there stood a temple of bronze in Sparta. As one can see, the exodos both re-evokes and reinstates the fraternity-in-arms, and in-ideals of the Spartans and Athenians, and from the moment the Spartans appear on-stage – from 1241, that is – awards great importance to these Spartan guests, to these erstwhile enemies. Those who maintain that the comedy once ended with an Athenian song in honour of Athena have understood little of the political and theatrical sense of this conclusion.[2]

The exodos of this feminist comedy, named after Lysistrata, in giving – positive – importance only to its male characters, is intended to show that the women's scheme has indeed restored the men, provided Athens and Sparta once more with men (cf. 528, 524). In such an atmosphere of male restoration it would hardly be appropriate were a woman, Lysistrata, to concede permission to the Spartans and Athenians to lead off their womenfolk, particularly when for these precise ends she has provoked an autonomous initiative on the part of the men (we, the women, shall now entertain you men on the Acropolis; there you must exchange oaths and promises) 'and then, each of you, having retaken his woman, is free to leave' (1186–7). She does not say, I will reconsign you the women, but rather: you, having sealed the pact of friendship, retake them and go.

Indeed, it is by means of this particular remark that Lysistrata prepares the spectators for a scene to come which is to involve active male characters and inactive female ones: the spectators know that the gates of the Acropolis will close at once behind Lysistrata and the men, and that the following scene will have somehow to 'repeat' the banquet and exchange of promises reserved for the men alone, and then set up their reunion with the women. It is symptomatic that as soon as the gates of the Acropolis open, men alone emerge and that their talk is exclusively of men. The mute women appear further on, and with them Lysistrata undoubtedly appears; for she too *must* abandon the Acropolis, the temporary site of action of the rebel women, and obviously must do so through the corridor, not from the wings.

The exodos requires three actors, one for the Athenian (thirty iambic trimeters), one for his companion (five iambic trimeters) and one for the Spartan Singer (three iambic trimeters and around forty lyrical lines). The part of the Spartan Singer, therefore, is the largest and most demanding. Who plays this important character? Certainly not the second actor, since prior to the exodos he has been playing the Athenian, and hence during the exodos will do the same. The third actor? In the course of the comedy, the third actor has been assigned very minor roles, with the sole exception of Myrrhine (around fifty iambic trimeters). It is highly improbable, therefore, that Aristophanes would have thought in particular of him for the principal and only lyrical character in the exodos. In truth, the role of the Spartan bears all the signs of having been written for the first actor: with Lysistrata-first actor having already done and said all that she had to do and say, Aristophanes must have considered it more convenient to eliminate Lysistrata as a speaking character and to employ the first actor for a new part of some importance and difficulty.

The first actor in *Lysistrata*, although he had indeed portrayed the main character, all told had lacked the chance to excel awarded to other Aristophanic protagonists: as mentioned previously, Lysistrata is a character whose role denies her much on-stage action after the prologue (whereas in the prologue she utters around 140 trimeters, between prologue and exodos she delivers no more than 230 lines). In the exodos, therefore, the first actor would undoubtedly have been pleased to be assigned a role which required him to deliver two solos, each of remarkable effect. The part of the mute Lysistrata would obviously have been taken by an extra, skilled enough to dance (given that Lysistrata forms part of one of the dancing couples), and it would also have been an extra who portrayed the mute Spartan Youth following the delegation. This passage from actor to extra, or extra to actor, is normal practice in Aristophanes from *Acharnians* to *Plutus*: this has already been discussed in regard to *Clouds* in particular, and will be discussed in later chapters.

4 Who speaks to the Spartan Herald?

A Proboulos, responded the Byzantines; a Prytanis, respond the editors of the last thirty years. What is absolutely certain is that the Herald does not speak to Kinesias, notes Victor Coulon, adopting the Wilamowitzian siglum of the Prytanis. Bentley thought of Kinesias, as did Jan van Leeuwen later, both on the basis of the scholion on 1014 (in the scholion on 992 and 1007 the interlocutor of the Herald is simply described as an 'Athenian').

The Spartan Herald appears in 980–1013, directly after the encounter between Kinesias and his wife, Myrrhine. The youthful Myrrhine is one of the Athenian women who, during the prologue, had decided to go on a sex-strike for pacifist ends and promptly enclosed themselves within the Acropolis. Of this extemporaneous sex-strike the men of Athens hear nothing at all, learning only that the women of Athens have occupied the Acropolis (cf. 259–65, 423): to protect the State treasure, explains Lysistrata to the Proboulos in 488–97, without saying a word, even in 551–60, about the sex-strike. While the Spartan Lampito has gone to Sparta to organize the strike of the women there, five days on from the occupation of the Acropolis Kinesias arrives in order to convince Myrrhine to abandon the other women and return home to her domestic tasks, and to their conjugal love (cf. 891–9). Myrrhine: 'I am not coming home, unless first you negotiate a truce and put an end to your wars.' Kinesias: 'all right, if that's what we want, we can even make peace'. Myrrhine: 'all right, if that's what we want, I'll even come home; but for the moment I've sworn to say no' (900–3). Kinesias then begs his wife to make love, there at least, close to the Acropolis, and to ignore her sworn oath to return untouched into the sacred Acropolis (cf. 904–15). In agreement by now, Myrrhine recommends her husband: 'But don't try to fool me on this business of the truce ... remember to vote for the truce.' And Kinesias: 'I'll think about it' (932, 950–1). At this precise juncture, however, Myrrhine slips off to the Acropolis, since this is exactly what Lysistrata had instructed her to do, to feign affection for her husband, but not to yield (cf. 839–41). Kinesias becomes desperate, cries out that he has been 'tricked' by his wife, and is detained by the coryphaeus of the Old Men (cf. 952–79).

Once the coryphaeus of the Old Men has augured for Kinesias the pleasure of hurling his wife into the air in such a way that she, falling back to earth, might impale herself at a stroke on his prick (cf. 972–9), a Spartan character appears: 'Where is the gerousia of Athens, or the Prytanes? I have something new to report.' An Athenian character: 'But who are you? man or Konislalos [a Priapistic demon]?' The Spartan: 'I'm a herald, young man, come from Sparta for the truce' (980–4). Hence, a Spartan has appeared, closer to a Priapus than a man, and has been apostrophized by an Athenian 'young man'. The youth, who seems rather amused, wants the Herald to admit that he has an erection, but the latter, embarrassed, insists on denying the evidence (cf. 985–91). So, the youth, demonstrating to the Herald that he too has an erection, exclaims: 'Come on, imagine that I already know and tell me the truth: how are things going in Sparta?' The Herald: 'All Sparta is erect.' The youth: 'How on earth has this affliction come upon you? Is it the fault of Pan?' The Herald: 'No, the instigator, I believe, was Lampito. Then the other women of Sparta, all in agreement, refused the men their cunts.' The youth: 'And how do you feel?' The Herald: 'It's pure torture. We're wandering bent over around the city. The women won't allow it even to be touched, unless first we seal a truce with all the Hellenes.' The youth: 'This is a plot sworn by the women everywhere: now at last I understand! Away, go and tell them to dispatch ambassadors plenipotentiary for the truce as soon as possible, and I will tell the Boulē, for its part, to elect other ambassadors, having shown them this prick I've got here!' The Herald: 'I'll fly. You have spoken excellently.' After an intermediate choral stasimon the ambassadors from Sparta and Athens arrive.

Which of the Athenians has spoken to the Spartan Herald? Or rather, who amongst the Athenians, when the Herald reveals the pacifist goals for which the women of Sparta are pursuing a sex-strike to the bitter end, could react by exclaiming: 'This is a plot sworn by the women everywhere: now at last I understand!'? Only Kinesias, the husband of Myrrhine, could react in such a way, since *only* Kinesias, amongst all the Athenians, has actually tried to approach an Athenian woman, and she has informed him of an oath binding her to the other women and in exchange for an act of love, eventually not conceded, required that her husband should swear to vote for peace. Kinesias now understands that this 'trickstress' is in fact bound to a sex-strike to the bitter end pledged by all the Hellenic women. When the Herald gives the news that the Spartan women are simply on a sex-strike, Kinesias as yet fails to grasp the situation, but once he has learned the motives for the strike, is the only Athenian man in a position to understand exactly why the Athenian women have insisted on remaining in the Acropolis, not come home and refused even for a moment to make love. Furthermore, an expression such as ἄρτι νυνὶ μανθάνω, 'now at last I understand', is suited *only* to a character who has been directly involved in the events which have since become clear to him: ἄρτι μανθάνω, for example, is uttered by Admetus in *Alcestis* 940, and in *Bacchae* 1296 by the previously insane Agave, when through the agency of her father she realizes that she has killed her own son as a punishment willed by Dionysos. In *Lysistrata*, the only other male character to enter into contact with the Athenian women is the Proboulos in 387–610; but the Proboulos does not come to the Acropolis to make love, nor have the women mentioned the sex-strike to him. Besides, the Proboulos is old (cf. 509–607 and Thucydides VIII.1), whereas whoever speaks to the Herald is a 'young man'.

Myrrhine leaves Kinesias in the lurch at 951, the Herald takes up his part at 980, and the coryphaeus of the Old Men, in the mean time, talks vivaciously and with pronounced explicitness to Kinesias (972–9). The coryphaeus, therefore, detains the solitary Kinesias (who, in any case, has said nothing about taking his leave), since Kinesias is a character with something essential and conclusive both to say and to do: the Priapistic envoy of the Spartan men, on their knees in the face of the pacifist strike of the Spartan women, must encounter an Athenian erotically and dramatically prepared to provoke the rapid capitulation of the Athenian men. It is also appropriate that this Athenian should be the husband of one of the women on the Acropolis, since the women of Athens' first and most immediate aim is the capitulation of their husbands (cf. 99–167). 'I'm not coming home', says the youthful Myrrhine at once to her youthful husband, 'unless you first negotiate a truce and put an end to your war.' At this precise juncture, Kinesias represents all the libidinous husbands of Athens, Myrrhine all their rebel wives.

175

In fact, the encounter between the amorous and provocative Myrrhine and her husband Kinesias, which takes place five days after the beginning of the sex-strike, is to all intents and purposes a dramatization of the basic hypothesis put forward by Lysistrata during the prologue:

O women, should we stay at home, all made up, and let them see us nude in our Amorgine tunics, nicely trimmed at the delta, our husbands will rear up and burn with desire; if, rather than accepting them, we should then refuse, they'll agree to a truce at once. I'm sure of it.

(149–54; cf. 839–41)

Were Kinesias also to have taken his leave once his seductress wife had refused him and then slipped away, his encounter with Myrrhine would have been rendered dramatically sterile, mutilated, so to speak. Kinesias, whose wife has not revealed to him the reason for the oath binding her to the other women, must now receive that revelation, since only the dreadful revelation of a sex-strike planned to last to the bitter end might convince the Athenian husbands to finish with their wars, as in the mean time it has convinced the Spartans, with whom Lampito and the others had been frank from the start (cf. previously 168–9). The spectators, who are acquainted with the conspiracy, at this point expect just that: that someone should inform that man called Kinesias why the women are refusing the men. And the appearance of the Herald provides a good excuse, since the news he brings from Sparta is the new fact destined to provoke the surrender of the Athenian men. Hence, the relation of an off-stage event – the public sex-strike of the Spartan women – leads in Athens to the discovery of the secret motives underlying the obstructionism of the Athenian women. It is also appropriate that the character to whom this news is addressed should previously have been the representative victim of the women's obstructionism. In *Assemblywomen*, too, Blepyros, the representative victim of female intrigue, procrastinates on-stage after 357 so that Chremes' relation of an off-stage event may be addressed to him, an event which has also led to the triumph of female intrigue.

Between the scene with Myrrhine and that with the Herald is a group of anapaestic dimeters uttered by Kinesias and the coryphaeus of the Old Men (954–79). The exit of Kinesias and the Herald is followed by a choral stasimon, and the scene involving Kinesias and Myrrhine is preceded by one (781–828). It is clear, therefore, that the complex 829–1013 constitutes an 'episode': the character who is continually present during this 'episode' is Kinesias. 'After scarcely a few lines uttered by the male chorus, there appears the very brief scene involving the representatives of Sparta and Athens ... although necessary for the dramatic action, this is no more than an extremely simple bridge-piece without any intrinsic merit ... the Athenian representative remains entirely schematic, despite being conceived as a character of rank'; 'the anapaestic pnigos which ends the scene involving Kinesias performs the task of dividing

176

the scenes, whereas this is achieved elsewhere by the use of a choral song'; 'the few anapaests spoken by the chorus here substitute a choral song calculated to divide the scenes, as no connection exists, merely a similarity': thus Wilamowitz. Yet, between one scene and another there is no choral song, but rather a non-antistrophic anapaestic period, since between the two scenes there is an intimate connection, similar to that between protasis and apodosis: as Lysistrata had foreseen in the prologue, 'If we women seduce our husbands and then refuse them, they'll agree to a truce at once.'

The root of Wilamowitz's generalized discontent clearly resides in his failure to identify Kinesias as the interlocutor of the Herald; hence he is at a loss as regards the character who might link the scenes. In 1893 he adopted the siglum of the Proboulos, and in 1927 invented the Prytanis; in each case, because he felt the need for an Athenian character of elevated rank. Why? Because a despairing and plaintive Kinesias – exclaimed the aristocratic Wilamowitz – could not represent the Athenian State before the foreigner and could not convoke the Boulē!

Yet Kinesias neither represents the Athenian State nor convokes the Boulē. Kinesias – who, in any case, might easily be a member of the Boulē – can certainly guarantee the Spartan Herald that the Boulē will elect ambassadors, because he knows what he is about (cf. 1012). Kinesias is to refer to the Boulē two clamorous novelties, each of public interest: that all the Hellenic women are united in a pacifist conspiracy and that the men of Sparta, having already yielded to the women's blackmail, are prepared to negotiate a truce with Athens. What else can the governors of Athens do when they have already been forced, days before, to register the political defeat of one of their Probouloi at the hands of Lysistrata (cf. 608–10)? Kinesias, fair enough, had been plaintive and desperate and, until a moment before, lying stretched out in expectation of his wife, but when he spies a foreigner looking more like a Priapistic demon than a man, it is perfectly natural that his mood should change and he should start to joke, all the more so when the coryphaeus has said something extremely comical to him in lines 972–9 (yet to Wilamowitz it remains perfectly clear that Kinesias exits at 971!). It is also natural that the Herald, in search of Athenian officials, should take time to speak to a 'young man'. Priapistic and confused, the Herald just cannot take it any more and has a burning desire to speak his mind – 'I've something new to report', he exclaims at once – and hence enters into conversation with whoever it is that addresses him, because this fellow puts his finger right on the wound, on the affliction which has sent him running from Sparta to Athens; and when the young Athenian demonstrates that he is suffering just as much, he tells him everything. Besides, a Prytanis who had entered the orchestra solely to give the Herald an official reception would hardly have responded to the Herald's announcement of the news from Sparta by enquiring, 'But who are you? Man or Priapistic demon?', nor would the Herald have replied to him, 'I'm a herald, young man.'

177

If the Herald's Athenian interlocutor were effectively an episodic Prytanis, the entire scene would appear stilted and mechanical, and the entrance of the Prytanis mechanical and puppet-like. 'The Prytanis', notes Wilamowitz,

> is obviously there in the orchestra the very moment the Herald mentions him; the comedy is spared a 'here comes a Prytanis' of the type one is accustomed to in tragedy and is here reserved for Lysistrata in 1106 . . . . The Prytanis is wearing the crown of an official personality, and hence is even easier to recognize.

So much easier to recognize that the Herald addresses him as a 'young man' . . . . In truth, while the lack of a 'here comes a Prytanis' would be disturbing in itself, it would be even more disturbing were the Prytanis, on command, to emerge in front of the Acropolis from the corridor, when the Acropolis is the scenic base of the Athenian women. An automatic appearance by the Prytanis might be considered natural only if he had his base in the scenic façade, which is actually the case for Lysistrata, whom Wilamowitz so inappropriately recalls.

The only remaining alternative is to assume that when the Herald appears, the Prytanis is already in front of the Acropolis, as a species of official observer of the rebel women's base. Yet this implies that a high-ranking personality such as he would be made to appear for no other reason than to receive the Herald, since it is not the Prytanis who leads the Athenian delegation in 1086–1188 and 1216–95, as Wilamowitz and, after him, Victor Coulon prefer to believe. It is beyond all doubt that the Athenian character who says to the Herald, 'away, go and tell them as soon as possible to dispatch ambassadors plenipotentiary for the truce, and I will tell the Boulē, for its part, to elect other ambassadors', is not also the leader of the Athenian delegation: 'Look here, the Spartan envoys are approaching . . . and there I can see the native ones, too', says the coryphaeus in 1072 and 1082. 'Why have you come here?', an Athenian character asks the Spartans (a question hardly appropriate on the lips of the supposed Prytanis of 1009–10). 'For the sake of peace, as ambassadors', replies the leader on one side; 'Well said, and us too', the leader on the other (1101–3). It is clear that on one side stand the ambassadors of Sparta, and on the other, those of Athens.

Yet here again Wilamowitz quibbles, for here again he finds himself confused:

> It does not make sense that the Athenians should elect ambassadors, when ambassadors are supposed to be on their way from Sparta . . . . The Athenians who then appear before Lysistrata do correspond to ambassadors, but are not characterized as such; hence, it is not in the least inconvenient that they should include the Prytanis and that he should take the floor.

However, it makes perfect sense that the Athenians, too, should elect fully fledged ambassadors, since one is dealing here with an encounter between the ambassadors of two cities at war before an impartial arbiter in 'neutral' territory (cf. 1103–11), and this impartial arbiter had himself foreseen that the war would be resolved by two separate delegations formed in response to the action undertaken by the women (569–70). It is also untrue that the Athenians are not characterized as ambassadors. After the banquet in the Acropolis, an Athenian character says: 'If with my words I manage to convince the Athenians, in delegation we'll be drunk wherever we go, since now when we go to Sparta on the dry . . .' (1229–31). The character speaking is obviously the leader of the Athenian delegation.

5 From the houses of the prologue to the Propylaea and the rocks of the Acropolis

In line 253, near the end of the prologue, the Athenian Acropolis becomes the scenic base of the characters who, earlier in the prologue, were to be found in the residences of Lysistrata and Kalonike, and of these residences no further mention is made. From 240 onwards, visual attention is focused exclusively on the Acropolis, whereas in line 250 there is an explicit reference to its gates (cf. previously 246).

The prologue ends, therefore, with a movement towards an existing element of the scene, to which one's attention had already been drawn in lines 176–9 (although at that point it was still invisible). The setting of the prologue is instead the residences of the two next-door neighbours Lysistrata and Kalonike (cf. 199 and 5), which form the site of the women's assembly (cf. 4–15 etc.). The latter is imagined as lying not far from the Acropolis, since the women gathered there can hear the uproar being caused by the other women who have occupied the Acropolis in an action occurring back-stage (240–2), and from this place of assembly the women of the prologue move swiftly to occupy a stable position on the Acropolis. Mention was made at the beginning of section 2 above of the reason why the scenic base of the subsequent action of the comedy should be established by back-stage characters, not by those of the prologue. As regards the scenic conception of the opening section of the prologue, one should note that the women who present themselves to Lysistrata with some delay between lines 64 and 76 all hail from far afield, some from Attica, others from the Peloponnese. Kalonike alone puts in an appearance as early as line 5, since she is conceived as the impatient Lysistrata's next-door neighbour: the timely appearance of Kalonike allows for a dialogue conveying the impatience and anxiety of the comedy's opening character.

The ephemeral residences of Lysistrata and Kalonike might have been represented by a pair of small doors located in the two wings which presumably flanked the scenic front of the theatre of Dionysos. Otherwise, one would have to assume that the two of the three entrances to the stage later to represent the gates of the Acropolis – or rather those of the Propylaea – would have been used in the mean time to represent the doorways of Kalonike and Lysistrata.[3]

It is certain that the scenic front of *Lysistrata* alludes by means of more than one solid door to the mighty central and four minor doors in the back wall of the vestibule of the real Propylaea, as throughout there is concrete mention of πύλαι and θύραι (250, 423, 248, 311; προπύλαια in 265). The more distinctive of the doors would be the central one, which would also be used for scenic purposes: in 1216, for instance, there is a request for 'the door' to be opened, and in 309 talk of breaking open 'the door'. Behind the stage-wall, representing the Propylaea, one must imagine the Acropolis (as regards the distinction between the Acropolis and the Propylaea, cf. 263–5) complete with its monuments: the statue of Athena Polias in the Erechtheum, the Parthenon and the Erechtheum itself (cf. 262, 345, 759). The top of the stage-wall would have to be accessible since, at one stage, Lysistrata and her companions are to be seen upon it: cf. 829–44, which implies the use of a back-stage ladder (as in *Wasps*).

Besides the gates of the real Propylaea, the scenic front of *Lysistrata* also alludes to the rocky landscape of the official Acropolis, since to one side of the scenic front lie rupestrian elements alluding to Pan's cave, which was located in the precipitous northern flank of the Acropolis, close to the Propylaea themselves. Once Myrrhine has decided to come out of the Acropolis, Kinesias persuades her to retire with him to Pan's cave and then to return to the Acropolis having first purified herself in the spring Klepsydra (cf. 910–17). Shortly before this scene, Lysistrata appears in the orchestra and speaks of having surprised a woman on the Acropolis who wanted to escape by 'attempting to widen the opening where Pan's cave is' (720–1). From Lysistrata's words alone, rupestrial elements cannot be inferred, since the cave might be situated back-stage (like the Erechtheum and the Parthenon etc.), nor can they from those of the Old Men in line 482: 'Why have they occupied the citadel of Kranaos, the inaccessible, high-cliffed Acropolis, the sacred enclosure?' In the episode involving Kinesias and Myrrhine, however, the setting, without the minimum of doubt, entails a rupestrian landscape adjacent to the gates of the Propylaea at least, i.e. against the back-stage wall. This landscape alludes to Pan's cave and to the nearby Klepsydra. One other element alluding to the environment of the official Acropolis might be a slightly inclined level in front of the door in the scenic front corresponding to the slope leading to the Acropolis (cf. 286–8, 294, but not 739), a factor discussed in section 11 of chapter 3 on *Acharnians*.

The off-stage environment of the Dionysian Lysistrata is also realistic: in line 835, from the height of the stage-wall, Lysistrata declares that beyond the precinct of the theatre she can see the temple of Demeter Chloe. This temple was situated at the foot of the same southern slope of the Acropolis on which the temple of Dionysos stood.

6 Distribution of parts. The mob of troublemakers

The nineteen characters of *Lysistrata* are portrayed by three actors and one amateur actor:

first actor, Lysistrata, delivering around 370 lines, 1–251, 430–613, 708–80, 829–64, 1112–87, Spartan Youth, with three iambic trimeters and around forty lyric lines, 1242–1320;

second actor, delivering around 312 lines, which include half a dozen lyric anapaestic dimeters in the passage 954–70: Kalonike, 6–253, Proboulos, 387–610, First Woman, 728–34, who retires into the Acropolis at 734 to reappear shortly as the Third Woman in 742–59, Kinesias, 845–1012, Athenian Ambassador, 1086–1188, 1216–95;

third actor, delivering around 105 lines: Myrrhine, 69–205, First Old Woman, 439–603, Second Woman, 735–9, Myrrhine, 837–951, Spartan Herald, 980–1013, Spartan Ambassador, 1076–1188, Athenian, 1221–41;

amateur actor: Lampito, 81–240 (twenty-seven trimeters), Second Old Woman, 443–604 (three trimeters), Fourth Woman, 760–1 (two trimeters), Fifth Woman, 830–6 (two trimeters). The part of Lampito might also be assigned to one of the choreutai, who do not appear until 319. The parts in the Laconian dialect would hence be performed first by an amateur actor or a choreutes (Lampito), then by the third actor (Herald, Ambassador), and lastly by the first actor (the Youth). The first actor, who plays the difficult role of the Spartan Youth in the exodos, would also be free for the Spartan Herald.

An ordinary *child* might have been used for Kinesias' Baby, appearing between 829 and 908, whose sole utterance is μαμμία μαμμία μαμμία in 879 (if the Baby is not a puppet and these three words spoken by Kinesias himself). The two women who appear beside Lysistrata in 439–44 and 505–604, and utter respectively eight and three lines (439–40, 505b, 515b, 556b, 561–4, 603; 443–4, 604), would be better assigned the sigla First Old Woman and Second Old Woman, rather than those of Kalonike and Myrrhine. In this way, the old women who have occupied the Acropolis in a back-stage action would appear at Lysistrata's side during the section of the comedy dedicated to the reasons why she had ordered them to do so. Indeed it would seem unnatural if these old women were to appear as extras (in 456–61, maybe), when they have already been ascribed marked back-stage vitality during the prologue and two of them have even been mentioned by name (cf. 177–9, 240–2, 245, 322–3; see also section 3b of chapter 5). One must also consider that during the prologue Kalonike had been played by the second actor, and that in 387–610 the second actor is taken up with the Proboulos. Besides, Kalonike and Myrrhine are both young, whereas at least one of the two women who appear in 505–604 is old (cf. 506; it is also impossible for her to be a member of the semi-chorus of the Old Women: cf. 486). Some scholars have deduced that Kalonike herself is old from the τέκνον she addresses to Lysistrata in line 7; yet an elevated term such as this could not be employed merely to indicate a character's age.

Hence, Kalonike and the other women from the prologue are all more or less young. Not only does Lysistrata distinguish herself and the others from the 'older women who in the mean time occupy the Acropolis' (177–9), but a number of her companions are explicitly described as young: the Spartan Lampito, for instance, the two girls from Boeotia and Corinth (cf. 79–91) and Myrrhine (cf. 885 and 955). Kalonike, too, speaks as if she is a youthful wife (cf. 17–19), and all of the women are the mothers of small children (99). The idea proposed in lines 149–51, moreover, is suited to such young married women alone, destined with eventual success to promote a sex-strike. Lysistrata herself speaks as if she is in the bloom of youth (551–2, 591, cf. 1126), and like the other women is undoubtedly married (cf. 514–15, 519, 592–3, etc.).

If it is unwise, therefore, to search for Kalonike and Myrrhine in the two women of 439–44 and 505–604, they might be two of the four who appear in 728–61. In that case, however, it would be rather strange if Lysistrata failed to remind these two in particular of their oaths from the prologue, as she reminds Myrrhine in line 841. During the prologue, Kalonike had been assigned a role of some importance: with 76 trimeters she came second to Lysistrata with 139, followed by Lampito with 27 and Myrrhine with 11 (these figures imply a division of the dialogue in some points distinct from that of Victor Coulon: briefly, Lysistrata, 74–76a, Myrrhine, 76b, Lysistrata, 77–81a, Myrrhine, 112b–114, Kalonike, 115–16, Myrrhine, 129, Kalonike, 130, Kalonike, 191b–192, Lysistrata, 193a, Kalonike, 193b–194a, Lysistrata, 194b–197a, Kalonike, 197b εἰς κτλ., Myrrhine, 200, Kalonike, 201, Myrrhine, 205). However, for reasons of economy in the use of the actors, and because of the presence on-stage of the twelve old women forming the semi-chorus, henceforth there are no enduring female roles of any importance except that of Lysistrata: Kalonike-second actor from the prologue is employed for male roles of relative importance, whereas of the women of the prologue only Myrrhine-third actor reappears episodically (with Kinesias-second actor). And on this occasion alone is there a precise mention of a female name, that of Myrrhine, obviously.

In this regard, one should note that the names of the four female characters appearing in the prologue are mentioned at once, and also that they recur quite frequently: Lysistrata, 6, 21, 69, 135, 186, 189, 216; Kalonike, 6, 9; Myrrhine, 70; Lampito, 77, 78, 181, 209, 242. Modern scholarship has since established that Lampito was the name of the mother of the contemporary King of Sparta, and Myrrhine that of the contemporary Athenian priestess of Athena Nike;

that Kalonike is a woman's name on a cup from the Athenian Acropolis dated around 480; that the contemporary Athenian priestess of Athena Polias was probably called Lysimacha; and that the names Lysistrata and Myrrhine appear on an Attic lekane from the late fifth century along with those of five other women. By using the names Lampito, Myrrhine and Lysistrata did Aristophanes wish to allude to real people? I should think not, but that one is dealing basically with a coincidence, and in the case of Lysistrata with a semi-coincidence. Moreover, the name Myrrhine seems to have been extremely common; and, in any case, with regard to the names Lysistrata and Myrrhine, what would have been the comic effect of a real allusion to the two priestesses? A name such as Lysistrata is above all a speaking name, like that of Lysimacha (cf. *Peace* 992): in contrast to other speaking names in Aristophanes, it is heard at once since Lysistrata is the comedy's title character.[4]

The crowd of *extras* is large and varied, particularly in the prologue and exodos. In the prologue, besides Lysistrata, Kalonike, Myrrhine and Lampito, there also appears 'a swarm of women' (93 and cf. 65 and 66): prominence is given to the women from the Attic deme of Anagyre (66–8), to the noble maiden from Boeotia going by the name of Ismenia (85–9; 697), and to the noble maiden from Corinth (90–2). Along with the Spartan Lampito, it is certain that other Spartan women appear (cf. 40 and 75), who then enclose themselves in the Acropolis with the women of Athens (cf. later 1186 and 1274; the two maidens from Boeotia and Corinth are instead forgotten). Lysistrata has one slave at least (184, cf. also 199). Between the prologue and the exodos there appear: Scythian Archers in 387–462 with the Proboulos (the archers are met by three women, not four, since 447–8 certainly belongs to Lysistrata, at that point speaking directly to an archer, whereas in 435–6 she had been addressing the Proboulos; and in each case she swears by Artemis); a host of women who emerge from, and then re-enter, the Acropolis between 455 and 462; a group of women on the summit of the scenic façade in 829–44; Kinesias' servant, Manes (908); Spartan and Athenian Delegates (from 1072 and 1082 onwards); and finally a girl portraying Reconciliation (1114–21). A mob of troublemakers appears at the beginning of the exodos (cf. 1217–40), followed by the delegations from Athens and Sparta, and by the women of Athens and Sparta. Other extras portray Lysistrata and the Spartan Ambassador during the exodos, while the presence of a *flautist* emerges explicitly from the text (1242).

The scene involving the mob of troublemakers in 1217–40 requires a separate comment, since the current interpretations are unacceptable. Invited by Lysistrata, the Spartan and Athenian delegations enter the Acropolis at 1188 to partake of the banquet, while the two reconciled semi-choruses sing the antistrophes in the orchestra (1189–1215). In 1216, the iambic trimeters resume once more: ἄνοιγε τὴν θύραν οὐ παραχωρεῖν θέλεις, reads the Ravenna manuscript, against the metre. Victor Coulon has adopted ἄνοιγε τὴν θύραν σύ. παραχωρεῖν σ' ἔδει, disregarding the far more simple emendation of Scaligero: ἄνοιγε τὴν θύραν. παραχωρεῖν οὐ θέλεις; (or rather 'θέλεις;).

The remark ἄνοιγε τὴν θύραν, 'open the door', must be delivered from the interior of the stage-edifice. In *Birds* 92 also, Hoopoe shouts to his Servant from within, ἄνοιγε τὴν ὕλην (πύλην, that is), ἵν' ἐξέλθω ποτέ, and then appears outdoors. After the imperious 'open the door! What, you won't stand aside?', when the character from *Lysistrata* appears outdoors, it is clear that he is carrying a torch (1217), and is also a bit tipsy (cf. later 1227–30). He is obviously one of the Athenian guests from the Acropolis (and has given his order to the concierge of the Propylaea). Cf. *Assemblywomen* 691–4: 'each with his crown and torch will come out tipsy, with the women at the crossroads hurling themselves at the men arriving from the banquet'; also *Wasps*, in which Philokleon returns from the banquet carrying a torch and makes use of it to threaten the mob at his rear (as regards the torch, cf. also *Plutus* 1041).

The guest in *Lysistrata*, as soon as he emerges from the Acropolis, threatens a group of people seated in front of the Propylaea: 'you lot, what are you doing sitting there? I'm not going to have to burn you with my torch, am I? . . . although, should it prove absolutely necessary, [to the spectators] to give pleasure to you, we'll undertake this toil' (1217–20). As the recipients of these threats are left with their mouths closed, another Athenian voice intervenes: 'Yes, and we too shall undertake this toil' (1221). What toil? That of expelling the undesirables by beating them with a torch. We are dealing, obviously, with a character speaking in the name of other guests carrying torches who have since emerged from the banquet behind the first (this is why the latter in 1220 says, 'we'll undertake this toil', and the others agree). The first guest continues with his threats: 'you don't intend to go? You're going to be tearing your hair about this for a long time! Won't you go away and allow the Laconians to come out in peace from the banquet?' (1222–4; for κωκύσεσθε τὰς τρίχας in 1222, addressed to men, cf. *Lysistrata* 448; κωκύσεσθε is in the elevated style, like ὄπωπα in 1225). The mob begins to move away (through the corridor, obviously) and the two guests begin a discussion about the banquet. The guest who appears first possesses the greatest authority: he is undoubtedly the Athenian Ambassador from the preceding scene, and his companion one of the Athenian delegates. On-stage, between character-actors and extras, the only characters are Athenians: the Spartans do not appear until 1241. As the two Athenians are discussing the banquet, the undesirables reappear: 'Here they come again, back to the very same place! Go to rack and ruin, gallows-bait!' (1239–40). These lines are clearly uttered by the same character as lines 1216–20 and 1222–4. The undesirables run away for good (through the corridor), and the Spartans emerge at once from the Acropolis.

Who are the undesirables? They are obviously not the choreutai, as a considerable number of modern scholars maintain: according to them, the choreutai are distanced from the stage in order to change costume, and then reappear at 1245 as the semi-choruses of Spartans and Athenians. This hypothesis is unacceptable: (1) there is absolutely no need for a Spartan semi-chorus, since the Spartan songs and dances in lines 1247–72 and 1296–1320 are performed by a single Spartan (cf. 1244, 1248, 1295); (2) there is also no need for an Athenian semi-chorus, since the two reconciled Athenian semi-choruses are already in the orchestra; (3) there would not have been enough time for twenty-four choreutai to exit by the corridor at line 1240 and then reappear from the scenic façade between 1241 and 1245 and, what is more, wearing new costumes; (4) the choreutai, who are not extras, would have to react verbally to the insults and threats of the Athenian; (5) the Aristophanic chorus never abandons the orchestra in the course of a comedy.

This mute mob, therefore, is composed of extras, who are also of base extraction, since in 1240 they are insultingly addressed as μαστιγίαι: in *Frogs* 756, ὁμομαστιγίαι is used in reference to slaves. In fact, we are dealing here with slaves, those of the Athenian delegation, who have since gathered outside the Acropolis waiting for their masters to emerge (cf. fragment 490 of Aristophanes).[5]

10

THESMOPHORIAZUSAE

1 Euripides, the Lenaia and the contest of the preceding year

'I am Echo . . . she who took part in the contest last year in this very same place, I too, for Euripides': *Thesmophoriazusae* 1059–61 on the lips of Echo, previously one of the characters of Euripides' *Andromeda*. *Thesmophoriazusae*, whose contest remains unknown, was thus presented 'in the same place' as *Andromeda*, and the theatre in which *Andromeda* was performed must have been the theatre of Dionysos, equipped with a flying-machine, not the Lenaia. *Andromeda* and *Thesmophoriazusae*, therefore, as dramas for the Dionysian theatre, were also dramas for the Dionysian contests, a factor discussed in chapter 1 which deals with the theatrical seasons.

On the *contest of Andromeda*, considerations of a different kind are possible, although in this regard the single fact to emerge, from the scholion on *Thesmophoriazusae* 1012, is that '*Andromeda* was presented along with *Helen*.' If instead one knew that Euripides, for instance, had competed with a third drama at least, or that two other poets had competed with him, then *Andromeda* and *Helen* might definitively be catalogued as Dionysian tragedies, for in the Dionysian contests during that period three poets took part with a tetralogy each. Regarding the Lenaian tragic contests, *IG* II².2319, 70–83 testifies that in the years 419 and 418 two tragic poets competed at the Lenaia with two tragedies each. It is not so difficult to concede that this conforms to the Lenaian norm – from the moment tragedy was actually admitted to the Lenaia, that is, from approximately 432.[1]

In the first half of the fourth century the regulations of the Lenaia – apart from those of the Dionysia prescribing three poets with a tetralogy each, in force from the beginning of the fifth century – must still have been the same, a factor evident in the case of Theodektes, active from approximately 365 to 350: 'Theodektes presented fifty dramas' (the *Suda*); 'Theodektes composed fifty tragedies' (Stephanus of Byzantium s.v. Φάσηλις); and 'in thirteen contests involving tragic choruses he obtained eight victories', as transmitted in the epitaph from his tomb quoted by Stephanus. From *IG* II².2325, 11, it emerges that Theodektes obtained altogether seven victories at the Dionysia;

186

the eighth must therefore have been Lenaian. Hence, the generally accepted figure of fifty dramas can be made to correspond only to twelve Dionysian tetralogies and two Lenaian tragedies (less evident, but still not to be overlooked, is the case of Sophocles the Younger, active from 396 to around 375: 'Sophocles presented forty dramas and won seven victories', the *Suda*: 'Sophocles won twelve victories', Diodorus XIV.53.6. If the difference in the number of victories is to be ascribed to the fact that seven were Dionysian and five Lenaian, then Sophocles must have competed seven times at the Dionysia and six at the Lenaia with 7 × 4 + 6 × 2 dramas. Regarding two victories at the Dionysia of this inveterate prize-winner, the grandson of Sophocles, information survives in *IG* II².2318, 199 and 244).

Did Sophocles and Euripides ever take part in the contests of the Lenaia? The *Suda* reports that 'Sophocles presented 123 dramas, though others would claim many more, and won twenty-four victories.' From *IG* II².2325, 5, it emerges that Sophocles won altogether eighteen times at the Dionysia, whilst Diodorus XIII.103.6 reports simply that 'Sophocles obtained eighteen victories.' The other six victories reported by the *Suda* (and in practice by the *Vita Sophoclis*, too) must have been Lenaian.[2]

Sophocles, therefore, won 18 + 6 victories with 18 × 4 + 6 × 2 dramas. The official dramas remaining must all have been Dionysian, for the *Vita Sophoclis* reports that 'Sophocles often gained second place, never third.' In the contest of the year 431, for example, Sophocles came second (Euripides was third); while another Sophoclean second place at the Dionysia is attested to by *Pap. Oxy.* 2256.3.

Euripides, in the course of almost fifty years, 'competed in twenty-two years altogether' (ἐπεδείξατο ὅλους ἐνιαυτούς κβ': thus the *Suda*, in which the figure of twenty-two is provided by the best manuscript), and obtained five victories *(Vita Euripidis,* the *Suda,* Varro). Of the twenty-two contests in which Euripides took part it is possible to provide the place-list and epoch of the following ten: three victories (contest of 441 – first victory; contest of 428; posthumous Dionysian contest with the trilogy *Iphigeneia in Aulis, Alcmaeon in Corinth* and *Bacchae*); three second places (the contest of 438 won by Sophocles; the contest of 415 won by Xenokles; and the contest of 410–409 whose victor remains unknown); two third places (his début in 455; contest of 431 won by Euphorion); second or third place in competition with Sophocles and Achaeus at a contest taking place between 447 and 444; and finally, second or third place when, as reported by the *Suda,* 'Nikomachos unexpectedly defeated Euripides and Theognis' (the idea that this contest is the same as that of 410–409 should be disregarded: as has correctly been deduced from the temporal ordering of Satyrus' biographical account, in the final years of his Athenian career, which closed definitively in 408 with *Orestes,* Euripides often found himself competing with mediocre poets such as Akestor, Doryleus, Morsimos, and Melanthius. Hence, the contest involving the equally mediocre Nikomachos and Theognis would have taken place before 410–409, clearly not immediately after Euripides' first victory in 441, but perhaps later than that of 428: the oldest mention of the frigid Theognis is to be found in *Acharnians*, which dates from the year 425).

The Euripidean prize-lists from the Dionysian–Lenaian period which we are in a position to reconstruct hence number five, or rather six, and they are all Dionysian. In truth, it is only in the case of the posthumous trilogy that mention of a Dionysian contest has actually survived, but in the five other cases this much can be deduced either from the lists containing three names or from the tetralogies: hence, list with three names and a Euripidean tetralogy in 431, list with three names in 428, a trio of poets in the contest won by Nikomachos, tetralogies by Xenokles and Euripides in 415, and a Euripidean tetralogy in 410–419.

So, to the ten reconstructable Euripidean contests there correspond ten tetralogies, or more precisely nine tetralogies and one trilogy – all told, thirty-nine dramas. The victorious tragic *trilogy* should provide no cause for amazement, since it was presented posthumously (it is significant that the two extant tragedies bear signs of incompleteness). Although in itself the thought is rather superfluous, it is also possible that on that particular occasion the other poets were requested a trilogy rather than a tetralogy.

Out of the twelve unidentified Euripidean contests remaining it is extremely easy to concede that four took place during the twenty-three-year Dionysian period spanning approximately 455–433, during which four of the ten reconstructable contests were certainly staged. The other eight would have been held, therefore, in the twenty-five-year Dionysian–Lenaian period lasting from around 432 to 408, to which four of the ten reconstructable contests definitely also belong, and almost definitely the contest won by Nikomachos; the sixth is posthumous. Dating the other four tetralogies to the pre-Lenaian period, one reaches a total of fifty-five Dionysian dramas.

If the eight unidentified contests from the Dionysian–Lenaian period include one that is Lenaian, then in official Athenian competitions Euripides would have presented 55 + 28 + 2 dramas; if the Lenaian contests are two, the dramas presented become 55 + 24 + 4; if, on the other hand, the eight contests are all Dionysian, the dramas presented are 55 + 32. Hence, 87 dramas = 22 Dionysian contests; 83 + 2 dramas = 21 Dionysian contests + 1 Lenaian; 79 + 4 dramas = 20 Dionysian contests + 2 Lenaian, and so on.

The Alexandrians were in agreement about a figure of 92 known Euripidean dramas (the *Suda*, *Vita Euripidis* at two different points), and were in possession of 78 (*Vita Euripidis* at two different points). The *Suda* reports that in some quarters the dramas composed by Euripides were held to be 75, and Varro, too, speaks of 75 tragedies. We are informed by *Vita Euripidis* that the 78 dramas preserved included the three apocryphal tragedies *Tennes*, *Rhadamanthys* and *Peirithous*, while the *Vita* elsewhere reports that along with the three tragedies a satyr play (from amongst the eight preserved) was also considered to be an apocryphal tragedy: it is clear that once the three tragedies had been proved apocryphal, some grammarians felt tempted also to contest the authenticity of a satyr play and hence, in practice, the authenticity of an entire tetralogy. Were 75 genuine dramas preserved, therefore, not 74? It would appear so, particularly when other sources, confusing dramas composed with dramas preserved, speak of 75 Euripidean dramas, having subtracted from the figure of 78, that is, only 3 tragedies.

The 75 Alexandrian dramas include *Andromache* and *Archelaus*, neither of which was presented at official Athenian contests, and should one accept the debatable testimony of Aelian, *Varia Historia* II.13 regarding Euripidean contests at Piraeus, it is also possible that the 75 may have included dramas presented at Piraeus. In such a case, the latter would not have been 'new' dramas like *Andromache* and *Archelaus*, however, but rather dramas identical to those previously presented at the official Athenian contests or, less probably, to dramas presented later in Athens, considering that in the fifth century the contests in Piraeus appear not to have been organized by the State. (The suspicion that Euripides presented dramas outside Athens, particularly in the years prior to *Thesmophoriazusae*, is based in part on *Thesmophoriazusae* 390–1, ὅπουπερ ἔμβραχυ εἰσὶν θεαταὶ καὶ τραγῳδοὶ καὶ χοροί. However, ὅπουπερ κτλ. does not mean that Euripides slandered women; 'wherever they are . . .', but, 'in every place where there are spectators, tragic poets and choruses' – in the theatre, in short.) It appears to modern scholars, therefore, that amongst the 75 Alexandrian dramas the only unofficial works are *Andromache* and *Archelaus*.

If the other 73 Alexandrian dramas were all official, as was undoubtedly the case of the 14 which have not been preserved (the Alexandrians were able to verify their existence through theatrical documents alone, and they also included the two satyr plays pertaining to the tetralogy of *Medea* and *Phoenissae*), then to the 87 official dramas can be made to correspond only twenty-one tetralogies and the posthumous trilogy: hence, the addition of even a single pair of Lenaian tragedies becomes mathematically inadmissible.[3]

In effect, the chance of Euripides' ever having taken part in the contests of the Lenaia seems, in itself, to be extremely slim. The unidentified Euripidean contests within the twenty-five-year Dionysian–Lenaian period are at a maximum eight, or rather eight is the figure that we have reached since out of the twelve unidentified contests in the entire career of Euripides we have managed to locate only four within the twenty-three-year pre-Lenaian period. The total itself has amounted to twelve because we have not accepted as indubitably Dionysian the two victorious contests of unrecorded date, although they are most probably Dionysian, given the close agreement which exists between the three ancient sources regarding the number of Euripides' victories, an agreement which does not exist in the case of Sophocles and Sophocles the Younger, both of whom must also have been victorious at the Lenaia. Hence, the unidentified Euripidean contests amount in reality to ten, and of these seven pertain to the Dionysian–Lenaian period, since at least one of the two presumably Dionysian victories must pertain to that twenty-five-year period, for which evidence exists only in the case of the victory in 428. If both of these victories took place, therefore, in the Dionysian–Lenaian period, then the number of unidentified contests during that period is reduced to six.

The apparent fact that Euripides never took part in the contests of the Lenaia is hardly surprising, since at the Lenaia in particular he could have expected neither victory nor public success. The environment of the Lenaia – in contrast to that of the Dionysia, itself so little favourable to Euripides – was dominated by anti-Euripidean comic dramatists and by a public, composed exclusively of Athenians, subject to the influence of these dramatists: Euripides would obviously have avoided competing in such an environment. Besides, since his competitive activity must certainly have been far less intense than that of Sophocles, it would also have been impossible for him to have appeared at the Lenaia: suffice it to say that in the twenty-five-year Dionysian–Lenaian period, he participated in a maximum of thirteen contests, given that in the twenty-three-year pre-Lenaian period he had competed in a total of eight. Lastly, if our distinction regarding the structure of the two Athenian theatres is indeed valid, then Euripides would have preferred the theatre of Dionysos to the Lenaia for technical reasons alone, since it allowed for the use of the flying-machine, so necessary for and congenial to many of his tragedies during the Dionysian–Lenaian period.

When the scholiast on *Thesmophoriazusae* 1012 remarks that '*Andromeda* was presented along with *Helen*', he naturally restricts himself to providing the information necessary for readers of *Thesmophoriazusae* as the comedy moves from its parody of *Helen* to that of its fellow-competitor, *Andromeda*. Moreover, the fact that *Thesmophoriazusae* presents parodies of characters from *Helen* and *Andromeda* alone, and not from the entire tragic trilogy of the preceding year, does not again imply that *Helen* and *Andromeda* are a pair of Lenaian tragedies. Aristophanes obviously draws from tragedies congenial to the dramatic situation of his imprisoned 'heroine' and, whereas he presents parodies of some of the characters from *Helen* and *Andromeda*, from other Euripidean tragedies he borrows, tacitly or explicitly, technical devices and utterances: the 'heroine' of *Thesmophoriazusae*, having tried in vain to entice Euripides, employing a strategy from *Palamedes*, exclaims: 'there's no doubt about it, Euripides is ashamed of that frigid *Palamedes*. But, with what drama might I entice him? I know: I'll imitate the new *Helen*: after all I've got the female clothes.' Later, the Aristophanic 'heroine' says: 'Euripides, who's come running out as Perseus, has let me understand that I should become Andromeda. After all, I've got the chains.'

'I am Echo ... she who took part in the contest last year in this very same place, I too, for Euripides', Εὐριπίδη καὐτὴ ξυνηγωνιζόμην *Thesmophoriazusae* 1059–61 on the lips of Echo, previously one of the characters of *Andromeda*. The words and tone of this brief report imply a net affirmation of

Euripides' actual participation in the contest, all the more so when one considers that the character delivering the report is the character of a comedy, and that that comedy harbours little tenderness for Euripides. The fact that Euripides was satisfied with the contest is also demonstrated by the counter-opposition mentioned above between a *Helen* capable of enticing Euripides and an ineffectual *Palamedes*, of which he is held to be ashamed: 'there's no doubt about it, Euripides is ashamed of that frigid *Palamedes*. But, with what drama might I entice him? I know: I'll imitate the new *Helen*.' Now, if a para-Euripidean character speaks respectfully of an extremely recent contest involving Euripides, if Aristophanes hastens to re-present in *Thesmophoriazusae* a number of characters from *Andromeda* and *Helen* and has some of them interpreted by Euripides himself, Euripides who remains unmoved in the face of a tragedy from a tetralogy of his own which had obtained second place in the Dionysia of 415 and is instead seduced by a *Helen* of novel type (the fellow-competitor of *Andromeda* which after a few years is to drive the god of the dramatic contests in search of Euripides in the infernal world of the *Frogs*), then, from many directions, the winds that blow are those of a Euripidean victory in the contest of the preceding year. In *Thesmophoriazusae*, moreover, the capital trial for which the alarmed women of Athens finally decide to prepare a case against Euripides, the misogynist dramatist, might also be a rejoinder to the weighty recognition which the men of Athens used to award to their poet in theatre at the end of the contests. In the world of the Athenian theatre a victory on the part of Euripides was a rarity: for the contemporaries of Aristophanes it was almost a novelty.

2 Euripides, the schemer and victim of *Thesmophoriazusae*. *Lysistrata* and *Thesmophoriazusae*, fellow-competitors

Euripides, who would, therefore, have been a much-discussed figure in Athens after the previous theatrical season, is the main character of the prologue and second part of *Thesmophoriazusae*, and throughout the comedy is at once subject and object, schemer and artistic victim. With the keenest of malice, Aristophanes presents Euripides, the man of the theatre, at the service of Euripides, the private citizen, as for his own practical salvation he puts the formulas and creatures of his repertoire to the proof, above all those of *Helen* and *Andromeda* from the preceding year (although the expedient which is eventually to have success, significantly, is an intensely prosaic one: see 1128–32).

In this respect, *Thesmophoriazusae* is rendered distinct from any other extant work of Aristophanes: not only because it is Euripidean as regards technique and device – the complicated plot, not unravelled until the end, and then by virtue of the artful rescue of a 'heroine' by a barbarian (Helen, Andromeda!) – but also because its dramatic milieu is strictly private, dominated as it is by the individual dilemma of Euripides: how he should resist the threatening offensive of the anti-Euripidean women. This, of course, is merely a pretext for an artistic experiment, an experiment that finds its structural justification in the refusal of Agathon, who alone might have resolved Euripides' dilemma with any degree of certainty (cf. 186–7, 191–2).

The play is an artistic experiment, let me repeat, so much so that, to cite just one example, it is Euripides in person who divulges on the city square the intensely secret plan he himself has devised to deceive the Athenian women (cf. 577–96; Agathon, the only witness, returns indoors to work at 265, and Euripides emerges from the corridor at 279). Through the artful failure of this scheme, an experimental field is created for the liberating expedients adopted by Euripides (a reason for his appearance can be found in 269–76), and the dilemma posed by the women's hate becomes altogether secondary. More precisely, to succeed truly in liberating his instrumental 'heroine' Euripides must in the end promise the women that he will no longer offend them in his tragedies (1160–9), thus accepting the practical consequences of his complicated and unsuccessful counter-offensive. Hence, Euripides is not only the artistic victim of this extremely private comedy, but also its practical victim.

The private nature of *Thesmophoriazusae* is undoubtedly related to the fact that its protagonists – Euripides and his Relative – provoke no alteration in the scenic milieu, nor do they affirm their presence by establishing an environment of exemplary value, but rather leave intact the site of their action, concerned as they are with problems devoid of public significance. In *Thesmophoriazusae* – a comedy whose action is set in motion by the pre-dramatic initiative of its future chorus (cf. 81–91) – the scenic milieu is defined, and remains defined, by the chorus of the thesmophoriazusae (and by the actors and extras who temporarily portray the other thesmophoriazusae), while the scenic façade neither is nor ever becomes, as elsewhere, the centre of operations of the actor-protagonists, but throughout remains relevant to the chorus alone (as seen further on, this might explain the comedy's lack of a choral parodos). The scenic milieu defined by the thesmophoriazusae is the occasional site of action of the actor-protagonists, and the thesmophoriazusae themselves the occasional background to a comedy whose principal scope is the artistic caricature of Euripides, not his dispute with the Athenian women. Indeed, the thesmophoriazusae quite swiftly lose their anti-Euripidean verve, and allow Euripides and his Relative to proceed undisturbed: the thesmophoriazusae, in effect, stand aside to allow the innocuous tragic artifices of Euripides to take the stage.

Because of the fact that it is dominated by Euripides, and is also para-Euripidean in style, *Thesmophoriazusae* is somewhat unusual as regards both formal and structural elements: first of all, it has a plot befitting the inventor of the 'novelty' of the Athenian theatre – the Euripidean drama of intrigue; its landscape is tragic in style – for instance, the temple and altar; its parabasis is delivered in the presence of its imprisoned 'heroine' and her guardian (and also explicitly renounces political satire: cf. 965); it contains a dialectical agon in the tragic manner – long polemical speeches delivered in trimeters, followed by a dispute in tetrameters (cf. 331–519, 533–73); its metrical-musical form is frequently tragic or paratragic; and lastly it proposes 'puppet-like characters' drawn from the repertoire of Euripides. In practice, it decomposes and then parodically recomposes the scenic and expressive forms of Euripidean theatre. Naturally, however, only the decomposition and recomposition of the extant *Helen* can be appreciated fully, and the subtle and mischievously accurate treatment which the tragedy receives implies that Aristophanes must have procured the manuscript immediately: this is discussed in section 2 of chapter 11 on *Frogs*.[4]

Thesmophoriazusae, which has been transmitted in the Ravenna manuscript and in a copy of that manuscript alone, yields no information whatsoever regarding the contest. This is also the case with respect to Euripides' *Helen*. The date of *Thesmophoriazusae*, however, may still be established with certainty as 411, inasmuch as it is a contemporary of *Lysistrata*, or rather its fellow-competitor: as noted previously, both comedies bear signs of having been conceived for the theatre of Dionysos, and hence for the contests of the Dionysia.

At the Lenaia of 422, Aristophanes had also presented two comedies, *Proagon* and *Wasps*, and Philonides had appeared as the author of *Proagon* (as proposed by Theodor Bergk in 1838, Phrynicos, too, presented a pair of comedies at the Dionysia of 414, one of which he ceded to Ameipsias). According to Argument I.35, *Lysistrata* 'was produced by Kallistratos' (εἰσῆκται διὰ Καλλιστράτου). This implies that Aristophanes himself remained its author: evidently, *Thesmophoriazusae* was ceded to Kallistratos or Philonides.

So these two comedies are from the same contest, both feminist, one politico-civil in character, the other literary and based on private intrigue. At the Lenaia of 422, Aristophanes had behaved in a similar manner, ceding the anti-Euripidean and probably literary *Proagon* to Philonides, whilst appearing himself with the politico-civil *Wasps*. Due as much to this marked difference between the two comedies (not to mention the difference at the level of actors and chorus), it is highly probable that first prize went to *Lysistrata* or *Thesmophoriazusae*.

'These women, enemies of Euripides and of all the gods', 'no poet is wiser than Euripides, for no brood exists more impudent than that of women': lines from *Lysistrata* (283, 368–9), or rather the embryo of the first section of *Thesmophoriazusae*. In *Thesmophoriazusae* the Athenian women settle their private account with Euripides alone, after the battle they had fought in the public interest in *Lysistrata*. As seen at the end of section 1 above, Euripides must have scored a notable success at the Dionysia of 412, and from that success the idea of *Thesmophoriazusae* was born, when plans had already been laid for the highly political and panhellenic *Lysistrata*.[5]

3 The scenic organization and stage-technique of *Thesmophoriazusae*

'Would you kindly let me know where you are taking me, O Euripides?' 'You don't in the least have to hear everything that you're shortly going to see in person' (3–6): these are the first remarks to be made by a pair of characters who have appeared in the orchestra from the corridor after a long journey begun at dawn (cf. 2).

Because of the actor's portrait mask, and above all the mention of him by name in line 4, the spectators' recognition of Euripides is as rapid as it is opportune (although out of sheer indifference Agathon and his Servant react inadequately before the most illustrious Euripides). In line 74, Euripides' companion, with intentional vagueness, identifies himself as a 'kinsman' of Euripides. What he was not to hear about at once, but rather to see in person, is the 'little door' of a house: 'here dwells the most illustrious Agathon, the tragedian' (26, 28–9). From line 26 to line 265, the action takes place near the residence of the 'youngster' Agathon. Regarding the stage-technique of this episode and the use of the *ekkyklema*, see sections 6 and 8 of chapter 3.

Agathon disappears in 265, and soon afterwards visual attention is focused on the Thesmophorium. Euripides says to his Relative: 'come, get a move on; the signal of the assembly has appeared over the Thesmophorium' (277–8). The Thesmophorium has already been mentioned in lines 83 and 89, and clearly as the site of an ensuing action fundamental to a comedy entitled *Thesmophoriazusae*. Even more than in *Lysistrata*, one's expectation regarding the fundamental scene of the comedy is aroused early, well before the end of the prologue, and like the Acropolis in *Lysistrata*, the Thesmophorium forms part of the opening scenery, juxtaposed with the house of Agathon.

Many scholars believe instead that there is a radical change of scene, since between lines 276 and 277 the Ravenna manuscript contains the following note: ὀλολύζουσί τε ἱερὸν ὠθεῖται (or, -ζουσι· τὸ κτλ., it would seem). This double note, in contrast to other stage-notes to be found in the manuscripts of theatrical works from Aeschylus to Menander, is normally considered genuine, since it is not suggested in any way by the surrounding text. But if the note ὀλολύζουσι were genuinely Aristophanes', Euripides and his Relative would be obliged to react to the din they hear after 276, as do the characters of *Lysistrata* 240 (cf. also *Peace* 232–5, *Frogs* 312–13 and 757–8). After 276, however, Euripides' reaction is a purely visual one, impressed as he is by the signal which has appeared over the Thesmophorium. Hence, while the note ὀλολύζουσι is inappropriate and therefore inauthentic (it is of little importance that papyrus 1194 of the Italian Society, from the second century, transmits an ολολυ[between 276 and 277), the other must be inauthentic too, since at the very least it is superfluous: it is improbable that Aristophanes would have included such an annotation in a text that with a phrase as clear as 'the signal has appeared over the Thesmophorium' had already ensured that even the most inexpert didaskalos or reader would have been in a position technically to have executed or understood the stage-action.[6]

There are analogies with the action and stage-technique of *Lysistrata*: just as Lampito in *Lysistrata* exits by the corridor as the women move from Lysistrata's house towards the Acropolis, here Euripides exits by the corridor as his Relative moves from Agathon's house towards the Thesmophorium (277–9). The singularity in *Thesmophoriazusae* is instead the appearance of the chorus, unaccompanied as it is by the usual kind of parodos: the chorus appears in silence as the Relative is delivering the final iambic trimeters of the prologue. The explanation for this phenomenon could reside in the quite exceptional fact that the comedy's scenic milieu is defined exclusively by the chorus. The chorus is at home, so to speak (even more obviously than the chorus of *Frogs*), and is neither provoked into making an appearance nor allows itself to be attracted by a scenic milieu defined by the actor-protagonists. It is perfectly natural, therefore, that the comedy should lack a parodos of the normally aggressive or at least animated kind. Yet once the chorus, master of the scenic façade and orchestra, starts to suspect that intruders have invaded its milieu, then movements and songs resembling those of a parodos begin (cf. 655–88).

'Look what a crowd is coming up here beneath the smoke of burning torches', says the Relative, disguised as a thesmophoriazusa, to his imaginary servant-girl in 280–1. The Relative is referring to the thesmophoriazusae, as they move from the corridor through the orchestra towards the Thesmophorium (although some of them might be entering the orchestra *from* the Thesmophorium, i.e. from the scenic façade). Having made his offering to the thesmophorian goddesses (282–91), the Relative undoubtedly mingles with the thesmophoriazusae of the chorus as they assemble to hear the thesmophorian oratresses (see 292), who address the chorus and the spectators (cf. prologue of *Acharnians*). Needless to say, the assembly takes place in the orchestra and not in the interior of the scenic façade-Thesmophorium. The latter thesis is still proposed by a considerable number of scholars, who confuse the interior of the scenic façade with the interior of a cathedral and, what is more, ancient theatre with the theatre of the Opera.[7]

During the prologue, Euripides did say that the women would hold an assembly 'in the Thesmophorium' and that it was necessary to try to 'enter the Thesmophorium' (83, 89), but it is still the orchestra that corresponds to the interior of the temple. The latter is at times effectively appreciable as such (cf. ἐσελήλυθε in 657), but normally seems to be more an open space from which one exits, for example, directly by means of the corridor, or else reaches from the Agora by means of the corridor once again (cf. 457, 572–8): an open space which even assumes the value of the sacred wood of the thesmophorian goddesses (cf. 1149). These latter the Relative would have favoured 'here'

(283), just as the assembled thesmophoriazusae would have the goddess Athena come 'here' (319), and come 'here' also whilst they are dancing (1138), etc.: 'here', which always refers to the orchestral space. The assembled thesmophoriazusae propose a search for the 'man seated amongst us' (600) and then, no longer in assembly, look around the orchestra to see if there is 'another man seated amongst us' (688).

In the orchestral space, perhaps close to the scenic façade, there appear to be some tents set up for the thesmophoriazusae (σκηναί, 658, cf. 624; the spaces between the tents are described as δίοδοι). In front of the scenic façade-Thesmophorium there definitely stands an altar (695, 888) bearing votive offerings in wood (773, 778), to which the Relative flees in 689 (cf. 693, 773, 886). The altar, along with the tents, is on-stage from the beginning of the comedy, unless it is brought out between 278 and 283.

The Thesmophorium (278, 880, 1046 and previously 83 and 89) rarely enters the action. In 726, there is talk of 'bringing out wood', and one of the thesmophoriazusae goes with her maidservant to fetch it (728). The wood has been prepared in advance (see the definitive article in 728), and is undoubtedly stored in some interior space – within the temple, presumably. When the Archer, following the order given in 930 (εἰσάγων), leads the Relative away to tie him up, the action takes place in an interior again, as it does when he goes to fetch a mat in 1007 (he returns quickly, but then falls asleep until 1081; and after 1135 until 1171 also). Between 1198 and 1209, the Archer dallies with a dancing-girl, certainly in an interior once again. In these cases, however, the interior cannot be that of the temple: the Archer employs a neutral opening in the scenic façade, since only the central opening is assigned to the Thesmophorium. In 1011, Euripides, too, emerges for a moment from this neutral opening (ἐκδραμών). This phenomenon – the use of a neutral stage-opening by actor-protagonists extraneous to the scenic façade – could be explained by the fact that the scenic façade in *Thesmophoriazusae* relates to the chorus.[8]

4 Role distribution

The comedy's ten characters are played by three actors and one amateur actor:

first actor, altogether around 350 lines, of which around 50 are lyrical: Euripides' Relative, 1–946, 1002–1209 (from 279, he is disguised as a woman);

second actor, altogether almost 290 lines: Euripides, 5–279, Mica, the oratress, 380–764 (over 100 in trimeters), Euripides as Menelaus, 871–927, Euripides back-stage as Echo, 1056–96, Euripides as Perseus, 1098–1132, Euripides, 1160–75, who then disguises himself on-stage and impersonates an aged bawd named Artemisia in 1177–1209;

third actor, all told around 220 lines, 101–29 lyrical: Agathon's Servant, 39–70,

Agathon, 101–265, a Widowed Flower-girl-oratress, 443–58, Kleisthenes, 574–654, Critylla, 759–935, Archer, 1001–7, 1082–1201, 1210–25;

amateur actor, with eight trimeters; Prytanis, 929–44.

NB: Victor Coulon attributes the prose lines 295–311 and trimeters 331–51 and 372–80 to a distinct female actor, whose functions alternate between those of priestess and heraldess. Yet, whereas these lines are undoubtedly uttered by a single voice (there are those who attribute 295–351 to a Priestess and 372–80 to a Heraldess), the voice is that of the coryphaea (it is quite typical that the coryphaeus should prepare himself to judge the orators: cf. 305–9): in *Frogs* 354–71, 382–3 and 394–6, the coryphaeus behaves in an analogous manner. One could perhaps allow for a Heraldess in *Thesmophoriazusae*, given that the comedy contains a parody of a political assembly (not of a religious ceremony, as in *Birds* 863–88). But in such a case the Heraldess would make herself heard again, whereas instead it is the coryphaea alone who delivers the remaining announcements and orders (cf. 571–3, 597–602, 607, etc.). Hence, it is the coryphaea who takes the floor when the prologue ends in 294, after which the actors dedicate themselves to the thesmophorian oratresses.

Like others before him, the French editor attributes the roles in 443–58 and 759–935 to the same 'Second Woman'. However, it is clear that the Widowed Flower-girl from 443–58, having gone to the Agora in line 458 to weave twenty garlands (cf. 457–8), would hardly be in a position to return to the theatre after fewer than two hundred lines; it would also be out of character were this industrious flower-seller to return to the assembly when she had already said all that she had to say and given all the advice that she had to give (cf. 443–5 and 453–4). The woman in 759–935, who is 'old' (896, cf. also 1024–5), may indeed be unaware of what has happened in the mean time (760–1, cf. also 893–4), but apparently, as is often the case, she has arrived late for the assembly (cf. 762). It would be imprudent, therefore, to attribute 759–935 to the hypothetical, or rather presumed, Priestess of 295–351.[9]

Extras: Agathon's Servants in the prologue, to carry the poet to his work-couch (one of his servants is invoked in 238). Other thesmophoriazusae-extras undoubtedly appear after the prologue, Philista in 568 and the Nursemaid in 608–9, for example, and perhaps the secretary in 432. The thesmophoriazusae are attended by Slave-girls (537, cf. also 726), one of whom is called Mania (728, 739, 754). An extra portrays the Archer in lines 923–46. The Archer is silently assisted by servants, or rather stage-hands, when he brings out the Relative bound to a pole. A dancing-girl, Little Fawn, appears in the finale (1172). The flautist, Teredon, invoked in 1175, is the usual comic flautist.

11

FROGS

1 A short account of the revision of *Frogs*

Frogs is known to have been produced at the Lenaia during the archontate of Kallias, who held office from the summer of 406 to the summer of 405. *Marmor Parium*, amongst other sources, reports that Sophocles died during this archontate. *Frogs* refers to the dead tragedian in the prologue, second prologue and exodos (76–82, 787–94, 1515–19): in the prologue and exodos, he is recalled in relation to Dionysos' anabasis from Hades with a tragic poet (see 71–85 and 1414–1533), in the second prologue, in relation to the dispute between Aeschylus and Euripides over the infernal throne of tragedy (see 757–1410).

Scholars have been in debate for some time as to whether the planning of *Frogs* followed the death of Euripides in the winter of 407–406, or that of Sophocles; and if *Frogs* was planned and written while Sophocles was still alive, to what extent his death obliged Aristophanes to revise the comedy. In recent times, one particular scholar, while he does tend to accept that Sophocles' death obliged Aristophanes to add to the already complete text Dionysos' anabasis from Hades with a fine poet, has still advised that the author's flexible and digressive comic game might, in such a case, make a joke of one's attempts at analysis. However, were an analysis of *Frogs* (of which, in fact, no sufficiently thorough examination has ever been made) to reveal a thread composed of essential logical, and artistic and structural deviations, and were these to have been directly or indirectly linked to an extremely recent and serious public event – the death of Sophocles, for instance – that which is truly illogical in the Aristophanic comic game would disdain to recognize itself in phenomena so logically and historically interconnected and artistically essential.

The results of my own analysis (*Storia delle Rane di Aristofane* (Padua, 1961)) indicate that Sophocles' death prompted the *reworking* of *Frogs* at a point when the comedy was already prepared for the stage. Here I shall restrict myself to providing the essential details.[1]

The reworking of *Frogs* hinges on trimeters 71–85 in the prologue. These fifteen trimeters – dealing with the following themes: (1) that Euripides is considered desirable by Dionysos in so far as he is a 'good poet'; (2) a conception of Dionysos as a conscientious patron of the dramatic arts; (3) the essential lack of a good tragic poet in Athens; (4) Dionysos' *anabasis* from Hades with Euripides, the fine poet, not with Sophocles, his better; (5) the defection from Athens to Macedonia of a good poet such as Agathon – were written as a consequence of Sophocles' death and replaced lines better adapted to the surrounding context. The latter, with biting malice, sets off a philo-Euripidean *catabasis* on the part of Dionysos (52–70, 86–107; 100 = 311), and sees Dionysos, comically masked as Herakles, confess to having been driven out on his infernal voyage by a morbid obsession with Euripides – that fearless poet, preferable by far to the sterile verse-mongers and poetlings left in his place, 'more loquacious than Euripides by a mile'.

With the death of Sophocles, who had been victorious for the twenty-fourth time at the very recent Dionysia of 406,[2] the last remaining poet of the old generation had passed away and the Athenian theatre, practically speaking, became a wasteland. Aristophanes, who had projected *Frogs* after the death of Euripides, was obliged to attempt an overall reworking of the motivation and scope of Dionysos' voyage into Hades. A simple updating on Sophocles would have proved inadequate in the light of the altered civil and theatrical conditions prevailing in Athens.

Hence, significant modifications were improvised in the opening dialogue between Dionysos and Herakles – trimeters 71–85 being substituted for the original lines – and consequently in the finale, too.

The original finale – which had quite certainly dealt with the pre-ordained consequences of the artistic duel between Euripides and Aeschylus *in the interest of the kingdom of the dead*: the assignment of the infernal throne of tragedy to the victor and the reception in the infernal Prytaneum (cf. 761–5, and also the final part of *Knights*, just after the conclusion of the political duel) – was deleted and replaced by a new finale which strove once and for all to make the late-sown seed of 71–85 blossom and mature, artificially at least. The great, and also purely comic, artistic encounter between Aeschylus and Euripides, touched on in *Clouds* 1364–79, readily deviated in the end towards a conscientious and unforeseen supplementary agon, motivated by the belated and conscientious need for an *anabasis* on the part of a poet in the interest of Athens, newly bereft of any fine tragic poets (1411–1533; 1418–21 → 77 and 71–2). At the end of the comedy, therefore, having charged Pluton to entrust his throne to Sophocles, Aeschylus could begin his voyage alongside Dionysos towards the light, to alter the theatrical and civil destiny of Athens.

The death of Sophocles, therefore, led to Aeschylus' resurrection, although of that particular resurrection, strictly speaking, Athens stood least in need, since Aeschylus' tragedy, and his alone, 'had not died with him' and Aeschylus himself 'was not in agreement with the Athenians' (868, 807). Euripides, moreover, for whom Dionysos had been forced quite significantly to compromise himself in the belated and serious lines of the prologue (before Herakles and the spectators at least), in the improvised and serious finale is hardly in the wrong when he cries out that he has been betrayed, as if Dionysos had led him personally to believe that it was he who would return to earth, a predicament from which Dionysos manages to extract himself only by recourse to witticisms (1469–78).

The improvised path taken at 1411 had indeed created some predicaments; it had also been followed with great hesitation and insufficient preparation. The entire passage, 1411–1533, is marked by rather crude technique: Pluton appears at 1414 with brusque timeliness, the famous throne of tragedy is never once brought out on-stage, after 1476 Euripides vanishes, the brief reception at Pluton's residence seems forced, Sophocles is notable for his absence, despite being the heir to the tragic throne of Aeschylus, and in the last fifty lines of the comedy Dionysos is left mute, indeed entirely ignored.

For the spectators and judges at the Lenaia of 405, however, the logical and scenic inconsistencies characterizing the improvised patriotic finale of *Frogs* would clearly not have been so disturbing. A sufficiently adroit presentation would have been enough to resolve many of them, and the spectators and judges were also well aware of the serious reasons why the author had been obliged to improvise both Aeschylus' resurrection and the altered conclusion of the comedy.

The new finale, 1411–1533, in which Euripides, too, is subjected to a serious interrogation by Dionysos in the context of a patriotic anabasis from Hades, obliged Aristophanes to bring the epirrhematic debate on the essence of the tragic arts well forward. From an analysis of the overall context of 860–1410, it emerges that this debate, the present lines 895–1098 (ending with Aeschylus' and Dionysos' stern judgement on the artistic, ethical and political merits of Euripides, 1065–98), once followed closely the inconclusive formal agons in 1099–1410. The anticipation of the epirrhematic debate had not only allowed for a new finale, containing an equal political agon between Aeschylus and the then already condemned Euripides, but had also compelled Aristophanes to suppress a scene dealing with the measuring of tragic language in which Aeschylus had come off worse. This had originally preceded the scene of the weighing of tragic language in which Aeschylus wins (1365–1410 → 797; the instruments of measurement are announced in 799–801), and had to be suppressed since in the revised version of the comedy it would have been too close to the new finale, where the intention was to resuscitate Aeschylus, and to do so with full honours. Besides, *after* his victory in the epirrhematic debate, it would have been inappropriate for Aeschylus to have suffered defeat in any form.

The original ending of *Frogs*, governed as it was by the harsh judgement of Aeschylus and Dionysos, was undoubtedly far more severe towards Euripides: not only had the anticipation of the epirrhematic debate allowed for an equal political agon between Aeschylus and the then already annihilated Euripides, but, to all intents and purposes, it had also deprived Aeschylus' and Dionysos' severe judgement of its element of decisiveness. The *anabasis with Euripides, the fine poet*, inserted into the prologue of *Frogs* as a consequence of Sophocles' death, obliged Aristophanes not only to treat Aeschylus even better (to resuscitate him and not even have him suffer defeat in his artistic encounter with Euripides), but consequently to relinquish, amongst other things, any cogent progression in the trial against Euripides' art. The anticipation of the epirrhematic debate, therefore, was effected as part of the general reworking, not solely to facilitate the substitution of the finale.

Naturally, Sophocles himself profited from the revision: apart from the honourable mentions in the prologue, second prologue (where trimeters 786b–795 were inserted) and new exodos, it would most probably have been his death which led Aristophanes to omit lines 1254–6, in which Aeschylus was defined as 'he who until the present day has written by far the most numerous and beautiful songs'. After the death of Sophocles, a definition such as this had come to sound disrespectful to a poet whom the revised *Frogs* was bound not to offend in any way whatsoever, not even indirectly. Hence, the original lines, 1252–6, had to be labelled as not being intended for performance (see section 2 below) and were replaced by lines 1257–60, which are only apparently dittographic.

The alterations made to *Frogs* are summarized in the following list, in which [< >] = substitutions, < > = additions, ⌐ ¬ = transpositions, ( ) = extant suppressions, [ ] = suppressions, and └──┘ = original positions of parts transposed:

1–70	<1257–1260>
[<71–85>]	1261–1364
86–786a	[ ]
<786b–795>	1365–1410
796–894	[ ]
⌐895–1098⌐	└895–1098┘
1099–1251	[<1411–1533>]
(1252–1256)	

The diacritic list itself shows that the alterations were made with regard to economy, so that the active alterations cover no more than 150 lines (71–85, 786b–795, 1257–60, 1411–1533), of which only about 30 are assigned to the members of the chorus. Amongst the passive alterations, the most striking, by virtue of its extreme economy, is the transposition of the lengthy scene 895–1098, which was achieved, moreover, without even the minimum of harmonistic retouching. Nor was this retouching done at other points, most noticeably in the case of the suppressed scene originally located between 1364

201

and 1365, of which, besides the advance mention in 799–801, there also remains a perceptible echo in 1366–72.

The revision of *Frogs* was clearly dominated by a sense of urgency.

Aristophanes had the comedy staged at the Lenaia of 405, either at the end of January or at the beginning of February. At the beginning of the summer of 406, the new archon had taken office, assuming the normal responsibilities. These included the prompt organization of the dramatic contests taking place in January–February and March–April (cf. Aristotle, *Athenaion Politeia* 56). Sophocles is known to have died during the archontate of Kallias, archon from the beginning of the summer of 406 to the end of the spring of 405, while the comedies' more or less definitive text, or at least their plots, would have been accepted by the archon (cf. Plato, *Laws* 817d) in autumn, or perhaps at the beginning of winter. As for the more or less definitive text or the plot, Aristophanes' opting for the Lenaia rather than the Dionysia, following later in March–April, might imply that the text of *Frogs* was already at an advanced stage of preparation (the text of *Peace*, staged in March–April 421, reveals that the comedy was first planned not earlier than October 422), and that the need to revise it had not as yet arisen.

Be that as it may, when this need did arise, no alternative remained other than to complete the revision with a certain degree of urgency. The spectators and judges, however, knowing that Sophocles had only recently died, would not have been perturbed in the least by its urgency and economy. Indeed, it was by means of this timely and significant revision alone that Aristophanes managed to redeem his comedy, and he did so with such success that the modern reader is left bewildered. (Regarding the adventures of the *Second Clouds*, see section 3b of the relevant chapter.)

2 The second production of *Frogs*. *Frogs* and the circulation of dramas

Frogs was produced by Philonides at the Lenaia of 405 and defeated the comedies entered against it by Phrynichos and Plato (see Argument I.36–8). Phrynichos also had to update his comedy, which was entitled *Muses*: 'blessed Sophocles, he died after a long life, a wise and happy man, composed many fine tragedies and had a sweet death, never once knowing illness'. The funeral elegy in this fragment implies that Sophocles was not one of the characters of *Muses*.

Not only did *Frogs* win first prize but, according to the Aristotelian Dikaiarchos, it also received the unusual honour of being given a second performance. When this was Dikaiarchos fails to mention, but it is clear, for technical, economical and administrative reasons alone, that the second performance must have involved the same actors and choreutai, choregos and didaskalos as the first. It would also have taken place in the environment most favourable to the exceptional second performance of a comedy, and of a Lenaian comedy in particular, and this could not have been the complex and rigorous environment of the springtime Dionysia, where comedy, in any case, was of minor importance (nor should one forget that at the Dionysia of 405 as it appeared to Aristotle, according to the scholiast on *Frogs* 404, the financing of *two* choregoi was required). Dikaiarchos' eloquent silence apart, it is clear therefore that the Lenaian *Frogs* also received its second performance under the administration of the Lenaia of 405, before the same audience and the same judges, and that the new production would have been practically identical to that deemed worthy of victory and of repetition.[3]

The fact that *Frogs* was put into circulation complete with lines not intended for performance (1252–6) might indicate that the text was not even minimally reconsidered after its performance.

With regard to this, it should be mentioned that some analytic readers in modern times (like certain Alexandrian philologists in theirs) have made deletions between lines 1437 and 1466. Yet in order to obtain a version of the text as reliable as the conditions allow, one must bear in mind the reasons for which lines 1411–1533 came to be drafted and also the manner in which the drafting actually took place: whereas on the one hand Aristophanes was obliged to present Euripides too in the new finale as a poet who might eventually have been of use to the Athenians, and hence to make him speak rather seriously, on the other he actually scripted this improvised finale in a rather crude and venturesome way, leaving it open to being circulated in an inadequate edition. For Aristophanes, the essential thing was to have brought the comedy safely into port, and for him that meant the theatre.[4]

An edition of the comedy was eventually circulated, yet this does not necessarily imply that it was first prepared or overseen *by the author*: for example, when around 417 Aristophanes abandoned his plans for the staging of the *Second Clouds*, throughout the years that followed he left the text of the comedy incomplete; and once he had brought *Assemblywomen* into port, in the year 392, he did not concern himself in the least with eliminating lines 1154–62, which had been improvised just before the comedy's performance and also made redundant by the verdict of the judges (as seen further on, in the edition eventually circulated these lines also appeared at an unsuitable point). It would seem, therefore, that the reader's editions of the comedies were based on versions which the author himself had never revised, either after the end of the contest or after his own decision not to compete – on versions which he himself had never technically prepared for public circulation.

Obviously, many specialists, for reasons associated with their work, procured written versions of theatrical texts, and one even went so far as transcribing a passage from the extremely bad tragedian Morsimos (*Frogs* 151): Aristophanes himself, for instance, must have immediately procured copies of *Helen* and *Andromeda* to have been in a position to parody them accurately the following year in *Thesmophoriazusae*, whereas in *Frogs* 52 Dionysos speaks of having read *Andromeda* aboard ship. But that the needs of the dramatists and public in fifth-century Athens gave birth to a wide and influential circulation of dramas in book form, that the spectators of *Frogs* held in their hands the works of Aeschylus and Euripides and that the success of the reader's version of the *Second Clouds* compared to that of the *First* can be explained only if it was prepared by Aristophanes in person: these are affirmations made by Wilamowitz, who, on this occasion at least, confused the fifth century BC with the nineteenth century AD.

It is true that the dramas were staged only once in Athens, and that on these occasions not all who were interested in seeing them could have been sure to attend. However, unofficial second performances, in and outside Athens, must have been quite normal events: 'Sophocles rarely went to the theatre, but when Euripides competed with a new tragedy, in that case he was sure to go', reports Aelian (*Varia Historia* II.13). Indeed, in an Athens accustomed each year to an extremely intense theatrical life and persistently in search of novelty, it is highly unlikely that a dramatist would have relied on the comparative novelty of the circulation of texts to have his drama better appreciated by a wider public after it had already been performed and had already been subjected to judgement – a drama, moreover, conceived for a single occasion, for judgement in a contest and for eventual perfection during its performance on-stage. After the failure of *Clouds* Aristophanes did not resort to circulating the text of the comedy, but attempted the theatre again with the *Second Clouds*.

So insignificant was the circulation of written texts in the fifth century that when a dramatist died, his work virtually died with him. The only exception was that of Aeschylus, which the Athenian State decreed should be performed posthumously.[5]

3 On the bipartite economy of *Frogs* and some artistic consequences of the revision

Frogs, a comedy of normal length containing a normal median parabasis, is dominated in its final seven hundred lines by the same three characters and at the end by a minor fourth (Aeschylus, Euripides, Dionysos, Pluton); it is also bereft of a single scenic diversion. Neither in the first part of *Birds* nor in a comedy such as *Knights* does one encounter such profound and sustained dependence on the actors, or such complete scenic immobility. It is also unusual that three of these four characters are *new* and that two of them – Aeschylus and Euripides – are protagonists in respect to Dionysos, who, disguised first as Herakles then as the slave, had himself been the protagonist up to the parabasis.

From the prologue to the parabasis, 'Dionysos' had been flanked constantly by an extremely active character (his slave, Xanthias), and gradually over half a dozen other extremely varied characters had appeared on-stage, not to mention the small chorus of Frogs and the chorus of the Initiated (temporarily filled out by elements extraneous to the chorus). From prologue to parabasis, the stage-technique had been distinguished by its mobility, exuberant variety and illusionistic extemporaneity, and the performance structure by its fluency and lightness. The first part of the comedy is concerned with the adventurous and multifarious voyage of 'Dionysos' and Xanthias from Athens to the house of Pluton (1–673): the origin of this voyage is a mania entertained by 'Dionysos' for the late Euripides and his fearless little phrases (cf. 52–106). The second part deals with the intensely complex artistic contest between Aeschylus and Euripides for the infernal throne of tragedy, judged by the then no longer ambiguous Dionysos (814–1410; regarding the finale, 1411–1533, where Pluton also appears, see section 1 above): advance notice of the contest is given after the parabasis by means of a dialogue between Aiakos and Xanthias, respectively the Slaves of Pluton and Dionysos (738–813). Its origin is the mania of the scoundrels of Hades for Euripides and his sophisms (see 771–786a). After the parabasis, the two Servants, inactive throughout the rest of the comedy, give an account of the back-stage issue of the scene preceding the parabasis (738–44 → 628–73).

The two sections of *Frogs*, therefore, deal with completely different subjects, are governed by different performance- and stage-techniques and involve two distinct sets of characters (with the exception of Dionysos, who in the first part, none the less, almost always keeps his identity concealed). The second section is introduced by a 'prologue', which initially functions as a link (the highly elevated parabasis is also a link, or rather a prelude; cf. previously the chorus in lines 354–8) and, conveniently, is performed by two characters active just before the parabasis. One of them, Xanthias, had in fact been the complementary protagonist of the entire first section of the comedy; the other, Aiakos, was the most important infernal character from the end of the parodos to the parabasis.[6]

The nonchalance with which Aristophanes juxtaposes and then skilfully links two such entirely distinct and effectively autonomous artistic organisms might be an indication of the dramaturgical problem inevitably posed by the representation of Aeschylus' and Euripides' encounter in Hades in the presence of a judge – an encounter, as *Frogs* 1109–18 implicitly admits, that from an exclusively theatrical point of view was ambitious and demanding in the extreme. Faced with the impossibility of staging and dramatizing the debate and the artistic sentence, it appears that Aristophanes wished to compensate the spectators in advance by offering them a major spectacle, animated and varied in style, involving a journey of great length. The staging of a journey is an undertaking of quite unusual significance in a theatrical work (this is discussed in section 4 below).

The prolongation of the voyage to Hades begins as early as the prologue: Dionysos-Herakles, who wants to reach Hades by the shortest route (118, cf. also 127–8), opts instead for a lengthy one (136). And this is not all: when the two wayfarers finally knock on Pluton's door (460, cf. previously 431–6), they do everything in their power to avoid being recognized. Hence, in marked contrast to the two expeditious wayfarers in *Birds*, this pair make contact with Pluton at an extremely late stage, and not out of any decision of their own: 'I would have preferred it if you had thought of this earlier [of bringing me to Pluton so that he could recognize me as a god], before giving me a beating' (672–3): with this mischievous remark the ambiguous Dionysos brings the first section of the comedy to a close. In line 805, towards the end of the metaparabatic prologue, dedicated from line 757 onwards to an account of the sensational encounter between Aeschylus and Euripides, Xanthias enquires of Aiakos: 'who on earth is going to judge such a contest?'. Aiakos: 'that was the difficult thing, given that Aeschylus and Euripides felt there was a dearth of connoisseurs, and since Aeschylus himself didn't get on with the Athenians and considered the others incapable of discerning the genius of a poet. Hence, they turned to your master, because he is an expert in the arts. But, let's get back indoors, for when our masters get down to things seriously, we can expect a beating.'

'That was the difficult thing', the problem that had arisen once the dispute broke out after the death of Euripides (cf. 771–80), to find a judge *in Hades*, acceptable to the fastidious Aeschylus as well. On the name of Dionysos, however, Aeschylus had at last voiced his assent. These conscientious considerations, made just at the end of the metaparabatic prologue and accepted without any objection by Xanthias, are intended to convey to the spectators the necessity of the serious new role henceforth to be assumed by a character who until recently had been carefree and unstable and had even descended into Hades in search of Euripides. The adventure in Hades in the first section of the comedy is given what amounts to a functional justification, in so far as the presence in Hades of this outsider (who has finally allowed himself to be identified as Dionysos during the parabasis: cf. 738–42) seems well-nigh providential in the attempt to decide which is the better poet, Aeschylus or Euripides, soon to make their first appearance on-stage portrayed by the actors engaged a short while previously for Xanthias and Aiakos.

The introduction of the authentic Dionysos as an impartial judge of the tragic arts (doubtless wearing a new costume) demonstrates that the pro-Euripidean motivation for the voyage into Hades, given in lines 52–106 of the prologue, was suited to the temporary protagonist of the first section alone. One should also note that during his voyage and adventure in Hades Dionysos hardly dwells upon his motivation (apart from the allusive reference in 311 = 100; 359, delivered by the chorus, is interesting too, since it might also refer to Euripides: cf. 1085 and 1521), and that in fact it was actually malicious with regard to Euripides. Indeed, the brief little Euripidean phrases, for which 'Dionysos' had developed such a craze and claimed to have undertaken his voyage into Hades, he himself deformed continually and hence, in practice, criticized (cf. 96–103, 105). And should any of the spectators have failed to understand that 'Dionysos' was lovingly criticizing his dear Euripides whilst at once professing to admire him, Herakles was there to remind them in 104: 'they're pure nonsense, and you think so too'.

Instead, it was in lines 71–85 of the prologue, the new lines of the revised *Frogs*, that the protagonist had gravely compromised himself for Euripides: not only, speaking as the conscientious patron of the dramatic arts, had he judged Euripides to be a 'fine poet', but he had also allowed himself to be ascribed a firm proposal to make an *anabasis* from Hades with Euripides – not with Sophocles (whereas of Aeschylus not a word is said!) – in the interest of the tragic theatre of Athens. If many readers, beginning in practice with the Byzantine Thomas Magister ('rather than bringing Euripides back up, Dionysos requests that a contest should be held between Aeschylus and Euripides': Argument III.6–7, p. 274 Dübner), have noticed an incongruity between the Dionysos who compromises himself for Euripides in the prologue, proposing to resurrect him in an Athens devoid of fine poets, and the Dionysos who subsequently agrees to be Aeschylus' and Euripides' judge in the dispute over the infernal throne of tragedy, this incongruity is entirely due to the weight and importance of the new and extremely binding trimeters 71–85, which are enough to eclipse the light and malicious surrounding context and to render somewhat less plausible – for the reader at least – the long and carefree adventure in Hades that follows on from the parodos (460–673).

The reader would also have been surprised to note that towards the end of the *first* artistic encounter between the two poets, Dionysos, so seriously pro-Euripidean in lines 71–85 of the prologue, should have lent his vigorous approval and support to Aeschylus' harsh anti-Euripidean closing speech (cf. 1065–98), and that despite this new resolutely anti-Euripidean stance he should on the whole have appeared comically impartial or have acted as Euripides' benevolent protector during the three succeeding biased contests (1119–1410), as he had also in 830–91, without even once expressing a judgement. This disharmony did not exist in the original *Frogs*, not only because of the absence of lines 71–85, but also because the artistic and political conviction of Euripides there took place extremely late, towards the end of the comedy: the epirrhematic debate, 895–1098, as seen in section 1 above, once followed closely the inconclusive contests in 1119–1410.

The anticipation of the epirrhematic debate created other inconveniences as well. In Aristophanes' epirrhematic debates, whoever first takes the floor, in this case Euripides in 907, is also destined to emerge as the loser. In practice, therefore, the spectators can always foresee the outcome of an epirrhematic debate, which in itself creates no problem. In the case of *Frogs*, however, where the two rivals appear on-stage at 830, it is inappropriate that the spectators should be able to foresee Euripides' defeat in the general debate on the tragic arts or, at any rate, that he should effectively be liquidated in 1065–98. The audience's foresight and its premature confirmation deprive the contests in 1119–1410 of dramatic interest, despite the fact that they are announced in 862a and 797. It is true that the epirrhematic debate in *Knights* 756–940, in which the Paphlagonian loses, is followed by two minor encounters. But, in *Knights* the Paphlagonian begs for these encounters and in each case they end in his defeat. Besides, the catastrophe of the ignoble Paphlagonian (the work of his still more ignoble rival) is governed implacably by an oracle, of whose existence the spectators have been aware since the prologue (nor should one forget that the epirrhematic debate in *Knights* follows two other inconclusive contests: cf. *Knights* 303–456 and 475–690). The decisive epirrhematic debate in the revised *Frogs*, followed as it is by three other inconclusive contests, is hence demonstrably premature, even from a purely dramatic point of view (here I shall avoid mentioning the various technical points which indicate that lines 895–1098 presuppose lines 1099–1410 and that the latter are strictly dependent on the context of 860–94).

Not to mention, of course, its ideological prematurity, and hence the ideological belatedness of the scene at 1099–1410, a progression whose ideological and dramatic abnormality was noticed by Max Pohlenz at least. In 1920, he voiced his dissatisfaction with an artistic contest that passed from general to particular arguments and failed to end with a discussion on the ethical influence of tragedy, as such a discussion would have been calculated to ensure Euripides' defeat. This had been the progression in the original *Frogs*, announced by Euripides himself in 862–4: τἄπη → 1099–1247; τὰ μέλη → 1248–1364; τὰ νεῦρα κτλ. → 895–1098 (between 1364 and 1411 come the two short scenes of the measuring and weighing of lines, announced by Aiakos in 797–801). Comprising two thorough examinations regarding formal aspects without any judgement from Dionysos, two technical scrutinies ending in mechanical and uncritical assessments favourable in one case to Euripides and in the other to Aeschylus, and a lengthy examination of artistic, ethical and political aspects culminating in Dionysos' judgement against Euripides (895–1098), the original progression had more in common with Aristophanes' own position regarding the poetics of tragedy.

The third point in Euripides' programme merits closer consideration. In lines 911–79, Euripides castigates the mechanism (911–924a) and also the expressive and interrelated thematical and ethical aspects of Aeschylus' tragedies (924b–938, cf. also 961b–963). Then, after a comment on the preliminary diet and refinement to which he had been obliged to subject the tragedy left to him by Aeschylus (939–44), he illustrates the mechanism (945–7, but see also 948–50) and also the expressive and interrelated thematic and ethical aspects of his own tragedies (948–79).

He keeps faithful, in short, to his declared intention to speak of his own ποίησις and of that of others (907–8), and in particular observes the programme outlined in 862b–864: δάκνειν . . . τὰ νεῦρα τῆς Τραγῳδίας καὶ νὴ Δία τὸν Πηλέα γε καὶ τὸν Αἴολον καὶ τὸν Μελέαγρον κἄτι μάλα τὸν Τήλεφον, to bite at 'the strings of tragedy' and also (καὶ . . . γε), by god, its substance, its themes and ethics. It was regarding the substance of his tragedies that Aeschylus had rebuked Euripides in 842, 846 and 849–50, whereas in 1008–88 his war-horse is this alone. Having at heart the φύσεις ποιητῶν (810), Aeschylus loses all interest in the 'strings of tragedy' and makes a few formal observations in 1060–4 alone.

Τὰ νεῦρα τῆς Τραγῳδίας are the strings on which tragedy moves, those which make it work. Euripides' criticism of Aeschylus is that he has no idea of how to manœuvre his characters, but leaves them sitting for long periods mute on-stage, and when he does decide to make them speak, what they say is incomprehensible (911–27). Euripides, on the other hand, knows how to make his characters work, and hence his dramas are better designed (945–50). Aeschylus, in short, cannot move the strings of tragedy. His characters, therefore, are so many immobile puppets (cf. 911–13), and the bases on which his dramas are built inconsistent, disconnected (cf. 923, 945): Aeschylus is ἀξύστατος, 'disconnected', in the words of the sophist Pheidippides in *Clouds* 1367.

In Plato, *Laws* 644e, there is an allusion to puppets on νεῦρα ἢ σμήρινθοι, *nervi* or *fila*, as the Romans put it. Ἀγάλματα νευρόσπαστα are encountered in Herodotus II.48; οἱ νευροσπάσται in Aristotle, *De Mundo* 6. Τὰ νεῦρα τῆς Τραγῳδίας therefore, and other expressions of its kind, must have been current in theatrical circles. However, the correct interpretation of the νεῦρα has escaped modern scholars, not only because the epirrhematic debate was moved forwards in the revised *Frogs*, but also because these scholars have failed to understand that lines 863–4 contain the second part of the third point outlined in the agonistic programme: the substance and interrelated thematic and ethical aspects of tragedy. These had formed the basis of Aeschylus' harsh anti-Euripidean closing speech, and of his and Dionysos' political and artistic condemnation of Euripides.[7]

Despite the radical anticipation of the epirrhematic debate, lines 1491–9 of the revised *Frogs* clearly echo the substance of Aeschylus' political, ethical and artistic closing speech. Fundamental and decisive as it is, the influence of this speech is to be felt in at least one section of the new finale: the antistrophe 1491–9, in mentioning 'the fundamental aspects of the tragic arts', strives to create some serious basis for the unmotivated anti-Euripidean outcome of the political contest in the finale of the revised *Frogs* (cf. 1468–78).

4 The journey in *Frogs* and the landscape. The revision of the comedy and its stage-technique

During the prologue and the parodos of *Frogs* a long journey takes place through a gradually changing landscape. Dionysos and Xanthias adopt the following route: Athens → the house of Herakles → the marshes → the pit of shadows and mire → the land of the monsters → the flower-clad plain, and end up in front of the house of Pluton (1–459). The progressive representation of a voyage, and of the landscape through which it passes, is unique in the extant corpus of ancient drama. In Aristophanes, an itinerant spectacle complete with alterations in the scenic milieu is to be encountered elsewhere only in *Peace*. One can hardly say that the representation there is gradual, however, since halfway through the prologue Trygaeus moves swiftly from earth to sky by means of a mechanical, paratragic device (although the account of his return 'on foot' to the earth, *Peace* 819–41, might also be the germ-cell for the comic representation of a voyage from earth to sky). In *Birds*, the action begins with a brief and intense itinerant spectacle; the landscape, however, is pre-constituted, as is that surrounding the entrance marches of the choruses in *Acharnians*, *Lysistrata* and *Assemblywomen*. In the parodos of *Wasps* there is a sketchy representation of a march through a partially extemporaneous landscape (the muddy terrain of the orchestra leading to the already operative house of Philokleon); yet the most outstanding example of a chorus affirming an extemporaneous landscape is, once again, that of *Frogs*.

The comedy's uniqueness in this respect amongst the extant ancient dramas – the fragmentary dramas, Aristophanes' *Gerytades* included, yield up nothing – would obviously have been casual. However, an itinerant spectacle does naturally have its own artistic dimension, and particularly in an ancient theatrical work the author would have been obliged to produce a flow of situations and images guaranteed to signify and evoke both the journey and the landscape through which it is taken with an adequate degree of intensity, whilst unnoticed, yet always in an appropriate manner, keeping this difficult and extremely unusual spectacle under way. The prolonged representation of a voyage and of a landscape is therefore a most ambitious undertaking, which the author would have taken on only if the economy of the drama definitely required it. As seen at the beginning of the previous section, this was exactly the case with *Frogs*.

The first station at which the two wayfarers arrive is the house of Herakles; the last, that of Pluton in Hades. The landscape in the long stretch between is made up consecutively of a marsh, a pit of shadows and mire, a land of monsters and an area of flower-clad grassland. Whereas the scenic façade represents unchangingly a house (attributed first to Herakles, presumably, and then to Pluton), the variable intermediate landscape is wholly imaginary, and is affirmed and evoked in the orchestra by the suggestiveness of the language and by the extremely intense dramatic action itself. Herakles' predictions regarding the landscape and the adventures to be met during the voyage (137–63 → 179–459) prepare the spectators for the marvellous phenomena that the dramatic action is to unveil. The two wayfarers continually refer to these predictions, in an apparent attempt to bolster up the extemporaneity of the action (182, 275, 279, 319). The only phenomenon which Herakles does not predict is the concert of the frogs, yet this is foreseen by Charon (205–7).

Herakles' house is reached in the opening section of the comedy (1–34), during a dialogue which takes its cue from the donkey ridden by the servant. Once Herakles' doorway is reached ('the voyage's first destination', cf. 36–7), the master orders his slave to dismount, and thereafter nothing more is heard of the donkey: it is apparently led off by some stage-hands. In *Birds*, the short opening spectacle is governed by the device of the two little compass-birds, which fly away just as soon as the two emigrants have reached their destination (*Birds* 1–91). Initially, the two wayfarers in *Frogs* behave more like ham-actors than dramatic characters, although their remarks always refer to itinerant spectacles in comedies by other authors (1–18). Amongst the three dramatists under attack, the first to be mentioned is Phrynichos, in contest at the same Lenaia with *Muses*.

The character addressed in the first line of the comedy as 'master' declares in line 22 that he is Dionysos. An explicit declaration is necessary, since the character is not actually recognizable as Dionysos: he has features typical of him, such as buskins and a yellow tunic, but is wearing a lion-skin over the latter and is also carrying a club (46–7). As he himself is to admit further on, he is impersonating Herakles (cf. 108–9), a club and a lion's pelt being enough for that purpose (cf. 495–503, 581, 589–93), the tunic notwithstanding (cf. 556–7). Obviously, in the second part of the comedy this no longer ambiguous character wears a costume suited to Dionysos, the god of the theatre. One should note that the Heraklean disguise, from which the adventures from the end of the parodos to the parabasis originate, is completely irrelevant during the preceding encounters with the Corpse, Charon and the Initiated (in line 298 there is an allusion to Dionysos-Herakles). Naturally, Dionysos-Herakles presents himself neutrally to the Initiated as a 'stranger' (433), and maintains his neutrality when the frogs recall their songs in honour of Dionysos and the Initiated invoke Iacchus.

Shortly after the interval at the house of Herakles – which should be imagined as lying in Athens or thereabouts, since the text never implies that its location is in any way remote (cf., for example, 127–9) – a Corpse accompanied by some grave-diggers appears on-stage *en route* for Hades (170–7). This brief scene is intended as physical demonstration of the fact that we are in a zone approaching hell. In fact, Dionysos commands, 'let's find the boat' (the boat has been foreseen by Herakles), and his command, which is so obviously a cue, is 'answered' by the remark typical of a helmsman heard in 180b. The latter is followed first by a pause, and then by an astonished question from Xanthias, through which other details emerge: 'what is that?'. Dionysos: 'That? That's a marsh, the one that [Herakles] mentioned, and I can also see a boat.' Xanthias: 'Yes, by Poseidon, and there's Charon himself' (181–3). Hence, in the orchestra (representing a marsh) a boat has appeared from the corridor bearing Charon.

The appearance of a boat on the comic stage is not a novelty in the least. In *Odysseis*, Kratinos had put one on-stage large enough to carry Odysseus and all his companions to the land of the Cyclops (his companions formed the chorus). Kratinos' boat would have been equipped with wheels, and so too is Charon's (also Euripides' and Agathon's pallets in *Acharnians* and

Thesmophoriazusae). Only Dionysos climbs aboard, since Xanthias is invited by Charon to 'take a run around the marsh', and then wait for his master at the station (193–5). This implies that as Charon gives Dionysos a lengthy explanation of how to row the boat (197–207), Xanthias runs around the orchestra and presumably waits for his master near the wall of the other corridor (cf. 194–5). As the Servant has been dismissed, the role of protagonist in the rowing scene goes to Dionysos, and simultaneously that of antagonist and interlocutor of the frogs. Charon, too, remains extraneous during this interlude, which is got under way by the frogs recalling their songs in honour of Dionysos in the Athenian sanctuary of the Marshland (211–19).

The allusive concert of these 'Dionysian' frogs is a remarkable invention aimed at evoking and filling with sound the non-existent marshland of hell and at allowing the crossing to be embarked upon unobserved. 'You will hear the exquisite songs ... of frog-swans, quite marvellous', promises Charon in 205–7. The frogs remain invisible, therefore, as can also be inferred from the succeeding context, creatures of voice and sound. Their songs, beginning with the 'command' in line 208, are heard back-stage, as is the song of the Initiated in lines 316–17 and 324–36: back-stage choral songs are also to be found in *Clouds*, whereas in *Birds* Hoopoe's serenade and monody are performed back-stage. In *Frogs*, there is also a dialogue between these invisible voices and Dionysos, a phenomenon encountered previously, in *Wasps* 144–73 and *Thesmophoriazusae* 1056–97.

The frogs' song is doubtless performed by the chorus, by the future Initiated (Μύσται), that is. If this is true, it is not at all strange that the title of the comedy should be linked to the chorus' first manifestation, particularly when the frogs are 'Dionysian' and a choral manifestation during the prologue is an unusual event in itself. The only possible alternative to the existing title would have been that of Μύσται, the proven title of a comedy by Phrynichos. If this comedy by Aristophanes' rival and peer dates, as is commonly maintained, to the year 407, then we can better understand the eccentric title that Aristophanes gave his own comedy from the year 405. The title is borrowed from a comedy written by the remote Magnes (scholion *Knights* 519), although in that comedy the frogs definitely formed the chorus (see *Knights* 525).

After the crossing, Charon and the boat disappear. Dionysos calls Xanthias immediately and asks him a question, again designed as a means to orientate the spectators: 'what's to be found around here?'. 'Darkness and mire.' 'Tell me, have you seen the parricides and perjurers he mentioned anywhere?' 'You haven't?' 'I certainly have, by Poseidon, and I still can.' The playful reference to the spectators demonstrates how illusory was the scenic value just that moment verbally attributed to the orchestra. A new value, the land of the monsters, is assigned, as normal, by indicative phrases in the body of the dialogue. Dionysos: 'Listen, what should we do now?' Xanthias: 'the best thing to do would be to keep moving, since according to him this place is filled with terrible monsters' (277–80; according to Herakles' predictions, the land of the monsters came after the pit of darkness and mire). A monster, Empusa, is promptly 'created', through Xanthias' blithe references to it and Dionysos' expressions of terror: he is too scared even to look at the monster 'seen' by Xanthias. Here again, the spectators are drawn into the dramatic game, since in order to save his skin Dionysos runs towards a priest seated in the proedria (297).

Towards the end of the prologue, what Herakles had predicted in 154–62 begins to occur: the breath of flutes, the fragrance of torches, and the songs of the Initiated (312–20). Herakles had predicted a landscape of myrtle-groves, and here the songs of the Initiated affirm and then reaffirm the existence of a 'flower-clad plain' in the orchestra (326, 352, 'marshy', 373–4, see then 441, 449 'full of roses'). Even more than in the case of the marshland and small chorus of frogs, there is a full-scale transposition into the theatre of a terrestrial ceremony and milieu (with an independent time dimension between the dramatic time of the comedy itself: cf. 342, 371, 387 and 446 with ἀρτίως in 433). The Initiated 'sing to Iacchus as they do all around the Agora' (320) and are accompanied by an array of women and girls (cf. 157). The latter are led away to the site of the vigil in honour of Demeter, while the Initiated remain within the sacred enclosure of the goddess (440–6). A terrestrial ceremony is therefore transferred into Hades, and at the same time continued outside the precinct of the theatre.

In 431, Dionysos and Xanthias enquire of the Initiated: 'Could you tell us where Pluton lives?' And, smiling almost at the superfluity of his question (cf. *Plutus* 962), the chorus replies: 'You don't have to go very far, or ask me again. Know then that you have already reached his door.' Once more, both question and reply are eloquent about the setting: Dionysos had already been told by Herakles that the Initiated 'lived near Pluton's door' (163), and at that very moment the Initiated were to be found in front of the scenic façade (this can be inferred from the reply and from lines 440–3). Hence, by means of the dialogue once more, a new value is assigned to the scenic façade: the house is no longer Herakles', but Pluton's. Dionysos orders his slave to fetch their baggage (437; the latter would have been laid down when the two withdrew at 315), and as the chorus moves from the scenic façade towards the orchestra, he and Xanthias approach the doorway.

Once Dionysos has knocked on Pluton's door in 460, the house becomes a frequent point of reference in the dramatic action (503, 514, 520, 669, 757, 799, 812, 847, 871, 1304, 1479), the orchestra is rendered neutral and the chorus ceases to be that of the Initiated in the flower-clad plain (the chorus's torches re-emerge at 1525). From the house, which symbolizes all of Hades (as the household in *Knights* symbolizes Athens), there gradually appear: Persephone's Servant in 502, the Hostess and Plathane in 549 and Aiakos with his three policemen in 605 (Aiakos has already been active in 464–78, albeit behind the door: see 492–3). Directly after the parabasis, Aiakos and Xanthias appear from the house, followed by Dionysos and the two new characters active in the second section of the comedy, Euripides and Aeschylus. Pluton, the third new character, appears in the finale, and rather abruptly at that. The crude stage-technique of the finale of the revised *Frogs* was discussed in section 1 above.

The four characters who appear in the second part of the comedy become vitally present back-stage in the course of the prologue, 738–813, and this is also the case with Sophocles (cf. particularly 791–4). The latter, however, never appears on-stage, despite the fact that the actor who plays Euripides is free from line 1482 onwards, and although in 1515 the departing Aeschylus advises Pluton to entrust his throne to him in Euripides' absence. Sophocles' perpetual absence, despite his vitality back-stage, is extremely unusual, particularly when other Aristophanic characters ascribed similar vitality back-stage (or off-stage) during the prologue do sooner or later appear before the spectators and assume roles of extremely great or great importance, or at the very least small parts such as that of Pluton-fourth actor in *Frogs*, a character announced in advance in 784 (cf. also 812; Persephone, whose name is mentioned in 671, goes entirely unrecalled during the second prologue). Regarding the announcement of Aristophanic characters during the prologue, see section 3b in chapter 5: there it is shown that in the *Second Clouds* Chaerephon never appears on-stage, for the simple reason that the *Second Clouds* was neither revised nor performed. Likewise, the abnormal absence of Sophocles in *Frogs* is due to the urgent revision which the comedy sustained (the non-appearance of the anonymous Chremilos' son is comically justified in *Plutus* 251–2).

The urgency of the revision of *Frogs* created yet another abnormality in its stage-technique, but only a rather minor one. The weighing of poetry on scales was once preceded, as lines 1371–2 make perfectly clear, by an equally prodigious mechanical inspection of the tragic arts. The announcement of the latter remains in the text: '(the art of poetry shall be weighed on a scale) . . . and rulers and measuring tapes for words shall be brought forth' (799–801). The announcement made here is a binding one, and it is disturbing to see it go unobserved: it is made by a character who belongs to the environment of Hades (not by an outsider), a serious and responsible character who would never make fun of the grave dispute between Aeschylus and Euripides and who does not respond to Xanthias' witticisms regarding the weighing of poetry and the instruments of measurement. His announcement is rendered even more binding by the fact that it is made during a prologue, and during a prologue, moreover, which is absolutely essential. It is also the rule that back-stage objects so firmly announced in prologues sooner or later appear on-stage. One need only think of the prologue of *Peace*, in which back-stage concreteness is ascribed to a realistic, yet surreal instrument: the indigenous Hermes informs the stranger Trygaeus of Polemos' 'mortar for the city', and Polemos subsequently carries his mortar out on-stage and dispatches Tumult to Athens and Sparta in search of a pestle (*Peace* 228–31, 238–88). In *Wasps* 937–9, five distinct kitchen utensils (and others left unidentified) are invited to present themselves as witnesses in favour of the Dog Labes. At least one of these utensils, the Cheese-grater, is subsequently interrogated (962–6): it is also the most important witness, in so far as the dog is accused of having eaten a sort of cheese. Here in *Frogs*, not even one of the five instruments of measurement appears.

5 Characters

Frogs is the only Aristophanic comedy to make almost constant and equal use of the first three actors, and to employ a single actor for two consecutive roles of major importance. This actor, certainly the first, plays the complementary protagonist of the first section – Xanthias – up to the metaparabatic prologue, and then assumes the role of Aeschylus. The role of Aeschylus is the most difficult in the comedy, followed by that of Euripides, whereas the large role assigned to the only permanent character, Dionysos, is fairly straightforward. It could have been played, therefore, by the third actor, unless one prefers to think that Dionysos, who is so different in the two sections of the comedy, is played by the second actor in the first section while the third actor takes the minor parts.

If one ignores this hypothesis, a possible distribution of the thirteen parts is as follows:

first actor, with around 370 lines, of which 65 are lyrical: Xanthias, 1–664 and 739–808 (almost 150 lines, of which 16 are lyrical), Aeschylus, 840–1465 and 1515–23 (almost 225 lines, of which 59 are lyrical);

second actor, with around 395 lines, of which 20 are lyrical in the passage 830–1476: Herakles (anonymous), 38–164, Charon, 180–270, Torch-bearer, 444–7, Aiakos (anonymous), 464–78, Persephone's Servant, 503–18, Hostess, 549–78, Aiakos (anonymous), 605–71 and 738–813 (these six characters deliver 208 lines altogether), Euripides, 830–1476 (186 lines altogether, of which 20 are lyrical);

third actor, delivering altogether around 390 lines, of which 36 are lyrical, in 3–673: Dionysos disguised, 3–673 (around 220 lines), Dionysos, 832–1481 (around 170 lines);

amateur actor, with 28 lines: Corpse, 173–7 (three trimeters), Plathane, 551–65 (three trimeters), Pluton (anonymous), 1414–80 and 1500–27 (four trimeters + eighteen anapaestic dimeters). The second actor would be available for the Corpse, the second and also the third for Pluton in 1500–27 (Dionysos in fact remains mute during the closing passage 1500–33).

Amongst the mute characters particular importance is ascribed to the Girls and Women mentioned in 445, who are certainly *dancers* temporarily added to the chorus. A preamble to the appearance of this female group – to which there is an allusion in 409–13, and perhaps in 338 also – is to be found in 157. Great significance is also ascribed to a Castanet girl, Euripides' Muse, in the scene 1305–64 (the dual number in 1364 is addressed to Aeschylus and her, not to Aeschylus and Euripides: cf. 1307): this woman, who dances too, is rather awkward on her feet, which gives rise to the ambiguous remarks made in 1323–4.

Extras: Corpse-bearers (cf. 170, 174), Ditylas, Skeblyas and Pardokas, Aiakos' policemen (608), Pluton's Servants.

Regarding the speaking characters, I have attributed 444–7 to the Torch-bearer rather than the coryphaeus (others have attributed a greater number of lines to the Torch-bearer, who is apostrophized by the chorus in 351–3). As for Aiakos in 738–13, see section 3 above. The distribution of lines of the individual characters provided here implies a division of the dialogue which is slightly different here and there from that adopted by Victor Coulon.

6 A fragment of Aeschylus. Oral poetry

Some remarks are offered, in other chapters, on the system of proportional-modular composition which has come to light in Aristophanes (although it was already operative in Homer), recognition of which has rendered the theatrical properties of his drama more amenable to study. Eric A. Havelock, 'The oral composition of Greek drama', in *The Literate Revolution* (Princeton, 1982), after a journey through *Frogs* in search of an 'oral' poet, finds that poet in Aeschylus and recommends that he should be studied more thoroughly. Let us take *Agamemnon*, therefore, and turn for some slight support to Henri Weil, who became a Greek philologist after his mathematical apprenticeship, following the teachings of *Republic* 522bc. It was Weil, in fact, who first glimpsed the linked formal and thematic principles underlying the scene with Cassandra (*Etudes sur le drame antique*, Paris, 1897).

When Cassandra's encounter with the chorus begins, she has been present for almost three hundred lines, but has been left mute and ignored. Aga-memnon has pointed her out to Clytaimnestra in vain. When the royal couple retire into the palace, and Cassandra is the only character left on-stage, she remains mute and ignored. Not even with the barbaric hand does she express herself when Clytaimnestra reappears imperiously and apostrophizes her, to lure her into the slaughter-house, their royal home.

In terms of the module, there is a 36-line scene with Clytaimnestra, a 108-line encounter between Cassandra and the chorus, a 135-line scene involving Cassandra and the coryphaeus, and finally a brief anapaestic farewell of 12 lines. From the moment Cassandra is apostrophized by Clytaimnestra, this entire thematic figure covers 291 lines divided into separate modular moments of differing length. The composition, in adopting a module, moves freely within that unit of measurement: one does not encounter terzinas, sextets, enneads, etc. That is as far as the module is concerned. The dynamic of the composition resides instead in the relations, and these are harmonic, geo-metrical and arithmetical. The coexistence of such concurrent relations provides the composition with the flexibility and variety that the author would otherwise appear to deny himself: rules cannot imprison the Muse. Naturally, the audience is not fully aware of all this: similarly, after a concert, it is only by looking at a copy of the score that one can form an idea of the deep structure of a piece. Modern scholars doubtless possess texts with only relative authority. However, in these exemplars more than the shadow of the author's libretto does remain, for the structural properties and main stage-directions are internal to the text, from Homer to the dramatists.

Cassandra's encounter with the chorus, 108 lines. For this encounter – the apex of the tragedy *Agamemnon* and the fulcrum of the entire *Oresteia* trilogy – Aeschylus chooses two materials: the usual iambic trimeters for spoken utterance and a series of other eminently singable metres. Little by little, these two heterogeneous ingredients are mixed, yet only in rigorously measured doses, such that in the entire preparation of 108 lines there are 72 lyrical lines and 36 trimeters. Seventy-two and 36 are the precise major and minor arithmetical sections of 108, forming respectively 2/3 and 1/3. In simpler terms, one can say that to every trimeter there correspond two lyrical lines. In the second book of the *Iliad* also, to each line of the characters there correspond two pertaining to the poet. In some modern editions, for example those of Gilbert Murray and Martin L. West, the lyrical lines are felicitously 72, not 70, for instance, as in other editions (e.g. that of Denys L. Page). This difference might seem trifling. Yet would it be trifling to see two terzinas of Dante in four lines?

And the theme? A glance at the many editions and commentaries available will allow us to see just how much difference of opinion exists in the attempt to recognize the development of the theme. The principles of composition assist us in this attempt. And how? The search for proportion amongst the materials adopted was by no means a piece of gratuitous gymnastics which ignored the theme. Quite the contrary: the theme is gradually moulded analogously to the dimensions of the materials. The analogical relation is a principle of mathematical poetics; the basic aspects and elements of the composition adopt analogical measurements. By analogy, indeed, the two historical moments of the amoibaion are 36 and 72, as the measurements of the materials. The theme, let us repeat, is scanned into two historical moments: the 36 moment, in which Cassandra witnesses the killing of Agamemnon in the palace, and the 72 moment, dealing with the destiny of Cassandra and of the family of Priam. The last, major moment also falls into two separate parts: an opening 28 and a closing 44. This linked thematic and musical division conforms to a musical relation, i.e. to the geometrical relation.

As for dramaturgy, the aspect which from a dramaturgical point of view resolves any problem of direction for Aeschylus – and is admired by everyone – is naturally the visionary 36 moment, in which Cassandra witnesses the killing of Agamemnon in the palace. This cosmos of 36 is privileged in form – 12 trimeters, 24 lyrical lines – hence providing the nucleus of the overall composition. Let us take up the compass or, more comfortably, the golden number: the preparations for the killing cover the first 14 lines, the killing itself the remaining 22. The relation is indeed golden, therefore. Likewise in the major historical moment, the first phase was 28 and the second 44.

The hammer of analogy falls twice more. There are 36 lines in a modular set, pertaining partly to Cassandra and partly to the chorus, and hence 72 in a non-modular set. Of the 36 in the modular set, Cassandra has 12 and the chorus therefore 24.

Solo and dialogue: is there any dialogue in this scene, a scene in which Cassandra is egocentric and visionary, and at one point even in a trance? Such a character would hardly be inclined to dialogue, even less to informal address. She is assigned two non-solo interventions alone, and they are signalled by altruistic particles. An extra metre begins the first, after line XVIII. Thenceforth, Cassandra's interventions are all solo. Even in the case of the nightingale, she is stimulated by a nightingale-flute in the theatre rather than by the voices of the chorus. The chorus tries more than once to initiate dialogue, but the dialogue remains the minor aspect: of 36 lines, only 6 belong to the egocentric Cassandra.

I shall conclude, leaving the skeleton of the first thematic phase of 28 and that of the last of 44 to rest in peace. Needless to say, this entire scene with Cassandra is merely a fragment, a fragment of a wider cosmos.

Remember the precision of the agonistic programme in *Frogs*: 'Now the real devilry's going to begin. Poetry's about to be weighed on a scale . . . – What, weighing tragedy like a leg of lamb? – and they'll drag out canons and cubits for the measure of lines and strange rectangular forms . . . – Is it bricks they're making? – wedges and compasses: Euripides says he wants tragedy weighed up line by line. – Aeschylus must be livid! – You're telling me! He was glaring at him with his head down like a bull. – But who on earth's going to judge such a contest? – That was the problem, since both of them thought there was a scarcity of connoisseurs.'

'Thanks to *Frogs* the historian has more complete data regarding tragedy at his disposal; in poetics the stakes are too high for it to be permissible by now to ignore the rules of the game', François Lasserre concluded in 1961 (see n. 1 to this chapter). However, the search for the oral in poetry, which is creative in the extreme, has since received splendid testimony: Homer, in fact, *presents himself* as the oral author of his own *Cypria*, when in 606 hexameters of the *Iliad* he makes oblique allusion to that precipitous, unlettered, Icarian composition, recounting how with the *Iliad* alone he had entered the writer's workshop and begun to dictate to an amanuensis of rank, Stasinos-Arctinos, the husband of his daughter Arsiphone: see 'Tradurre Icaro, tempi nuovi', *La traduzione dei testi classici*, (Naples, 1992), pp. 55–6 and 'Notizie stilate a Chio vinta l'Olimpiade del 724', *Tradizione e innovazione nella cultura Greca* (Roma, 1993). The Athenian dramatists are all scholars of the pro-grammatic Homer.

12

ASSEMBLYWOMEN

1 *Assemblywomen* and the draw for position on the programme

'I would like to make a little suggestion to the judges: whoever is serious should give me the prize remembering my seriousness; whoever laughs his heart out should give me the prize because he has laughed. It is clear, therefore, that I am inviting more or less everyone to give me the prize. Nor should it be to my disfavour that I have been awarded priority in the draw. Instead, recalling each single thing, you should keep to your oaths and judge the choruses with equanimity, always: do not behave like the wanton hetairai, who can only ever remember the last to arrive': thus the coryphaea towards the end of *Assembly-women* (1154–62). This passage implies that *Assemblywomen* was drawn first in the order of performance. The contest's outcome remains unknown, since no information has survived at all regarding this particular contest (the year was definitely 392).

> We do not know exactly when the draw took place, but it is clear that while he was working on the first rehearsals the poet could not have known in what order the comedy was to be performed. The draw undoubtedly took place during the final rehearsals, since lines 1154–62 of *Assemblywomen* are a last-minute addition to the comedy. These lines, which the coryphaeus would have been obliged to learn with great haste, interrupt drastically the close-knit relationship 1151–3 → 1163–6.

So drastically in fact do lines 1154–62 offend the unity and rhythm of the stage-action that it is by no means unreasonable to suspect that they were intended to follow 1150 or 1148.[1]

Despite the fact that they were linked to the ephemeral contingency of the draw, lines 1154–62 were eventually put into circulation: this implies that, as discussed in section 2 of chapter 11 on *Frogs*, the texts of the comedies were not even minimally revised after their performance.

219

2 Dramaturgical decline and structural action in *Assemblywomen*

Assemblywomen, which dates from 392, is perceptibly different from the earlier extant works of Aristophanes: it is perhaps enough to say that out of the comedy's 1,183 lines, 900 are in iambic trimeters and 140 or a little more are lyrical, and that only around 60 of the latter are sung by the chorus. The artistic rift separating *Assemblywomen* from the earlier comedies becomes particularly evident from line 729 onwards:

> after line 729, when it would have been natural for the parabasis to appear, the chorus, although it is to a considerable extent responsible for the title and the subject of the comedy, limits its already meagre participation to little more than a pair of dancing interludes (the presumable absence of a simultaneous choral song is discussed further on);

> after line 729, lyrical song is performed almost exclusively by the actors, since only the four closing lyrical lines are sung by the chorus, whereas around eighty lyric lines are delivered by the three actors (in the new roles of First Old Woman, Young Girl, Youth and Maidservant);

> after line 729, the most important character in the first section of the comedy – Praxagora – distances herself permanently from the stage-action (and not for any urgent reason of economy with respect to the actors); one of the other characters from the first section reappears in 730–876, another at the end of the comedy;

> between lines 729 and 1111 the use of the scenic façade is somewhat unusual, whereas between 877 and 1111 it is quite clear that it is attributed to new, episodic characters.

These features might lead one to define *Assemblywomen* as a comedy divided into two formally distinct acts. Other phenomena – such as the weakening of the role of the chorus (which causes greater involvement of the actors, including in the lyrical passages as well), the premature disappearance of the protagonist (resulting in an episodic concentration on the individuality of other characters) and finally the dominance of the garrulous iambic trimeters – might lead one to believe that *Assemblywomen* is a comedy containing only some moderate dramatic and imaginative complications, that it is fairly talkative and smooth-running, and that it has a tendency to produce rather autonomous scenes (which constrains some of the characters to appear in a somewhat puppet-like manner: cf. 746, 1049, 1065).

To understand fully the ethical and political rift separating *Assemblywomen* from the earlier comedies one need only recall, apart from the already significant weakening of the chorus, that the women succeed the men in the government of the State because of the male disguise they assume in the People's Assembly – a disguise of which the men remain permanently ignorant. An intrigue based on the fruits of a machination which never comes to light is again a unique artistic feature of *Assemblywomen*, bespeaking a resigned and satirical evaluation of Athenian society and a somewhat abstract comic design, bereft of practical intent (this is also the case in *Plutus*). *Assemblywomen* is concerned above all with the satirical experimenting of a social theory, comparable to the satirical experimentation of Euripides' art in *Thesmophoriazusae*. The social theory experimented with in *Assemblywomen* would also have been a novelty for the Athenian theatre (cf. 578–80, 583–5).

The long and extremely well-conceived prologue, 1–284, is performed by Praxagora and a group of other women who have assembled shortly before dawn close to her and her Neighbour's homes for a meticulous general rehearsal prior to taking themselves to the Assembly (116–17, cf. 160–2). The prologue is followed by the intervention of the chorus, already on-stage during the prologue and directed towards the Assembly as well (285–310). Apart from this unusual treatment of the chorus, then, which is discussed further on, there is also the fact that the entire, extremely large cast of the opening scene are made to assemble on-stage in view of their departure for a destination off-stage.

The protagonists of the lengthy iambic scene which follows, 311–477, are the husbands of Praxagora and of her Neighbour and a citizen on his way back from the Assembly; its background is still Praxagora and her Neighbour's homes. The prologue is opened by a monologue (delivered by Praxagora) and followed by an intervention of the chorus (an exodos); the iambic scene is also opened by a monologue (delivered by Praxagora's husband) and followed by an intervention of the chorus (a parodos, 478–503). The latter scene is dramaturgically parallel to its predecessor, a species of 'second prologue' involving the men, which also dramatizes and exemplifies the criticism made of them by the women of the prologue.[2]

In the course of this 'second prologue', Chremes provides an account of what has taken place in the People's Assembly. From a dramatic and ethical point of view it is remarkable that Chremes should not immediately inform his interlocutor Blepyros – Praxagora's husband, that is – that the Assembly has entrusted the government of the State to the women: the statement about the Assembly begins in 376, whereas an account of the clamorous feminist decision does not appear until 455–7 – and then with the most perfect ease. It might perhaps be said that calm and prolix conversation is to the liking of the dramatist of *Assemblywomen*, and in this case, as throughout the 'second prologue', is employed as a means of showing just how indifferent the men really are to public affairs.

The men's indifference renders Praxagora's exposition of the revolutionary programme during the epirrhematic agon 571–709 a simple and smooth-running affair. It is normally observed that the revolutionary programme is a surprising novelty in the comedy, since in the prologue the women's declared intention had been merely to seize power, and they had also put themselves forward as conservatives. However, those favourable to this observation have clearly not taken into account that the women's programme could not have been expounded during the prologue since at that stage they were pretending to be men (in this respect lines 229–32 are of some importance), and that in order to have the women seize power these 'men' tended naturally to depict them as innocuous conservatives.

The epirrhematic agon proceeds smoothly in the form of an oration (nor is it bipartite as in the earlier comedies), and evolves from the coryphaea's incitement to a 'rapidity preferred by the spectators' (581–2), and from Praxagora's injunction to Blepyros and Chremes, 'no objections and no interruptions until ...' (588). Once she has expounded her programme, Praxagora abandons the site of the stage-action for the Agora and no longer appears on-stage: she is mentioned indirectly in 835 and 870 (and during the exodos also).

It should be noted that although Praxagora has been elected 'stratega' by the women of the prologue (246–7, see also 517), not by the Assembly, she still speaks before Blepyros and Chremes as though she were a political leader and in the end actually declares to them that she has been elected to run the State (714–15), and Blepyros later describes his wife as a 'stratega' (727). This is an inevitable incongruity (or rather a dramatic 'short-cut'), which is attenuated none the less by the political investiture Praxagora receives from the women of the chorus in front of the two men in lines 571–82 (Blepyros, in any case, was already prepared to consider his wife a governor of the new State in 563–4). The new laws – of which everyone has already heard (cf. 759, 762–3, 766, 767, 854, 944, etc.) – are also considered to be incongruous: evidently they were proclaimed off-stage after Praxagora had gone to the Agora (hence her immediate search for a heraldess with a strong voice, 713).

In her exposition of the revolutionary programme, Praxagora had insisted particularly on three points: the depositing and communal division of goods (590–610), the regulation of sexual activity (611–50, 693–709), and free meals for all (599–652, 675–90). Before abandoning the stage, she recalls exclusively the depositing of goods (712), the free meals (715–17) and the regulation of sexual activity (718–24). During the second part of the comedy, in lines 730–1111, two elaborate scenes playfully dramatize two of the three salient points of this 'communistic' programme: the depositing of goods (730–833/853–76) and the regulation of sexual activity (877–1111).

The third point of the programme – free meals for all – is put into effect off-stage, and the event is evoked rapidly during the exodos (1112–83). The free meals had been announced by Praxagora as a predominantly off-stage event (715–16, cf. 675–86), and later a Herald had appeared bearing news that the tables were set and that all the citizens were expected by Praxagora (834–52).

After the scene 877–1111 – which implies that a banquet is held (cf. 877, 948 and 988 with 691–709) – the Maidservant of a 'most blessed mistress' (i.e. Praxagora, cf. 1112–13 with 558–9) appears on-stage heady with wine in search of her master (Blepyros), who is late, and urges him and the girls with him, the spectators, the benevolent judges and the women of the chorus to go to the banquet, where there are food and drink remaining (1139–40). All the characters on-stage – the Maidservant, the master, the girls and the chorus (cf. 1164–8) – begin to dance in response to the Maidservant's invitation and leave the theatre.

The 'communistic' off-stage meal, evoked on-stage with Blepyros' lateness as a pretext, gives rise to a traditional exodos containing a hopeful allusion to the feast in honour of the victorious chorus (1182). The intensity and outright festiveness of the exodos are conveyed, amongst other means, by the girls who appear with Blepyros – undoubtedly hetairai-dancers called to take part in the elaborate dancing with which the comedy ends.

Scholars have been in dispute for over a century as to whether there are actually girls on-stage, or more precisely women distinguishable from those of the chorus. Clearly they have paid little attention to the Greek text: 'your wife has ordered me to lead away you and τασδὶ μετὰ σοῦ τὰς μείρακας' (1138), i.e. 'these girls who are with you' (cf. *Plutus* 843), not 'to lead you away and, along with you, these girls'.[3]

3 The treatment of the chorus. Characters and actors

The title Ἐκκλησιάζουσαι, like Θεσμοφοριάζουσαι, takes in both the chorus and the 'women at the assembly' portrayed by the actors; neither is it a coincidence that in both comedies the appearance of the chorus is somewhat unusual. In *Thesmophoriazusae*, the thesmophoriazusae women-choreutai and the thesmophoriazusae women-actors appear silently and simultaneously at the end of the prologue, and the chorus begins to sing after a prose passage has been delivered by the coryphaea, only later making sounds and movements similar to those of a parodos (*Thesmophoriazusae* 655–88); in *Assemblywomen* the genesis of the chorus is no less unusual.

The future choreutai of *Assemblywomen* appear in groups as early as the beginning of the prologue (cf. 41–53 and maybe 30–1) and then remain *mute* on-stage as though they were extras (see, for example, 72), while the women-actors deliver the prologue. Towards the end of the prologue, the mute women receive orders from Praxagora to disguise themselves as men and to sing in the peasant style (268–79), and the women-actors, already disguised as men (cf. 118–27), exit for the Assembly (279–82). Once the actors have disappeared in 284, the mute women disguise themselves (or rather, finally organize themselves into a chorus, and on the orders of an actor), parade in the orchestra singing like peasants (289–310, cf. 299; 285–8 are delivered by the coryphaea) and then exit in 310 for the Assembly. The chorus re-enters the theatre at 478, when a kind of parodos takes place (478–503). Whereas the choreutai are still masked as men, Praxagora and her friends, when they enter around 500, have removed their male disguise (cf. 499–510, 514).

The future chorus, therefore, is on-stage during the prologue (for reasons of intrigue), organizes itself into a chorus at the end of the prologue on the orders of an actor, sings an exit march, and after this unusual off-stage action following the actors, reappears on-stage singing an entrance march. From this point onwards, the chorus, already barely autonomous, slowly loses its importance: although Praxagora does resolve to seek advice from the chorus (cf. 517–18), in fact she does not address it again; and Blepyros, so critical of his wife, fails even to notice that there are another twenty-four women on-stage. Despite the fact that it introduces the epirrhematic debate with a song (571–80 and then 581–2), the chorus is gradually slipping out of the dramatic action; when Praxagora disappears for good, it does not represent her in any way whatsoever. Apart from the two choral interventions indicated by the XOPOY between 729–30 and 876–7, altogether the coryphaea delivers two iambic trimeters (1127, 1134) and the chorus the four closing lyrical lines (1180–3). Aristophanes improvised lines 1154–62 for the coryphaea shortly before the comedy's performance.

As mentioned previously, the chorus of *Assemblywomen* is one which is invited to sing (277), and one which sings (289–310 and then 477–503). After the song at 571–80, however, it sings no more than the four short closing lines, the remaining song being delivered by the actors. The first of the actors to sing introduces his rendition as follows: 'although singing may be boring for the spectators, it does have something pleasant and comical about it' (888–9). So complete is the abdication of the chorus that there is good reason to suspect that the XOPOY between 729–30 and 876–7 were intended to indicate merely interludes with music and dance.

It is improbable, moreover, that those responsible for the first public circulation of the comedy would have omitted songs already performed on-stage, even should these songs have been extraneous to the dramatic action. Are there not other Aristophanic choral songs equally extraneous to the dramatic action? It is still more improbable that Aristophanes would have judged these songs to be ephemeral and hence unworthy of being put into circulation. The simple truth is that from a certain point onwards the chorus of *Assemblywomen* has nothing left to sing or to say, apart from the four short standard lines with which the comedy ends. This is discussed again in chapter 13, on *Plutus*.

According to the modern interpretation of the dialogue of *Assemblywomen* there are fifteen characters in the comedy. A possible subdivision of the parts might be as follows:

first actor, uttering altogether around 505 lines, of which more than 20 are lyrical, in the passage 938–75: Praxagora, 1–284, 504–724, Man who prefers not to deposit, 746–876, Youth, 938–1111 (the Youth is apparently called Epigenes: cf. 931–4, 951);

second actor, uttering altogether around 325 lines, of which approximately 30 are lyrical, in the passages 893–945 and 1163–78: First Woman, 30–282 (see further on, however), Blepyros' Neighbour, 327–56 (the first actor would also be available for this character), Chremes, 372–477, 564–729 (including lines 631–4), 730–871 (anonymous in 564–729 and 730–871), First Old Woman, 877–1044, Second Old Woman, 1049–95, Maidservant, 1112–78;

third actor, uttering altogether more than 260 lines, of which over 30 are lyrical, in the passage 900–59: Second Woman-Praxagora's Neighbour, 35–265, Blepyros, 311–477, 519–728, Herald (or rather Heraldess), 834–52, Young Girl, 884–1042, Third Old Woman, 1065–97, Blepyros (anonymous), 1129–79.

It is conceivable that an *amateur actor* might play the Second Old Woman in 1049–95 (eleven trimeters), should the time available for the costume changes between 1044–8 and 1107–11 seem too short. During the prologue, the Third Woman in 54–6 is portrayed by an amateur actor. It must be said, however, that the sigla currently assigned in the prologue, in which, unusually, the entire chorus is on-stage, are not entirely convincing: some of the remarks in the first place seem more suited to the *coryphaea* (30–1, for instance), and 41–5 are not particularly well adapted to Praxagora (because of 44–5). Moreover, it is unlikely that an amateur actor would have been employed for lines 54–6 alone: it seems to me that the so-called Third Woman, on account of the importance she assumes with 54–6 (which are parallel to 37–9, uttered by the so-called Second Woman), might well be retained as one of Praxagora's constant interlocutors. In short, I would conceive of a prologue subdivided between Praxagora, her Next-door Neighbour (second or third actor) and the Woman from 54–6 (third or second actor), with some passage given up to the coryphaea after 30–1 (which would mean that she intervenes again between 40 and 54). Naturally, the future coryphaea cannot but express herself for the moment in iambic trimeters.[4]

Dancing-girls appear in the finale, as mentioned at the end of section 2 above. As usual there is also a *flautist* (891).

Extras: Chremes' two servants, whose names are Sicon and Parmeno (867, 868, cf. 833 and also 730–45). At least two women accompany Praxagora on her return from the Assembly (see 503); they might be her two interlocutors from the prologue, here portrayed by extras.

4 The rotation of tenants in the scenic façade

Assemblywomen provides an incontrovertible example of the progressive attribution of the scenic façade to new tenants, which could only be admitted as a hypothesis in the Lenaian *Acharnians* (house of Euripides → house of Lamachus) and Lenaian *Frogs* (house of Herakles → house of Pluton). In *Assemblywomen* the five tenants clearly do not occupy five different houses.

It emerges from the text that the following are undoubtedly tenants of the scenic façade:

Praxagora's 'Neighbour' (33–6) and the latter's husband (327–56, cf. 35–40);

Blepyros, Praxagora's husband (311–477, cf. 510–20), who is apostrophized as 'neighbour' by Praxagora's Neighbour's husband (327), and Praxagora herself (cf. 489–92 and 510–13);

The Obsequious Citizen (730–45, cf. 754, 833);

First Old Woman (877–1037);

Young Girl (884–1055, cf. 1080).

The tenants are rotated during the choral interludes at 729 and 876 (the Obsequious Citizen in 730–45 is definitely the Chremes of 372–477, and also of 564–729, since he could easily have become a tenant of the scenic façade at the end of the 'second prologue' rather than after 729). The simultaneous occupation of the scenic façade by two different sets of tenants takes place in the case of Praxagora and Blepyros and their Next-door Neighbours, and in that of the Old Woman and the Young Girl. The scenic façade therefore never represents more than *two* houses. The existence and use of two different houses is implicit throughout the symmetrically litigious scene involving the Old Woman and the Young Girl, since trimeters 976–7 do not imply that there is only one door: the Old Woman merely pretends that the Youth has knocked on her door rather than that of the Young Girl. The action of the Second Old Woman (cf. 1062) is apparently set against the house of the First (who disappears in 1037), and this also seems to be true of the action of the Third (cf. 1093). The Young Girl disappears in 1055, although there is a concrete reference to her house in 1080.

Regarding the scene with the Old Woman and the Young Girl, it emerges from the text that the Young Girl initially appears at a higher level than that of her doorway: the Youth begs her to 'come down and open the door' (962–3). A symmetrical performance on the part of the Old Woman can be inferred from the first words that the Young Girl addresses to her: 'This time it was you who leant out first' (884, παρακύψασα προὔφθης). The Young Girl upbraids the Old Woman again for her tendency to παρακύπτειν like a little cat (924), to διακύπτειν (929), or rather to lean out of an opening. In *Thesmophoriazusae* 797 there is mention of wanton women leaning out of windows (ἐκ θυρίδος παρακύπτειν and then in 799 παρακύπτειν), and in *Peace* 982 and 985 of women peeping out of half-closed doors. Here in *Assemblywomen* it is clear that for much of their appearance the two rivals are at their *windows*.[5]

It is highly probable that Blepyros' Neighbour, too, was at his window in 327–56.

In the finale of the comedy the scenic façade is neutral in value.

13

PLUTUS

1 The last contest

Plutus was performed under the archon Antipater [in 388, therefore]; Aristophanes' opponents were Nicochares with *Laconians*, Aristomenes with *Admetus*, Nicophon with *Adonis* and Alcaeus with *Pasiphae*. Having presented this comedy as the last under his own name [see also scholion *Plutus* 173], and since he wished to recommend his son Araros to the audience with some dramas in hand, it was through Araros that he entered the remaining two, *Kokalos* and *Aiolosikon*.

Argument III

The Argument's considerations regarding Aristophanes' desire to recommend his son to the audience are certainly no more than the opinion of a scholar who happened to have theatrical information relative to the two comedies succeeding *Plutus* (and perhaps noticed that they had been a great success: see further on). It is instead admissible to assume that Aristophanes died after *Plutus* and that his son brought the two comedies his father had left him to the stage, particularly when the *Suda* reports that Araros made his début (with comedies of his own) no earlier than 375–372. It seems almost definite that one of the two Aristophanic comedies was staged by Araros at the Dionysia of 387, inasmuch as the Fasti that year ascribe a victory to him: this was discussed at the end of section 6 of chapter 2, *Chronology*.

The Argument quoted above, as can be inferred from the complete (yet not alphabetical) list of authors and of their works, must once have provided an explicit place-list: first, second, third, fourth and fifth. For clearly expository reasons, however, the place-list true and proper was subsequently omitted (this is not meant to imply that Aristophanes was the winner, although the Argument's outlining of the situation does seem to be prompted by a conclusive success of his). No information has survived about the contest either. However, if, as seems to be the case, the contest was Lenaian, then *Kokalos* might already have been staged at the Dionysia of 388. The five poets in competition are discussed in section 7 of chapter 2 and at the end of section 3 of the present chapter.

It is an established fact that the extant *Plutus* from 388 is a *Second Plutus*, since it is known that Aristophanes presented another *Plutus* under the archon Diocles in 408 (scholia on *Plutus* 173 and 179). *Aiolosikon* was also a 'second comedy': in two of his last three comedies, therefore, Aristophanes returned at least to the themes and masks of earlier works; this is discussed below, at the end of section 2. Here, one might simply draw attention to the fact that one of the characters of *Plutus* – Plutus himself – is assigned a remark typical of Aristophanes in former times, when he used to polemize on the comic arts: 'in this manner we shall also avoid vulgarity, since it is unfitting for the comic poet to fling dried figs and comfits at the spectators, thus constraining them to laughter' (796–9). 'For the comic poet', or rather for Aristophanes. Like Dikaiopolis in *Acharnians* and the slave-prologuist in *Wasps*, Plutus is here the personal spokesman of the dramatist, in the fortieth year of his theatrical career.

2 The two alternating protagonists of *Plutus* and the comedy's artistic economy

As previously in *Wasps*, throughout *Plutus* the setting is a bourgeois home in Athens. The two comedies are also alike in the perpetual coexistence of their two protagonists, who belong in each case to the comedy's single scenic milieu. Whereas the two protagonists of *Wasps* are mutually antagonistic and in continual disagreement, Chremylos and Karion – respectively master and servant in *Plutus* – are complementary and like-minded, so that *after the prologue* they never perform together and indeed alternate with precise regularity. When Chremylos is inactive, Karion takes the stage (253–321, 627–770, 802–958, 1097–1170), and when Karion is inactive Chremylos does (322–626, 771–801, 959–1096, 1171–1207). The individual scenes with Karion and with Chremylos – in the course of which Karion utters altogether around 255 lines, Chremylos around 200 – are always distinguished by the appearance of new scenic personnel, normally episodic: in 253–321 Karion is active with the coryphaeus and the choreutai; in 322–626 Chremylos is active with the episodic Blepsidemos and Poverty; in 627–770 Karion is active with Chremylos' Wife; in 771–801 there is a brief scene with Plutus restored (new mask etc.), Chremylos and Chremylos' Wife; in 802–958, after a message from the chorus, Karion is active with the episodic characters of the Just Man and Sycophant; in 959–1096 Chremylos is active with the Old Woman and the episodic Youth; in 1097–1170 Karion is active with the episodic Hermes; and lastly Chremylos and a Priest of Zeus get the exodos under way.

A performance regimen of this kind produces distinct scenes tending towards the episodic, which are always governed none the less by one of the two long-term protagonists of the comedy; in *Assemblywomen* the protagonist Praxagora instead disappears half-way through the comedy, after which a series of new well-drawn episodic characters appear. In *Assembly-*

women and *Plutus* the weakening of the role of the chorus alone – or rather the reduction of both the dramatic milieu and the political engagement of the comedy – seems to have created problems in the elaboration of the pro- tagonists and characters, which in *Plutus* resulted in a conception involving a pair of long-term alternating protagonists. The latter's functions and char- acteristics are so clearly distinct that it would be inappropriate – other considerations apart – to think that the dramatist might have invented the roles of Chremylos and Karion, after the prologue, in order to entrust them alternatively to the same actor.

If Aristophanes' intention in introducing two complementary protagonists alternating on-stage in the company of new, normally episodic characters was therefore to render the comedy more mobile and varied, such mobility and variety, as remarked previously, create a tendency towards the episodic, to the scene in itself and for itself, towards delay and dramatic fragmentation: it is perfectly natural that a comedy built on a stylistic preoccupation with the alteration of two main characters should show little concern for the organic development of its thematic substance and the steady progression of its structural action.

In fact, the scenes dominated by Karion are always relevant enough to the main thread of the comedy, yet those successively dominated by Chremylos are not always so. It is significant, for example, that after the prologue both Karion and Chremylos should delay in revealing the advent of Plutus, one to the countrymen, the other to Blepsidemos; however, Chremylos' pro- crastination, in contrast to Karion's, gives rise to a dialogue unconnected with the dramatic situation of the comedy, albeit of considerable interest regarding the characterization of Blepsidemos (cf. 343–90). Once the matter has been cleared up, Poverty appears, and, like Plutus during the prologue, pro- crastinates in revealing her identity (415–35, cf. 56–78). The ensuing debate between Chremylos and Poverty – during which Poverty comes up with some extremely acute ideas (although it has been observed that they are of little pertinence to the preceding enunciations) – remains completely extraneous to the dramatic context: not so much because an important character such as Poverty is made to appear and disappear like a marionette, but because some of the closing remarks of the contestants themselves provide reason to suspect that the debate bears little weight in the dramatic action. Backed into a corner by Poverty, the confused Chremylos has no alternative other than to shout out: 'you won't convince me, even should you convince me' (600), and the acute, but suddenly compliant Poverty: 'you'll call me back one day'. Chremylos: 'and that day you will return. For the moment, however, go to hell!' (608–10).

The first part of the comedy ends here, with off-stage action lasting an entire night: Chremylos, Blepsidemos and Karion conduct Plutus to the temple of Aesculapius. This was once the position of the parabasis, but now there is activity involving the chorus indicated by a ΧΟΡΟΥ (discussed in section 3 below). After this interlude, Karion appears: it falls to him to provide an account of Plutus' healing in the temple of Aesculapius, since he alone has remained awake during that miraculous night (cf. 669–72, 739–40). This extremely long account – the message extends from 653 to 759 – is one of the most outstanding pieces of Aristophanic theatre; the personality of the crafty Karion, in contact with a listener such as the superstitious Wife of Chremylos, is extraordinarily effective.

The dramatist was clearly inspired when he wrote the part of Karion, since he is far more of a flesh-and-blood character than his modest and judicious master: the scenes dominated by the verve and energy of Karion are followed by those with less verve and energy involving Chremylos, which, as already mentioned, are at times less organically connected to the main thread of the comedy. This has previously been noted in regard to the scene with Blepsidemos and Poverty, and is also true of the scene in the demonstrative section of the comedy involving the Old Woman, Chremylos and the Youth, 959–1096 (although the part of the Old Woman is highly original). The two demonstrative scenes governed by Karion, 823–958 and 1097–1170, are on the contrary vivacious, pungent and pertinent.

In this demonstrative section of the comedy the most thematically and ethically important scene is 823–958, with Karion, the Just Man and the Sycophant. The ethical weight and spiritual energy which Karion displays during this scene are so striking as to have led a number of scholiasts and copyists to ascribe the episode to his master Chremylos instead.

Undoubtedly, Karion's function in this scene is spiritually unusual for a slave. Yet this is one of the main features of *Plutus*: the Servant's promotion to the rank of autonomous character, or rather the division of the traditional comic hero – a 'free' man – into two separate characters bearing complementary characteristics. The premonitory signs of this development are to be found in *Frogs*, from the year 405, where the fearful master Dionysos-Herakles and the courageous and lucid servant Xanthias, to whom from time to time Dionysos-Herakles passes his mask and delegates his prerogatives, voyage side by side in Hades. In the bourgeois milieu of *Plutus*, however, the sustained dramatic and spiritual weight ascribed to the Servant could be the sign of an entirely new ethical and comic design in which the typical figure of the energetic comic hero disintegrates to find a new equilibrium. The energetic Praxagora in *Assemblywomen* has not yet found this equilibrium since she disappears half-way through the stage-action and makes herself heard again only indirectly when at the end of the comedy she sends her Maidservant to pull the strings of the exodos. In respect to *Assemblywomen*, *Plutus* has found some equilibrium in its treatment of the chorus also: this is discussed in the following section.

In the *Plutus* of 408, the Servant would not have had the role of long-term, autonomous and complementary protagonist assigned to Karion in the extant *Second Plutus*. However, there are situations and masks in the good-natured

388 comedy which recall those of earlier comedies: the countryfied milieu, the polemic against Zeus, the biting parody of a dithyramb by Aristophanes' contemporary Philoxenos, the sophistic and Euripidean vigour of Poverty's argumentation, and the demonstrative parade of a variety of 'characters', particularly the Sycophant, Hermes and the Priest of Zeus. Echoes of *Plutus*?[1]

In the two later comedies, according to the benevolent ancient critics, Aristophanes beat a new path: 'in *Kokalos* he was the first to show the manner of new comedy ... presenting a seduction, a recognition and all the other characteristics so typical of Menander' (*Vita Aristophanis* 1.1–6 and 46–51); 'the [*Second*] *Aiolosikon* bears all the features of middle comedy' (Platonios 7). Another critic, who apparently did not have recourse to the two last comedies, nevertheless found some 'new' characteristics in the extant *Plutus* as well (cf. Koster, *Prol.* V).

3 The coryphaeus and the choreutai in *Plutus*. Characters and actors

As mentioned before, the presence of two long-term alternating protagonists might be a result of the weakening of the role of the chorus. At any rate, the chorus of *Plutus*, which is even more modest than that of *Assemblywomen*, remains passive throughout the comedy. In order to have it appear at the site of the stage action, the chorus of *Plutus* – made up of a group of countrymen, Chremylos' fellow-workers (223) – is both collected by Karion (222–6) and enters the theatre guided and incited by him. Karion incites the chorus in iambic tetrameters (253–6), the coryphaeus replies in iambic tetrameters and the dialogue continues in this metre (257–87). The coryphaeus exclaims: 'I feel like dancing for joy' (288–9), and Karion conducts the dance and song (290–315). Karion then gives orders for the dancing and satirical song to end, invites the choreutai 'to turn to another show' (ἐπ' ἄλλ' εἶδος τρέπεσθε) and goes indoors (316–21). In the Venetus manuscript the invitation is followed by a XOPOY, itself succeeded by a brief dialogue between Chremylos and the coryphaeus (322–31).

After trimeters 328–31, the coryphaeus' activity is slighter but more sustained (487–8, anapaestic tetrameters, 631–2 and 637/639–40, two iambic trimeters and three dochmiac trimeters, 962–3, iambic trimeters, 1208–9, two closing anapaestic tetrameters). The characters also focus their attention fairly constantly on the chorus and the coryphaeus: apart from 627–30, 802–22, 959–61 and 1171, addressed to the chorus, see the indirect mention of the chorus and the coryphaeus in 341 and 641. One should note that this did not take place in *Assemblywomen*, where the chorus is remembered in the finale alone. In *Plutus*, therefore, the treatment of the chorus is more coherent: whilst it may be more modest, it has found a new equilibrium.

Recent scholars are in agreement in attributing the melic iambs 296–301 and 309–15 to the coryphaeus alone rather than to the entire chorus, since these passages 'respond' to the iambs delivered by Karion in 291–5 and 302–8: a

231

'response' delivered by the coryphaeus alone is appropriate to a song delivered by Karion alone. The exultant coryphaeus intervenes separately again – in dochmiacs – when he learns from Karion of the healing of Plutus (637, 639–40). It is strange, however, that in this moment of exultation the *chorus* should not intone a song: also when the restored Plutus re-enters the theatre after 770. Although Karion's exhortation in 761, 'skip and leap and dance in a circle' (ὀρχεῖσθε καὶ σκιρτᾶτε καὶ χορεύετε), might lead one to expect a song, Karion does not explicitly exhort the chorus to salute the god or to sing and dance in his honour, as did Trygaeus in *Peace* 581, the Nuptial Herald in *Birds* 1719 and the Athenian Ambassador in *Lysistrata* 1277.

In the manuscripts of *Plutus* there is a KOMMATION XOPOY between lines 770 and 771. Could it be that this KOMMATION XOPOY indicates a choral song, as many scholars maintain? I believe not, for reasons already given in chapter 12. The thought is rendered even more unlikely by the fact that the chorus of *Plutus* – in contrast to that of *Assemblywomen* – remains significantly mute during the epirrhematic debate: the coryphaeus alone makes his presence felt with the two anapaestic tetrameters 487–8. This·is the only Aristophanic epirrhematic debate not introduced by the traditional choral song, which in itself provides some cause for reflection. Is it really admissible that the chorus should renounce its lyrical introduction of the epirrhematic debate and sing between 770 and 771 instead (and that it should also sing between 321 and 322, 626 and 627 and 801 and 802, at least)?

Is it not also significant that the chorus should be led into the theatre by an actor, an unusual event in itself, and that the coryphaeus should engage in dialogue with this actor and not with the choreutai as well? And why should the XOPOY appear only when there are no characters on-stage? Why should the premisses be denied, in short, for a lyrical interchange between the chorus and the actors? It is neither economically nor theatrically credible that an entire corps of singers would have been paid and then instructed not to sing when there were actors on-stage. It is also clear that the chorus does not sing during the exodos: the coryphaeus does promise a song for the entire chorus (1208–9), but it is performed outside the theatre during the procession towards the Acropolis (although this took place in the finale of *Frogs* also: cf. *Frogs* 1528).

It would appear, therefore, that *Plutus* does not use traditional choreutai but choreutai who limit themselves to dancing when the characters have abandoned the stage (not a single source refers to an interlude of this kind between 1170 and 1171, however). It is the coryphaeus alone who sings – once only, in practice, and nothing of great importance, simply the parody of Philoxenos' dithyramb. The comedy naturally employs a flautist.

What has been said here about the choreutai is a hypothesis, and not an original one at that. It is based, none the less, on internal evidence, on the comedy's particular artistic economy and on its distribution of roles (hence the impropriety of evoking Plato's general definition of the χορεία as a performance made up of dance and song: *Laws* 654b). It is a hypothesis relevant perhaps to *Plutus* alone, and to its four fellow-competitors in the contest of 388 (three of which, like *Plutus*, draw their titles from characters' names).

In the contest of 388 there were in fact five poets in competition, whereas in the contests from *Acharnians* in 425 to *Frogs* in 405 there were only three (regarding *Assemblywomen* from 392 no theatrical information survives): the normal regulations of the Dionysia and Lenaia had obviously been revived (cf. Aristotle, *Athenaion Politeia* 56). On this occasion, whilst on the one hand more poets were allowed to compete, there might also have been a reform as regards the choruses, a reform based, however, on the interpretation of an existing artistic situation: in 392, *Assemblywomen* did use a chorus of twenty-four choreutai-singers, but it did not employ it fully.

If in accordance with the Byzantine scholia one places XOPOY after *Plutus* 958 and 1096, then only three actors are required to portray the comedy's twelve characters (after 1170 a dancing interlude is not strictly necessary, at least in terms of economy in the use of the actors, since the actor involved has enough time to change his mask between 1168 and 1172)[2]:

first actor (or second actor), delivering altogether almost 495 lines, of which 20 are lyrical in 290–321: Karion, 1–228, 253–321, Poverty, 415–609, Karion, 627–770, Plutus Restored, 771–99, Karion, 802–958, Old Woman, 959–1094, Karion, 1097–1170, Old Woman, 1197–1203;

second actor (or first actor), delivering altogether almost 420 lines: Chremylos, 22–252, 322–626, 782–7, Just Man, 823–954, Chremylos, 965–1096, Hermes, 1099–1168, Chremylos, 1172–1207;

third actor, delivering altogether around 250 lines: Plutus Blind, 58–251, Blepsidemos, 335–623, Chremylos' Wife, 641–769, 788–801, Sycophant, 850–950, Youth, 1042–93, Priest of Zeus, 1171–96;

Extras: Baby with the Just Man (823–43), Sycophant's Witness (933), Chremylos' Slaves (1194, 1196). An extra portrays the mute Plutus when he is carried out of his house in 626 and 1196.

The division of the role of Plutus between the third and first actor (the only example of the division of a character between two actors in Aristophanes) was discussed in section 3 of chapter 5.

14

ELEMENTS OF A
THEATRICAL CAREER

'Ever since the Virtuous and the Inverted received great praise in this theatre from people whom it is in itself a pleasure to entertain, and I had to expose them – I was still unmarried and not allowed to give birth – and another girl took them and adopted them instead': Aristophanes' 'secret' début, which these lines from the *Second Clouds* re-evoke in 419–417, took place in the year 427. The comedy of the Virtuous and the Inverted, *Banqueters*, came second, having been staged by the didaskalos Kallistratos. The theatre was that of Dionysos, in which dramas were staged exclusively for the contests of the Dionysia (these included *Clouds*): the début was Dionysian, therefore.

In Athens during that period a new generation of playwrights had come to the fore, whose appearance provoked the rapid decline – within the period 428–424 – of the poets who had dominated the contests of the Lenaia and of the Dionysia for the previous ten years. Phrynichos made his début in 429 and won the Lenaian contest in 428. Eupolis made his début at 17 years of age in 429, and won the Lenaian contest in 426 and the Dionysian in 424. Aristophanes made his début, at an equally tender age, in 427 and distinguished himself: with *Acharnians* at the Lenaia of 425, with an unknown comedy at the Dionysia of 425 and at the Lenaia again with *Knights* in 424. Until then, no new poet had succeeded in overthrowing the supremacy of the old and mature masters such as Kratinos, Telekleides, Pherekrates and Hermippus. After 424, however, it was extremely rare for the latter to emerge. The great Kratinos, whom Aristophanes defeated with *Acharnians* and *Knights*, distinguished himself with the *Bottle* over Ameipsias' *Konnos* and Aristophanes' *Clouds* at the Dionysia of 423. Subsequently, however, as an analysis of the marble lists of the winning poets makes perfectly clear, the surviving old and mature masters (Kratinos died shortly after 423) won at most a couple of times. In *Knights*, Aristophanes justly distinguishes himself, after his two consecutive victories in 425, from the old, once fortunate generation of poets.

In these years, the stable Athenian public had been notably altered by the mass of people displaced from country to city in 430 by the Peloponnesian war. Poets making their début, some of whom, such as Eupolis and Aristophanes, for instance, were extremely young, asserted themselves at once in this period, before this public, in an epoch in which – from 425 at least – only three poets were admitted to the comic contests, and no longer five.

Aristophanes, who in the spring of 425 was the first to overthrow the supremacy of the old masters in the environment of the more ancient Dionysian contests (as far as one can deduce from the *Acharnians*, which followed immediately, the Dionysian *Babylonians* from the year 426 was not victorious), a few months later decided to request a chorus personally from the archon for the Lenaian *Knights* of 424. His 'secret' career, therefore, lasted three years, with five Aristophanic comedies competing in five contests, piloted in the theatre by Kallistratos (*Banqueters*, *Babylonians* and *Acharnians*) and another didaskalos (two unknown titles). At a certain point, however, 'many came in total amazement to the poet to ask him why for some time he had not requested a chorus in his own name': the coryphaeus of *Knights*.

The delay – which Aristophanes explains fully in *Knights*: the art of comedy is the most difficult of all; the public is fickle and demanding; first, one must be an oarsman, then take the helm, next scrutinize the winds from the prow, and lastly pilot oneself – certainly depended, at least after the noted Kleonian affair provoked by *Babylonians* in 426, on a calculated desire to appear officially with a highly political chorus such as that of the authoritative Knights. Anticipation of this is to be found in *Acharnians* from the year 425, when in a context other than the parabasis the coryphaeus, as though he were the poet (but he certainly was . . .), exclaims and announces: 'I hate you even more than Kleon, whose hide I'll have to make shoes for the Knights!' Likewise, the coryphaeus of *Knights*:

> if one of the old comic poets had tried to constrain us Knights to address the public in the parabasis he wouldn't have got away with it so lightly. But this time the poet is worthy, for he hates the same people as we do, and dares to speak the truth, and marches generously against Typhon and Hurricane.

In *Wasps*, performed in January–February 422, Aristophanes reminds the spectators that his official career began with his violent attack on the monstrous Kleon:

> when the poet first began to present comedies, he didn't pick on normal men, but with Heraklean wrath attacked the mighty and powerful, and from the very beginning clashed audaciously with the Jag-toothed one: his eyes flashed with the tremendous radiance of the harlot Cynna, the heads of a hundred execrable adulators licked rings around his head, he had the voice of a torrent disseminating massacre, the fetid stench of a seal, foul balls from Lamia and a camel's arse.

It is worth repeating that in *Knights*, regarding his three-year apprenticeship, Aristophanes says that 'one must first be an oarsman, next the helmsman and then scrutinize the winds from the prow'. The man of the theatre is saying: 'in that period, I first exercised myself amongst the choreutai, next stood at the head of a semi-chorus, and then became the coryphaeus myself' (the latter was certainly the case in *Acharnians*). In *Knights*, however, the captain follows in the tracks of Odysseus, and his refined and formally structured comedy returned rigorously to Homer and to the physiognomy of the first canto of the *Iliad*, in which Odysseus is the seaborne captain of a 'parabasis'. Over half a century before, this revered Homeric physiognomy would have been employed to legitimize the savage child of comedy, and thus have it admitted to the official contests. Such an event, from the year 487–486, is evoked at the end of *Knights*, from the marvellous times of Aristides and Miltiades and of the trophy of Marathon. Aristophanes, newly appointed captain and twice victorious, desires to excel as the historian of comedy from its very earliest days, in a comedy piloted by him alone, after much shrewd delay, on the model of Odysseus among the Phaeacians.

The Monster died in 422, and in *Peace*, performed the following March–April, Aristophanes repeated the lines quoted above from *Wasps*, which by then had been transformed into a monumental epigraph of farewell, in a comedy where the whole intention was to bid farewell to Kleon, and in which the countrymen-choreutai complain of 'lacking the same rough grit as before'. Aristophanes had intuited that with Kleon dead and peace imminent between Athens and Sparta – the truce was in fact sealed a few days after the performance of *Peace* – a chapter of his career had come to a close. Indeed, in the parabasis of *Peace* he provides what amounts to a euphoric résumé of his own artistic merits, all the more so as that particular year his competitors included Eupolis, with his aggressive and satirical *Flatterers*, while he himself – after autumn and on the threshold of peace – had put together a comedy 'lacking the same rough grit as before'. First prize went to Eupolis. Aristophanes came second.

The choice of the Lenaia for a début with an extremely political and domestic comedy such as *Knights* is perfectly understandable. 'This time' – in the words of the protagonist of the Lenaian *Acharnians*, after the incident provoked by the Dionysian *Babylonians* – 'Kleon won't be able to slander me, accusing me of speaking ill of the city in the presence of foreigners. We are here alone, the contest is in the Lenaion, and no foreigners are present: as you know, no tributes have arrived, and not even our allies from the cities. Today, we're here alone, the purest wheaten flour.' In the confidential atmosphere of the Lenaia, the coryphaeus of *Knights* in the parabasis asks the spectators to applaud 'with propitious Lenaite clamour, such that the poet may depart joyful at the outcome he desired'. It is also possible that the comedy might have been brought to completion by a pre-planned demonstration in favour of Aristophanes, the new didaskalos. 'Today, O goddess, as never before, you must do everything in your power to ensure that victory goes to our men', insists the coryphaeus of *Knights*.

Like *Acharnians*, *Knights* makes implicit reference to the site of the other dramatic contests, the theatre of Dionysos, in which the Dionysian contests were held in springtime and at which the tragedies were the main item on the programme. The contests of the Dionysia were more ancient and rigorous than those of the Lenaia, and the audience included the foreigners and allies that *Acharnians* and *Knights* presuppose are absent from the Lenaian contest: 'sweetest shall be the light of day for you who are present and for those to come, should Kleon die', words sung by the Knights. When Aristophanes repeats a group of lines from the Lenaian *Wasps* of 422 in the Dionysian *Peace* of 421, he adds: 'and all along I stood up to the Monster, fighting for you and for the islands'. He adds 'for the islands' because the audience this time includes the allies from the islands, not the Athenians alone. The chorus of the Dionysian *Clouds* salutes 'the Athenians and their allies', and the coryphaeus makes it clear that the site of the performance of *Clouds* is not the Lenaion: 'this, the most acute of my comedies [*Clouds*], I felt that you should be the first to relish', you, the spectators of the Dionysia, not of the Lenaia, with which the theatrical season began. 'In every season' – sing the Clouds – 'there are processions in Athens, sacrifices and banquets; and when spring arrives it's time for the feast of Bromios, the excitement of resounding choruses, the deep-quivering muse of the flauts.' The springtime Dionysia was the feast *par excellence*, and a comedy as aerial as *Birds*, performed at the Dionysia of 414, provides just reflection of its unique character.

Displaying his awareness of the differing politico-civil environments of the Lenaia and of the Dionysia, Aristophanes staged uninhibited and domestic comedies such as *Acharnians*, *Knights* and *Wasps* at the former and more ambitious comedies such as *Clouds*, *Peace* and *Birds* at the latter. The six comedies were presented within twelve years, which implies that the different political and artistic vein of the Lenaian playwright, as compared to the Dionysian, was by no means casual. Neither Friedrich Leo nor Theodor Bergk has omitted to remark upon this point.

The six comedies from 425 to 414 – to those who read them as works for the theatre rather than for the coffee-table – are distinguished by a range of differing stage-properties. Perfectly natural in comedies conceived for two radically differing theatres. In the case of the Lenaia, 'the contest is in the Lenaion' (uttered clearly by the protagonist of *Acharnians*!), in a precinct, perhaps lying in the area of the Agora, in which the theatre was improvised each year. The Dionysian contest took place in the solemn theatre of Dionysos, on the southern slopes of the Acropolis.

Differing stage-properties, Lenaian and Dionysian, are to be found in later comedies also, regarding whose contests no information survives. The comedies in question are *Lysistrata* and *Thesmophoriazusae*, both from 411, which appear to have been conceived for the theatre of Dionysos, and *Assembly-women* (392) and *Plutus* (388), which bear the signs of having been composed for the Lenaion. The highly political *Frogs* from 405 has been transmitted as a Lenaian comedy, and its stage-technique is typical of the Lenaion.

Acharnians, Knights, Wasps, Frogs, Assemblywomen and *Plutus*; *Clouds, Peace, Birds, Lysistrata* and *Thesmophoriazusae*: altogether eleven extant comedies out of the forty that Aristophanes wrote in as many years. During these forty years, because of the intensity of his output and the fact that he was free to request admission to either contest, or to both, Aristophanes would regularly have planned one or the other kind of comedy for one or the other theatre. This is perfectly normal conduct on the part of an author for the stage, who wrote for the audience alone and for specific competitive events, although the stylistic and ideological variants between the Lenaian and Dionysian comedies would not always have been as striking as their differing .stage-properties. It is significant, none the less, that Aristophanes had the Dionysia in mind for the *Second Clouds* when the unsuccessful *Clouds* had competed there a few years before, or that a comedy such as *Birds* should have been staged at the Dionysia when that same year another comedy had been presented at the Lenaia.

In *Thesmophoriazusae*, whose stage-properties are typically Dionysian, a character declares: 'I am Echo ... she who took part in the contest last year, in this very same place, I too, for Euripides [as a character from *Andromeda*].' 'This very same place' has to be the theatre of Dionysos, if only because Euripides apparently competed in that theatre alone. In the theatre of Dionysos, from the beginning of the fifth century, three tragedians competed with four dramas each, whereas at the Lenaian contests, inaugurated around 432, two tragedians took part with no more than two tragedies each. Sophocles must have competed six times at the Lenaia, inasmuch as six of his twenty-four victories were not Dionysian. It is possible that Euripides might never have competed at the Lenaia, a possibility which may be deduced from the number of his official dramas and contests (22 contests, 84 dramas and a posthumous trilogy). Already so unlucky at the Dionysia, Euripides would have avoided an environment dominated by the comic dramatists, of whom he was a favoured target. He would also have nursed a technical preference for the theatre of Dionysos, since it alone had use of the flying-machine, so necessary for and congenial to so many of his tragedies, including *Andromeda*, parodied in *Thesmophoriazusae* 'in the same theatre'.

When Aristophanes competed in the theatre of Dionysos, the theatre *par excellence*, it was almost as if he desired to give a lesson in dramaturgical virtue to his colleagues, the tragedians: whereas one characteristic of the comedies designed for the improvised theatre of the Lenaia is that the protagonist and other characters are also active 'outside the theatre' (apart from *Frogs*, which is set in Hades), in the Dionysian comedies the protagonist remains within the environment of the theatre from start to finish, and if any of the other characters exit by the corridor, they are never seen again. This, the theatrical unity of the site on which the dramas were performed, perhaps made possible by the existence of a stable theatre at the city boundaries, is unknown in Euripides (not to mention Aeschylus), and evident only in Sophocles' later tragedies (with respect to the protagonists alone).

Such rigour on the part of Aristophanes, and of Sophocles, must have been the fruit of a dramaturgical debate taking place in contemporary Athens (it is known that Sophocles wrote a treatise on the chorus and was also the author of various reforms regarding stage-technique and acting style). Sophocles and Aristophanes are also remarkably attentive to the verisimilitude of their characters' appearances and to that of dramatic time (Aristophanes, for instance, always attempts to shorten the lengthy interval generated by the parabasis). Dramaturgical speculation is also frequently given explicit expression in Aristophanes, from *Acharnians* to *Assemblywomen*. One of the more renowned examples is the moment in *Frogs* when Euripides criticizes what he describes as the 'strings of tragedy'. Aeschylus, according to Euripides (and Aristophanes) has no idea about how to move his characters and leaves them sitting for too long mute on-stage, allowing the chorus to lay down the law in its songs: the bases of Aeschylus' dramas are disconnected, therefore, yet Aeschylus does not react.

Aristophanes, on the other hand, moves the strings of comedy to perfection. He is not the anarchic and casual dramatist that the amateurism and laziness of so many scholars have portrayed for us; quite the contrary: Aristophanes, at least as emerges from *Peace*, wrote to a geometrical design, in the same way as Homer. When the strings of one of his comedies fail to respond to his commands, the reason is to be found in serious dramatic events. Chaerephon and Sophocles may never appear on-stage in *Clouds* and *Frogs*, although they have been ascribed intense vital force back-stage; yet this is because the extant *Clouds* is the *second* version of the comedy, which the Alexandrians held was never performed – and which, on analysis, indeed proves to be impossible to perform – and, whereas *Frogs* did reach the stage, an analysis of the comedy demonstrates that Sophocles' death provoked its urgent revision at a point when it was already prepared for performance.

Aristophanes' flexible and digressive comic game might indeed make a joke of our attempts at analysis, but not if they conform to the solid properties of a text designed for the stage and for a specific theatrical contest. An analysis of *Frogs* demonstrates that all the logical, and artistic and structural, deviations in the comedy depend on an extremely recent and serious public and theatrical event, while an analysis of *Clouds* reveals that the famous debate between the two Arguments does not conform to the rigorous norm prescribing three actors then in force in the Athenian theatre, since the debate and surrounding contest require five front-ranking actors. The debate between the two Arguments in the *Second Clouds* is therefore an innovation, and an imperfect one, with respect to *Clouds*, whose characters included Chaerephon. It would indeed have been the plan to put on a comedy not very different from that already performed and negatively received which prevented the *Second*

Clouds from being performed (by contrast, the fragments of the *Second Thesmophoriazusae*, from the prologue onwards, provide evidence of a thorough revision of *Thesmophoriazusae*, both in substance and in the distribution of roles).

After the rout of *Clouds* at the Dionysia of 423, Aristophanes presented two comedies at the Lenaia the following year, *Proagon* and *Wasps*, absenting himself from the Dionysia (and from the Lenaia of 421). However, as the law did not allow him to appear as the author of more than one comedy, he ceded *Proagon* to his didaskalos Philonides. He himself preferred to appear with *Wasps*, a politico-civil comedy like the successful *Knights*, characterized even more than *Knights* by a concentration of the greater weight of the performance on two antagonistic characters alone, each of a clear and elementary type. In a preamble, *Wasps* sets out to present itself as a measured and accessible comedy, although it cannot conceal what appears to be a slight polemical flicker with regard to its fellow-competitor *Proagon*, an anti-Euripidean, literary comedy. Aristophanes' experience with *Clouds* governed his choice of subject and structure in *Wasps*, and after enlivening the parodos with a boy-singer, he devised a novelty for the conclusion as well: 'Go ahead, if you wish, lead us out while you dance; for no one's ever done that before, sent off the chorus of a comedy dancing.' However, the entire conclusion, entrusted to three dancing dwarfs, the sons of Karkinos, cannot have been received enthusiastically if a year later in *Peace* Aristophanes protests: 'O Muse, if Karkinos comes begging you to dance with his sons, pay him no heed, don't enter into their company.' This implies that *Peace*, performed at the Dionysia of 421, is the direct successor of *Wasps* and its severe dicasts: 'You will no longer find in me a sour and intractable dicast', says the idyllic chorus of *Peace*. *Wasps* came second (thanks to the sons of Karkinos?), whereas *Proagon*, ceded to Philonides, came first.

Aristophanes ceded a second comedy to his didaskalos on at least one other occasion. *Lysistrata* and *Thesmophoriazusae*, both from the year 411, are clearly designed for the contests of the Dionysia. However, although both are feminist comedies, one is politico-civil and panhellenic in character, the other literary and occupied with an intensely private intrigue, so private that the actors leave the site of their action intact (unique in Aristophanes), concerned as they are with problems devoid of all public significance. The deep rift separating the two comedies is also evident in the treatment of the choreutai and actors. *Lysistrata*, for instance, has *two* choral entrance marches, whereas *Thesmophoriazusae* does not even have one. This time, too, Aristophanes figured as the author of the more political comedy, *Lysistrata*.

In *Thesmophoriazusae* the subject and object, schemer and artistic victim is Euripides: Euripides, the man of the theatre, at the service of Euripides, the private citizen. Euripides had a remarkable success at the Dionysia of 412 (a victory on his part was almost a novelty for Aristophanes' contemporaries), a success from which *Thesmophoriazusae* was born, when plans for the highly political and panhellenic *Lysistrata* must already have been under way. *Lysistrata* is a panhellenic comedy to such an extent that in the lyrical finale in the Laconian dialect Aristophanes eliminates Lysistrata as a speaking character and assigns the first actor the demanding new role of the Spartan Singer. From a technical point of view, this phenomenon, like that planned in the *Second Clouds* to facilitate the definitive introduction of the two Arguments, and another which emerges in *Plutus*, demonstrates that for important episodic roles Aristophanes had no alternative than to resort to one of the first three actors. He did have a fourth actor at his disposal, but one of extremely modest status with functions clearly distinct from those of the first three, performing exclusively in iambic trimeters. The later aesthetic theory of performance structures involving three characters and no more was drawn from tragedy, but with fair reason might equally have been drawn from Aristophanic comedy. Clearly, it was drawn from tragedy, conceived as a literary form, that is, not as stage drama subject to a presumable State law governing the actors, which, needless to say, was no more than the official sanctioning of an artistic syntax relative to the actors developed gradually by the dramatists.

Frogs, from the year 405, provides an outstanding example of the depth of Aristophanes' dramatic resources, as *Birds* had before. The dramatic coherence of *Birds*, which was presented at the Dionysia of 414 with an abundance of original features, is quite remarkable: the stage-illusion is established at the very beginning of the comedy by, amongst other things, the inclusion within the dramatic landscape of a normally neutral element such as the corridors; the two opening characters are non-functional, one of the reasons why the comedy is so well structured; the chorus remains consistent with its mask throughout (even during the parabasis); the dramatic landscape is convincingly presented as extending back-stage, by virtue of the comedy's 'open' façade (which represents a copse); the three actors are kept in use almost constantly; the lyrical tendency of the entire comedy is manifested at the end of the prologue by the evident back-stage substitution of the third actor with a singer; finally, the sustained creative vein of the piece comes to a climax in the exodos with the appearance on-stage of an exclusively Aristophanic goddess.

Frogs is not notable for its dramatic coherence. It is notable, however, for the progressive staging of a journey and of a landscape almost throughout the first section of the comedy: this itinerant spectacle, unique amongst the extant ancient dramas, was clearly intended by Aristophanes to compensate for the inevitable scenic immobility of the second section of the comedy, which is devoted to the great artistic and political duel between Aeschylus and Euripides. Because of the revision the comedy sustained shortly before its performance the analytic reader will notice certain incongruities in the logical progression and stage-technique of the second section: this is especially true of the finale, improvised as it was in order to return Aeschylus to Athens after Sophocles' death. However, it was by virtue of this timely and significant revision alone that Aristophanes managed to save his comedy (it won first prize and was later restaged), and to save it so thoroughly that the modern reader is left bewildered. In 1920, stimulated by the analytic observations of Eduard Fraenkel, Max Pohlenz at least noticed that the progression of the artistic duel between Aeschylus and Euripides was far from normal. Today, one can distinguish the original progression, and see how much it favoured Aristophanes' own position regarding the poetics of tragedy.

Appearing thirteen years after the bipartite *Frogs*, *Assemblywomen* is genuinely divided into two formally distinct acts. The weakening of the role of the chorus, brought to completion in *Plutus* in the year 388, posed new problems with respect to the elaboration of characters and scenes. Implying a reduction of the comedy's dramatic milieu and political commitment, it also led to a situation in which comic intrigue was completely stripped of its practical intent: in *Assemblywomen*, indeed, the intrigue is based on a hoax which never comes to light. In *Plutus*, the traditional comic hero – a 'free' man – is divided into two separate, yet complementary characters alternating on-stage: the shrewd master and the carefree slave. Whereas in *Assemblywomen* the protagonist, Praxagora, disappears half-way through the comedy, *Plutus* sustains a single main role throughout, divided alternately between two characters. The comedy also attains a degree of equilibrium in its treatment of the chorus: although only the coryphaeus sings, and the choreutai are dancers only, the comedy always pays some slight attention to this ghost of a chorus.

In the year in which *Plutus* was performed, 388, the number of dramatists admitted to the contest was no longer three, but five. This alteration in the number of dramatists might have led to a remodelling of the chorus as well, advance symptoms of which are to be gleaned from *Assemblywomen*, staged in 392.

Although Aristophanes' last two comedies were written in an age in which reading and the cirulation of texts were gaining influence, they are none the less intrinsically conceived for the spectator. Indeed, the text of *Assemblywomen*, like that of (the disorderly) *Wasps*, *Second Clouds* and *Frogs*, seems to have been left untouched by the author after it had been performed (or after its performance had been abandoned, as in the case of the *Second Clouds*): these texts demonstrate that the comedies were left to circulate without having been prepared for this purpose *by the author*. The theory which Wilamowitz upheld until the last years of his life, that the Athenian dramatists also edited their texts to meet the demands of the reading public, still continues to gain ground. However, there are other factors in the textual tradition of the works of the Greek theatre which warn against such a modernistic and bibliocratic idea, and induce one instead to maintain that the transformation of the theatrical text into a text designed to be read was generally a rather haphazard affair.

15

THE DISORDERLY *WASPS*
AND
AN 18 × 2 TETRAMETER MODULE

1 'How could two choral songs have been transposed?'
The paralysis of the bibliocrat

In his 1964 Penguin translation of *Wasps*, David Barrett notes: 'I have followed Zieliński and other editors in reversing the respective positions of this chorus (lines 1450–1473) and the "second parabasis" (lines 1265–1291).' Victor Coulon's edition of *Wasps* reads: '*1265–1291* et *1450–1473* inter se commut. Müller-Strübing, Textor, Zieliński'. And in 1909, a Belgian scholar wrote: 'Il est de la dernière evidence que l'ordre des deux morceaux a été interverti' (Alphonse Willems, *Aristophane* (Paris–Bruxelles 1919), I, p. 509, n. 1).

In the Byzantine manuscripts, lines 1265–91 do in fact occupy the position of 1450–73, and 1450–73 are in a position extremely well suited to 1265–91.

This exchange of position between two non-adjacent textual units is unique in the tradition of the works of Greek theatre. In 1911, Ulrich von Wilamowitz-Moellendorff issued the following warning from the Prussian Academy:

> wie sollen denn zwei Chorpartien in der Überlieferung vertauscht sein? Was berechtigt zu solcher kritischen Manipulation? Das ist das Charakteristische: man fragt gar nicht nach ihrer Berechtigung. Diese Umstellung ist ein Survival aus den Zeiten der durch Grössenwahn tollgewordenen Methode, die immer andere Leute dafür verantwortlich machte, wenn sie etwas nicht verstand.

'How could two choral songs have been transposed in the course of the tradition?', enquired Wilamowitz indignantly of the 'crazed megalomaniacs' who had proposed and adopted the transposition. To Wilamowitz, such a phenomenon would have seemed to collide directly with his own idea that the Athenian dramas, after staging, were issued as books published and annotated by their authors to meet the demands of the 'publicum' of readers and of the dramatists themselves (a factor considered in *Frogs*). Despite his realistic and historicist intentions, in the chapter 'Die Tragödie ein Buch' Wilamowitz nurtured the fantasy of this *bibliocracy* for over twenty years, and allowed himself to be won over again in *Hellenistische Dichtung* (1924)

(I, p. 98 with n. 4). Just such a bibliocracy, modernistic in the extreme, went on to dominate in a considerable number of influential textbooks about the Greek theatre (e.g. Thomas B. L. Webster, *Greek Theatre Production* (London, 1956), pp. xi and xii: 'the Greek playwright could not be certain of more than a single production, and therefore he always wrote for a reading public as well as his audience', 'already in the fifth century the tragic poet at least could count on a reading public', Albin Lesky, *Die tragische Dichtung der Hellenen* (Göttingen, 1964²), p. 54, and *Geschichte der griech. Literatur* (Bern–München, 1971³), p. 16). Hegel, on the other hand, saw things correctly when in the third edition of *Vorlesungen über die Aesthetik*, considering the reading and performance of dramatic works, he wrote: 'ja meiner Meinung nach sollte eigentlich kein Schauspiel gedruckt werden, sondern, ohngefähr wie bei den Alten [here, Hegel was obviously theorizing on the opinions of contemporary classicists: theatre manuscript, insignificant circulation] als Manuscript dem Bühnenrepertoir anheimfallen, und nur eine höchst unbedeutende Cirkulation erhalten'.

In 1911, whilst the 'irresponsible manipulators' of the two choral songs of *Wasps* were being pitied in Berlin, in Paris Louis Havet wrote in section VIII ('Les Fautes Princeps'), chapter XLIV ('Editeurs posthumes') of his *Manuel de critique verbale appliquée aux textes latins*: 'Il n'y a pas de raison pour que les exemplaires de théâtre aient eu la forme du *volumen*'(§ 1104 A), and referred back to § 55: 'L'antiquité n'avait pas ignoré les *codices*, mais ils jouaient le rôle de nos cahiers manuscrits, carnets, etc.; cf. 1104 A.' In February 1944, at the Ecole Normale Supérieure, Alphonse Dain, imagining the compilation of an author's manuscript as 'une opération multiforme', said:

> Quoi qu'il en soit, la confection de l'original a toujours été une entreprise moins simple qu'on ne le croit. Comment Hérodote ou Xénophon, comment Stace ou Lucain ont-ils confectionné leur original? C'est que nous n'entrevoyons que fort mal. On peut dire que l'original de Thucydide était fait de la suite des rouleaux au bas desquels il avait apposé sa signature; mais qu'en était-il pour les autres auteurs? Que de problèmes de composition d'une œuvre ancienne trouveraient peut-être leur solution si nous étions mieux renseignés sur ces faits! Qu'on retienne en tout cas que, dès le point de départ, l'histoire du texte est liée aux conditions matérielles qui constituent ce que nous appellerions aujourd'hui 'la mise en page' de l'ouvrage.
>
> (*Les Manuscrits* (Paris, 1949), p. 93; (1975³), p. 105)

For a Louis Havet and an Alphonse Dain, both aware that a textual tradition is not complete in itself but ensues from a *preliminary 'domestic' phase*, the encounter with *Wasps* would not have produced the paralytic effect it did for Wilamowitz, whose lifelong objective was the author's manuscript: 'Es soll seine Hand von den Texten lassen, wer es nicht versteht, den Weg von

der erhaltenen Handschrift bis auf die des Verfassers zurückzuverfolgen'
(*Geschichte der Philologie* (1927), p. 76).

The two choral songs might easily have been transposed, since 'Il n'y a pas de
raison pour que les exemplaires de théâtre aient eu la forme du *volumen*.' The
transposition would have occurred when the single parts of the manuscript of
Wasps, prepared and organized in accordance with the drama's various
economies and stage-directions, were being copied on to a papyrus scroll (in
Aristophanes' time, naturally, and within his circle). In *Wasps*, the artistic
economy governing the last six hundred lines or more is quite striking (the
actors' lines are in roman type, the chorus' in italics; K = two iambic trimeters
assigned to the coryphaeus): 891–1008, *1009–1121*, 1122–1264, *1450–73*,
1292–1449 + K *1265–91*, 1474–1515, *1516–37*. Dialogue on the one hand and
parts for the chorus alone on the other.

The transposition, therefore, is really quite simple to understand:

> in both cases one is dealing with pieces written for the chorus alone (and
> with the only two choral passages between the parabasis and exodos), to
> be inserted, in both cases, between two remarks delivered by the first
> two actors as they exit from the stage, and a remark made by the third as
> he enters.[1]

2 Actors, choreutai and youths: another accident *chez* Aristophanes

The disharmony which the late appearance of lines 290–316 creates in the
parodos of *Wasps* was noted in the second half of the nineteenth century by
Wilhelm Nesemann, Emil Brentano and Jan van Leeuwen. However, the
dramaturgy of the parodos became recognizable in its genuine form only
when the Polish scholar Stefan Srebrny relocated lines 290–316 between
lines 265 and 266.[2]

An analysis might make it easier to recognize the verbal, logical and scenic
harmony of 230–47/248–65 → 290–316, 266–89 → 317–33. Here it is enough
to bear in mind the following:

290: The coryphaeus orders the lantern-bearing Youth to move on; *291–316*:
as they march (299), the Youth and the coryphaeus converse in lyric metres
(in 248–65 they had been speaking in tetrameters);

266–72: the coryphaeus points out Philokleon's house (cf. 214–29) and invites
his companions, the chorus, to stop and entice Philokleon outdoors with a
melody; *273–89*: a choral song for Philokleon, invoked directly in 286–9;

317–33: Philokleon (first actor, inactive after trimeter 197) responds with a
monody to the choral song, which he has been enjoying since it first began
(cf. 317–18).

In the Byzantine manuscripts, therefore, lines 266–89 (coryphaeus + chorus) occupy the position of lines 290–316 and lines 290–316 (coryphaeus + Youth) that of 266–89. Not only was an entire scenic unit at some time copied prior to the unit meant to precede it, but this advance copying must also have taken place in an exemplar authoritative enough to determine the entire course of the textual tradition, direct and indirect, extant and reconstructable.

Such an exemplar could only have been the original exemplar on the scroll of *Wasps*, mentioned in section 1 above. There is very little reason why the continuous text, already transcribed on to the scroll (and no longer performed on-stage), would have induced some unknown hand to transcribe in advance a group of lines which were: (a) quite distant, (b) numerous enough and (c) marvellously coincident with an entire scenic unit. The two groups of lines, moreover, although adjacent, were of different length and in addition diacritically unequivocal: one contained at least twelve paragraphoi, whereas the other was either devoid of paragraphoi or contained only one, before tetrameter 266 (as in the Ravenna manuscript).[3]

If the switching of the two adjacent units took place during the first transcription on to the scroll, the decisive factor might have been the attraction exerted over the seven iambityphallic tetrameters 266–72 by the eighteen iambic tetrameters 230–47, or, still more, by the succeeding eighteen iambityphallic tetrameters 248–65. *In such a case, tetrameter XXXVI (= line 265) would have been the last of the unit transcribed on to the scroll and a different unit would have contained the scene with the youth and the coryphaeus (= lines 290–316) and another the seven tetrameters + choral song (= lines 266–72 + 273–89).*

In any case, the unit on which the opening tetrameters (= lines 230–47, or 230–65) were originally written was quite certainly an autonomous one, since the 'preceding' lines 1–229 were concerned with the instruction of the three actors alone, after which the tetrameters would have inaugurated the action and instruction of the chorus, of the para-choral personnel (the Lantern-bearing Youth), and probably of the flautist, too.

3 A structural form dominated by rhythm

In 1886, reviewing *Die Gliederung der altattischen Komödie* by Thadeusz Zieliński, Konrad Zacher wrote of *Wasps* (here translated into English):

> Lines 266–272 are drastically detached from those preceding them (on p. 269 Zieliński himself described the shift from considerations regarding the weather to expressions of wonder at Philokleon's non-appearance as 'very abrupt') and seem rather to be the introduction to a song; lines 248–265, on the other hand, constitute a coherent whole. Whether or not *it is a coincidence* [my italics] that this passage is made up of exactly the

same number of tetrameters as the passage preceding it (lines 230–247), eighteen, that is, I would prefer to leave undecided.

> (*Wochenschrift f. klass. Philologie* 50, c. 1573; for the 18 and 18 in symmetry cf. Rudolph Westphal, *Prolegomena zu Aeschylus Tragödien* (Leipzig, 1869), p. 34)

Today, we can affirm that it is not *a coincidence*. Indeed, it is easy to see that the second eighteen tetrameters are the stylistic and metrical antithesis of the first: the first eighteen are iambic, the second iambithyphallic; in the first, the coryphaeus addresses the choreutai, while in the second he converses with a youth. The Youth opens the dialogue (248), and the coryphaeus closes it (258–65); whereas both make three interventions, the Youth has only six tetrameters, the coryphaeus twelve. Between the 18 and 18, moreover, an extra metre points up the opposition: the Youth draws attention to himself with an ὤ, and from Aeschylus to Aristophanes exclamations such as this are often in a specially planned position.

Similarly, the other parodoi of this kind – in which the coryphaeus, on his first appearance with the chorus, converses with an actor – open with *thirty-six* tetrameters. The year after *Wasps*, 421, Aristophanes drafted a dialogic opening to the parodos of *Peace* which was composed of thirty-six (trochaic) tetrameters delivered by the coryphaeus and the first actor (301–36). After more than thirty years, the dialogic parodos of *Plutus* from the year 388 is composed, once again, of thirty-six (iambic) tetrameters delivered by the first actor and the coryphaeus (253–89); it is also followed by an amoibaion sung by the first actor – who has led the chorus' march into the theatre and is still leading them – and the coryphaeus (290–5 = 296–301, 302–8 = 309–15). In *Wasps*, which was performed at the Lenaia of 422, the thirty-six tetrameters are also followed by an amoibaion sung by the Youth – who has just led the chorus' march into the theatre and is still leading them – and the coryphaeus (291–302 = 303–16; in *Wasps* 266 and *Plutus* 318, after the amoibaion, the scenic façade comes into play). In the single other dialogic parodos, that of *Knights* from the year 424, the opening trochaic tetrameters are thirty-seven in number (247–83) and form a dialogue between no fewer than four voices. In the other comedies, after the prologue the chorus performs and sings alone on-stage (*Acharnians*, *Lysistrata*, *Assemblywomen*), sings back-stage (*Clouds*, *Frogs*), or, as in the case of *Birds* and *Thesmophoriazusae*, files silently into the theatre. In *Frogs*, however, when the parodos towards the orchestra really begins the coryphaeus delivers *eighteen* anapaestic tetrameters (354–71).

In *Peace*, the module of thirty-six tetrameters is set within a minor symmetrical framework of two pairs of tetrameters uttered by the first actor, 299–300 and 337–8; the distinguished metrician Heliodorus made a critical distinction between the two tetrameters 299–300 – 'uttered still by the old man' – and 'the thirty-six equally trochaic tetrameters from the moment the chorus arrives'. After this thirty-six-line dialogic complex Heliodorus isolated the two trochaic tetrameters 337–8, which he defined as a 'prelude' to the 'song' in dimeters subsequently performed by the first actor (scholia on *Peace* 299–336 White).

It would have been unlike Heliodorus, on this as on so many other occasions, to have simply bunched all the equal lines together, as the majority of modern 'analysts' do. To give just one example: in contrast to Heliodorus (scholion *Knights* 247–83 White), and to Aristophanes, the moderns include tetrameters 242–6 in the parodos of *Knights*. Heliodorus knew well how to recognize the intrinsic characteristics of a theatrical text edited in accordance with this intended destination or use.

4 Next to the parabasis and to the epirrhematic agon

An analysis of the tetrameter module, in synthesis, provides the following results:

(a) In *Wasps*, *Peace* and *Plutus*, the module is symmetrically epirrhematic (tetrameters 18 × 2). *Wasps*, in which the 18 × 2 structure is also metrical, was discussed at the beginning of section 3. In *Peace*, the first unit is governed by the motif of the forbidden cry, the second by that of the forbidden dance (see tetrameters XVII and XIX of the module only); in the first unit the coryphaeus and actor are assigned three interventions each (twelve tetrameters against six), and in the second seven each (eleven against seven). In the two units of *Plutus*, the equal numbers of interventions and tetrameters assigned to the coryphaeus and to the actor are symmetrically antithetical (first unit: actor – four interventions and eleven tetrameters; coryphaeus – three and seven; second unit: coryphaeus – five interventions and eleven tetrameters; actor – four and seven). In the thirty-seven-tetrameter module in *Knights* it seems possible to distinguish a first unit of *8.3.8* lines and a second of *3.4.1.1.1.2.2.2.2.* (the interventions of the coryphaeus are in italics); in the first unit the coryphaeus is assigned two interventions and the actor one, while in the second the coryphaeus has three and the three actors six; in the second unit the numerical relationship of eleven lines to seven is that to be found in the second unit of *Peace* and in the first and second of *Plutus*. The coryphaeus is therefore assigned twenty-three lines altogether, like the coryphaeus of *Peace*. In *Frogs*, the module is monological and composed of eighteen tetrameters.

NB: in *Peace* 553–70, there is a dialogic module for a choral 'parodos' composed of eighteen trochaic tetrameters (9 × 2) which stands out quite clearly from the surrounding context inasmuch as it erupts from the trimeters.

(b) The second unit of the trochaic module in *Peace* is the only (dialogic) tetrameter scene in Aristophanes in which the chorus and coryphaeus explicitly *dance*. The symmetry of the module's epirrhemata would seem to favour a kinetic interpretation (if not actually an orchestic one) in two separate phases, as in *Wasps* certainly and also in *Peace* 553–61/562–70 (in *Plutus*, the interventions of the coryphaeus are symmetrical, in italics: *4.4.3.1.3.2.1./ 2.2.2.2.4.2.1.1.2*). Vocal interpretation is assigned to the coryphaeus and the first actor (*Peace, Plutus*), to the coryphaeus and more than one actor (*Knights, Peace* 553–70), to the coryphaeus alone (first unit of *Wasps, Frogs*) and to the coryphaeus and the para-choral personnel (second unit of *Wasps*).

(c) In *Knights* and *Peace* the module is opened by eight tetrameters delivered by the coryphaeus, divided into two equal units (*Knights* 247–50, 251–4, *Peace* 301–4, 305–8), in *Plutus* by 4 + 4 tetrameters delivered by the actor and the coryphaeus.

NB: some parodoi performed by the chorus alone on-stage are opened by units composed of four tetrameters: *Acharnians* 204–7, *Lysistrata* 254–5 + 319–20 (semi-chorus + semi-chorus), *Assemblywomen* 285–8; cf. also *Thesmophoriazusae* 655–62 (4 × 2), which bear the characteristics of a parodos: *Thesmophoriazusae* 660–2 → *Knights* 242, *Wasps* 246, *Peace* 299–300, *Plutus* 255–6. Cf. moreover *Assemblywomen* 489–92 and 500–3. Also in *Clouds* 263–6, the prologue is followed by a unit of four tetrameters (delivered by the actor).

(d) In three comedies the module has a circular structure, and is opened and closed by lines expressing the specific themes of the agon: *Knights* 247–50 → 278–83, *Peace* 303–4 → 336 and 553–5 → 569–70, *Plutus* 262–3 → 284–9; one encounters verbal circularity in *Wasps* 230 → 246 and *Frogs* 354 → 370.

(e) There are some extremely strong verbal similarities between the modules of *Peace* and *Plutus*: it is enough to compare the XXXV tetrameter of each module (*Peace* 335, *Plutus* 288) and the first tetrameters of the coryphaei (*Peace* 301, *Plutus* 257; see also *Wasps* 230). In *Wasps* 250–8, *Peace* 301–31 and *Plutus* 261–82 polemical skirmishes take place between the coryphaeus and the actor, in *Knights* there is a violent clash and in *Frogs* the coryphaeus speaks polemically.

(f) In *Knights* 242–6 and *Peace* 299–300 the actor, by extemporaneously including the chorus in the stage-action, establishes the metre of the module; in *Plutus* 253–6 the actor, by leading the entrance march of the chorus, both opens and establishes the module; in *Wasps*, the actor establishes the new metre of the second unit of the module; in *Wasps* and *Plutus*, the actor starts up an amoibaic song with the coryphaeus after the module.

Anapaestic, iambithyphallic, iambic, trochaic tetrameters in canonical number (36, 18), symmetric epirrhemata (18 × 2, 9 × 2), kinetic or orchestic symmetry or eurhythmy on the part of the chorus, vocal interpretation by the coryphaeus and the first actor, verbal circularity, dramatic action and dialogic agonism in miniature, verbal and gestural stereotypy even within the same lines of the module, an actor who draws the chorus into the performance, establishes the metre of the module and of its second unit and intones a lyrical amoibaic coda with the coryphaeus: these features make the module under analysis a noble element of Aristophanic comedy.[4]

NOTES

2 Chronology of an apprenticeship

1 οἷς ἡδὺ κτλ. is interpreted accurately by A. Willems, *Aristophane* (Paris–Brussels, 1919), I, p. 393. 'Im Dionysostheater', 'on this spot' and 'in the theatre', as translations of ἐνθάδε, are to be found in the commentaries on *Clouds* by W. S. Teuffel and O. Kaehler (Leipzig, 1887), W. J. M. Starkie (London, 1911) and K. J. Dover (Oxford, 1968); but see also *Clouds* by G. Hermann (Lipsiae, 1830), p. xxvi. A fresh approach to *Banqueters*, as a Dionysian comedy, is proposed by D. Gilula, 'P. Oxy. 2737 and Aristophanes' early career', *Zeitschr. Papyr. Epigr.* 81 (1990), 101–2:

> The explanation of the scholiasts (*Clouds* 530c, Tzetzes *Clouds* 518ab, 530b, *Vita* XXXIIb, p. 145, 5–7 Koster) that Aristophanes was prevented from producing the *Banqueters* in his own name by a law which prescribed a minimum age, though in itself suspect of being an explanation inferred from the text of *Clouds* 530–1, seems nevertheless to imply that the secrecy resulted from some sort of a transgression, if not of law then of custom, which it was necessary to cover up. P. Oxy. 2737, 44–51 allows us to surmise that this transgression had something to do with producing plays at the Dionysia when one was not yet entitled to compete at that festival .... Callistratus was not a beginner and could compete, therefore, at the Dionysia. It was precisely because Callistratus produced Aristophanes' plays where and when Aristophanes himself was not entitled to do so that the authorship of Aristophanes had to be kept secret.

P. Oxy. 2737 = fr. 590 (Plato comicus, *test.* 7), published by E. Lobel in 1968, has provoked some reflection on the considerable social and administrative rift separating the Dionysia from the Lenaia. The papyrus has also sparked off a discussion as to the number of participants in the contest (three or five): see R. M. Rosen, 'Trouble in the early career of Plato comicus', *Zeitschr. Papyr. Epigr.* 76 (1989), 223–8, complete with bibliography.

2 Some doubt is evident in P. Geissler, *Chronologie altatt. Komödie* (Berlin, 1979, 1925), p. 5: '*Babylonians* received first prize; but the poet did not pronounce on his success, at least in any of the extant comedies.' H. Ollacher also, 'Chronologie altatt. Komödie', *Wien. Studien* 38 (1916), 101f., recognized that the parabasis of *Acharnians* implies no more than that *Babylonians* had enjoyed a certain degree of success. This notwithstanding, he opted for victory. Wilamowitz, *Lysistrate* (Berlin, 1927), p. 41, refers back to Geissler and writes, 'one must now recognize that *Babylonians* was victorious: the evidence provided by the list is decisive, *schlägt durch*'. In 1919, however, before falling under Geissler's influence,

Wilamowitz had written about *Babylonians*: 'wie töricht an einen Sieg dieses Stückes zu glauben' (*Platon*, II, p. 17) (communicated by Eduard Fraenkel). Later, Geissler took notice of the parabasis of *Acharnians*. R. Kassel and C. Austin in 1984 still maintained (*Testimonia*, p. 9): 'Dionysiis vicit fortasse a. 426 (Babyloniis)', omitting the Dionysia of 425 from their list.

3 Hence, Argument III to *Plutus*. For the three operations relative to the didaskalos, or to the poet-didaskalos, cf. respectively (a) *Acharnians* 11, (b) *Vita Sophoclis* 14 and Aristides, *Rhet.* 1 and 2, and (c) Aristides, op. cit., Plutarch, *Moralia* 785b, Alciphron, *Ep.* IV.18.16, Athenaeus 241f., etc. *Acharnians* 1224 might allude to the third operation.

4 See also *Clouds* 549. Regarding the period of the apprenticeship, one should consider that in an epoch in which the competition had become far more severe (six poets, not ten), there is all the more reason to understand why a poet making his début might have preferred to entrust his work to an established didaskalos: the *Suda* χορὸν δίδωμι and the scholiast on Plato's *Republic* 383c point out that 'not all the tragic and comic poets obtained a chorus, only those εὐδοκιμοῦντες καὶ δοκιμασθέντες ἄξιοι': evidence, if you wish, unfavourable to the victory of *Babylonians*. The scholar who interpreted πάλαι as 'after having reached the legal age' was M. Pohlenz, 'Aristophanes *Ritter*', *Nachr. Ak. Wiss. Göttingen* (1952), 113 n. 36 (*Kleine Schriften*, II). As everybody knows, one may only hypothesize regarding Aristophanes' date of birth: the least imprudent approach is to keep to the *Suda* (the scholion on *Frogs* 501 could be an interpretation of *Clouds* 530).

5 D. Gilula, 'A career in the navy (Arist. *Knights* 541–4)', *Classical Quarterly* 81 (1989), 259–61, has clarified the issue of the *three* stages in the seafaring career (oarsman, helmsman, at the prow), referring to R. Porson and A. Cartault, *La Trière athénienne* (Paris, 1881), pp. 226–7, and H. Schrader, 'Kleon und Aristophanes *Babylonier*', *Philologus* 36 (1877), 405–6 (on the seafaring apprenticeship in *Knights* and the mask of *Peace*, see W. Helbig, *Quaestiones scenicae* (Bonn, 1861), p. 23). F. Perusino, *Dalla commedia antica alla commedia di mezzo* (Urbino, 1988), pp. 37–57, offers a critical overview entitled *I registi di Aristofane*.

The didaskalos Philonides must have had a close relationship with Aristophanes. Indeed, Aristophanes was probably in contact with a thiasus of Herakles in his own deme, the Kydathenion, of which Philonides, Amphitheos (*Acharnians* 45), the priest Simon (*Knights* 242) and others formed part: see Th. Gelzer 'Aristophanes der Komiker', *Paulys Real. Suppl.* XII (1970), c. 1398, 14–56 and H. Lind, 'Neues aus Kydathen, Beobachtungen zum Hintergrund der *Daitales* und der *Ritter* des Aristophanes', *Museum Helveticum* 42 (1985), 249–61, reprinted in *Der Gerber Kleon in den 'Rittern' des Aristophanes* (Frankfurt on Main, 1990).

6 As to the nature of Aristophanes' relationship with his didaskaloi, particularly during the period of his apprenticeship, the question is still open, notwithstanding the rigorous article by K. Zacher, Διὰ Καλλιστράτου, in *Philologus* 49 (1890), 313–37. With respect to Aristophanes and Aegina, it is known that criticism is based on the first conjectural explanation provided by the scholion on *Acharnians* 654, on which the local historian Theogenes apparently also drew, fr. 2 Jacoby IIIB (complete with commentary (Leiden, 1955), p. 8). It has been proved that Athenian cleruchs were installed on Aegina from 431 onwards, whence the moderns prefer to think of Aristophanes' father, Philippos. Regarding the Spartans' vague requests relative to Aegina, see Thucydides I.139. On the life of Aristophanes, see also M. R. Lefkowitz, *The Lives of Greek Poets* (London, 1981), ch. X.

3 Acharnians

1 On two separate occasions, Dikaiopolis speaks with the voice of Aristophanes regarding the comedy last performed, whereas in a context other than the parabasis the comedy's unusual coryphaeus heralds *Knights*. In the wake of the seafaring passage from *Knights*, it is inappropriate to conceive of Aristophanes as an actor; this is also because the actors, unlike the freelance choreutai, were employed by the State. The characters speak in the name of the poet on other occasions too: *Wasps* 55–66, 648–9, fr. 488. Aristophanes' mask might have alluded to his renowned premature balding (*Knights* 550, *Peace* 767–74, Eupolis fr. 89). The expedient employed in *Acharnians*, 'secret author-didaskalos/coryphaeus' (*the coryphaeus is a didaskalos also*), conforms to the species of theatrical invention recommended by the coryphaeus himself in lines 389–91. On the interchangeable terms διδάσκαλος and ποιητής, see Th. K. Hubbard, *The Mask of Comedy: Aristophanes and the Intertextual Parabasis* (Ithaca and London, 1991), p. 229; regarding Aristophanes as coryphaeus see P. Thiercy, 'Deux variations sur *Les Acharniens* (et *Cavaliers* 542–544)', *Cahiers du Gita*, no. 5 (December 1989), 34–8. C. Bailey, 'Who played "Dicaeopolis"?', in *Greek Poetry and Life* presented to G. Murray (Oxford, 1936), pp. 231–40 places Aristophanes as the first actor of *Acharnians*, influenced also by the fact that in Pindar, *Pyth.* 8.31 δικαιόπολις is an epithet for Aegina:

> is not Δικαιόπολις besides its primary meaning [a 'just city', according to Cyril Bailey], intended to suggest the 'Aeginetan', just as a character called Ἰοστέφανος would inevitably be an Athenian? And if it is the 'Aeginetan', then it is Aristophanes; the hero's name was a clue to his actor.

Agreement is voiced by O. Weinreich, *Aristophanes* (Zürich, 1968, 1952), p. lxxii, K. Lever, *The Art of Greek Comedy* (London, 1956), pp. 107, 131, and others (the first to make this proposal was W. Merry in his 1893 Oxford commentary, line 377). It is amusing also that Aristophanes' friend and rival was named Εὔπολις: see E. L. Bowie, 'Who is Dicaeopolis?', *Journal of Hellenic Studies* 108 (1988), 183–5, followed by L. P. E. Parker, 'Eupolis or Dicaeopolis?', *Journal of Hellenic Studies* 111 (1991), 203–8. On Eupolis and Eupolis-Aristophanes, see J. C. Storey, 'Notus est omnibus Eupolis', in *Tragedy, Comedy and the Polis*, Greek Drama Conference, Nottingham 1990, ed. A. H. Sommerstein *et al.* (Bari, 1993), pp. 373–96. Names and naming in Aristophanic comedy: see S. Douglas Olson, *Class. Quart.* 42 (1992), 304–19.

2 These are the conclusions which he reaches in pp. 345–8 of his book *Le Dialogue antique* (Paris, 1954). Anyone who knows this rich volume in its entirety needs only consult pp. 170, 192–8 and 273–81. Regarding Plato's dialogues, which are discussed briefly further on, see particularly pp. 304–15, and for the inauthenticity of the sigla, pp. 214–18 and 269–72. The various manuscripts which Jean Andrieu examined led him to distinguish three stages in the evolution of the text: the author's manuscript, a version containing stage-notes for the didaskalos, if the choreutai and actors were not being instructed by the author himself (on this exemplar, see the observations of Karl Holzinger referred to in n. 5 below), and lastly the edition designed to be read, which Andrieu discusses on pp. 183–92 and 345–6. Andrieu deals with the character lists, which are of hypothetical Alexandrian origin, on pp. 93–5. 'The only safe guide is the text', concludes the distinguished J. C. B. Lowe, 'The manuscript evidence for changes of speaker in Aristophanes', *Bull. Inst. Class. Studies*, London 9 (1962), 27–42; sections: 'Codices recentiores', 'Codices vetusti', 'The archetype', 'The Aristophanes papyri', 'Other papyri of the Roman and Byzantine period', 'Papyri of the Hellenistic period', 'The earliest

texts', 'The scholia', 'Value of the manuscript tradition'; one should also consult Lowe's 'Some questions of attribution in Aristophanes', *Hermes* 95 (1967), 53–71. See also Th. Gelzer, *Aristophanes der Komiker* (1970), cc. 1548–63.

3 See Andrieu, *Le Dialogue*, pp. 249–69, who also studied more ancient papyri of Greek mime, with algebraic sigla. Clearly, Andrieu was unaware of the Hibeh papyrus 180, published by E. G. Turner in the second volume of his collection (London, 1955) (in this papyrus, there are algebraic sigla in the margins before lines 22 and 23 of the second column). See Lowe, 'The manuscript evidence', 35.

4 The sources relative to the proagon are all well known: a scholion to Aeschines, *Ctes.* 27, a passage from the Life of Euripides and a scholion on *Wasps* 1109. Despite P. W. Harsh, *Class. Phil.* 44 (1949), 116f., it is probable that Plato's *Symposium* 194b reflects the tragic proagon. E. Rohde, *Rhein. Mus.* 38 (1883), 251–68, and in *Kl. Schriften*, II (Tübingen–Leipzig, 1901) is mostly valid regarding the proagon. Let us repeat that there is no evidence of a proagon being held for comedy, whereas for tragedy there is evidence for the Dionysian contests alone. See S. Srebrny, *Studia scaenica* (Wrocław, 1960), pp. 98–113 and A. W. Pickard-Cambridge, *The Dramatic Festivals of Athens* (Oxford, 1968, 1953), pp. 67–8.

5 K. Holzinger, 'Kritische Bemerkungen spätbyz. Aristophanesscholien', in *Charisteria Rzach* (Reichenburg, 1930), p. 70 n. 18, observes that Aristophanes must somehow have distinguished the κῶλα in his manuscript, expression as they were of an original and elaborate creation. The Alexandrians were the first to discover them, and also invented a system of colometric signs. It is by no means certain, however, that their colometry was always correct. In the few exemplars first circulated the κῶλα were perhaps indicated by a small blank space, destined soon to disappear. In his commentary on *Plutus* (Vienna–Leipzig, 1940) pp. 201f., Holzinger observes that in the theatre exemplar a slanting line or a small blank space would have indicated a pause for stylistically ambiguous remarks. 'The unwieldy and impractical manner' – concludes Karl Holzinger, with reason – 'in which a private scholar transcribed Timotheos' *Persians* excludes any deduction regarding the appearance of the papyrus rolls which Aristophanes prepared for the actors.'

6 Euripides, fr. 706. Strictly speaking, there is no documentation to suggest that these words are uttered by Telephus, although it remains highly probable that the attribution is valid. The fragments of *Telephus*, enhanced by new and old scraps of papyrus, have been published along with a commentary by E. W. Handley and J. Rea, 'The *Telephus* of Euripides', *Bull. Inst. Class. Studies*, London 5 (1957).

7 The existence of the *ekkyklema* in the fifth century is denied by E. Reisch in W. Dörpfeld-E. Reisch, *Das griechische Theater* (1896, repr. 1966), pp. 234–48, and in Pauly–Wissowa, 1905, cc. 2202–7. The amendment of E. Bethe, in *Rhein. Museum* 83 (1934), 21–32, is of some importance relative to his own *Prolegomena Geschichte Theaters* (Leipzig, 1896): Bethe realized that the platform, or rather the *ekkyklema*-device, in the Thesmophorium would have been subjected to a not insignificant load, weighing altogether two tons. Both Reisch and Bethe remarked that the later, technical acceptation of ἐκκυκλεῖν could have been transferred to Aristophanes' ἐκκυκλεῖσθαι. There are other arguments against the *ekkyklema* in Pickard-Cambridge, *The Theatre of Dionysus in Athens* (1946), pp. 100–22, in which one may also consult all the relevant scholastic and erudite documentation. A more moderate approach is that of A. M. Dale, 'Seen and unseen on the Greek stage: a study in scenic conventions', *Wiener Studien* 69 (1956), 98–101 (also in *Collected Papers*, London, 1969, in an article composed of observations regarding

the stage-technique of tragedy, which are almost always appropriate and take their cue from Fensterbusch's observations regarding Aeschylus in the final pages 66–71 of his well-known dissertation on Aristophanes (Fensterbusch favoured the *ekkyklema* of the scholiasts). The first to propose the *ekkyklema* for the cavern of the goddess in *Peace* was T. B. L. Webster, *Greek Theatre Production* (Oxford, 1970, 1956), p. 19. For the *ekkyklema* in Greek theatre, see N. C. Hourmouziades, *Production and Imagination in Euripides: Form and Function of the Scenic Space* (Athens, 1965), W. Jens, *Die Bauformen der griechischen Tragödie* (Munich, 1971), pp. 410–12 (K. Joerden) and O. Taplin, *The Stagecraft of Aeschylus* (Oxford, 1989, 1977). A critical overview is provided in H.-J. Newiger, 'Ekkyklema e mechané nella messa in scena del dramma greco', *Dioniso* 59 (1989), 173–85. The ancestor of the *ekkyklema* is recognizable in the mobile wooden horse of Troy (communicated by Francesco De Martino, Bari).

8   A modern dramatist theoretically most attentive to unity of time would have nothing to object to such incongruities in the epilogue:

> je voudrais que les huit heures de l'action excédant les deux heures de la représentation se consumassent dans les intervalles des actes, et que chacun d'eux n'eût en son particulier que ce que la représentation en consume, principalement lorsqu'il y a liaison de scènes perpétuelles, car cette liaison ne souffre point de vide entre deux scènes. J'estime toutefois que le cinquième . . . a quelque droit de presser en peu le temps, en sorte que la part de l'action qu'il représente en tienne davantage qu'il n'en faut pour sa représentation. La raison en est que le spectateur est alors dans l'impatience de voir la fin, et que quand elle dépend d'acteurs qui sont sortis du théâtre tout l'entretien qu'on donne à ceux qui demeurent . . . ne fait que languir.

> (Corneille, *Troisième discours du poème dramatique*)

9   Andrieu, *Le Dialogue* (1954), pp. 68f. Jean Andrieu swam against a tide which had culminated in the schematic dissertation of the American R. T. Weissinger, 'A Study of Act Division in Classical Drama', Univ. of Iowa, 1940. The content of one tragedy is divided into five μέρη, in the sense of acts true and proper, by a late second-century ὑπόθεσις = *Pap. Oxy.* 2257, published in 1952, when it was too late for Jean Andrieu to have become aware of it. Regarding Aristophanes and Aeschylus, see A. H. Sommerstein, 'Act division in old comedy', *Bull. Inst. Class. Studies*, London 31 (1984), 139–52, and Taplin, *The Stagecraft of Aeschylus*, s.v. 'Structural technique'.

10 A. M. Dale, *Journ. Hell. Studies* 77 (1957), 207–11, and later in the *Collected Papers* (1969), goes as far as trying to establish that Aristophanes had available, and used, a *single* door, which would have been assigned first one scenic value, then another: this singular hypothesis, which takes its cue from tragedy, is discussed in chapter 12.

11 In the pseudo-Aristophanic *Islands*, fr. 403, the Islandwomen: 'where are they? They are those whom you see κατ' αὐτὴν . . . τὴν εἴσοδον.' On each of these three occasions, one is dealing with a particularly original chorus: for a brief remark to this effect see section 5 of chapter 5. It is known that there is no proof for the existence of the term πάροδος in the fifth century. On the texts of the comedies and tragedies, K. Rees, *Am. Journ. Phil.* 32 (1911), 377–402 denies that the two corridors had any conventional value (but see also at least Bodensteiner, 'Szenische Fragen', *Jahrbb. class. Phil.*, Suppl. 19 (1893), 646f.); Rees observed that the contrast between countryside and city in comedies such as *Assemblywomen* and *Plutus* might later have led to conventional values being assigned. This opinion is shared

by Fensterbusch in *Philologus* 81 (1926), 480–2. The symbolic use of the two corridors, a theory which has enjoyed such success amongst a majority of scholars, is affirmed by Pollux IV.128, and also by Anonymous, *De comoedia* XI b.c. Regarding tragedy, see W. Jens, *Die Bauformen der griechischen Tragödie* (Munich, 1971), pp. 409–10 (K. Joerden).

12 The terminology relative to entrances and exits is collected in E. Droysen, 'Quaestiones de Aristophanis re scaenica', Diss. Bonn 1868, pp. 3–14, with a few flaws; the most outstanding is that there is no mention whatsoever of the use which is made in this respect of simple verbs such as ἔρχεσθαι, φέρειν and so forth. For example, ἔρχεσθαι, when it is used technically, is equivalent to προσέρχεσθαι (cf. *Wasps* 1505 with *Wasps* 1508f.), whereas φέρειν is equivalent to ἐκφέρειν (see section 4 of chapter 4). Regarding terms of characterizing the orchestra as a closed space, see section 7. In the case of disappearances out of the theatre, the most common terms are ἀπιέναι and ἀπέρχεσθαι. However, these terms are not strictly technical, since they are also used to indicate a simple distancing from the zone in which the character is performing.

13 On Aristophanes' normal practice with regard to the actors, from the protagonists to the multiple roles, see K. McLeish, *The Theatre of Aristophanes* (London, 1980), pp. 111–56. On the comedy's economy of roles and scenic organization C. W. Dearden, *The Stage of Aristophanes* (London, 1976), adds his rather feeble voice. The limits of Dearden, who neglects a scenic archaeologist such as Fensterbusch, have been pointed out by K. J. Dover and H.-J. Newiger, *Journ. Hell. Studies* 97 (1977), 177–8, *Gnomon* 55 (1983), 197–201. An illustrated collection: P. Ghiron-Bistagne, *Recherches sur les acteurs dans la Grèce antique* (Paris, 1976).

4 *Knights*

1 The new fragment 590 of an Aristophanic parabasis reads: ἀλλ' ἐχρῆν χορὸν διδόντας τὸν ἐπὶ Ληναίῳ σκοπεῖν. Regarding *Acharnians* 504 οὑπὶ Ληναίῳ τ' ἀγών, see chapter 1, p. 2. Even more interesting is a fragment of *Gelos* by Sannyrion – writing around 400 – in which the tragedian Meletus is described as 'the corpse *of the Lenaion*' (Μέλητον τὸν ἀπὸ Ληναίου νεκρόν), the selfsame Meletus who in fragment 156 of Aristophanes' *Gerytades* – a comedy from the last years of the fifth century – had descended into Hades in the company of other poets of moribund appearance. Whether Sannyrion is alluding to the 'moribund' Meletus of *Gerytades* or not, he still refers to Meletus as a character, or rather a corpse, *of the Lenaian theatre*, since ἀπὸ Ληναίου in relation to a dramatist cannot but refer to the presence of that dramatist within the precinct of the Lenaian theatre. H.-J. Newiger, *Gnomon* 64 (1992), p. 99 reviews Pherekrates fr. 69 (σκηνή and περίβολος, Lenaian perhaps). Nor should one overlook the fact that Pollux IV.121, the only ancient source actually to name the 'theatre' of the Lenaion as θέατρον Ληναϊκόν, distinguishes between the two Athenian theatres when he begins to deal with their structures themselves:

ἐπεὶ δὲ καὶ τὸ θέατρον οὐ μικρὸν μέρος ἐστὶ τῶν μουσικῶν, αὐτὸ μὲν ἂν εἴποις θέατρον καὶ Διονυσιακὸν θέατρον καὶ Ληναϊκόν, καὶ τὸ πλῆθος θεατάς. Ἀριστοφάνης δὲ συνθεάτριαν εἴρηκεν, ὥστ'οὐ θεατὴν μόνον εἴποις ἂν ἀλλὰ καὶ θεάτριαν, κατὰ δὲ Πλάτωνα καὶ θεατροκρατίαν. τοὺς δ'ἀναβασμοὺς καὶ βάθρα καὶ ἕδρας καὶ ἐδώλια, καὶ ἐδωλιάζειν τὸ συγκαθίζειν κτλ.

Apart from Albin Lesky (1968), already cited in the preface and chapter 1, attention is paid to the Aristophanic Lenaion by: C. Fensterbusch, *Theatron*, Pauly–Wissowa (1934), c. 1392, P. Geissler, *Chronologie d. altattischen Komödie* (Berlin, 1979, 1925), p. xvi, and D. M. MacDowell, *The Wasps* (Oxford, 1971), p. 18: 'The festival of the Lenaia was held each year in Gamelion (the month corresponding approximately to January). In early times the plays at this festival were performed at the precinct of the Lenaion. Later the performances were transferred to the theatre of Dionysos, beside the Akropolis. It is not known at what date this transfer took place. Some scholars believe that it was before the career of Aristophanes began, but there is no clear evidence for this; and *the question remains open.*' And in a note: 'For recent discussions see W. B. Stanford in *Hermathena* 89 (1957), 65, C. F. Russo, *Aristofane autore di teatro* (1962), *Dram. Fest.*[2] 39–40.' In addition, besides M. Bieber, *History of Greek and Roman Theater* (Princeton, 1966, 1939), pp. 69–70, see R. G. Ussher, *Ecclesiazusae* (Oxford, 1973), p. 113, K. McLeish, *The Theatre of Aristophanes* (London, 1980), pp. 22–9, N. W. Slater, 'The Lenaean theatre', *Zeitschr. Papyr. Epigr.* 66 (1986), 225–64, P. Thiercy, *Aristophane: fiction et dramaturgie* (Paris, 1986), p. 24, J. Henderson, *Lysistrata* (Oxford, 1987), pp. xv–xvi, D. Del Corno, *Antologia della letteratura greca* (Milan, 1991), I, pp. 279–80. Passing attention is given to the matter in the second edition of Pickard-Cambridge, pp. 39–40 (but see Lesky, cited in chapter 1). Lexicographical material by C. F. Russo, 'I due teatri di Aristophane', *Rendiconti Accad. lincei* XI (1956), 27, n. 1.

2 Thus O. Kaehler, *De partibus servorum, qui sunt in Aristophanis Equitibus, Vespis, Pace* (Weimar, 1877), p. 12. Regarding the Servants and the development of the comedy, see W. Kraus, *Aristophanes' politische Komödien. Die Acharner/Die Ritter* (Vienna, 1985). Regarding the masks: K. J. Dover, *Portrait-Masks in Aristophanes*, Studia Koster (Amstelodami, 1968), pp. 16–28 (also to be found in *Greek and the Greeks* (Oxford, 1967) and in Newiger's well-known anthology.

3 As discussed in section 5 below, the Knights tend to absorb the character of Demosthenes. One scholar inclined to interpret the abdication of Demosthenes and Nikias in typological terms is S. Hess, in the unpublished dissertation 'Studien zum Prolog att. Komödie', Heidelberg, 1953, p. 21; he does none the less distinguish the Servants in *Knights* from those in *Wasps* and *Peace* when he observes that it is they who are suffering, not their master, and they, too, who provoke the action which leads to their liberation.

4 See P. Mazon, *Essai sur la composition des comédies d'Aristophane* (Paris, 1904), pp. 37f., 44.

5 See also H.-J. Newiger, *Metapher und Allegorie* (Munich, 1957), p. 105, n. 3, who would content himself with two dancing-girls. Exhibitions by naked women in Aristophanes cannot be proved, and are, in any case, improbable: see K. Holzinger, *Erklärungen umstrittener Stellen des Aristophanes* (Vienna–Leipzig, 1928), pp. 36–54.

6 See also the considerations on p. 30 of chapter 2. The relationship between audience and dramatist in general is discussed in section 5 of chapter 3.

7 ἐκφέρω in 998, εἴσω in 1110, and previously ἔνεγκε in 970, since ἔνεγκε and ἐνεγκάτω are always used in relation to an interior. Good judgement from M. Pohlenz, 'Aristophanes *Ritter*', *Nachr. Ak. Wiss. Göttingen* (1952), p. 117, n. 41 (*Kleine Schriften*, II). Rogers, in his commentary, undoubtedly exaggerates, at least in the passage in which he postulates three distinct houses – that of Demos in the centre and the others assigned to the two antagonists (1001 is devoid of scenic

value). However, he is the only scholar who correctly denies that the orchestra represents the Agora, a matter discussed directly below.

8 Cf. Th. K. Hubbard, 'The Knights' Eleven Oars (Aristophanes, *Equites* 546–547)', *Classical Journal* 85 (1989), 115–18 (the idea of the eleven choreutai was first voiced by E. Rothert, 'Zu den Rittern des Aristophanes', Program Cleve 1866, p. 19, and taken up by the commentator R. A. Neil (Cambridge, 1901), p. 82). In the previously discussed finale, the choreutai would have been provided with oars.

9 Others have offered the same interpretation, but without the necessary documentation: Hess, *Studien*, pp. 14–16, for example, effectively limits himself to citing *Thesmophoriazusae* 228–9. The scholar who reattributed line 234 to the Sausage-seller is the often-cited Pohlenz, p. 110, n. 30.

5 *Clouds*

1 Thus H. Erbse, *Hermes* 82 (1954), 397–400, while for H.-J. Newiger, *Metapher und Allegorie* (Munich, 1957), pp. 143–52, there are four actors on-stage in Socrates' absence. Erbse refers to K. Rees, *The So-called Rule of Three Actors in the Greek Classical Drama* (Chicago, 1908), pp. 41–6, the successful opponent of C. Beer, *Über die Zahl der Schauspieler bei Aristophanes* (Leipzig, 1844), pp. 128–30. Erbse returned to *Clouds* in 1969, in *Opus nobile, Ulf Jantzen* (Wiesbaden), pp. 35–41. An analytical contribution from M. Landfester, *Handlungsverlauf und Komik in den frühen Komödien des Aristophanes* (Berlin, 1977), pp. 95–102.

2 At the end of his 1968 Oxford commentary on *Clouds*, K. J. Dover adds: 'p. lxxix, *On the work required of the fourth actor*. In the light of passages pointed out to me by Mr. J. C. B. Lowe I have some misgivings on what I have said, but have not yet come to a conclusion.' A. Pickard-Cambridge, in the revised edition of *The Dramatic Festivals of Athens* (1968), pp. 150–1, following C. F. Russo, acknowledges the scene of the two Arguments: 'The scene as a whole, then, appears to call for five actors, and the fourth and fifth actors would have parts wholly in excess of what is given to such actors elsewhere in extant Aristophanes.' Dover, in *Aristophanic Comedy* (London, 1972), pp. 26–8 and 104–6, draws close to the company of the three actors, but without distancing himself too far from that occasional voice which he insists on calling 'the fourth actor'. A. C. Schlesinger, although he denies the existence of an economic law for the three actors (but whether or not such a law existed is of secondary importance), arrives at extremely judicious conclusions in his 'Three actors and poetry', *Class. Phil.* 46 (1951), 33. The following observation from Andrieu, *Le Dialogue* (1954), p. 307, n. 2, is also of interest: 'il y a une certaine coïncidence entre le théâtre grec qui limite le nombre des acteurs à trois, et le dialogue dramatique [of Plato] qui dépasse difficilement trois à quatre acteurs actifs. Rencontre fortuite sans doute: la limitation du théâtre tient à l'influence de la tradition; celle du dialogue aux nécessités de l'expression claire.' Regarding the tragedians' normal use of the actors, one should refer to the rigorous dissertation of H. Kaffenberger, 'Das Dreischauspielergesetz', Darmstadt, 1911, to Roy C. Flickinger, *The Greek Theater and its Drama* (Chicago, 1936, 1918), p. 182, and to Pickard-Cambridge, *The Dramatic Festivals* (1968), pp. 135–49. Finally, the expert E. Fraenkel, *Beobachtungen zu Aristophanes* (Rome, 1962), p. 167, n. 3, indicated that although Pluton is the householder in *Frogs*, he is assigned an extremely insignificant role. This, he wrote, can be explained by the fact that only an amateur actor, the so-called 'fourth actor', would have been

available for the part. Other observations on the *Second Clouds*: Th. Gelzer, *Der epirrhematische Agon bei Aristophanes* (Munich, 1960), p. 62, 2, and 'Aristophanes der Komiker', *Paulys Real.*, Suppl. XII (Stuttgart, 1970), cc. 1434–41.

3　B. Heidhues, 'Über die Wolken des Aristophanes', Program Köln, 1897, p. 21, gave the siglum of the Student in the prologue to Chaerephon, a Student who speaks of Chaerephon in the third person . . . Heidhues, the standard-bearer of the unitarian critics, was less superficial than his modern followers; on p. 19, for example, he took care to free the third actor-Pheidippides in line 888, in order to entrust him the role of the Strong Argument (wearing the mask of Chaerephon). Evidently, he assigned the minor role of Pheidippides to a 'fourth actor'. According to Heidhues, Socrates is not on-stage during the agon (on Plato, Comedy and Aristophanes: K. J. Reckford, *Aristophanes' Old-and-New Comedy* (Chapel Hill, 1987), p. 392 and passim).

4　In 1958, D. Holwerda, 'De novo priorum Aristophanis Nubium indicio', *Mnemosyne*, 32–41, announced that in the fourteenth-century Vatican Barb. manuscript 126, f. 43v, a scholiast refers to a metrical comment of his own regarding the *First Clouds*. This new document, therefore, provides additional indirect proof of the existence of two distinct and complete editions of the *First* and *Second Clouds*. The metrician is almost certainly Heliodorus, from the end of the first century of the common era. In 1968, the list of Oxy. Pap. n. 2659 was published, containing the titles the *First Plutus* and the *Second Clouds*; this implies that *first* and *second* comedies did exist. Th. K. Hubbard, 'Parabatic Self-criticism and the two versions of Aristophanes' *Clouds*', *Classical Antiquity* 5 (1986), 182–97, maintains that the revision of *Clouds* is alluded to in the new parabasis, which contains self-criticism concerning the first version (537–544). On the date of the second version, see E. Ch. Kopff, *American Journ. Phil.* 111 (1990), 318–29. When and by whom was the *Second Clouds* put into circulation? 'By Aristophanes, a few years after the revision', maintains Wilamowitz, 'Der Chor der *Wolken*', *Sitzb. Berl. Ak.* (1921), 738 (in Newiger's well-known 1975 anthology). In *Hellenistische Dichtung* (Berlin, 1924), I, p. 98, n. 4, Wilamowitz adds that the successful circulation of the *Second Clouds* is explicable only should the comedy have been prepared by Aristophanes himself, not by someone else after his death. Considerations of this kind are ultramodernistic! In this regard, see section 2 of chapter 11, *Frogs*.

5　See E. Fraenkel, 'Dramaturgical problems' (Murray) (1936), p. 258 (*Kleine Beiträge* (Rome, 1964), I, p. 470), and O. Weinreich, *Aristophanes, Sämtliche Komödien* (Zürich, 1952), p. lxxxi. Scenic tableaux prepared before the beginning of the comedy are discussed in chapter 6, *Wasps*.

6　On the parodos, see some of the observations of Wilamowitz, 'Der Chor der *Wolken*', 739. Regarding the personification of the Clouds, see Newiger, *Metapher und Allegorie*, pp. 50–74. At a certain point, the Clouds become so depersonalized that in line 1352 the coryphaeus invites Strepsiades to 'tell the *Chorus* what has happened'. Elsewhere, the Chorus qualifies as a χορός in lyric passages alone, or else at technically appropriate points (see also C. Segal, 'Aristophanes' Cloud-chorus', *Aretusa* 2 (1969), 143–61, reprinted by Newiger).

7　On the personification of the Two Arguments, see Newiger, *Metapher und Allegorie*, pp. 134–43. Regarding lines 889–1104, and the attendant artistic and dramaturgical questions, see section 3 of this chapter.

8　For κρεμάθρα as a suspending device, cf. again Aristotle, *Rhet.* 1412a with the comment of E. M. Cope (Cambridge, 1877). Regarding the uncertain κρεμαθρῶν in *Clouds* 869, see W. Kraus, *Testimonia Aristophanea cum scholiorum lectionibus* (Vienna–Leipzig, 1931), p. 22.

9 The new division of the dialogue was proposed by H. Kruse, *Hermes* 63 (1928), 231–6. Regarding the characters in the finale, see also the remarks at the end of section 3b of this chapter.

6 *Wasps*

1 At a point when *Wasps* was prepared for the stage, it had to be updated by Aristophanes on account of a legal affair ongoing in Athens (the sensational trial of the pacifist strategos Laches). See G. Mastromarco, *Storia di una commedia di Atene*, with a foreword by C. F. Russo (Florence, 1974), pp. 47–101, which analyses the passages composed at the last moment: 240–7, 281–9, 826–47, 891–1008.

2 See S. Srebrny, *Eos* 50 (1959–1960), 43–5. Regarding the exchange of the two units, see chapter 15, with note 2 to that chapter. The incongruity between the sensational account provided in the prologue and the scenes which follow is pointed out solely by B. B. Rogers, *The Wasps* (London, 1912, 1876), pp. xii–xiii. Regarding the dramaturgy of Xanthias' account in 54–135, see Mastromarco, op. cit., pp. 103–7. For Wilamowitz's judgement on the parodos, see *Sitzb. Berl. Ak.* (1911), 476 and 486 (= *Kl. Schriften*, I (1935), pp. 302 and 314).

3 These affirmations are based on the results of the extremely skilful and abundant research conducted by E. Roos, *Die tragische Orchestik im Zerrbild altatt. Komödie* (Lund, 1951); I would refer particularly to pp. 75–6, 94–106, 114–60, 201 and 202. With respect to line 1537, I have chosen to follow the Venetus manuscript. On the finale, see 'Mimica e danza sulla scena comica greca' by L. E. Rossi, *Rivista di cultura classica e medievale* 20 (1978), 1149–70.

4 The exchangeability of lines 1265–91 and 1450–73 was intuited by H. Müller-Strübing, *Aristophanes und die hist. Kritik* (Leipzig, 1873), p. 170n. (J. Stanger, *Über Umarbeitung einiger Aristoph. Komödien* (Leipzig, 1870), pp. 48–9, noticed the tardiness of lines 1450–73). 'Wie sollen denn zwei Chorpartien in der Überlieferung vertauscht sein?', objected Wilamowitz, op. cit., p. 480 (= p. 308). The exchange is easily explained if it took place in the first phase of the circulation of the text (in this regard, see section 2 of chapter 11): in both cases one is dealing with pieces written for the chorus alone (and with the only two choral passages between parabasis and exodos), to be inserted, in both cases, between two remarks delivered by the first two actors as they exit from the stage, and a remark made by the third as he enters. See chapter 15, *The Disorderly Wasps*.

5 For the scenic organization of *Wasps* according to Wilamowitz, see pp. 472–86 (= pp. 299–314) of his previously cited 1911 essay. For different positions regarding the door-shutters in *Wasps*, see W. Beare, *The Roman Stage* (London, 1964, 1950), pp. 279–82, and A. M. Dale in *Journ. of Hell. Studies* 77 (1957), 205–6 (also in *Collected Papers*, London, 1969). The house-prison is illustrated in MacDowell's commentary (1971). Because of the existence of animated and clearly pre-prepared opening scenes such as those in *Wasps*, and also in some tragedies, there has been a tendency to assume that from the beginning of the last quarter of the fifth century, Athenian theatre employed a curtain designed to conceal pre-dramatic activity from the spectators: see E. Bethe, *Prolegomena Gesch. des Theaters im Altertum* (Leipzig, 1896), pp. 186–203, E. Bethe, 'Die Theaterfrage', in Gercke-

Norden, *Einleitung* . . . (Leipzig, 1927), pp. 61–2, E. Reisch in W. Dörpfeld and E. Reisch, *Das griechische Theater* (Athens, 1896, reprint, 1966), pp. 252–5. Pickard-Cambridge, in *The Theatre of Dionysus* (1946), pp. 128–30, is extremely reserved in this regard, if not openly sceptical. Surely a spectacle would have been held in the orchestra during the intervals between one drama and another of such a kind as to effectively constitute a curtain? One should not forget that actions performed by the chorus in the course of the dramas would have distracted the audience's attention as the value of the scenic façade was being changed.

7 Peace

1   As remarked in chapter 1, Polemos' extra-metre roar between 235 and 236 divides the celestial prologue into two tableaux containing 63 trimeters each, themselves divided into 25/38 lines in accordance with the golden section. The same is true of the terrestrial prologue: after having remained unseen for 81 lines, Trygaeus appears astride the beetle and inaugurates the new metre; this is followed by another analogical moment, made up of 72/90 lines. The elasticity of the latter division, 72/90, is due to the 18 concluding anapaests, an arietta between earth and sky, scanned 9×2 (163 must be classified as extraneous, since a refined stercoral beetle would hardly be interested in 'all human foods'). Both the dialogue and the monologue are modelled on the basic measures of the prologue: the dialogue is modelled on the terrestrial dimension 153 (or rather the dialogue-lines number 153), the monologue on the celestial dimension 144 (18 + 126). Lines 96–101 are delivered in monologue form, hence φράσον is φράζω. The materials employed in the prologue end in 298 (= 297), when the choral metre begins. Apart from D. Holwerda, 'De Heliodori commentario metrico in Aristophanem', *Mnemosyne* 17 (1964), 117–18, see the critical notes in the edition of Mastromarco (1983), pp. 98–9. In *Peace* 657–728, Trygaeus and Hermes gradually give form to an outline of 72 trimeters, scanned midway by an ὦ ὤ, as remarked naturally by Heliodorus. For O. Hense, *Heliodoreische Untersuchungen* (Leipzig, 1870) (dedicated to Friedrich Ritschl), pp. 78–80, the first thirty-six trimeters deal with Attic politics, Kleon and Hyperbolus, the second with artistic life, Sophocles and Kratinos. In each case, the two XIV trimeters represent a turning-point with ἴθι νυν: *Angry Peace* (13), *Political life* (23), *Artistic life* (13) and *Happy Peace* (23); this 23/13 section is golden. Hense, pp. 75 and 87, adds that with his responsive analyses Heliodorus had worked back to the editorial signs of the Alexandrians, and that it was a short step from the Alexandrians to the signs of the Athenian dramatists themselves. Mathematical poetics is recognizable in the prologues, but elsewhere the sophisticated lyric metres impede its sure recognition. However, Cassandra's kommos in *Agamemnon* is easily recognizable: in the relationship between the iambic and lyrical materials (36 and 72 Murray and West); in the theme; in the theatrical properties; and in the dialogue and monologue, etc. Regarding Aeschylus and Homer, see section 6 of chapter 11 and n. 4 to chapter 15.

2   With respect to the scenic organization of *Peace*, the best-founded analysis remains that of Fensterbusch, *Die Bühne von Aristophanes* (Borna–Leipzig, 1912), pp. 31–46. See also Pickard-Cambridge, *The Theatre of Dionysus* (1946), pp. 61–5, who again denies that beneath the orchestra of the theatre of Dionysos there lay a subterranean chamber linked to the stage-edifice by a corridor. The existence of two stage levels is reproposed by S. Srebrny, *Studia scaenica* (Wrocław, 1960), pp. 113–26; three levels, earth–cave–sky, are suggested by A. Vallois, *Rev. Etudes Anciennes* 49 (1947), 58–64, H. Kenner, *Das Theater und der Realismus in der griech. Kunst* (Vienna, 1954), pp. 118–20, and F. Robert, *Rev. Etudes Grecques* 68

(1955), ix–xi. A discussion in H.-J. Newiger, 'Retraktationen zu Aristophanes' *Frieden*', *Rhein Mus.* 108 (1965), pp. 229–54, collected in the author's anthology. For a review of the nineteenth-century bibliography, see the commented edition of H. Sharpley (Edinburgh–London, 1905), pp. 16–31. Anyone who thinks of two (or three) levels, practicably conjoined, has clearly not paused to think, amongst other things, of why Trygaeus should fail to make use of the junction when ascending into the sky, and has also forgotten *Peace* 69–71. W. Jobst, *Die Höhle im griechischen Theater* (Vienna, 1970), pp. 61–8: about *Peace*, and then *Birds* and *Lysistrata*.

3 The scholars opposed to the idea of personnel extraneous to the chorus in *Peace* include R. Arnoldt, *Die Chorpartien bei Aristophanes* (Leipzig, 1873), p. 55, B. B. Rogers, *The Peace* (London, 1913), nn. 296–8 and 466, and V. Ehrenberg, *The People of Aristophanes* (Oxford, 1951, 1943), p. 55, I. Guil. Westphal, 'Quaestiones scaenicae', Diss. Halis Saxonum 1919, p. 53, although opposed to the stage-presence of a series of apostrophized characters (for instance, he denies that the Prytanes are on-stage in the prologue of *Acharnians*), nevertheless observes that in the case of *Peace* one has no other alternative than to admit that extras must have portrayed the foreigners and other Athenians.

4 The scholion reads: τὰ τοιαῦτα παραχορηγήματα καλοῦσιν, οἷα νῦν τὰ παιδία ποιεῖ καλοῦντα τὸν πατέρα. εἶτα πρὸς οὐδὲν ἔτι τούτοις χρήσεται. The Aristophanic scholiasts mention παραχορηγήματα again, improperly, with reference to *Frogs* 209. Regarding the documentation and acceptation of the term, see Pickard-Cambridge, *The Dramatic Festivals* (1968, 1953), pp. 143–4 and p. 89, 2. Boys from the dithyrambic choruses are also suggested by A. C. Schlesinger, *Class. Phil.* 46 (1951), p. 33 (and see C. Beer, *Über die Zahl der Schauspieler bei Aristophanes* (Leipzig, 1844, p. 15 and pp. 44–5 and C. Heym, *De puerorum in re scaenica Graecorum partibus*, Dissertationes Phil. Halenses, vol. XIII (1897), pp. 275–6). Naturally, Trygaeus' little daughter is also portrayed by a boy from the dithyrambic choruses, although H. Devrient, *Das Kind auf der antiken Bühne* (Weimar, 1904), pp. 15–16, maintains that she, like other Euripidean children, is portrayed by a normal actor.

5 On the text of Argument III, see N. W. Slater, 'Problems in the hypothesis to Aristophanes' *Peace*', *Zeitschrift Papyr. Epigr.* 74 (1988), 43–57, and previously, A. C. Cassio, *Commedia e partecipazione. 'La Pace' di Aristofane* (Naples, 1985), pp. 21–5.

8 *Birds*

1 The relationship between *Birds* and the two Dionysian ceremonies involving orphans and outlaws is pointed out in B. B. Rogers, *The Birds* (London, 1906), notes to 1072–87 and 1361. Regarding the ceremony of the orphans, however, one should also see the earlier note of A. Willems (1903), later reproduced in *Aristophane* (1919), II, pp. 314–15.

2 The latter observation was made by S. Hess, 'Studien zum Prolog att. Komödie', unpublished dissertation, Heidelberg, 1953, pp. 37–9 (in this regard, see also section 3 of chapter 11). It was N. Terzaghi, *Boll. Filol. class.* 25 (1918), 6–7, who first noted that lines 155–156a do not pertain to the distracted Euelpides, but to the thoughtful and constructive Peisetairos. Furthermore, the strong apostrophe οὗτος δὲ δή in 155a suits Peisetairos alone: having kept silent for some time, this is the *first occasion* on which he addresses Hoopoe directly. The speaking names of the two

protagonists are not revealed until 644–5: see section 2 of chapter 3. It is untrue that the protagonist's name is Stilbonides first (139) and Peisetairos later. Besides, Stilbonides is not even a name.

3 For an analogous interpretation see J. Muhl, *Symbolae ad rem scaenicam Acharnensium Aviumque* (Augustae Vindelicorum, 1879), pp. 39–41: Muhl maintains that of the three normal stage-openings, one was used by the terrestrial characters, the central one by Hoopoe and the other by the 'aerial' and 'aetherial' characters. Regarding the use of the corridors, see at least *Birds* 1034–50, and also section 11 of chapter 3. More recently, scholars have not been much concerned with this problem, although Wilamowitz at least, analysing the final scene of *Birds*, in *Hermes* 63 (1928), 372–5 (= *Kl. Schriften*, IV (1962), pp. 457–60), had observed that Peisetairos makes his way to the sky through the copse. With respect to *Birds* 278, 990–1 and 1169 see section 7 of chapter 3; in the same chapter see section 11 for προσέρχεσθαι and also section 4 of chapter 4.

4 C. Robert, *Hermes* 33 (1898), 571–4, was the first to observe that Hoopoe reappears with a panoply, which he later removes. However, scholars have since not paid much attention to this, with the sole exception of Th. Kock and O. Schroeder in their fine commentary on *Birds* (Berlin, 1927), notes to lines 208–69, 270 and 434. The only modern critic to be aware that line 267 pertains to Hoopoe is Rogers, cited above (see also E. Fraenkel, *Eranos* 48 (1950), 82–4, reprinted in *Kleine Beiträge*, I (Rome, 1964), pp. 459–61, and also Newiger's anthology). Rogers also observes that the serenade and monody were definitely performed by an appropriate singer (Schroeder attributes only the monody to a singer). R. Pretagostini has written on word, metre and music in the monody (*La Musica in Grecia*, ed. B. Gentili and the author, Bari, 1988). In relation to these back-stage songs performed by a singer, cf. Pollux IV.109, and also Pickard-Cambridge, *The Theatre of Dionysus* (1946), p. 170. Regarding the annotation αὐλεῖ after line 223, see n. 6 to chapter 10.

5 The first to add the four birds in 268–93 to the chorus, indeed to make them its 'leading ladies', was the aforementioned Willems, *Aristophane* (1919), II, pp. 259–64. This thesis was adopted more recently by J. Carrière in *Rev. Etudes Anciennes* 58 (1956), 211–35. Starting from an inexact scholion on *Knights* 589, W. E. Blake, *Am. Journ. Phil.* 64 (1943), 87–91, took the four 'male' birds in 268–93, thus obtaining a chorus of fourteen males + fourteen females: but see also H. L. Crosby, in *Hesperia*, suppl. 8 (Studies Shear) (1949), pp. 75–81, who on his part prefers the four flautist-birds first conjectured by F. Wieseler, *Adversaria in Aristophanis Aves* (Gottingae, 1843), pp. 33–72 (followed, amongst others, by Robert, op. cit., p. 567). The hypothesis of four dancer-birds is put forward by L. B. Lawler, in *Trans. Am. Ph. Ass.* 73 (1942), 58–63, but see also Fraenkel, op. cit., p. 84, n. 3. See J. Irigoin, *Remarques sur la composition formelle des 'Oiseaux' d'Aristophane (vers 1–433)*, Σχόλια D. Holwerda (Groningen, 1985), p. 51, n. 21.

6 The lightning-machine, which may also have been used in *Prometheus* 1082, Pollux IV.130 calls κεραυνοσκοπεῖον, without providing a description. According to modern scholars, the machine was simply a wooden board bearing a painted lightning-bolt, which would have been allowed to fall down violently from a height (see C. Fensterbusch, *Das Theater im Altertum* (Leipzig–Berlin, 1930), p. 16), or else a species of rotating prism with a metal surface which flashed in the sun (see Pickard-Cambridge, *The Theatre of Dionysus* (1946), p. 236). Regarding the thunder-machine, see section 6 of chapter 5. Close above, in regard to Iris, we referred to A.-M. Desrousseaux, *Les Oiseaux* (Paris, 1950), p. 112 (cf. also *Rev. de Phil.* 27 (1953), 14). The interpreters who deny Iris the services of the flying-

machine include Fensterbusch, *Die Bühne* (1912), p. 61 and Th. Kock and O. Schroeder, *Die Vögel* (1927), p. 140, with some interesting considerations on πλοῖον ἢ κυνῆ.

7 Lines 1726–30 and 1743–7 were first attributed to the Herald by Robert, op. cit., p. 589, followed by Kock and Schroeder, note to lines 1743ff. H.-J. Newiger provides a synthesis regarding the dramaturgy in a 1970 essay collected in his anthology.

9 *Lysistrata*

1 Regarding the historical background, J. Henderson, *Aristophanes' Lysistrata* (Oxford, 1987), pp. xv–xvi, is in favour of the Lenaia and adds: 'It is still uncertain whether Lenaian plays were in Aristophanes' time performed at the Lenaion (location unknown) or in the theatre of Dionysos by the Akropolis: for a recent discussion see N. W. Slater, *Zeitschr. Papyr. Epigr.* 66 (1986), 255. The theatrical topicality of *Lys.*, whose action is centred on the Akropolis, might be thought to be enhanced if the play was performed in the Dionysos theatre.'

2 See, for example, Wilamowitz, *Lysistrate* (Berlin, 1927), p. 199. Like J. van Leeuwen in his 1903 commentary, S. Srebrny, *Eos* 51 (1961), 39–43 (reprinted in Newiger's anthology), believes that lines 1273–94 should follow line 1321 (and, like Coulon in *Rhein. Mus.* 99 (1956), 250, he attributes lines 1273–8 and 1295 to Lysistrata). At most, one might imagine that the comedy ended with the two short standard lines 1291–4 (cf. *Assemblywomen* 1180–3). We read these brief choral lines after the choral passage 1279–90, since in the first phase they would have been written after the only other group of lines to have been assigned to the chorus, with instructions that they should be sung at the end (for an analogous phenomenon, see n. 4 to chapter 6). Th. Bergk, in his edition of Aristophanes (Leipzig, 1872, 1851), II p. xii, maintained that at the end of *Lysistrata* there were 'interjectiones aliquot haud dubie simillimae iis quae leguntur supra 1291 seqq., quas librariorum socordia praetermisit'. O. Schroeder, *Aristophanis cantica* (Lipsiae, 1930, 1909), p. 57, observes: 'periodorum concentum si spectas nihil desideratur. Ultimis vero fabulae verbis τὰν πάμμαχον, quantopere Athenis sub ipsam arcem deaeque Προμάχου quasi in conspectu et agentes commoti sint et audientes sponte intelligitur.' See also B. Zimmermann, 'Aristophanes, *Lysistrate*, v. 1295', *Hermes* 113 (1985), 374–6, Henderson, *Aristophanes' Lysistrata*, lines 1273–1321, and A. H. Sommerstein, *Lysistrata* (1990), lines 1273–90.

3 On the hypothetical practicability of the two wings which presumably flanked the scenic front, see A. W. Pickard-Cambridge, *The Theatre of Dionysus in Athens* (1946), pp. 52 and 54.

4 This was discussed in section 2 of chapter 3 (although it seems that Lysistrata's name has already begun to 'speak' in lines 46–50). D. M. Lewis, *Annual Br. School Athens* 50 (1955), 1–12, prefers an allusion to the two priestesses, conjecturing that in 411 the priestess of Athena Polias might have been called Lysimacha; Myrrhine, in any case, was definitely a priestess (*SEG* XII.80). On the late-fifth-century Attic lekane, there are seven female figures: two seated mistresses, ΚΑΛΛΙΣΤΩ and ΑΡΧ[ΕΣΤΡΑΤΗ, and five handmaidens, including ΛΥΣΙΣΤΡΑΤΑ and ΜΥΡΡΙΝΗ. Today, the lekane is to be found at Ruvo (Jatta 1526) and is published in G. Minervini, *Bull. arch. Nap.* 5 (1847), 25–7 and plate I. Attention was drawn to this lekane by J. D. Beazley, *Am. Journ. Arch.* 54 (1950), 319. Beazley, ''Αρχ. 'Εφημ.' 92–3 (1953–1954), 204, speaks also of ΚΑΛΟΝΙ[on a cup by the Attic

painter Makron. On dialogue-division in the prologue, see W. Süss in *Rh. Mus.* 97 (1954), 242–9, and on line 197, K. J. Dover, *Lustrum* 2 (1957), 93.

5 For interpretations radically opposed to my own, which is effectively the same as that proposed by Wilamowitz, see A. Willems, *Aristophane* (Paris–Brussels, 1919), II, pp. 450–2, and H. van Daele in Coulon's edition. For yet another interpretation, see H. Kruse, *Quaestiones Aristophaneae* (Berolini, 1874), pp. 115–17. Kruse, like C. Beer before him, *Über die Zahl der Schauspieler bei Aristophanes* (Leipzig, 1844), pp. 92–3, is one of those scholars who identify Kinesias as the interlocutor of the Spartan Herald, an issue discussed in section 4 of the present chapter. (For Kinesias, see also Henderson, *Aristophanes' Lysistrata*, lines 980–1013).

10 *Thesmophoriazusae*

1 As to the reliability of this date, which has been reached through a comparative analysis of the lists of tragic actors at the Lenaia and Dionysia, and through a reckoning of the lost beginning of the list of tragic poets at the Lenaia, see J. B. O'Connor, *Chapters in the History of Actors* (Chicago, 1908, reprinted 1966), pp. 46 and 47; K. Schneider, 'Σκηνικοὶ ἀγῶνες', in Pauly–Wissowa (1927), c. 504, proposes a date between 436 and 426. Regarding the Lenaian contests of 419 and 418, we are indebted to A. Wilhelm, *Urkunden dram. Aufführungen* (Vienna, 1906), for the rigorous conclusion that 'two poets staged two tragedies each, without any satyr plays' (p. 53), a conclusion of which a sizeable number of Greek drama experts are apparently unaware, given that they equate the rules of the Lenaia with those of the Dionysia (at least for P. Mazon, *Sophocle* (Paris, 1955), I, p. ix, n. 1, 'at the Lenaia only two or three tragedies were staged'. Why 'three' also? Perhaps because at the end of the last century some scholars filled in lines 71, 74, 78 and 81 of *IG* II².2319 with the titles of three tragedies. As demonstrated by Wilhelm, however, the space available allows for no more than two).

2 Thus Th. Bergk in *Rhein. Mus.* 34 (1879), 298, who also observed that the figure of 'twenty' victories in *Vita Sophoclis* 8 can easily be restored to 'twenty-four'; see also the commentary of F. Jacoby on Apollodorus fr. 35 = Diodorus XIII.103.6 (Leiden, 1930). It might have been Sophocles who won at the Lenaia of 418 with the two tragedies ΤΥΡΟΙ ΤΡ[ΩΙΛΩΙ = *IG* II².2319, 78, surmises H. Hoffmann, *Chronologie der att. Tragödie* (Hamburg, 1951), p. 53.

3 '. . . if the Alexandrians thought that they could calculate the overall total of Euripides' dramas by multiplying 22 contests by 4, this implies that they either supposed or knew that Euripides had competed at the Dionysia alone . . . . I therefore maintain that Euripides never took part in the contests of the Lenaia': thus Hoffmann, op. cit., p. 82. It would be pleasant to be able to exclude Euripides' participation at the Lenaia by virtue of this simple hypothesis (albeit a second-degree hypothesis), yet it is inappropriate to attribute the multiplication of 22 by 4 to grammarians who, in their work on Euripides, had a substantial and varied bank of information to use: these grammarians possessed no fewer than seventy-eight Euripidean and pseudo-Euripidean dramas and had at their disposal documentation from which they could infer, amongst other things, the unofficial status of *Andromache*, the titles of the lost satyr plays from the tetralogies of *Medea* and *Phoenissae*, the existence of a juvenile *Rhesus*, which they confused with an inauthentic extant *Rhesus*, the number of contests in which Euripides competed and of those in which he came first, the didaskalos of the posthumous trilogy, and so forth. It would be equally difficult to accept that some grammarians

contested Euripides' authorship of three tragedies and one satyr play, out of an overall total of 92 dramas and titles, induced to do so, once more, by 22 × 4 = 88.

4 Regarding the treatment undergone by *Helen*, see E. W. Handley in Handley–Rea, *The Telephus of Euripides* (London, 1957), pp. 23–5, P. Rau, *Paratragodia* (Munich, 1967), pp. 53–89, and 'Das Tragödienspiel' (1971), in Newiger's anthology.

5 *Thesmophoriazusae* also refers to events which took place outside Attica at the end of December 412 (*Thesm.* 804→ Thucydides VIII.39). When the comedy was staged, 'in that period Karminos was strategos at Samos along with Phrynichos' (scholion on 804). Since the two were strategoi together during the archontate of Kallias of 412–411 alone (Thucydides VIII.25 and 30), the scholion presupposes that the comedy was performed during Kallias' archontate. This is confirmed by the scholiast on 190 (Euripides died ἕκτῳ ἔτει ὕστερον, he died quite definitely under Antigenes, archon in 407–406) and by the scholion on *Frogs* 53 (*Andromeda* ὀγδόῳ ἔτει προεισῆλθεν, *Frogs* is from 406–405, hence *Andromeda* and *Helen* are from 413–412). By contrast, the scholion on *Thesmophoriazusae* 841 (Lamachus died τετάρτῳ ἔτει πρότερον) would appear to assume that the comedy was staged in 411–410, since Lamachus died in 414–413 under Tysandros (Diodorus XIII.7–8), and not in 415–414 under Karias. But the error, if not merely graphical, can be explained by the fact that Lamachus died in summer (Thucydides VI.101), at the end of one Attic year and the beginning of another. Lines 808–9 do not allude to an event occurring in May 411 (Thucydides VIII.69–70), but more probably to one in 413–412 (Thucydides VIII.1, and see K. O. Müller, *Gesch. griech. Lit.* (Breslau, 1841), II, p. 246, Wilamowitz, *Aristoteles und Athen* (Berlin, 1893), II, p. 344, and also M. Croiset, *Aristophane et les partis à Athènes* (Paris, 1906), p. 238). The scholion on 32 might refer to Agathon's début at the Dionysia. Later, Aristophanes wrote the *Second Thesmophoriazusae*, which contains allusions to his own art (fr. 346). In the parabasis, indeed, the poet becomes quite unusually personal, informing the judges and spectators of the illness which had afflicted him in the four months preceding the comedy's performance. In this regard, see the interesting data provided by K. Deichgräber, *Parabasenverse aus Thesmophoriazousae II bei Galen* (Berlin, 1957) (*Sitzb. Berl. Ak.*, 1956, Nr 2), who argues most convincingly that the *Second Thesmophoriazusae* was staged at the Dionysia (see particularly pp. 19 and 24). Aristophanes' illness would have been of a 'political' nature, and would also have watered down and enfeebled the comedy: cf. Th. Gelzer, *Aristophanes der Komiker* (1970), c. 1416, and by contrast A. C. Cassio, 'I tempi di composizione delle commedie attiche e una parafrasi di Aristofane in Galeno (Ar. *fr.* 346)', *Rivista di filol. e d'istruzione classica* 115 (1987), 5–11. The anthologist of the eleven Aristophanic comedies who chose the *Second Clouds* and the *Second Plutus* was not equally impressed by the *Second Thesmophoriazusae*. Perhaps the *Thesmophoriazusae* of 411 was preferred for its ample and exact citation of Euripides?

6 τὸ ἱερὸν ὠθεῖται was interpreted by the scholiast as ἐκκυκλεῖται ἐπὶ τὸ ἔξω τὸ Θεσμοφόριον. Regarding the improbability of such a technique, see particularly n. 7 to chapter 3. The musical- and stage-annotations to the dramatic texts are collected, and generally well evaluated, in J. Andrieu, *Le Dialogue antique* (1954), pp. 185–9 (W. J. W. Koster, *Acme* 8 (1956), 96–102, once more pronounces himself in favour of the authenticity of these annotations). A new and judicious collection is to be found in O. Taplin, 'Did Greek dramatists write stage instructions?', *Proceedings Cambridge Phil. Society* 202 (1976), 121–31.

7 Those who maintain that from 280 to 645 the thesmophoriazusae are shown inside

the temple interpret lines 280–1 as 'was für ein grosses Ding der brennenden Fackeln, ein wie grosser Schein der brennenden Fackeln hebt sich auf Qualm' (E. Bethe, *Rhein. Mus.* 83 (1934), 29; likewise V. Coulon, *Rhein. Mus.* 100 (1957), 188, who still maintains that one is dealing with torches which the Relative pretends to set alight). However, for ὅσον τὸ χρῆμα cf. *Peace* 1192, and for ἀνέρχεται, cf. the following note. 'Interiors' in Aristophanes are discussed in section 7 of chapter 3, *Acharnians*.

8 See section 11 of chapter 3 for verbs of ascent (and not of descent!) in *Thesmophoriazusae* 281, 585, 623, 893, 1045. Ὀρθὴν ἄ ν ω δίωκε in *Thesmophoriazusae* 1223 does not imply that there is a difference in height, but simply one sense of direction opposed to another, as in the locution ἄνω καὶ κάτω (here, the opposing sense of direction is expressed by πάλιν in 1223b; cf. also 1224b). Apparently, line 784, as well as 1222b alludes to the *two* corridors.

9 Subsequently, Coulon, *Rev. Etudes Grecques* 44 (1931), 13–15, attributed lines 295–311, 331–51 and 372–80 to a Heraldess (see also H. Kleinknecht, *Die Gebetsparodie in der Antike* (Stuttgart–Berlin, 1937), pp. 33–5). S. Srebrny, *Eos* 50 (1959–1960), 48–9, thought once more of a Priestess true and proper for 295–311 and 331–51 (and for 759–935), basing his arguments too trustingly on the teasing remarks heard in 758 (likewise C. Beer, *Über die Zahl der Schauspieler bei Aristophanes* (Leipzig, 1844), pp. 61–7, and Wilamowitz, *Hermes* 64 (1929), 468–9 = *Kl. Schriften*, IV (1962), pp. 486–7).

11 *Frogs*

1 In my *Storia delle Rane di Aristofane* (Padua, 1961; a summary in English in *Greece and Rome* 13 (1966), 1–13), five chapters in turn are dedicated to an analysis of lines 786–96, 69–117, 797–813 and 1364–73, 895–1128, 1251–60. The analysis is examined by F. Lasserre, *L'Antiquité classique* 30 (1961), 558–60, by H. Dörrie, *Riv. fil. istruz. class.* 92 (1964), 83–5 and by Th. Gelzer, *Aristophanes der Komiker* (1970), cc. 1486–91. Much attention is paid to that analysis in K. J. Dover's commentary, *The Frogs* (Oxford, 1993), pp. 8–9. For analytic hypotheses regarding *Frogs*, see J. van Leeuwen in the preface to his 1896 commentary (and previously, his 1876 dissertation on Aristophanes), Wilamowitz on pp. 2–3 of the preface to his commentary on *Herakles* (1889, but see also *Hermes* 64 (1929), 470–6 = *Kl. Schriften*, IV (1962), pp. 488–94), B. B. Rogers, *The Frogs* (London, 1902), pp. xvi–xviii, E. Fraenkel in *Sokrates* 42 (1916), 134–42 (regarding this fine analytic exploration, see M. Pohlenz in *Nachr. Gött. Ges.* (1920), 145, I = *Kl. Schriften*, II, 1965, K. Kunst, *Studien griech. röm. Komödie* (Vienna–Leipzig, 1919), p. 53, I, H. Drexler in *Jahresb. Schles. Ges.* 100 (1927), 122–75, and finally Th. Gelzer, *Der epirrhem. Agon bei Aristophanes* (Munich, 1960), pp. 26–31. For anti-analytic positions, see C. O. Zuretti, in *Atti Acc. Scienze Torino* 33 (1898), 1058–66, A. Ruppel, *Konzeption und Ausarbeitung der Aristophanes Komödie*, Diss. Giessen (Darmstadt, 1913), pp. 40–7, W. Kranz in *Hermes* 52 (1917), 584–91, F. Richter, *Die Frösche und der Typ der arist. Komödie*, Diss. Frankfurt am Main (Düren, 1930), pp. 1–28, H. Erbse, *Gnomon* 28 (1956), 273, and lastly the careful D. Del Corno, *Le Rane* (1985), pp. xiv–xv. The scholar who had advised on the risks of analysis was O. Seel, *Aristophanes* (Stuttgart, 1960), pp. 47–8. E. Fraenkel passes from an analytical position to a unitary one in *Beobachtungen zu Aristophanes* (Rome, 1962), pp. 163–88. I discussed *Frogs* with Piero Pucci, Ithaca.

2 See H. Hoffmann, *Chronologie der att. Tragödie* (Hamburg, 1951), pp. 48–9.

3 For theatrical data on *Frogs*, see Argument I.36–40 (regarding the variants for lines 36–7 in the Ambrosianus and the Aldine, which should not be overlooked, see n. 1 to chapter 4 and section 1 of chapter 6). Lines 39–40 read: οὕτω δὲ ἐθαυμάσθη τὸ δρᾶμα διὰ τὴν ἐν αὐτῷ παράβασιν ὥστε καὶ ἀνεδιδάχθη, ὥς φησι Δικαίαρχος = fr. 84 in F. Wehrli, *Dikaiarchos* (Basel, 1944). Wehrli notes: 'the restaging emerged from the documents, the rest is a piece of arbitrary embroidery typical of Dikaiarchos'. And this is undoubtedly true, in so far as it is most improbable that the parabasis alone would have inspired the restaging of an entire comedy. See A. H. Sommerstein, 'Kleophon and the restaging of *Frogs*', in *Tragedy, Comedy and the Polis*, Nottingham, 1990, Bari, 1993), pp. 461–76, and Dover, *The Frogs* (1993), pp. 75 and 373–6 ('The play was performed again early in 404'). With respect to the conjecture of the scholiast on *Frogs* 404 regarding the synchoregia of the comedy, see E. Capps, *Hesperia* 12 (1943), 5–8.

4 Cf. H.-J. Newiger, 'Zum Text der *Frösche* des Aristophanes', *Hermes* 113 (1985), 429–48, with n. 69: 'Wir müssen ja für die Schauspieler und den Chor mit einzelnen Blättern rechnen, die z.T. nur ihre Partien enthielten, vgl. Russo, *Belfagor* 23, 1968, 317ff. (= Aristophanes u.d. alte Komödie, Darmstadt 1975, 219ff.) zu den in den "Wespen" möglicherweise vertauschten Partien, mit Hinweisen auf L. Havet und A. Dain.'

5 Cf. the scholia on *Acharnians* 10 and *Frogs* 868, and *Frogs* 868–9 (and see also section 3 of chapter 3). Wilamowitz's well-known modernistic theory goes back to 1889, and is generally accepted (it can be read in unaltered form in *Einleitung in die griech. Tragödie* (Berlin, 1921), pp. 121–8; regarding the successful circulation of the *Second Clouds*, see the work cited in n. 4 to chapter 5). See also W. B. Sedgwick, *Classica et Med.* 9 (1947), 1–9, and E. G. Turner, *Athenian Books in the Fifth and Fourth Centuries B.C.* (London, 1957), pp. 16–23. With respect to the finale of *Frogs*, an analysis of lines 1433–67 has led H. Dörrie, *Hermes* 84 (1956), 296–319, to the conclusion that lines 1451–62 have been transmitted out of place, through a purely mechanical accident occurring in a pre-Alexandrian epoch (see particularly Dörrie, 318–19, and also D. M. MacDowell, *Class. Quart.* 53 (1959), 266 and Dover, *The Frogs*, p. 375). A phenomenon such as that mentioned in n. 4 to chapter 6 (see also n. 2 to chapter 9) may also be explained with reference to the fortuitous and haphazard phase during which the theatrical version was made up for a limited circulation.

6 The character in 738–813 whom the most recent scholars and editors identify as a 'Servant' is certainly the Aiakos of 464–78 and 605–73 (605 → 464–78): cf. solely 738–44 with 628–73, and particularly 738 with 640, and 746 and 812 with 670 (see also section 9 of chapter 3). In this regard, one should refer to the unpublished dissertation of S. Hess, 'Studien zum Prolog att. Komödie', Heidelberg, 1953, pp. 40–55: it would be more worth while to take Hess's example and to examine the link between the two parts of *Frogs* than to search for the comedy's unity in a celebration of various aspects of the cult of Dionysos, as C. Segal does once again in *Harv. St. in Class. Phil.* 65 (1961), 207–42. One should perhaps note that the investigation aimed at distinguishing between two personalities (Aeschylus and Euripides) is a motif which also arose just before the parabasis in the attempt to distinguish between Dionysos and Xanthias. And one κρίσις follows another κρίσις.

7 In 1920, the aforementioned M. Pohlenz came close to interpreting the νεῦρα correctly: 'the strings of Tragedy can only be whatever governs the parts and ensures an organic whole . . . . The progress, announced in line 862, from the ἔπη and μέλη to the general composition (τὰ νεῦρα) would have been extremely fine,

NOTES

and a discussion on the ethical influence of Tragedy have guaranteed Euripides' final defeat. Aristophanes did not behave in this way, and the technique of composition is not examined until 911 and 945.' Wilamowitz, *Hermes* 64 (1929), 476 (= *Kl. Schriften*, IV (1962), p. 494 and in Newiger's anthology), interprets the νεῦρα as 'Mythos und οἰκονομία'. To interpret, as is often the case, τά νεῦρα as in apposition to τἄπη and τὰ μέλη is improper, for stylistic motives alone (Dover, *The Frogs*, p. 300).

12 *Assemblywomen*

1 Strictly speaking, it would have been preferable to locate these lines between 1111 and 1112. Another appropriate point would have been after 1143 (cf. 1142), yet this would have necessitated the revision of the succeeding context. Wilamowitz is therefore rather hasty in his affirmation that, for lines 1154–62, 'it was clear by then that no better position could be found' (*Lysistrate* (1927), p. 218). The passage quoted in the text is taken from C. Robert, *Hermes* 67 (1922), 346–7 (although the fact that lines 1154–62 were a last-minute addition had already been mentioned by Wilamowitz in *Sitzb. Berl. Ak.* (1903), 454). Regarding 392 as the year of the comedy's performance (which is better than 391, in any case), cf. Philochorus, fr. 148 (= scholion on *Assemblywomen* 193) and fr. 149 Jacoby III (with relative commentary (Leiden, 1954), I, pp. 514 and 519, II, p. 416). See also R. G. Ussher, *Ecclesiazusae* (1973), p. xxv. With respect to the contest, 'the overwhelming presence of characters exposed to derision, of whose personal features only the Athenians could have been aware, does seem to indicate that the comedy was performed at the Lenaia' (M. Vetta, *Donne all'assemblea* (1989), p. xxxi). In the course of the comedy, the chorus, too, has an extra-theatrical action.

2 The features characterizing lines 311–477 as a prologue, or as an exemplary scene, have been pointed out by K.-D. Koch, *Kritische Idee und komisches Thema* (Bremen, 1965), pp. 109–11. According to P. Mazon, *Essai sur la composition des comédies d'Aristophane* (Paris, 1904), pp. 151–3, the prologue lasts until line 477. Regarding the particular dramaturgy of *Assemblywomen* and *Plutus*, see H. Flashar, 'Zur Eigenart des Aristophanischen Spätwerks', *Poetica* 1 (1967), 154–75; the article is also in Newiger's anthology.

3 The first to interpret μείρακες as referring to female dancers was J. W. White, *The Verse of Greek Comedy* (London, 1912), pp. 147–9 (but see earlier note of F. H. Bothe to line 1149 (Leipzig, 1845, 1830)). White was followed by E. Fraenkel, 'Dramaturgical problems' (Murray) (1936), pp. 269–70 (*Kleine Beiträge* (Rome, 1964), I, pp. 480–1). According to Fraenkel, the Anonymous Husband in the finale is Chremes. With regard to Blepyros, lines 725–8 do not imply that he withdraws definitively from the stage-action. On presumed satirical intentions in the exodos of *Assemblywomen*, see K. J. Dover, *Lustrum* 2 (1957), 101–2.

4 See C. Beer, *Über die Zahl der Schauspieler bei Aristophanes* (Leipzig, 1844), pp. 103–6, and F. Kaehler, *De Eccl. tempore et choro* (Ienae, 1889), pp. 41–50. J. van Leeuwen (1905), and C. Robert, *Hermes* 67 (1922), 344, attribute trimeters 54–6 to the First Woman.

5 According to E. Fraenkel, *Dramaturgical Problems*, pp. 262–5 (*Kleine Beiträge*, I, pp. 473–4), the two rivals are both on the roof, in so far as ἕστηκα in 879 would seem to imply that the Old Woman is visible from head to toe, in an erect position. However, as we learn from *Birds* 206 and 1308 and *Lysistrata* 424, ἕστηκα could be intended here as 'I'm staying inactive' (whether or not ἕστηκα is then strictly

NOTES

qualified by ἀργός in 880, cf. *Peace* 256). Fraenkel is followed by Pickard-Cambridge, *The Theatre of Dionysus* (1946), p. 67, but not by A. M. Dale, *Journ. Hell. Studies* 77 (1957), 208 (reprinted in *Collected Papers*, London, 1969), or by S. Srebrny, *Studia scaenica* (Wrocław, 1960), p. 119. Dale, basing her conclusions on *Assemblywomen* 976–7, maintains that the two rivals live in the same house, behind the one door, and consequently that all the assemblywomen use a single door and a single house throughout the comedy. Dale, as previously remarked, is firmly convinced that Aristophanic theatre employed only one door; one is also indebted to Ussher for 'The staging of *Assemblywomen*', *Hermes* 97 (1969), 22–37, reprinted by Newiger.

13 *Plutus*

1 With respect to the importance of Karion see Dover, *The Frogs* (1993), p. 47.

2 Regarding the tradition of the XOPOY in *Plutus*, Victor Coulon's edition is seriously flawed. In reality, the Venetus manuscript transmits XOPOY in the left margin of lines 321, 627 and 802, and KOMMATION XOPOY between lines 769 and 770. The Ravenna manuscript transmits KOMMATION XOPOY between 770 and 771, and has a XOPOY, received second hand, between 801 and 802. Byzantine scholia and manuscripts read XOPOY at 252–3, 626–7, 770–1 (KOMMATION XOPOY), 801–2, 958–9, 1096–7: a precise description of this material is given in E. W. Handley, *Class. Quart.* 47 (1953), 55–61, whereas other Byzantine material has been indicated and discussed by W. J. W. Koster, *Autour d'un manuscrit d'Aristophane écrit par Démétrius Triclinius* (Groningen, 1957), pp. 116–35. Regarding KOMMATION XOPOY, see K. Holzinger, *Plutos* (Vienna, 1940), pp. 236–7. For other hypotheses regarding the interpretation of the XOPOY, see A. Körte, in *Hermes* 43 (1908), 39–41, and the entry *Komödie* in Pauly–Wissowa (1921, c. 1259, although the first to think of XOPOY = uncirculated songs was F. Ritter, *De Aristophanis Pluto* (Bonn, 1828), p. 18) and K. J. Maidment in *Class. Quart.* 29 (1935), 1–24. Our thesis had already been proposed by, amongst others, D. Comparetti in his preface to the translation of *Plutus* by A. Franchetti, Città di Castello 1900 (= *Poesia e pensiero del mondo antico* (Naples, 1944), pp. 134 and 142) and P. Mazon, *Essai sur la composition des comédies d'Aristophane* (Paris, 1904), pp. 155–6. See also W. Beare, *Class. Quart.* 49 (1955), 49–52, P. Händel, *Formen und Darstellungsweisen in der aristophanischen Komödie* (Heidelberg, 1963), pp. 126–39, Th. Gelzer, *Aristophanes der Komiker* (1970), cc. 1507–8, and R. L. Hunter, 'The comic chorus in the fourth century', *Zeitschr. Papyr. Epigr.* 36 (1979), 23–38. In the unperformed, and never retouched, *Second Clouds*, the XOPOΣ or XOPOY in the margin of 889 refers, as mentioned in its place, to a planned choral song which eventually was not written.

15 The Disorderly *Wasps* and an 18 × 2 tetrameter module

1 As already remarked in chapter 6. Th. Zieliński, *Die Gliederung der altattischen Komödie* (Leipzig, 1885), p. 203, limited himself to observing that the two choral songs in *Wasps* had been exchanged 'durch ein Versehen'. An accident 'in the course of the tradition' was proposed explicitly, in his second edition, by J. van Leeuwen, *Vespae* (Leiden, 1909), p. 196 (cf. *Prolegomena ad Aristophanem* (Leiden, 1908), p. 311) and W. Schmid, *Geschichte der griech. Literatur* (Munich, 1946), IV, p. 278, n. 7. In brief: thanks to an observation of Stanger (1870) regarding the notable belatedness of *Wasps* 1450–73, Müller-Strübing (1873) intuited that the

two choral songs were indeed interchangeable. The inversion was proposed, independently, by Textor and Zieliński in 1885 and by Couat in 1898. The significant belatedness of the 'second' choral song was again noticed by Brentano (1871) and Hoekstra (1878). The two choral songs were published in their original order by Starkie (1897), Leeuwen (1909) and Willems (1909). Opposed by Wilamowitz (1911), the exchange found favour again with Kunst (1919), Schmid (1946), Weinreich (1952), Russo (1962), Barrett (1964), Gelzer (1971) and Mastromarco (1983). See also the highly attentive Newiger, cited in the notes to chapter 6 and 11.

2   In *Eos* 50 (1959–1960), fasc. I, pp. 43–5, independently of W. F. E. Nesemann, *De episodiis Aristophaneis* (Berolini, 1862), p. 18, n. 8, of E. W. H. Brentano, *Untersuchungen über das griech. Drama* (Frankfurt on Main, 1871), p. 178, and of J. van Leeuwen in his first (and only in his first) edition with commentary of *Wasps* (Leiden, 1893), pp. xxiii–xxiv and 36; this is mentioned in section 2 of chapter 6. Recent approval comes from Romano (1992), Mastromarco (1983, pp. 92–3, 96), Newiger (1972), Gelzer (1970, 1993), to Perusino (F. Perusino, *Il tetrametro giambico catalettico nella commedia greca* (Rome, 1968), p. 35, n. 2), and much attention in the 1971 commentary of MacDowell.

3   F.146ᵛ. The only information on this paragraphos is to be found in J. W. White and E. Cary, 'Collations of the manuscripts of Aristophanes' *Vespae*', *Harvard Studies*, XXX (1919), p. 8 (besides MacDowell's commentary). In *Wasps* 230–72 the Ravenna (R) and Venetus (V) bear sigla before 230, and paragraphoi before 231 R, 242 R, 248 R, 249 R, 250 RV, 251 R, 254 RV and 266 R. Following the example of Gottfried Hermann (1843), some scholars attribute lines 266–72 to one of the choreutai.

4   'The disorderly *Wasps* and an 18 × 2 tetrameter module' was published in 1968 in *Belfagor* (Florence, Olschki); since then, the marching-unit has stridden ahead on the energy of the 18 tetrameters of *Peace* 553. At the end of the *Belfagor* article, I indicated the 36 × 2 trimeter outline of *Peace* 657, divided by an extra metre, and the third idyll of Theocritus; in the version prepared in 1971 and published in 1975 at Darmstadt in *Aristophanes und die alte Komödie* edited by H.-J. Newiger under the title '*Die Wespen* "im Umbruch" und ein Modul von 18 × 2 Tetrametern', translated by Frank Regen, I indicated the prologue of *Peace* and the kommos of *Agamemnon*, *Iliad* A.1–487 (in 1973, with the entire *Iliad* in mind, I opened a brief article with τρὶς ἓξ βαλούσης τῆσδέ μοι φρυκτωρίας). Regarding *Peace* and Aeschylus, see chapter 7 and note 1 to that chapter. Regarding Homer, with the collaboration of the fine Bari philologists Francesco De Martino and Onofrio Vox: C. F. Russo, *Die Gestalt einer archaischen Handschrift (und einer kyklischen Ilias)*, Mélanges Delebecque (Aix-en-Provence, 1983), pp. 343–7, 'La formula della forma agli albori dell'Occidente', *Forma Struttura Rappresentazione*, University of Padua Institute of Philosophical Studies (Naples, 1989), pp. 155–68, 'Cherchez l'Olympiade chez Homère', *La componente autobiografica nella poesia greca e latina* (University of Pisa, 1993), pp. 93–9, 'Notizie stilate a Chio vinta l'Olimpiade del 724', in *Tradizione e innovazione nella cultura greca* (Rome, 1993), pp. 45–50, 'Dante e Omero al paragone', *Omaggio a Gianfranco Folena* (Padua, 1993), pp. 33–7. Also Seneca, the Invisible Hand of the State, wrote following a geometric design, making use of lines of poetry: C. F. Russo (ed.), *Apocolocyntosis* (Florence, 1985⁶), pp. 161–5.

BIBLIOGRAPHY

I Editions with commentaries. Translations
II Language and metre
III Theatre and dramaturgy
IV Critical anthologies. Reviews

I   Editions with commentaries; translations

Oxford University Press: *Peace*, M. Platnauer (1964, repr. 1981); *Clouds*, K. J. Dover (1968, *editio minor* 1970); *Wasps*, D. M. MacDowell (1971); *Ecclesiazusae*, R. G. Ussher (1973); *Lysistrata*, J. Henderson (1987); *Frogs*, K. J. Dover (1993).

Fondazione Valla/Mondadori, Milan: *Rane*, D. Del Corno (1985); *Uccelli*, G. Zanetto (1992, 1987); *Donne all'assemblea*, M. Vetta (1989): with translations by Del Corno.

Warminster, 1981–90: from *Acharnians* to *Lysistrata*, A. H. Sommerstein, with translations of the seven comedies.

Essential companions: *Acharnians, Clouds, Wasps*, W. J. Starkie (London, 1897–1911, repr. 1968), with translations; *Knights*, R. A. Neil (Cambridge, 1901, repr. 1966), *Acharnians*, W. Rennie (London, 1909); *Die Vögel*, Th. Kock and O. Schroeder (Berlin, 1927) (Kock also wrote commentaries on *Knights, Clouds* and *Frogs*, 1876/1881); *Lysistrate*, U. von Wilamowitz-Moellendorff (Berlin, 1927, repr. 1964); *Plutos*, K. Holzinger (Vienna, 1940); *Die Frösche*, L. Radermacher and W. Kraus (Vienna, 1967, 1922); *Frogs*, W. B. Stanford (London, 1963, 1958).

The eleven comedies: B. B. Rogers (London, 1902–16), with translations; J. van Leeuwen, in Latin (Lugduni Batavorum, 1896–1909, 1893–); St. Bergler, with Latin translations and metrical notes (Lugduni Batavorum, 1760); L. Küster (Amstelodami, 1710) with Bentley's notes.

Text and translation: V. Coulon and H. van Daele (Paris, 1923–30); G. Mastromarco (Turin, 1983), from *Acharnians* to *Peace*, with critical notes.

Critical editions of single comedies: *Pax*, K. Zacher, prefaced by O. Bachmann, with the Heliodorean scholia (Leipzig, 1909); *Acharnians*, R. Th. Elliott (Oxford, 1914).
Poëtae Comici Graeci, R. Kassel and C. Austin (Berlin–New York, 1984): *Aristophanes, Testimonia et Fragmenta* III, 2.

Scholia: W. J. W. Koster, *Prolegomena de comoedia*, and D. Holwerda have published the scholia of the first six comedies (Groningen, 1969–91); otherwise F. Dübner (Paris, 1877, 1842). One comedy: J. W. White, *Aves* (Boston–London, 1914). Papyri: G. Zuntz, *Die Aristophanes-Scholien der Papyri* (Berlin, 1975, 1938–9).

271

Translations: B. B. Rogers's version, in The Loeb Classical Library (1924 and reprints). Ann Arbor, 1961–7: W. Arrowsmith and D. Parker, *The Complete Greek Comedy*; Harmondsworth, Penguin Books: D. Barrett and A. H. Sommerstein, 1964–78. Noteworthy: A. Willems, *Aristophane* (Paris–Brussels, 1919). L. Seeger's version (Weinreich →) was revised by H.-J. Newiger and P. Rau (Munich, 1968).

II Language and metre

O. J. Todd, *Index Aristophaneus* (Cambridge, Mass., 1932, repr. 1962); A. Dunbar, *A Complete Concordance to the Comedies and Fragments of Aristophanes* (Oxford, 1883, revised 1973); H. A. Holden, *Onomasticon Aristophaneum* (Cambridge, 1902, 1883, repr. 1970).

J. Taillardat, *Les Images d'Aristophane. Etudes de langue et de style* (Paris, 1965, 1962); K. J. Dover, 'Lo stile di Aristofane', *Quaderni urbinati cultura class.* 9 (1970), 7–23 (in German by Newiger →, in English in *Greek and the Greeks*, Oxford, 1987); J. Henderson, *The Maculate Muse. Obscene Language in Attic Comedy* (New York–Oxford, 1991, 1975).

J. M. White, *The Verse of Greek Comedy* (London, 1912, repr. 1969); O. Schroeder, *Aristophanis Cantica* (Lipsiae, 1930, 1909); P. Pucci, 'Aristofane ed Euripide: ricerche metriche e stilistiche', *Atti Lincei, Memorie* (Rome, 1961), pp. 277–422; A. M. Dale, *The Lyric Metres of Greek Drama* (Cambridge, 1968, 1948); B. Zimmermann, *Untersuchungen zur Form und dramatischen Technik der Aristophanischen Komödien* (Königstein im Taurus, 1985–7); C. Romano, *Responsioni libere nei canti di Aristofane* (Rome, 1992).

III Theatre and dramaturgy

Albini, U. *Nel nome di Dioniso. Vita teatrale nell'Atene classica*, Milan 1991.
Andrieu, J. *Le Dialogue antique. Structure et présentation*, Paris 1954.
Arnott, P. D. *Public and Performance in the Greek Theatre*, London 1989.
Blume, H.-D. *Einführung in das antike Theaterwesen*, Darmstadt 1991 (1978).
Dover, K. J. *Aristophanic Comedy*, London 1972.
Fensterbusch, C. *Die Bühne des Aristophanes*, Borna–Leipzig 1912.
Finley, M. I. *The Idea of a Theatre: The Greek Experience*, London: British Museum 1980.
Fraenkel, E. *Beobachtungen zu Aristophanes*, Rome 1962.
Gelzer, Th. *Der epirrhematische Agon bei Aristophanes. Untersuchungen zur Struktur der attischen Komödie*, Munich 1960.
—— 'Aristophanes der Komiker', *Pauly's Real.*, Suppl. XII, Stuttgart 1970, cc. 1393–1570.
—— *Feste Strukturen in der Komödie des Aristophanes*, Entretiens Hardt XXXVIII, Vandœuvres-Genève 1993, pp. 51–90.
Gould, J. 'Tragedy in performance', *Cambridge History Class. Lit.*, Cambridge 1985, I, pp. 263–80.
Handley, E. W. *Aristophanes and his Theatre*, Entretiens Hardt, XXXVIII, Vandœuvres-Genève 1993, pp. 97–117.
Kindermann, H. *Il teatro greco e il suo pubblico*, a cura di A. Andrisano, Florence 1991 (Salzburg, 1979).
Kolb, F. *Polis und Theater*, 1979, pp. 504–45 (by Seeck →).
Landfester, M. *Handlungsverlauf und Komik in den frühen Komödien des Aristophanes*, Berlin 1977.

Lowe, J. C. B. 'The manuscript evidence for changes of speakers in Aristophanes', *Bull. Inst. Class. Studies*, London 9 (1962), 27–42.

McLeish, K. *The Theatre of Aristophanes*, London 1980.

Mazon, P. *Essai sur la composition des comédies d'Aristophane*, Paris 1904.

Melchinger, S. *Das Theater der Tragödie. Aischylos, Sophokles, Euripides auf der Bühne ihrer Zeit*, Munich 1974.

Mette, H.-J. *Urkunden dramatischer Aufführungen in Athen*, Berlin–New York 1977.

Newiger, H.-J. *Metapher und Allegorie. Studien zu Aristophanes*, Munich 1957.

—— *Aristophanes und die alte Komödie* →; *Drama und Theater*, pp. 434–503 (Seeck →).

Pickard-Cambridge, A. W. *The Theatre of Dionysus in Athens*, Oxford 1946, repr. 1956.

—— *Dithyramb, Tragedy and Comedy*, revised by T. B. L. Webster, Oxford 1966 (1927).

—— *The Dramatic Festivals of Athens*, revised by J. Gould and D. M. Lewis, Oxford 1968 and 1988 (1953).

Russo, C. F. *Gli Acarnesi*, translation, commentary and notes on stagecraft, Bari 1953.

—— *Storia delle Rane di Aristofane*, Padua 1961 (*Greece and Rome* 13 (1966), 1–13).

—— *Aristofane autore di teatro*, Florence 1962, revised 1984 (repr. 1992).

—— 'Il prologo e il proto comico', *Dioniso* 57 (1987), 65–74.

Seale, D. *Vision and Stagecraft in Sophocles*, Chicago 1982.

Sifakis, G. M. *Parabasis and Animal Choruses, A Contribution to the History of Attic Comedy*, London 1971.

Simon, E. *The Ancient Theatre*, London 1985 (Heidelberg 1975, revised 1981).

Srebrny, S. *Studia scaenica*, Wrocław 1960.

Taplin, O. *Greek Tragedy in Action*, London 1978.

—— *The Stagecraft of Aeschylus. The Dramatic Use of Exits and Entrances in Greek Tragedy*, Oxford 1989 (1977).

—— *Comic Angels and other Approaches to Greek Drama through Vase-paintings*, Oxford 1993.

Thiercy, P. *Aristophane: fiction et dramaturgie*, Paris 1986.

Travlos, J. *Pictorial Dictionary of Ancient Athens*, New York 1971.

Trendall, A. D. and Webster, T. B. L. *Illustrations of Greek Drama*, London 1971.

Weinreich, O. 'Zur Geschichte und zum Nachleben der griechischen Komödie' (197 pages), in *Aristophanes, Sämtliche Komödien*, übertragen von L. Seeger (1845–8), Zürich 1968 (1952–3).

IV Critical anthologies; reviews

Die Bauformen der griechischen Tragödie, ed. W. Jens (Munich, 1971).

Aristophanes und die alte Komödie, ed. H.-J. Newiger (Darmstadt, 1975).

Das griechische Drama, ed. G. A. Seeck (Darmstadt, 1979).

K. J. Dover, 'Greek Comedy', in *Fifty Years (and Twelve) of Classical Scholarship* (Oxford, 1968) (London, 1954; *Greek and the Greeks,* Oxford, 1987), pp. 123–58; 'Aristophanes 1938–1955', *Lustrum* 2 (1957), 52–112.

W. Kraus, 'Alte Komödie und Epicharm', *Anzeiger Altertums*. 24 (1971), 161–80.

J. R. Green, 'Theatre production: 1971–1986', *Lustrum* 31 (1989), 7–95.

W. Schmid (and O. Stählin), *Geschichte der griechischen Literatur* (Munich, 1946), IV, pp. 1–470 with *Nachleben der alten Komödie, besonders des Aristophanes* (with W. Süss, *Aristophanes und die Nachwelt*, Leipzig, 1911, and L. E. Lord, *Aristophanes, His Plays and His Influence*, London, 1925, repr. 1963; a recent essay:

BIBLIOGRAPHY

W. D. Howarth, *Comic Drama, the European Heritage*, London, 1978; the fortune of the single comedies and of the genre in Weinreich's valuable study, pp. cxxxv–cxcvii).

A. Lesky, *Geschichte der griechischen Literatur* (Bern, 1971, 1957–8), pp. 471–509 (London 1966).

R. G. Ussher, *Aristophanes* (Oxford: JACT, 1979).

E. W. Handley, 'Comedy', *Cambridge History Class. Lit.* (Cambridge, 1985), I, pp. 355–425.

AN INDEX OF
DOMINANT THEMES

The single themes of the book are listed chapter by chapter in the *Contents* and are synthesized in chapter 14, *Elements of a Theatrical Career*. This Index is intended to provide an elementary overview: 'The Secret Apprentice', 'The Workshop', 'The Festivals', 'The Performers', 'Dramaturgy'. Occasionally the words of the dramatist are directly quoted.

The Secret Apprentice. *Knights*, 'the poet was first an oarsman, then a helmsman; he then observed the winds at the prow and lastly governed the ship himself'; *Clouds*, 'still an unmarried girl'; *Wasps*, 'soothsayer': 29–31 ◊ *Acharnians*, at the prow as coryphaeus, 'our didaskalos, who is at the head of the chorus': 30, 33, 60; *Peace*, 'I gathered my mask/my costume': 30 ◊ *Babylonians*, no first prize. Victory in 425 at Dionysia: 17–26 ◊ Didaskaloi: 13–32 ◊ New public, new poets: 17–32.

The Workshop. *Clouds, Frogs*, an idea of the manuscript: 105–9, 201–2 ◊ *Assemblywomen*, the last moments: 203, 219 ◊ *Wasps*, transpositions in the domestic draft, the dramaturgical pagination: 243–6 ◊ *Clouds, Wasps, Frogs*, revised plays: 92–109, 124[1], 198–209 ◊ Critical signs, symmetrical extra-metra, colometry: 7–8, 40[5], 137[1], 218, 246–9 ◊ XOPOY: *Clouds, Assembly-women, Plutus* ◊ Nominal sigla missing: 37–43 ◊ *Wasps, Peace*, identical 'anapaests' with one variant: 3, 133–4 ◊ Euripides and Agathon at work: 50–5, 194 ◊ Copies, Dionysos reading *Andromeda*: 40, 106[4], 203–4, 243–4.

The Festivals. *Clouds*, 'in every season there are processions, sacrifices and banquets in Athens; and when springtime arrives, it is time for the feast of Bromios, the excitement of resounding choruses, the deep-quivering Muse of flutes', 'on this spot . . . I felt it was right that you should be the first to relish my comedy': 1, 17 ◊ *Thesmophoriazusae*, 'I am Echo: she who in this very same place took part in the contest last year for Euripides', 'Euripides slandered women in every place where there are spectators, tragic poets and choruses': 190–1 ◊ Pericles, 'By celebrating games and festivals throughout the year, we have procured the greatest distraction for our minds, providing relief from fatigue': 3 ◊ *Knights*, 'a roar proper to the Lenaion' 78–9 ◊ *Acharnians*, 'the contest is in the Lenaion'; Aristophanes fr. 590, 'chorus for the Lenaion'; Sannyrion, 'Meletus, the corpse of the Lenaion'; Pollux, 'the Lenaian theatre': 1–2, 79[1].

The theatre of Dionysos, the precinct of the Lenaion: 1–5, 43, 59, 79[1], 147–8, 186–91 ◊ *Wasps* Lenaia – *Peace* Dionysia, identical 'anapaests' with one variant for a different audience: 3, 133–4 ◊ The two festivals: 1–5, 23, 60, 82, 84, 90, 147–8, 165, 186–91, 202–3 ◊ The last season, the last four months: 23, 44, 186, 194[5] ◊ Choice of poets, two comedies: 3–4, 17–24, 121–2, 193–4, 233 ◊ Choregia proagon programme judges: 3, 31–2, 39, 40[4], 150, 186–91, 202–4, 219 ◊ Winners' list, Aristoteles: 17–20, 40.

The Performers. Choreutai, twenty-four distinct: 159, eleven oars: 30, 88 ◊ Choruses at the Dionysia, 1165 singers: 3 ◊ Three actors: 70–2, 92–109, 135–6, 173 ◊ The actor spokesman of the poet: 33[1], 44 ◊ Special performance regimens: Hoopoe *Birds*, Lysistrata *Lysistrata*, Plutus *Plutus*.

Characters, number of: *Knights* five, *Birds* twenty-two ◊ Identity: 34–7, 67–8, 73–4, 110–11 ◊ Named, but absent: 102, 201 ◊ Servants: *Frogs*, *Plutus* ◊ Homeric Paphlagonian Harpalion: 9.

Dramaturgy. Homer, the dawn of Comedy, Aristoteles: 7–10, 218, 249[4] ◊ Euripides, 'spoken lines, sung lyrics, strings of Tragedy ...': 204–9 ◊ Aristophanes, 'The art of Comedy is the most difficult of all': 29.

Modular composition, comedy written in blocks, extra-metra, trimeters 36 × 2 and 63 × 2, tetrameters 18 and 18 × 2: 5–8, 137[1], 216–18, 246–9 ◊ Prologue/parabasis, Homeric 'parabasis': 5–10 ◊ Euripides, *Thesmophoriazusae*, 'the spectator should not hear immediately everything that he's shortly going to see with his own eyes': 38, 194 ◊ The style of New Comedy: 42, 109–13 ◊ Second prologue/The bipartite *Frogs*: 204–14 ◊ *Wasps*, *Peace*, *Plutus*, parodos of 18 × 2 tetrameters: 216–18 ◊ Exodos: *Knights*, *Wasps*, *Lysistrata* ◊ XOPOY: *Clouds*, *Assemblywomen*, *Plutus*.

Extra-theatrical actions, Time structuring, Acts: 4–5, 60–4, 223–4, 229 ◊ Illusion: 49–50, 124–5 ◊ Missing stage directions: 194–5[6] ◊ On-stage journeys: *Peace*, *Frogs* ◊ Back-stage vocal display: 113, 118, 156–8, 212.

Orchestra, façade, statue of Dionysos: 5–6, 48–9, 66–70, 192, 225–6 ◊ Ekkyklema, 'curtain': 43, 50–8, 131[5], 196 ◊ Machines: 3, 58, 117–18, 138, 161–2 ◊ Corridors: 66–7, 153–5, 196[8].

Aeschylus 'oral poet': 216–18 ◊ Tragedians at Lenaia: 186–91 ◊ Sophocles, Euripides: 58, 69, 73, 145, 198–9, 238–9 ◊ Seneca's geometrical composition: 249[4] ◊ Shakespeare's theatres: 5 ◊ Corneille as critic: 61[8].

INDEX OF MODERN AUTHORS

Other scholars are listed in the Bibliography .